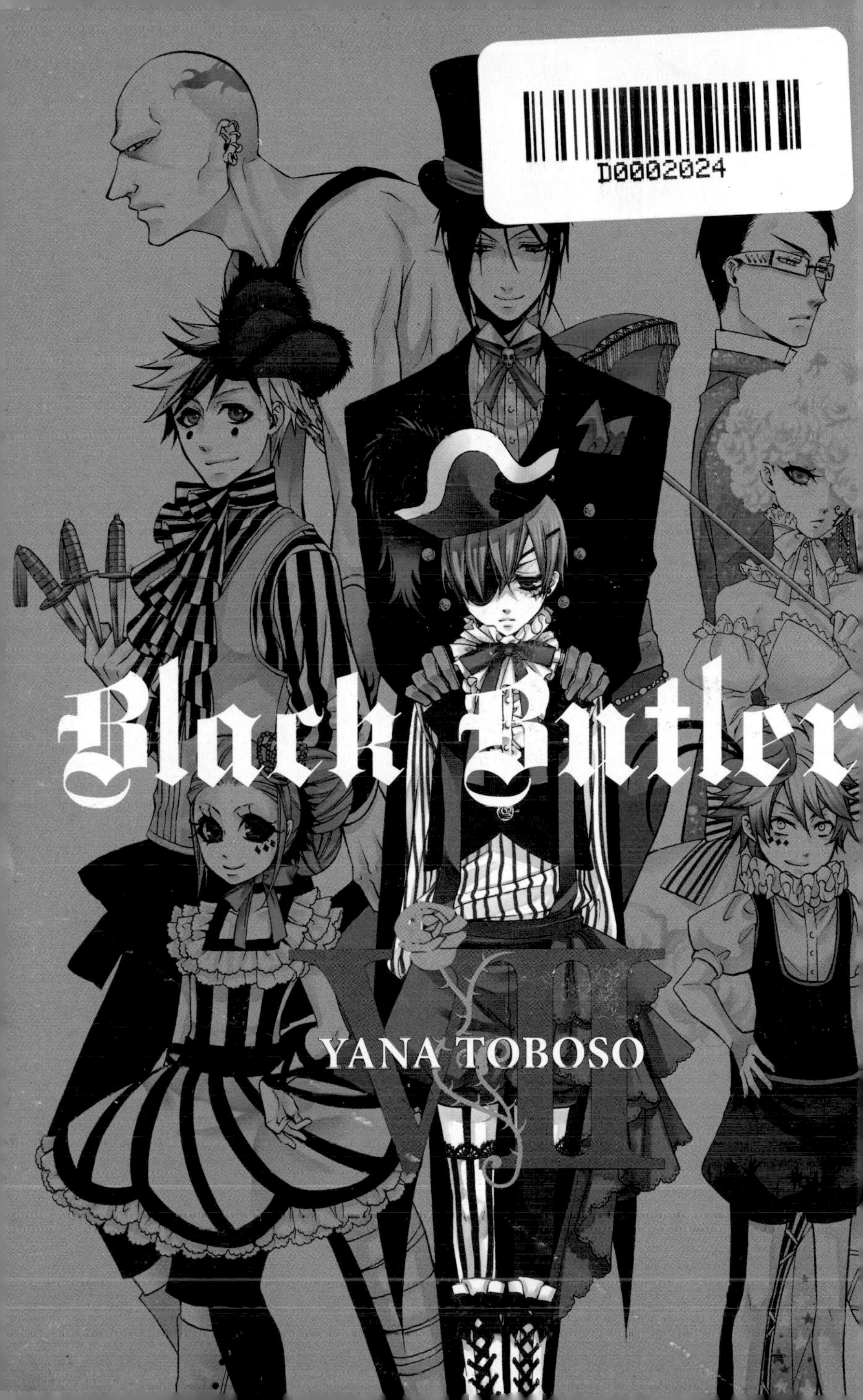
Black Butler
VIII
YANA TOBOSO

Contents

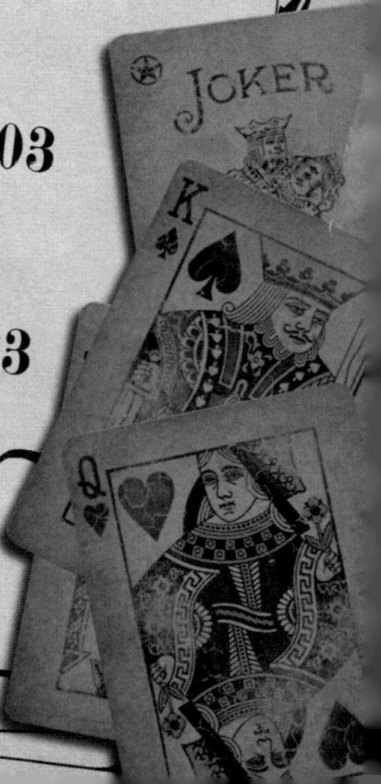

JOKER

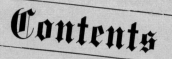

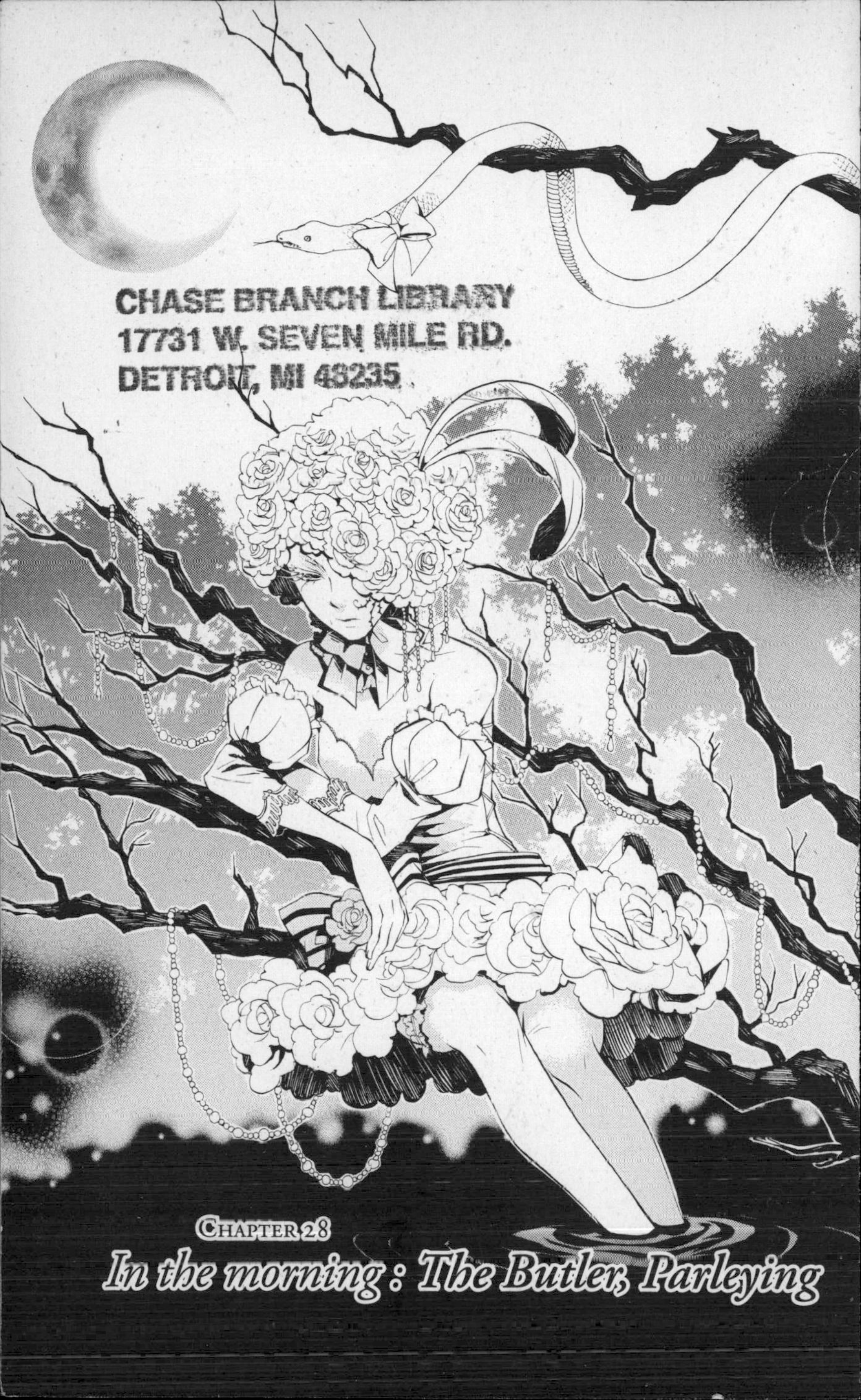
CHAPTER 28
In the morning : The Butler, Parleying

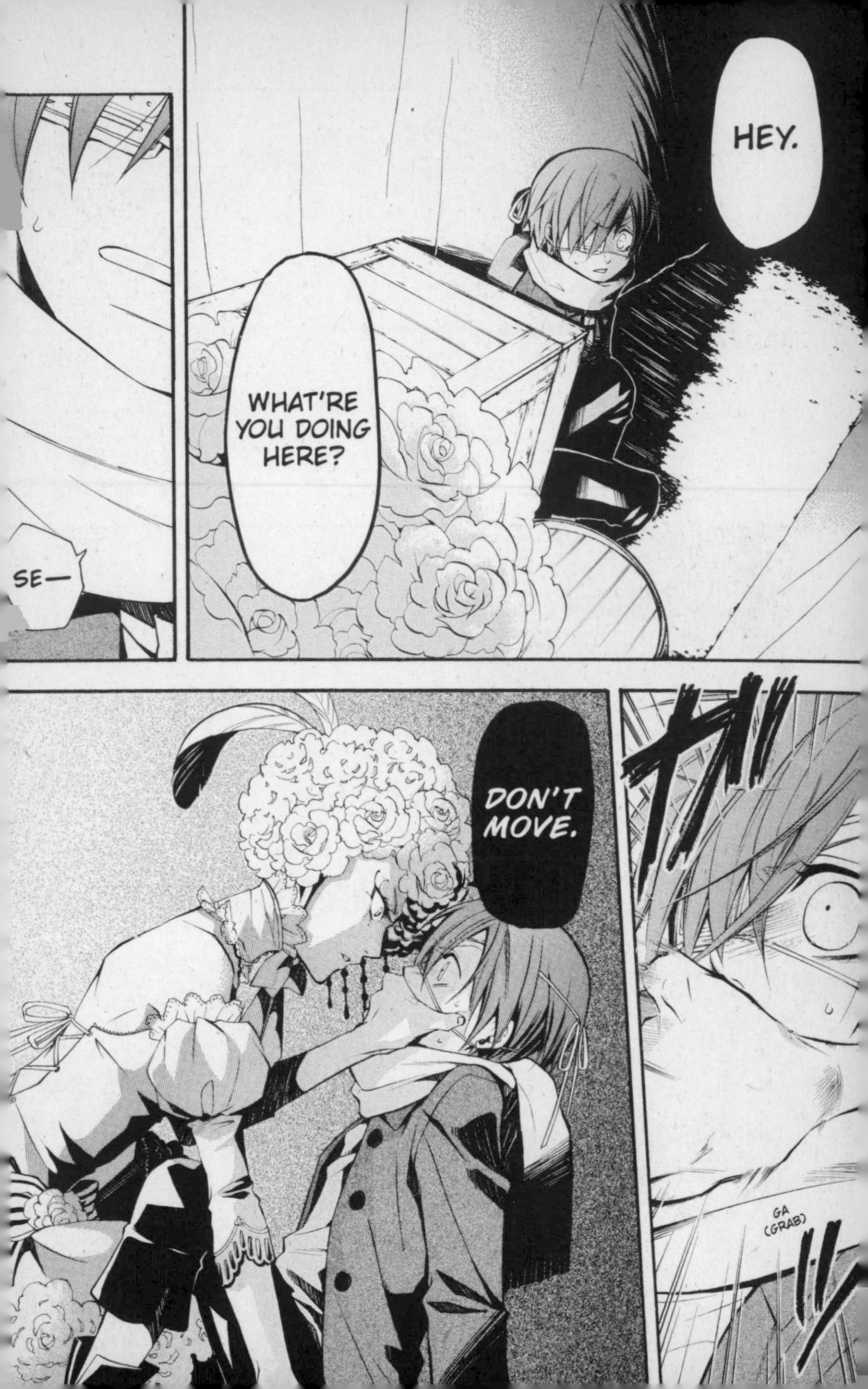
HEY.
WHAT'RE YOU DOING HERE?
SE—
GA (GRAB)
DON'T MOVE.

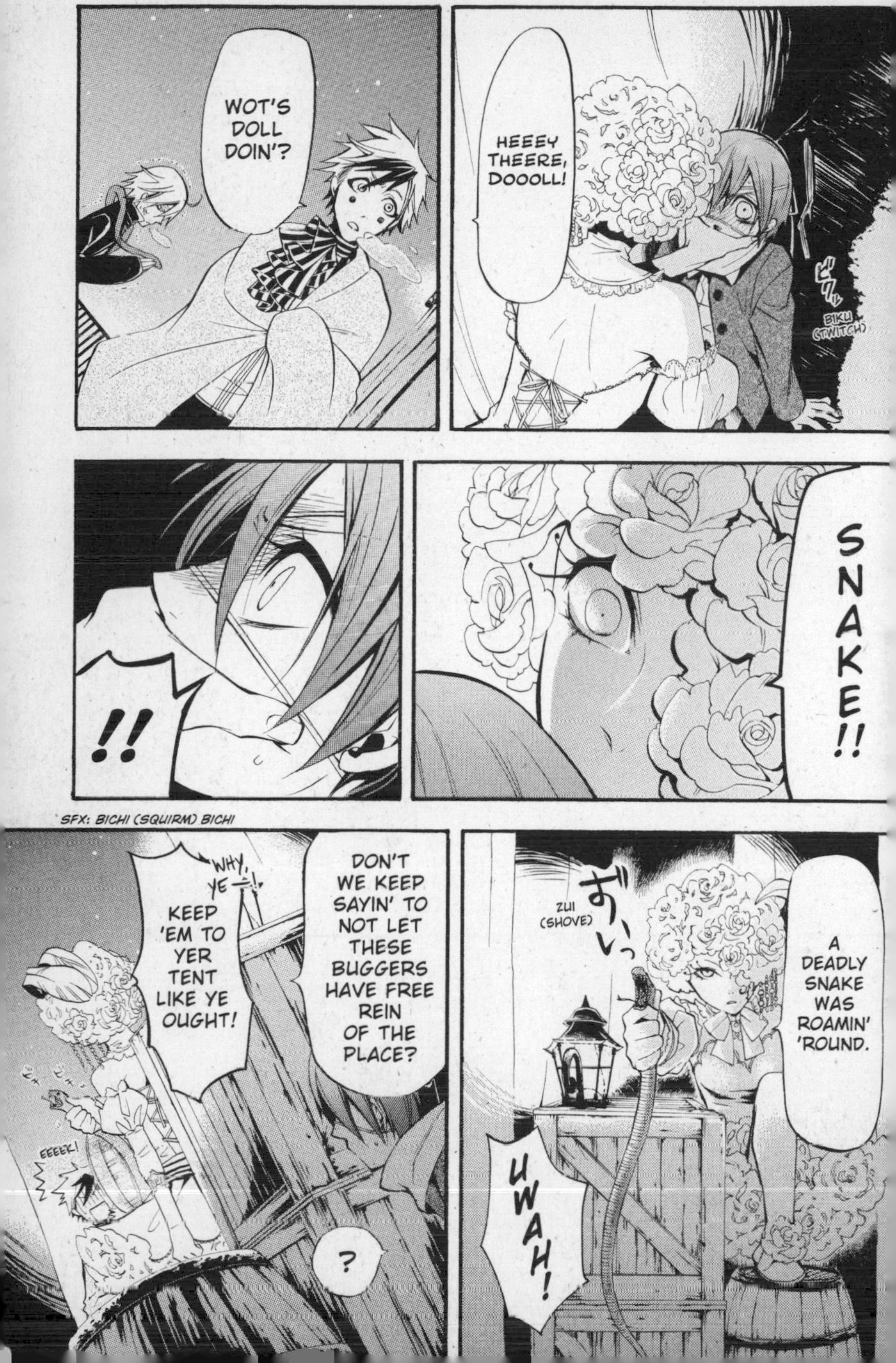
HEEEY THEERE, DOOOLL!
BIKU (TWITCH)
WOT'S DOLL DOIN'?
SNAKE!!
!!
SFX: BICHI (SQUIRM) BICHI
A DEADLY SNAKE WAS ROAMIN' 'ROUND.
ZUI (SHOVE)
UWAH!
DON'T WE KEEP SAYIN' TO NOT LET THESE BUGGERS HAVE FREE REIN OF THE PLACE?
WHY, YE—!
KEEP 'EM TO YER TENT LIKE YE OUGHT!
EEEEK!
?

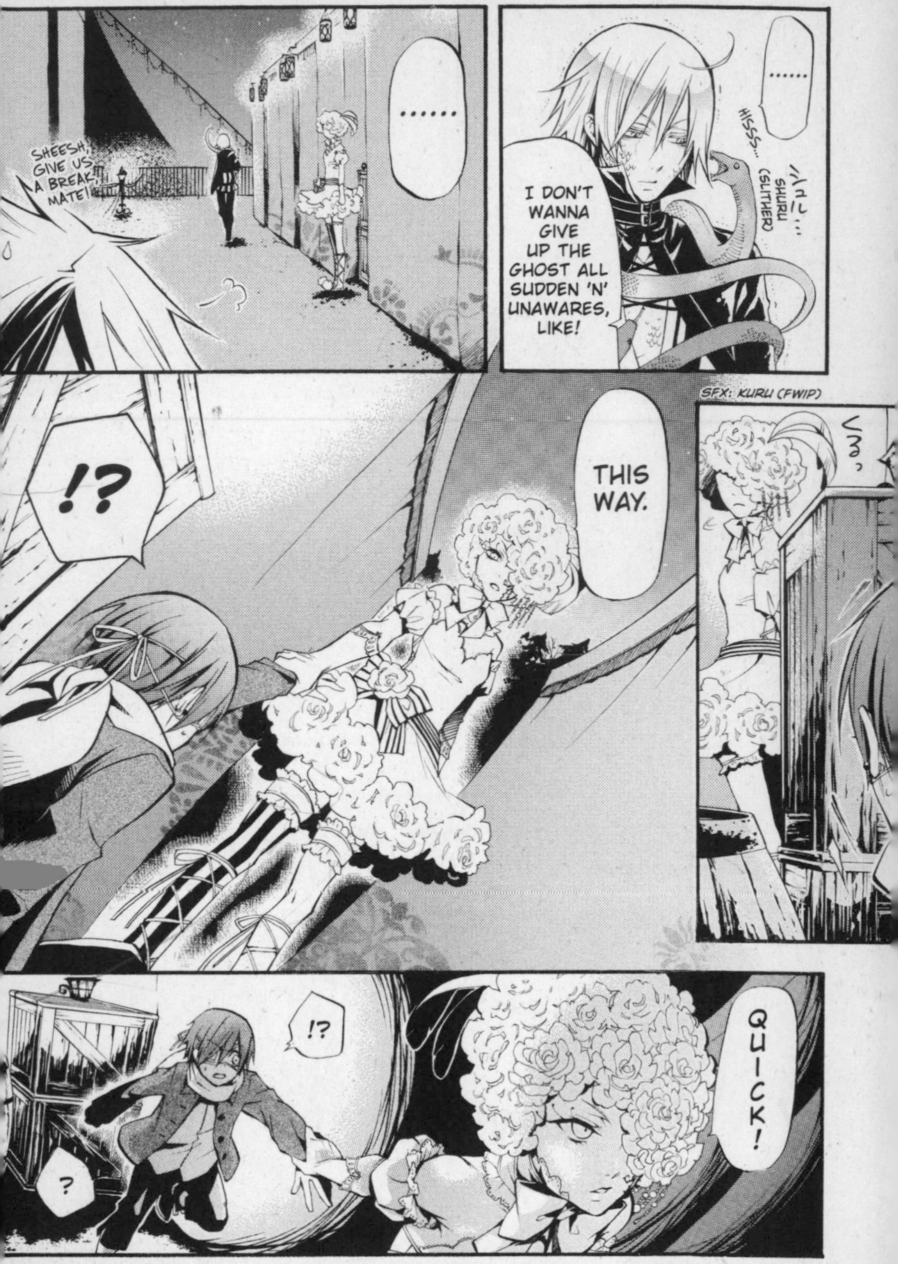
……
HISS…
シュル…
SHURU (SLITHER)
I DON'T WANNA GIVE UP THE GHOST ALL SUDDEN 'N' UNAWARES, LIKE!
……
SHEESH, GIVE US A BREAK, MATE!
SFX: KURU (FWIP)
くるっ
THIS WAY.
!?
QUICK!
!?
?

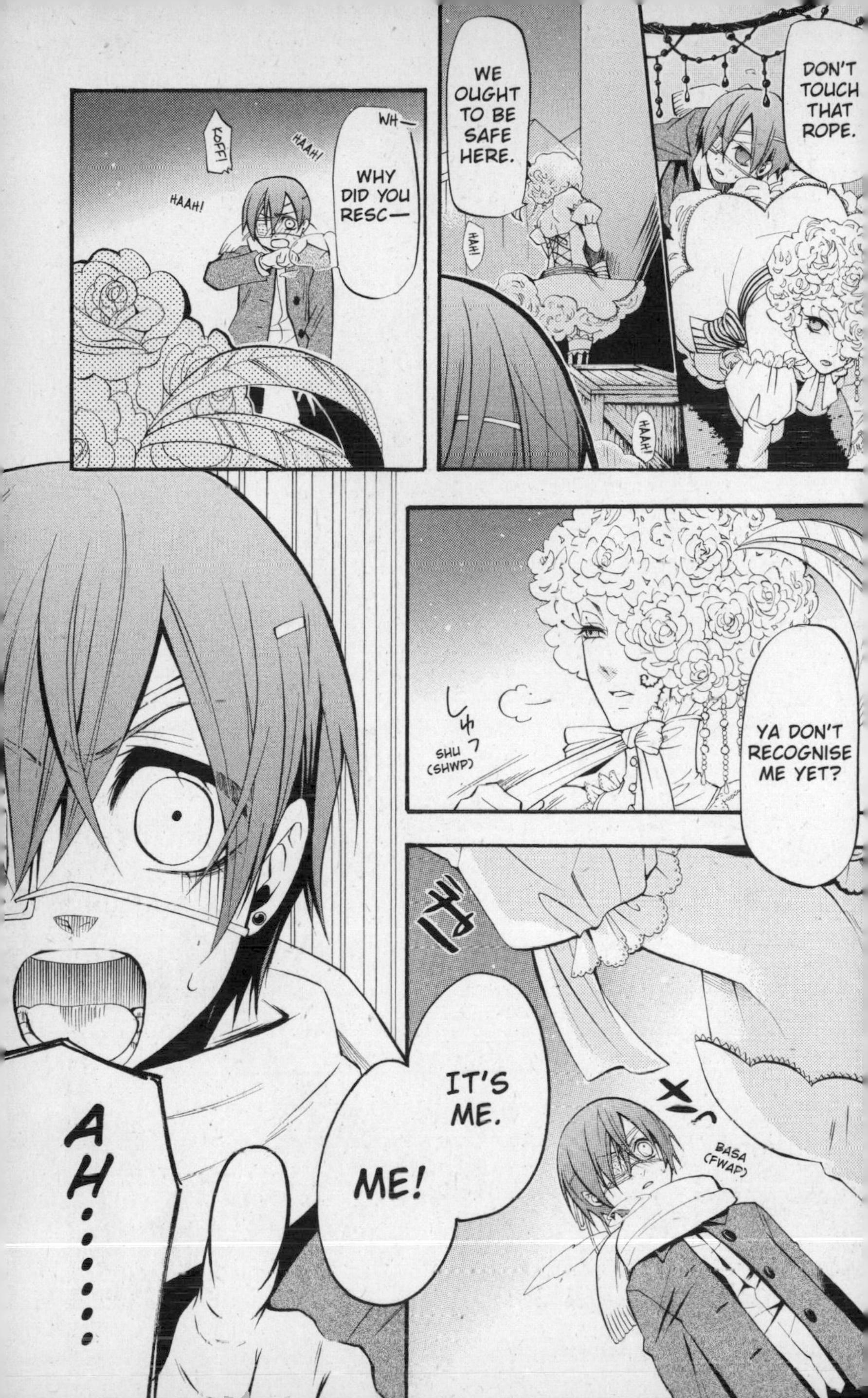

DON'T TOUCH THAT ROPE.
WE OUGHT TO BE SAFE HERE.
HAH!
HAAH!
WH—
WHY DID YOU RESC—
HAAH!
KOFF!
HAAH!
YA DON'T RECOGNISE ME YET?
SHU (SHWP)
IT'S ME.
ME!
BASA (FWAP)
AH......

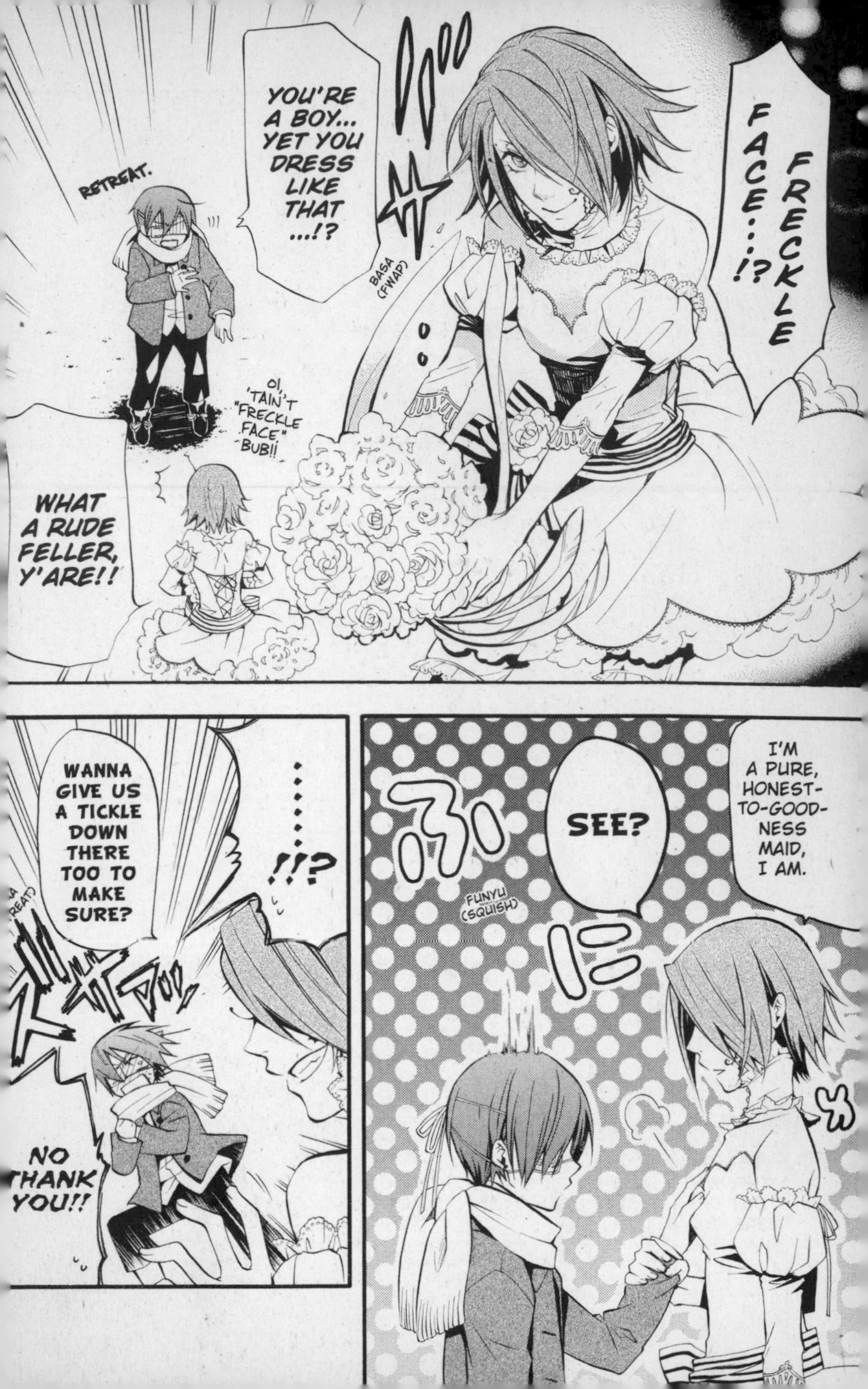
FRECKLE FACE...!?
BASA (FWAP)
YOU'RE A BOY... YET YOU DRESS LIKE THAT ...!?
RETREAT.
OI, 'TAIN'T "FRECKLE FACE," BUB!!
WHAT A RUDE FELLER, Y'ARE!!
I'M A PURE, HONEST-TO-GOODNESS MAID, I AM.
SEE?
FUNYU (SQUISH)
......!!?
WANNA GIVE US A TICKLE DOWN THERE TOO TO MAKE SURE?
NO THANK YOU!!

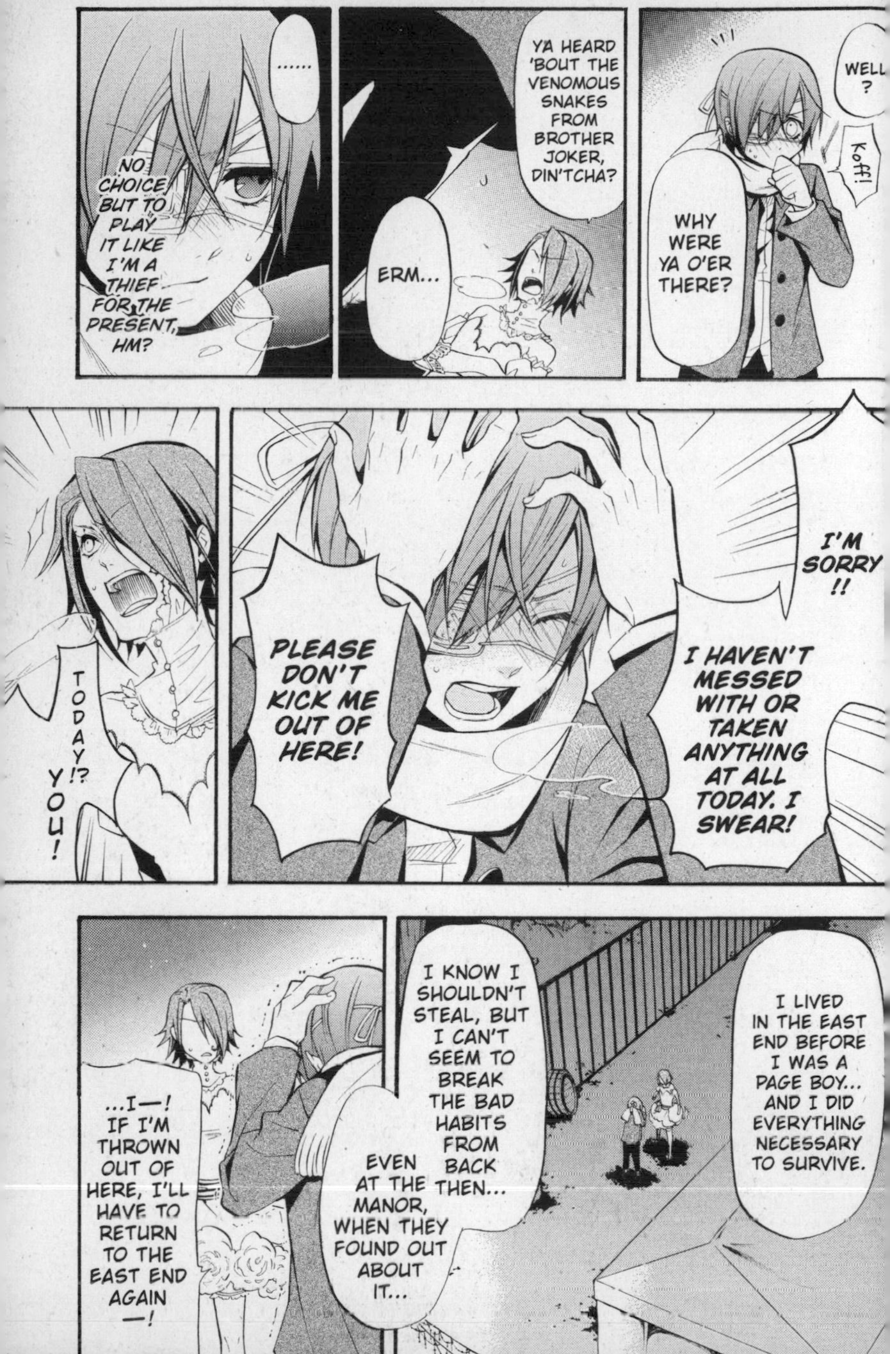
WELL?
Koff!
WHY WERE YA O'ER THERE?
YA HEARD 'BOUT THE VENOMOUS SNAKES FROM BROTHER JOKER, DIN'TCHA?
ERM...
......
NO CHOICE BUT TO PLAY IT LIKE I'M A THIEF FOR THE PRESENT, HM?
I'M SORRY!!
I HAVEN'T MESSED WITH OR TAKEN ANYTHING AT ALL TODAY. I SWEAR!
PLEASE DON'T KICK ME OUT OF HERE!
TODAY!?
YOU!
I LIVED IN THE EAST END BEFORE I WAS A PAGE BOY... AND I DID EVERYTHING NECESSARY TO SURVIVE.
I KNOW I SHOULDN'T STEAL, BUT I CAN'T SEEM TO BREAK THE BAD HABITS FROM BACK THEN...
EVEN AT THE MANOR, WHEN THEY FOUND OUT ABOUT IT...
...I—! IF I'M THROWN OUT OF HERE, I'LL HAVE TO RETURN TO THE EAST END AGAIN—!

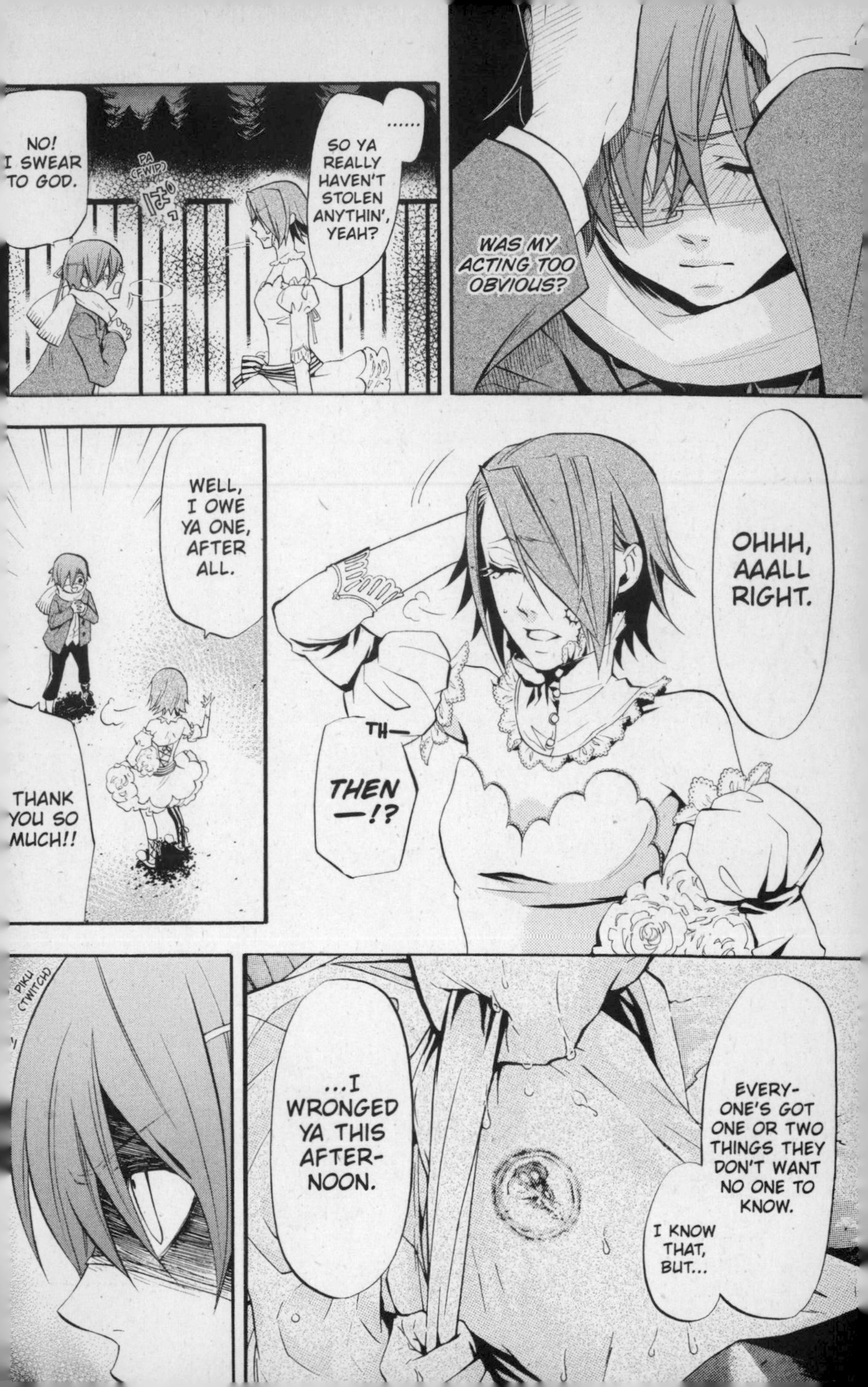
WAS MY ACTING TOO OBVIOUS?
......
SO YA REALLY HAVEN'T STOLEN ANYTHIN', YEAH?
PA (FWIP)
NO! I SWEAR TO GOD.
OHHH, AAALL RIGHT.
TH— THEN—!?
WELL, I OWE YA ONE, AFTER ALL.
THANK YOU SO MUCH!!
EVERY-ONE'S GOT ONE OR TWO THINGS THEY DON'T WANT NO ONE TO KNOW.
I KNOW THAT, BUT...
...I WRONGED YA THIS AFTER-NOON.
PIKU (TWITCH)

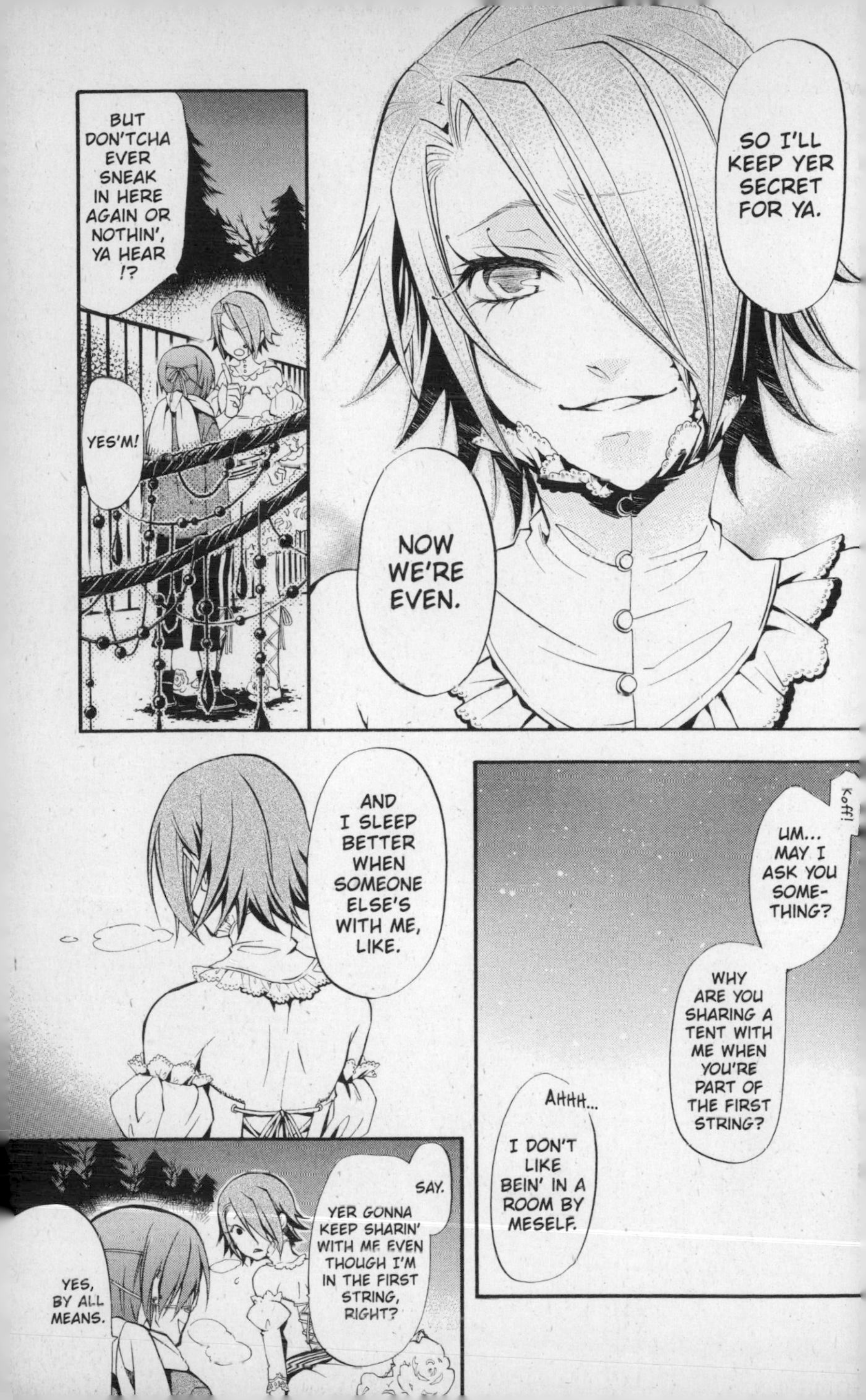
SO I'LL KEEP YER SECRET FOR YA.
NOW WE'RE EVEN.
BUT DON'TCHA EVER SNEAK IN HERE AGAIN OR NOTHIN', YA HEAR!?
YES'M!
Koff!
UM... MAY I ASK YOU SOME-THING?
WHY ARE YOU SHARING A TENT WITH ME WHEN YOU'RE PART OF THE FIRST STRING?
AHHH...
I DON'T LIKE BEIN' IN A ROOM BY MESELF.
AND I SLEEP BETTER WHEN SOMEONE ELSE'S WITH ME, LIKE.
SAY.
YER GONNA KEEP SHARIN' WITH ME EVEN THOUGH I'M IN THE FIRST STRING, RIGHT?
YES, BY ALL MEANS.

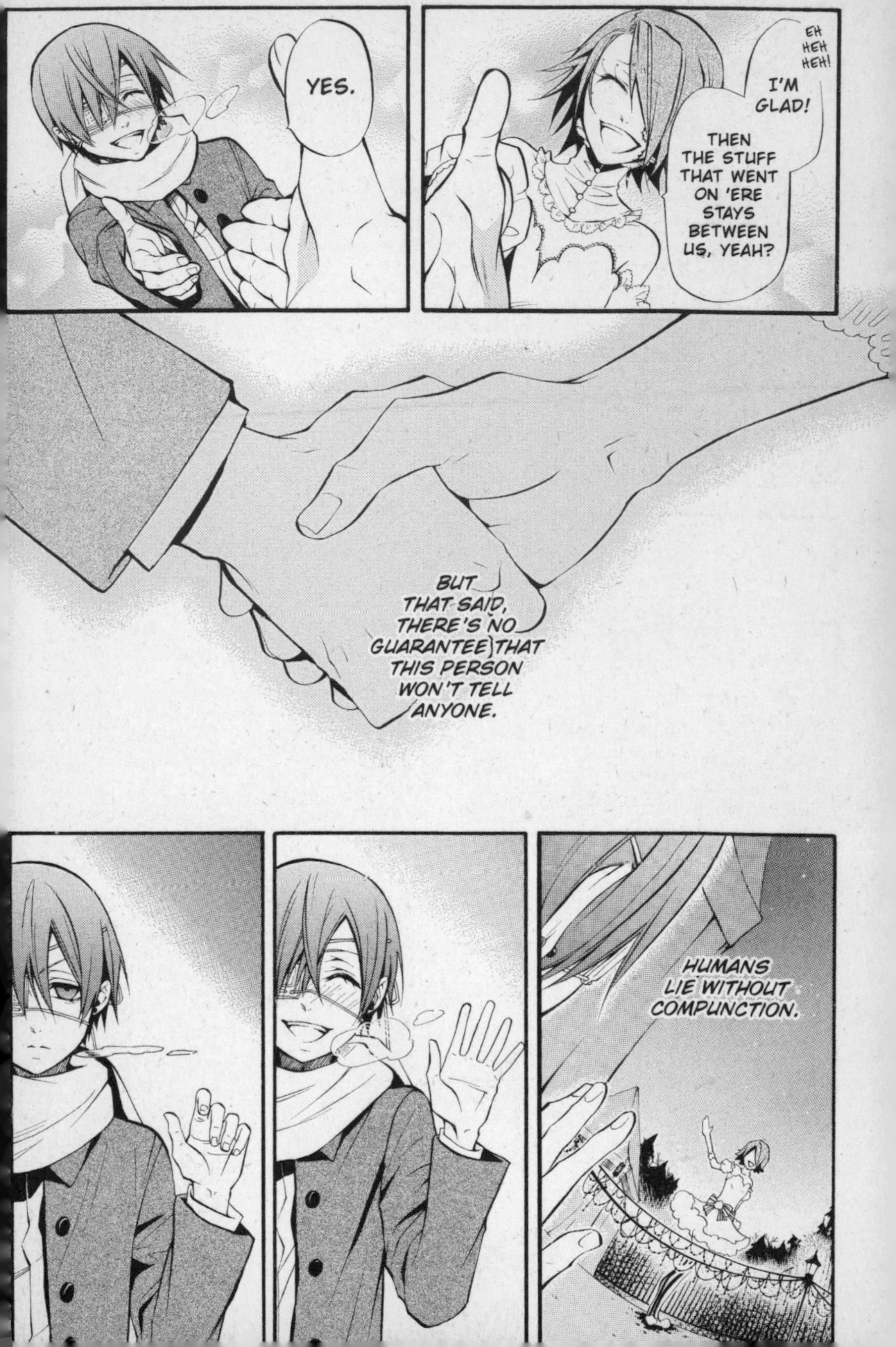
EH HEH HEH!
I'M GLAD!
THEN THE STUFF THAT WENT ON 'ERE STAYS BETWEEN US, YEAH?
YES.
BUT THAT SAID, THERE'S NO GUARANTEE THAT THIS PERSON WON'T TELL ANYONE.
HUMANS LIE WITHOUT COMPUNCTION.

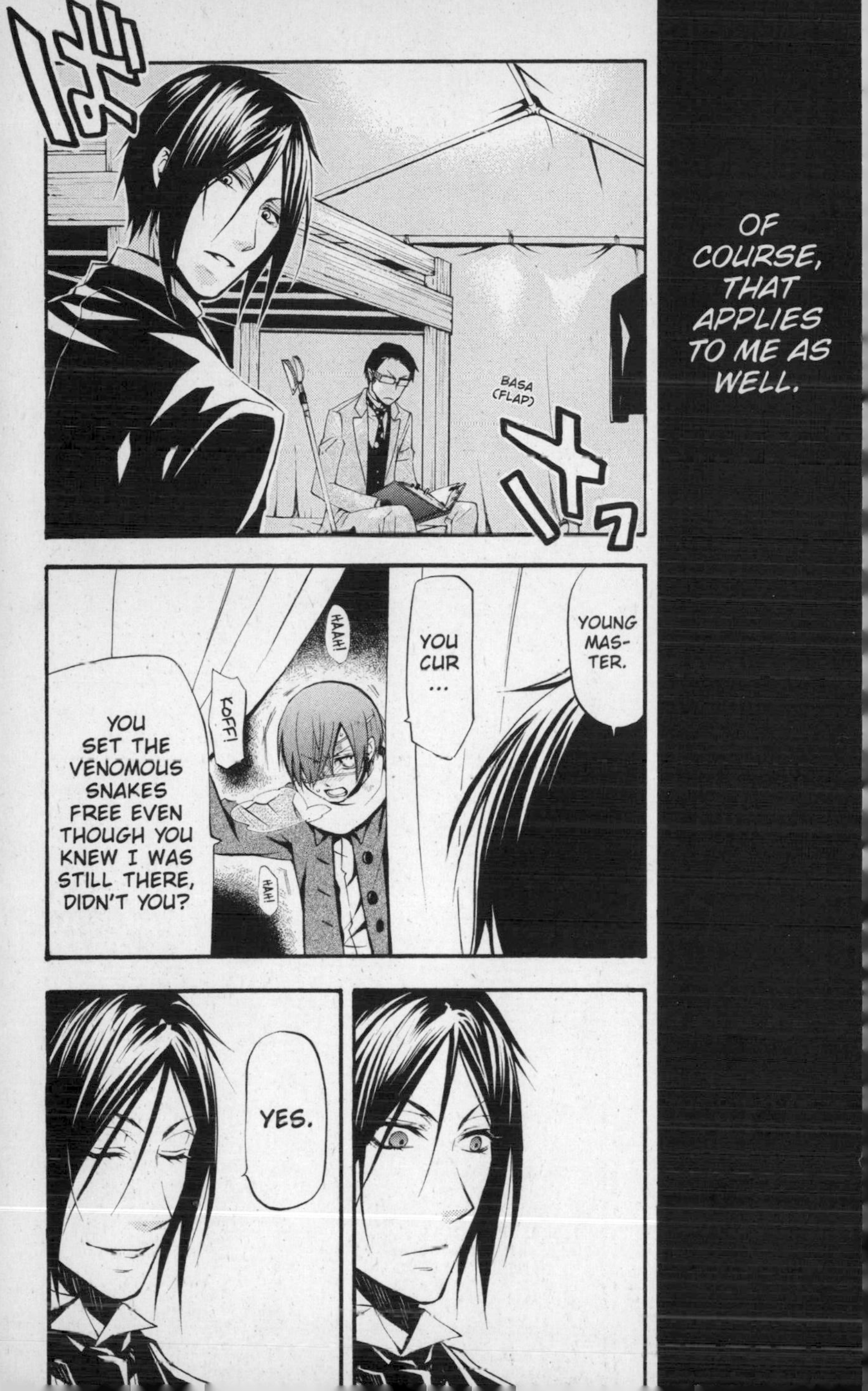
OF COURSE, THAT APPLIES TO ME AS WELL.
BASA (FLAP)
YOUNG MAS- TER.
YOU CUR ...
HAAH!
KOFF!
YOU SET THE VENOMOUS SNAKES FREE EVEN THOUGH YOU KNEW I WAS STILL THERE, DIDN'T YOU?
HAH!
YES.

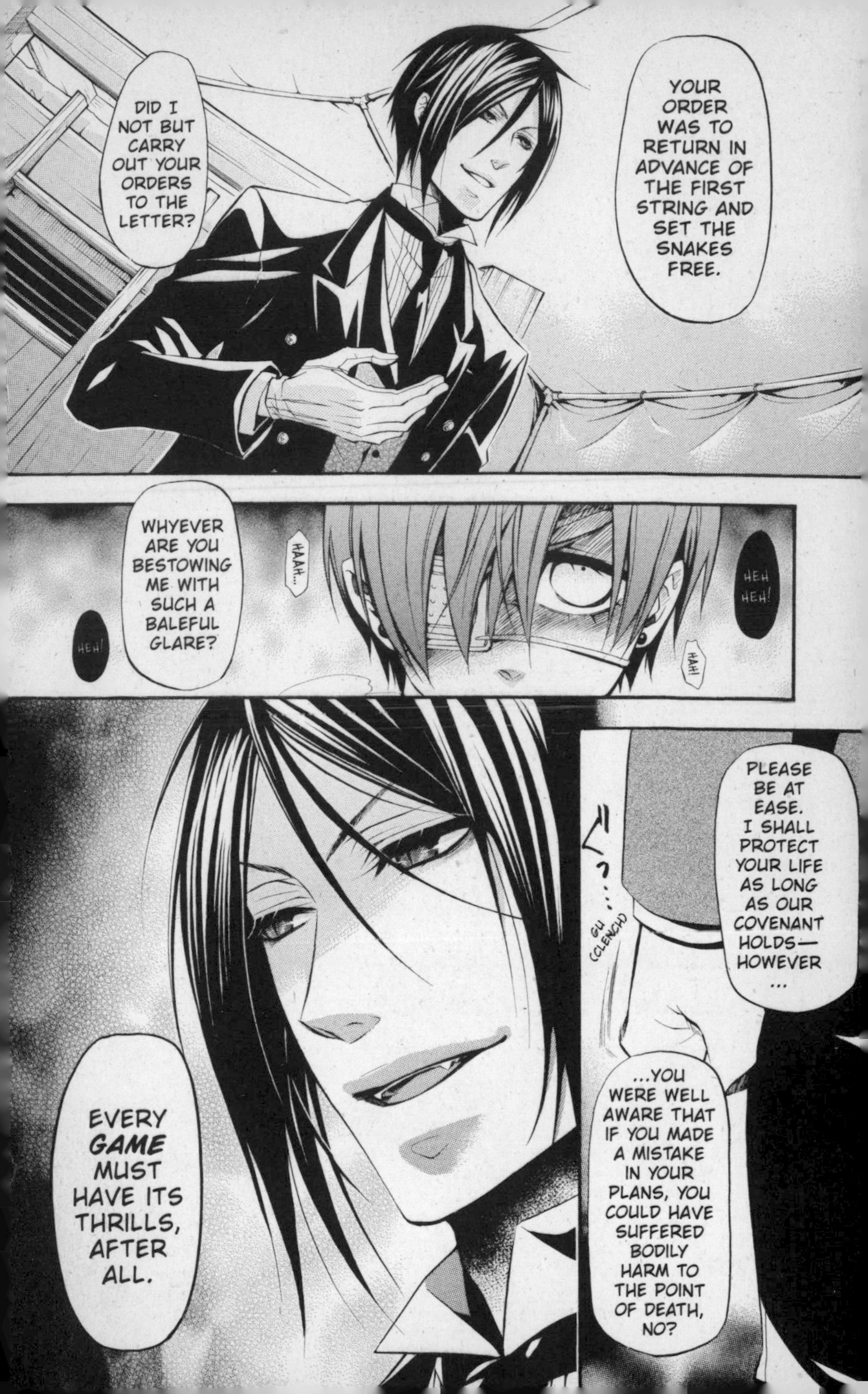
YOUR ORDER WAS TO RETURN IN ADVANCE OF THE FIRST STRING AND SET THE SNAKES FREE.
DID I NOT BUT CARRY OUT YOUR ORDERS TO THE LETTER?
HEH HEH!
HAH!
HAAH...
WHYEVER ARE YOU BESTOWING ME WITH SUCH A BALEFUL GLARE?
HEH!
PLEASE BE AT EASE. I SHALL PROTECT YOUR LIFE AS LONG AS OUR COVENANT HOLDS—HOWEVER...
GU (CLENCH)
...YOU WERE WELL AWARE THAT IF YOU MADE A MISTAKE IN YOUR PLANS, YOU COULD HAVE SUFFERED BODILY HARM TO THE POINT OF DEATH, NO?
EVERY GAME MUST HAVE ITS THRILLS, AFTER ALL.

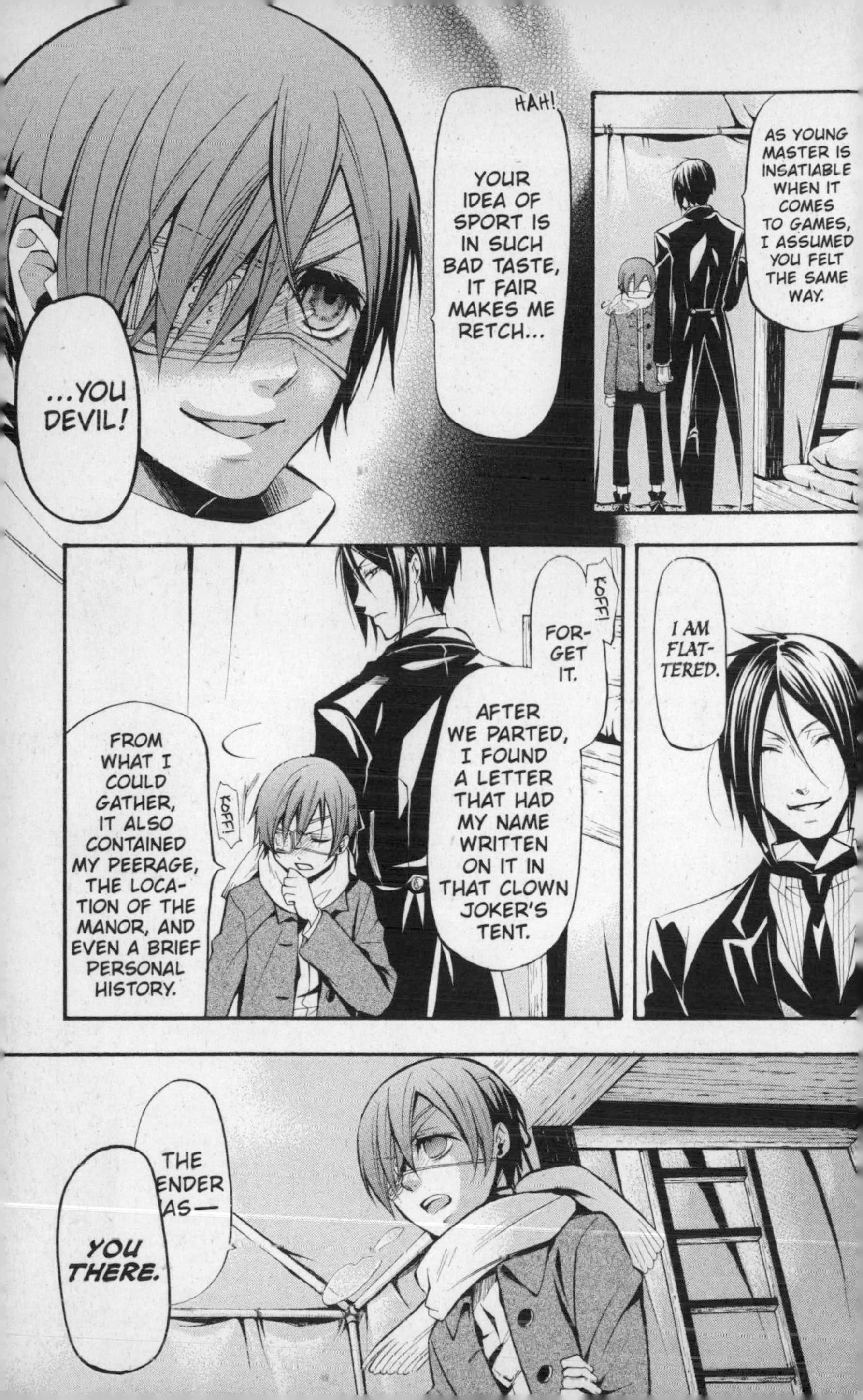
AS YOUNG MASTER IS INSATIABLE WHEN IT COMES TO GAMES, I ASSUMED YOU FELT THE SAME WAY.
HAH!
YOUR IDEA OF SPORT IS IN SUCH BAD TASTE, IT FAIR MAKES ME RETCH...
...YOU DEVIL!
I AM FLATTERED.
KOFF!
FOR-GET IT.
AFTER WE PARTED, I FOUND A LETTER THAT HAD MY NAME WRITTEN ON IT IN THAT CLOWN JOKER'S TENT.
KOFF!
FROM WHAT I COULD GATHER, IT ALSO CONTAINED MY PEERAGE, THE LOCA-TION OF THE MANOR, AND EVEN A BRIEF PERSONAL HISTORY.
THE ENDER AS—
YOU THERE.

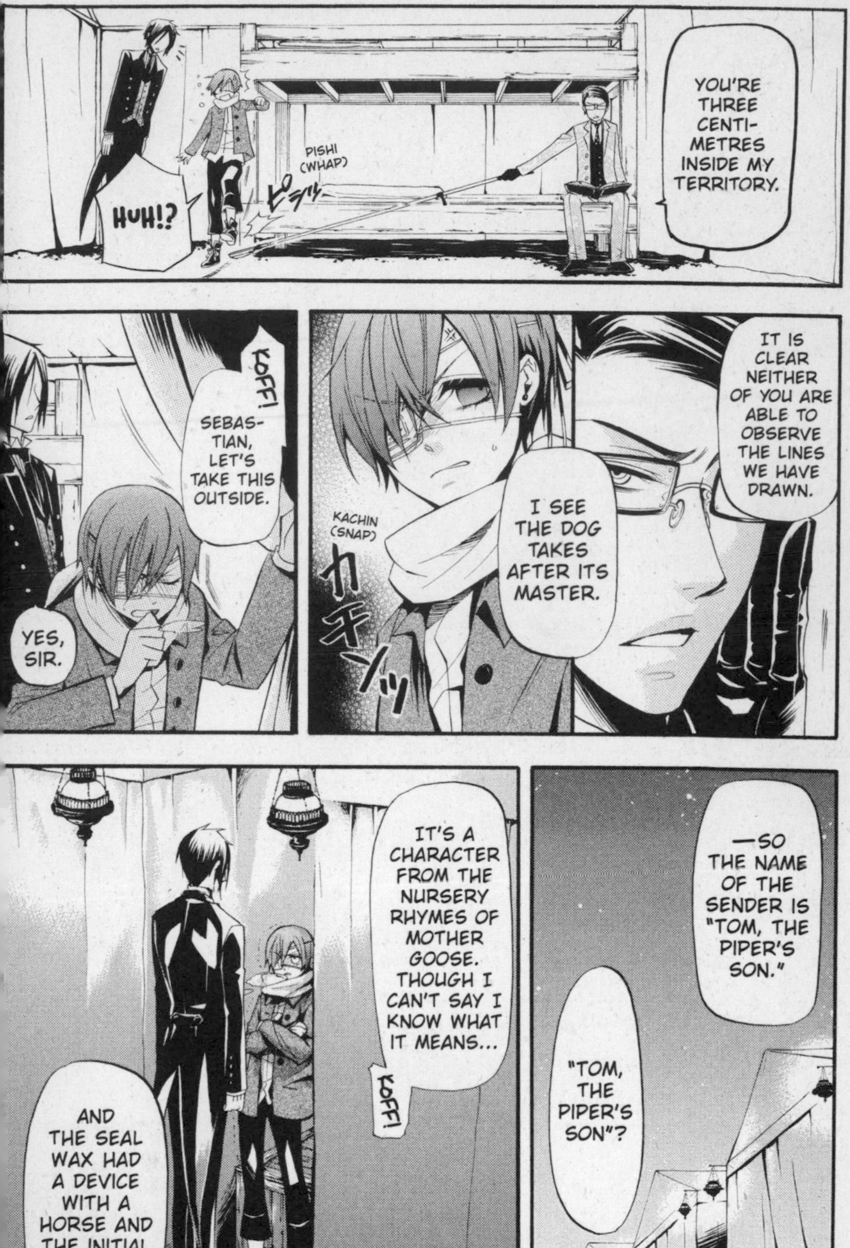
YOU'RE THREE CENTI-METRES INSIDE MY TERRITORY.
PISHI (WHAP)
HUH!?
IT IS CLEAR NEITHER OF YOU ARE ABLE TO OBSERVE THE LINES WE HAVE DRAWN.
I SEE THE DOG TAKES AFTER ITS MASTER.
KACHIN (SNAP)
KOFF!
SEBAS-TIAN, LET'S TAKE THIS OUTSIDE.
YES, SIR.
—SO THE NAME OF THE SENDER IS "TOM, THE PIPER'S SON."
"TOM, THE PIPER'S SON"?
IT'S A CHARACTER FROM THE NURSERY RHYMES OF MOTHER GOOSE. THOUGH I CAN'T SAY I KNOW WHAT IT MEANS...
KOFF!
AND THE SEAL WAX HAD A DEVICE WITH A HORSE AND THE INITIAL "K" ON IT.

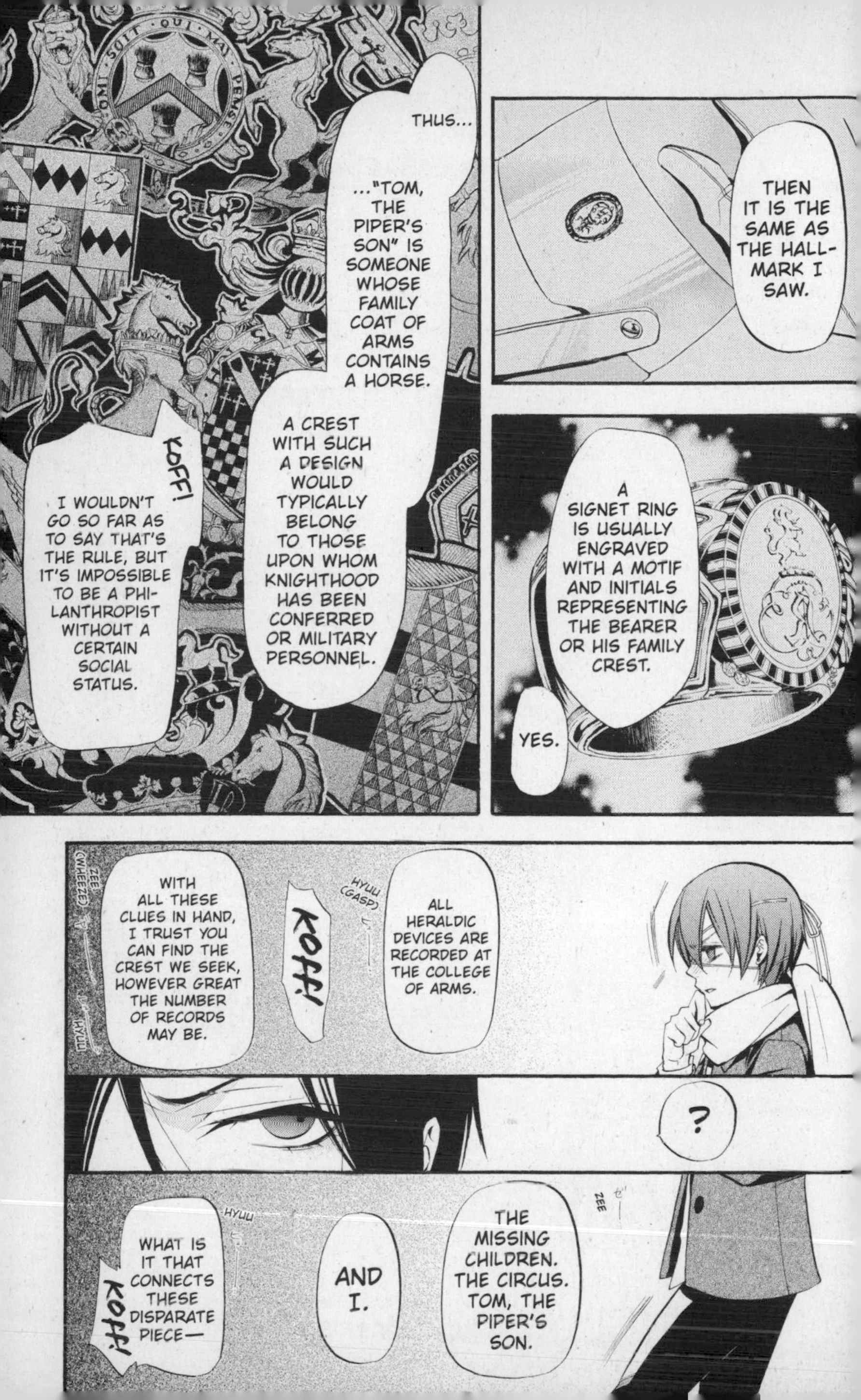
THEN IT IS THE SAME AS THE HALL-MARK I SAW.
A SIGNET RING IS USUALLY ENGRAVED WITH A MOTIF AND INITIALS REPRESENTING THE BEARER OR HIS FAMILY CREST.
YES.
THUS...
..."TOM, THE PIPER'S SON" IS SOMEONE WHOSE FAMILY COAT OF ARMS CONTAINS A HORSE.
A CREST WITH SUCH A DESIGN WOULD TYPICALLY BELONG TO THOSE UPON WHOM KNIGHTHOOD HAS BEEN CONFERRED OR MILITARY PERSONNEL.
KOFF!
I WOULDN'T GO SO FAR AS TO SAY THAT'S THE RULE, BUT IT'S IMPOSSIBLE TO BE A PHI-LANTHROPIST WITHOUT A CERTAIN SOCIAL STATUS.
ALL HERALDIC DEVICES ARE RECORDED AT THE COLLEGE OF ARMS.
HYUU (GASP)
KOFF!
WITH ALL THESE CLUES IN HAND, I TRUST YOU CAN FIND THE CREST WE SEEK, HOWEVER GREAT THE NUMBER OF RECORDS MAY BE.
ZEE (WHEEZE)
HYUU
?
ZEE
THE MISSING CHILDREN. THE CIRCUS. TOM, THE PIPER'S SON.
AND I.
HYUU
WHAT IS IT THAT CONNECTS THESE DISPARATE PIECE—
KOFF!

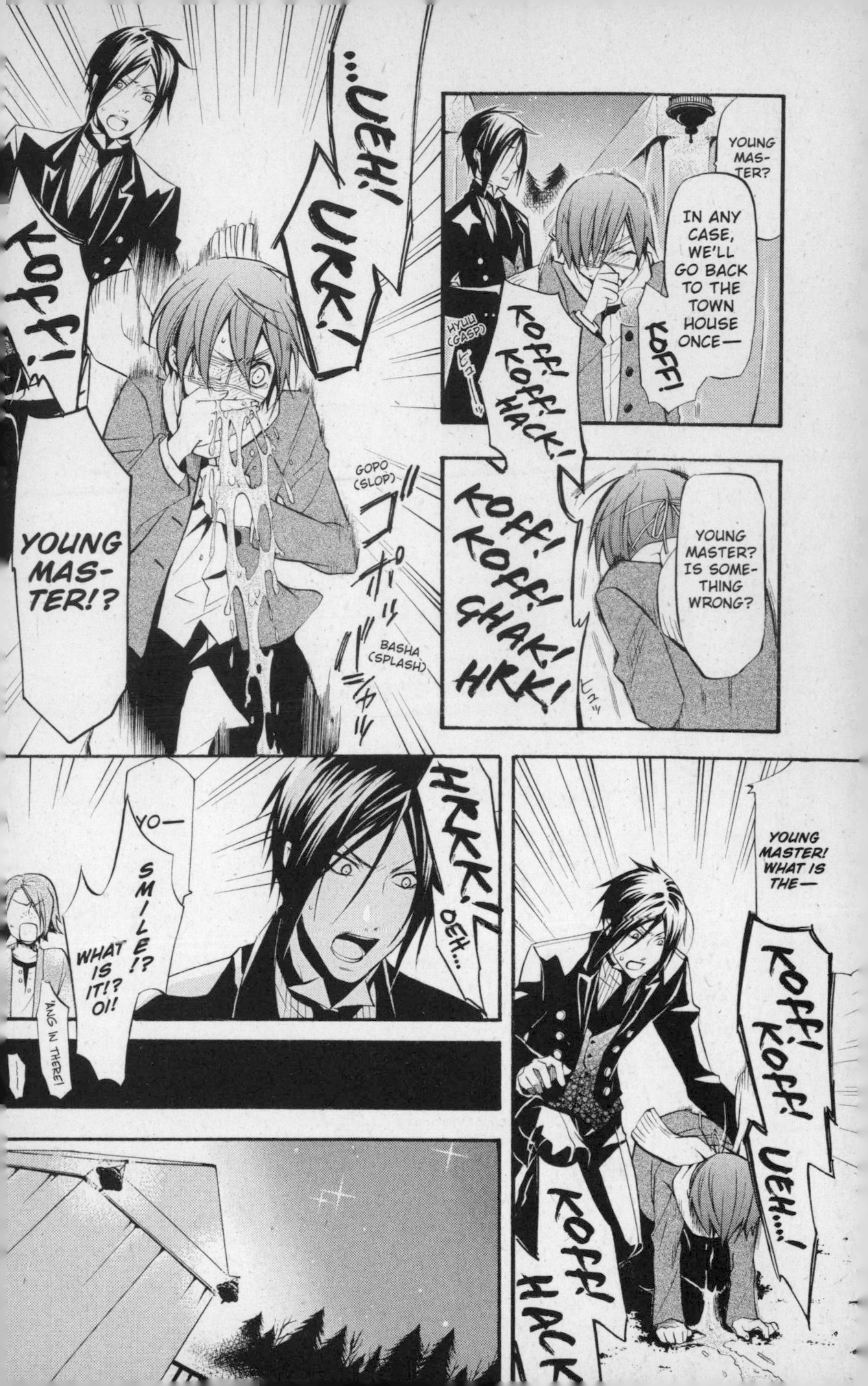

YOUNG MASTER?
IN ANY CASE, WE'LL GO BACK TO THE TOWN HOUSE ONCE—
KOFF!
HYUU (GASP)
KOFF! KOFF! HACK!
YOUNG MASTER? IS SOMETHING WRONG?
KOFF! KOFF! GHAK! HRK!
...UEH! UKK!
GOPO (SLOP)
BASHA (SPLASH)
KOFF!
YOUNG MASTER!?
YOUNG MASTER! WHAT IS THE—
KOFF! KOFF! UEH...!
KOFF! HACK
HRKK!!
OEH...
YO—
SMILE!?
WHAT IS IT!? OI!
'ANG IN THERE!

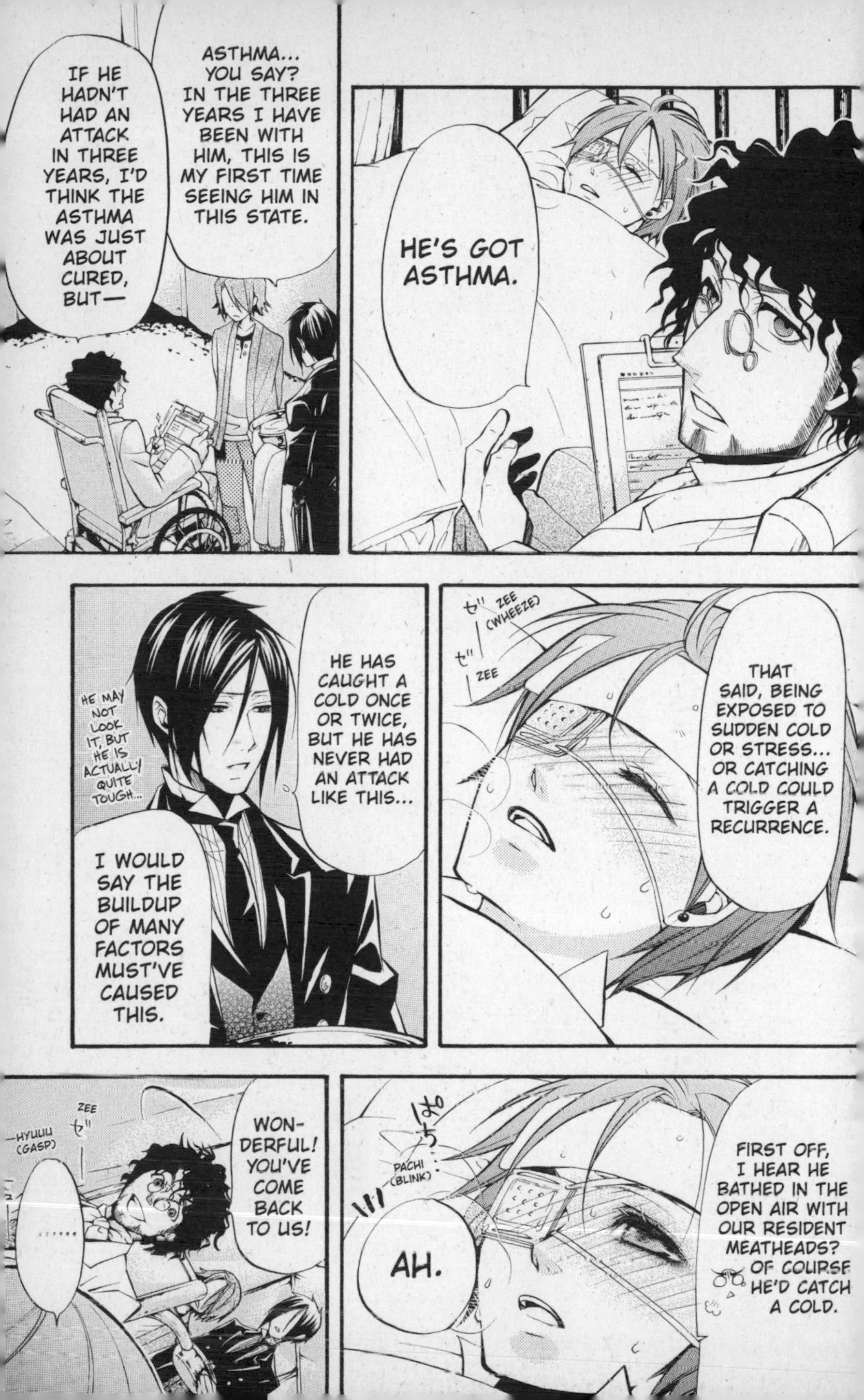
HE'S GOT ASTHMA.
ASTHMA... YOU SAY? IN THE THREE YEARS I HAVE BEEN WITH HIM, THIS IS MY FIRST TIME SEEING HIM IN THIS STATE.
IF HE HADN'T HAD AN ATTACK IN THREE YEARS, I'D THINK THE ASTHMA WAS JUST ABOUT CURED, BUT—
THAT SAID, BEING EXPOSED TO SUDDEN COLD OR STRESS... OR CATCHING A COLD COULD TRIGGER A RECURRENCE.
ZEE (WHEEZE)
ZEE
HE HAS CAUGHT A COLD ONCE OR TWICE, BUT HE HAS NEVER HAD AN ATTACK LIKE THIS...
HE MAY NOT LOOK IT, BUT HE IS ACTUALLY QUITE TOUGH...
I WOULD SAY THE BUILDUP OF MANY FACTORS MUST'VE CAUSED THIS.
FIRST OFF, I HEAR HE BATHED IN THE OPEN AIR WITH OUR RESIDENT MEATHEADS? OF COURSE HE'D CATCH A COLD.
PACHI (BLINK)
AH.
WON-DERFUL! YOU'VE COME BACK TO US!
ZEE
HYUUU (GASP)
......

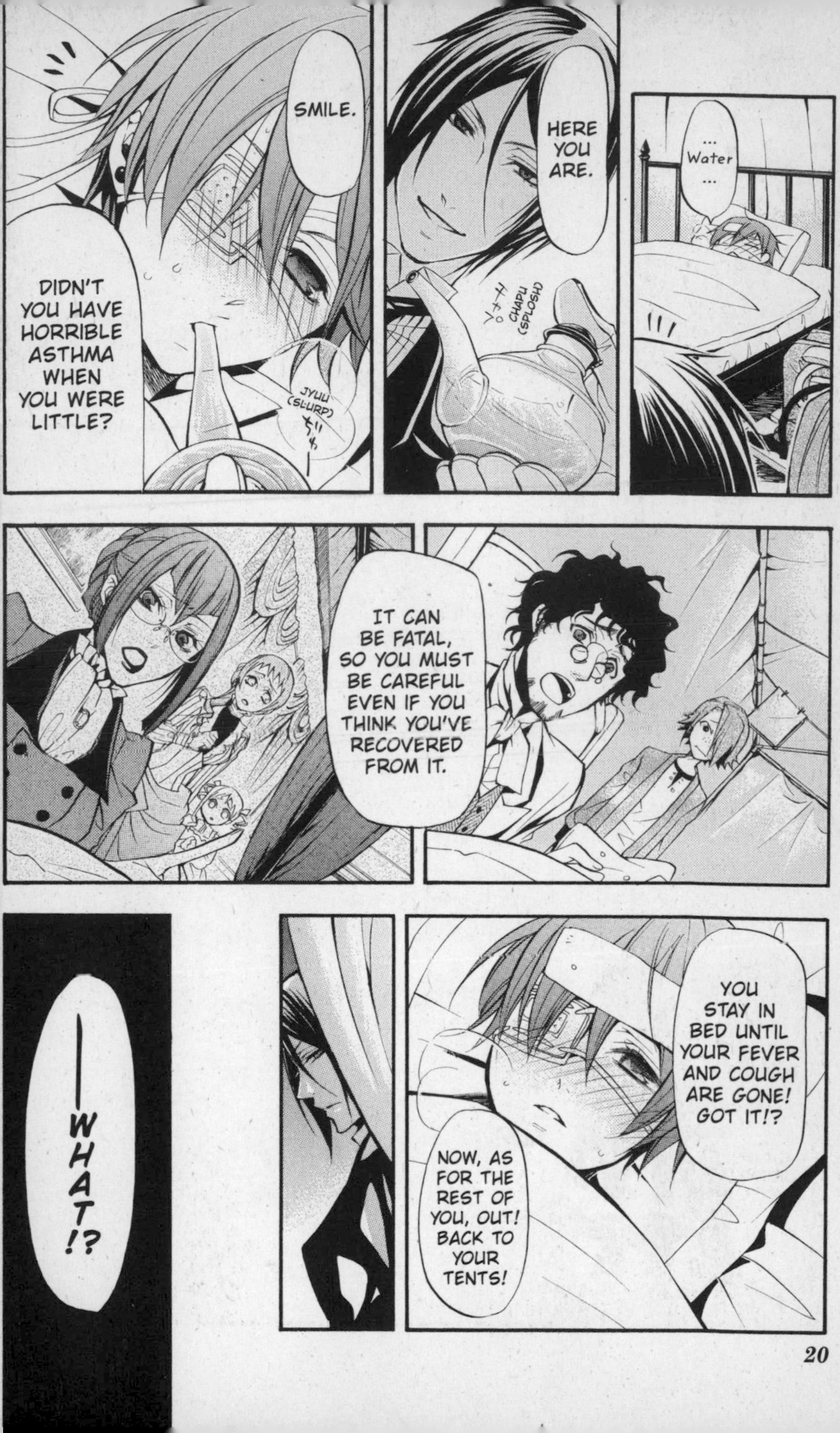
... Water ...
HERE YOU ARE.
CHAPU (SPLOSH)
SMILE.
JYUU (SLURP)
DIDN'T YOU HAVE HORRIBLE ASTHMA WHEN YOU WERE LITTLE?
IT CAN BE FATAL, SO YOU MUST BE CAREFUL EVEN IF YOU THINK YOU'VE RECOVERED FROM IT.
YOU STAY IN BED UNTIL YOUR FEVER AND COUGH ARE GONE! GOT IT!?
NOW, AS FOR THE REST OF YOU, OUT! BACK TO YOUR TENTS!
—WHAT!?

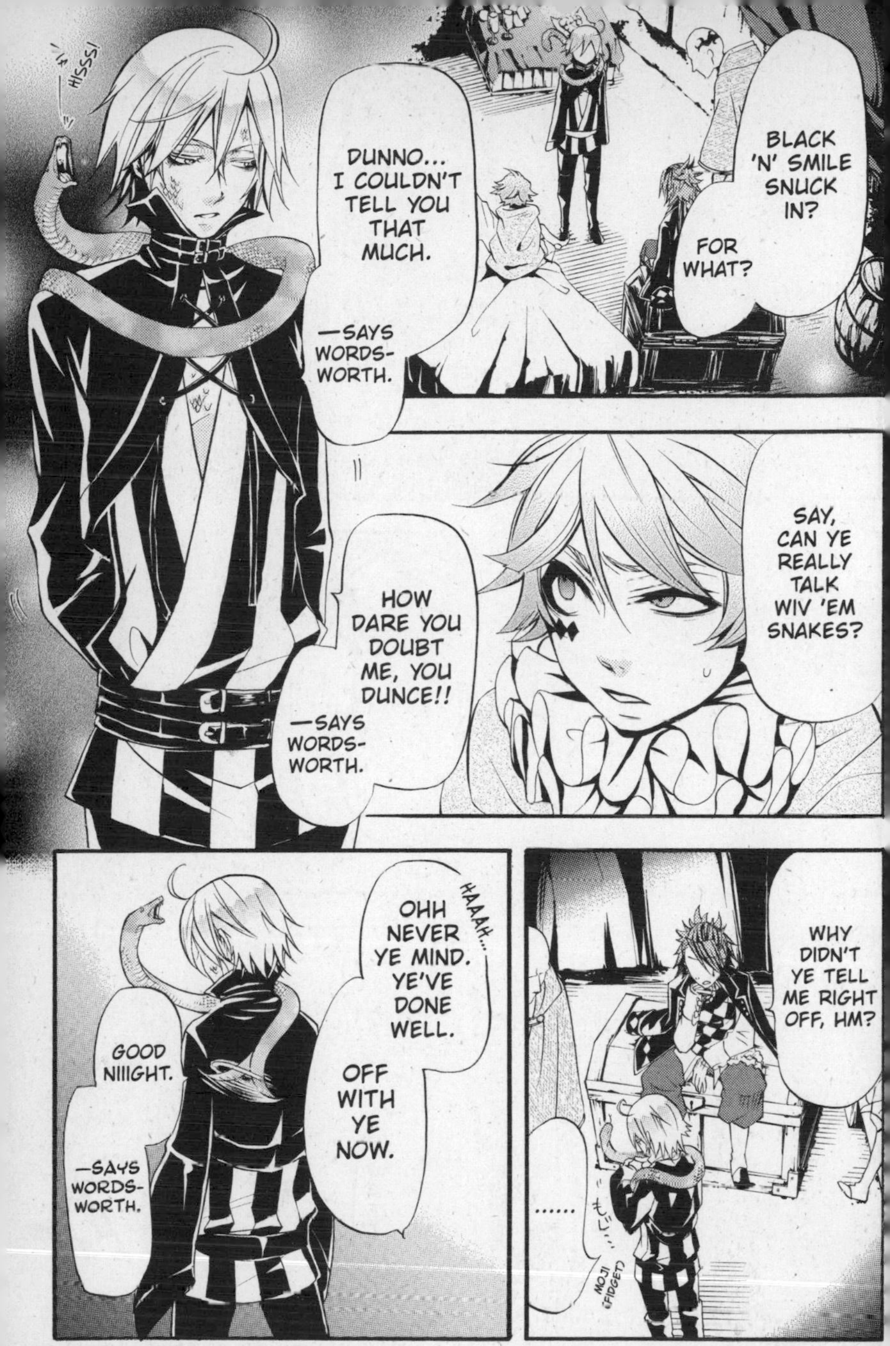
BLACK 'N' SMILE SNUCK IN?
FOR WHAT?
SAY, CAN YE REALLY TALK WIV 'EM SNAKES?
HISSS!
DUNNO... I COULDN'T TELL YOU THAT MUCH.
—SAYS WORDS-WORTH.
HOW DARE YOU DOUBT ME, YOU DUNCE!!
—SAYS WORDS-WORTH.
WHY DIDN'T YE TELL ME RIGHT OFF, HM?
......
MOJI (FIDGET)
HAAAH...
OHH NEVER YE MIND. YE'VE DONE WELL.
OFF WITH YE NOW.
GOOD NIIIGHT.
—SAYS WORDS-WORTH.

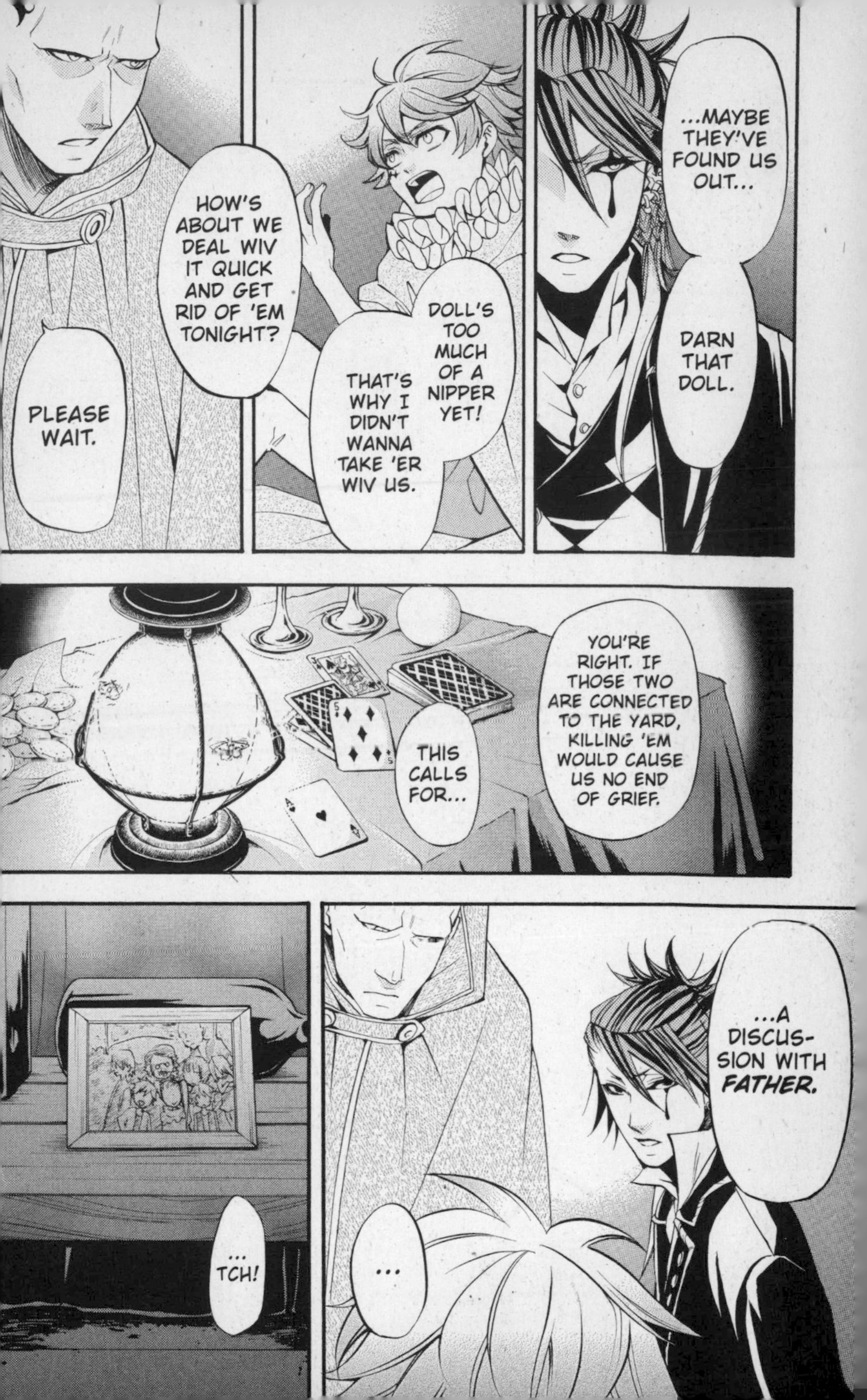
...MAYBE THEY'VE FOUND US OUT...
DARN THAT DOLL.
HOW'S ABOUT WE DEAL WIV IT QUICK AND GET RID OF 'EM TONIGHT?
DOLL'S TOO MUCH OF A NIPPER YET!
THAT'S WHY I DIDN'T WANNA TAKE 'ER WIV US.
PLEASE WAIT.
YOU'RE RIGHT. IF THOSE TWO ARE CONNECTED TO THE YARD, KILLING 'EM WOULD CAUSE US NO END OF GRIEF.
THIS CALLS FOR...
...A DISCUSSION WITH ***FATHER.***
...
...TCH!

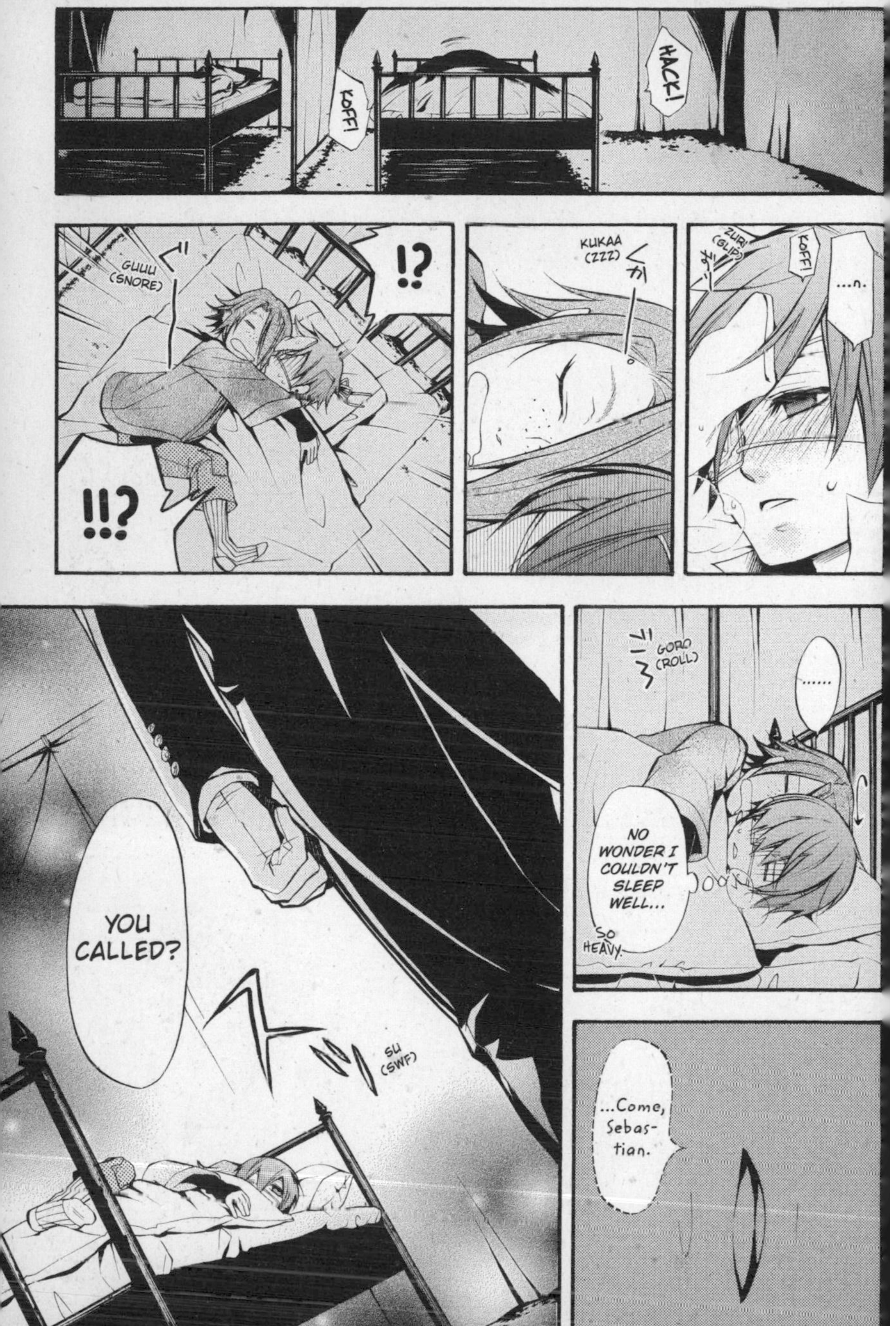

HACK!
KOFF!
ZURI (GLIP)
KOFF!
...n.
KUKAA (ZZZ)
!?
GUUU (SNORE)
!!?
GORO (ROLL)
......
NO WONDER I COULDN'T SLEEP WELL...
SO HEAVY.
...Come, Sebas-tian.
YOU CALLED?
SU (SWF)

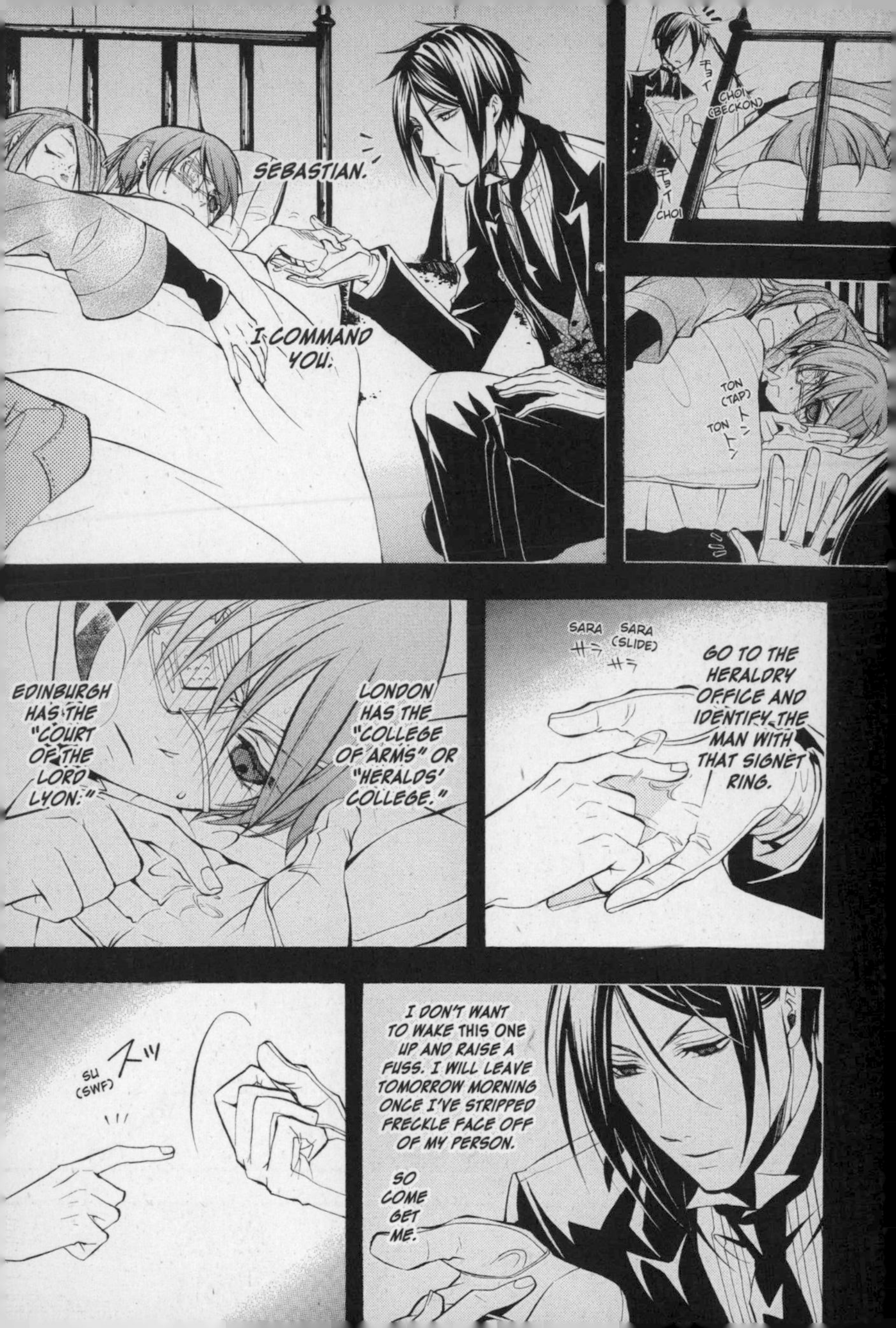

CHOI (BECKON)
CHOI
TON (TAP)
TON
SEBASTIAN.
I COMMAND YOU.
SARA SARA (SLIDE)
GO TO THE HERALDRY OFFICE AND IDENTIFY THE MAN WITH THAT SIGNET RING.
LONDON HAS THE "COLLEGE OF ARMS" OR "HERALDS' COLLEGE."
EDINBURGH HAS THE "COURT OF THE LORD LYON."
I DON'T WANT TO WAKE THIS ONE UP AND RAISE A FUSS. I WILL LEAVE TOMORROW MORNING ONCE I'VE STRIPPED FRECKLE FACE OFF OF MY PERSON.
SO COME GET ME.
SU (SWF)

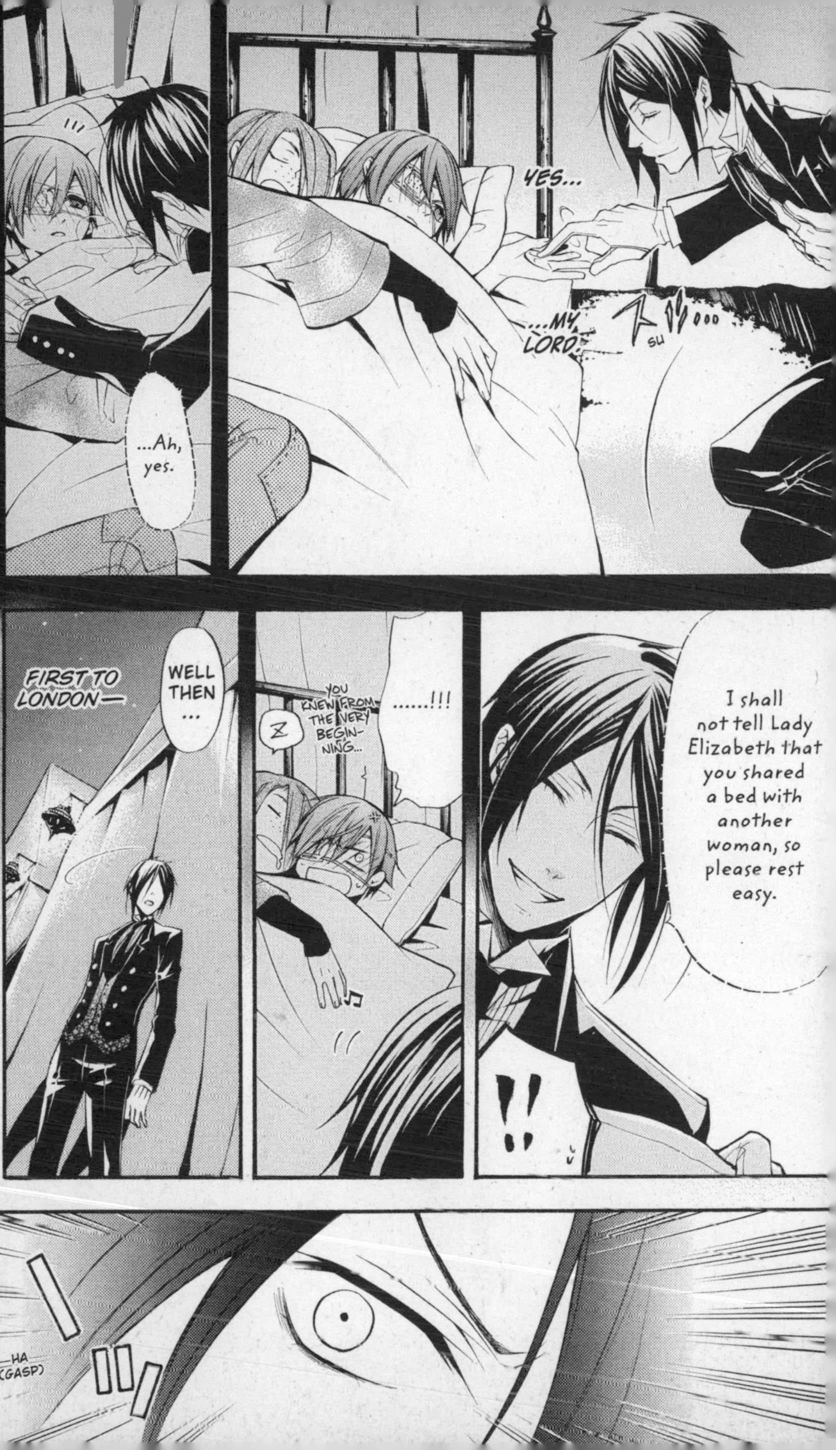
YES...
...MY LORD
SU
...Ah, yes.
I shall not tell Lady Elizabeth that you shared a bed with another woman, so please rest easy.
......!!!
YOU KNEW FROM THE VERY BEGIN-NING...
Z
WELL THEN ...
FIRST TO LONDON—
HA (GASP)

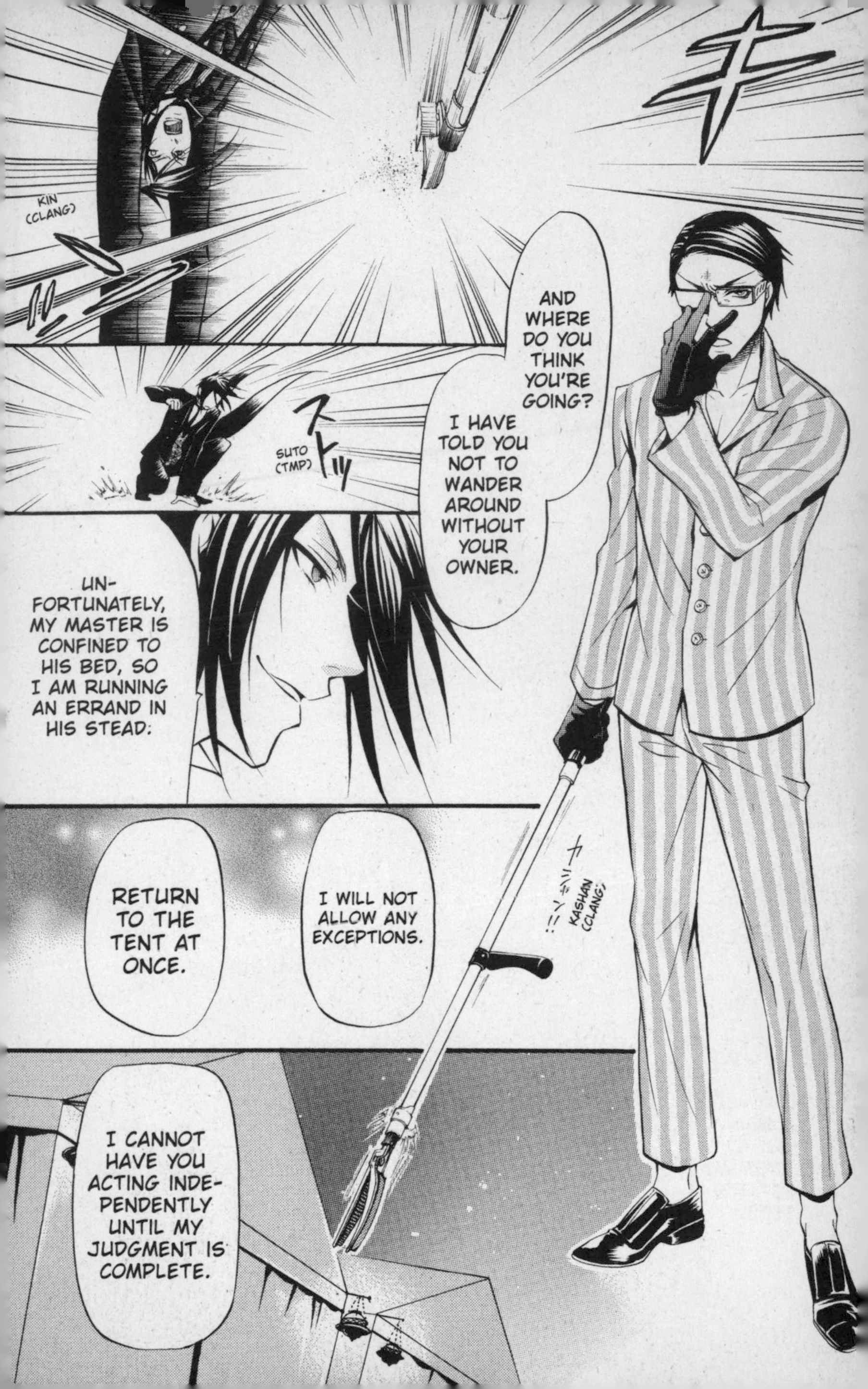
KIN (CLANG)
AND WHERE DO YOU THINK YOU'RE GOING?
I HAVE TOLD YOU NOT TO WANDER AROUND WITHOUT YOUR OWNER.
KASHAN (CLANG)
SUTO (TMP)
UN-FORTUNATELY, MY MASTER IS CONFINED TO HIS BED, SO I AM RUNNING AN ERRAND IN HIS STEAD.
I WILL NOT ALLOW ANY EXCEPTIONS.
RETURN TO THE TENT AT ONCE.
I CANNOT HAVE YOU ACTING INDE-PENDENTLY UNTIL MY JUDGMENT IS COMPLETE.

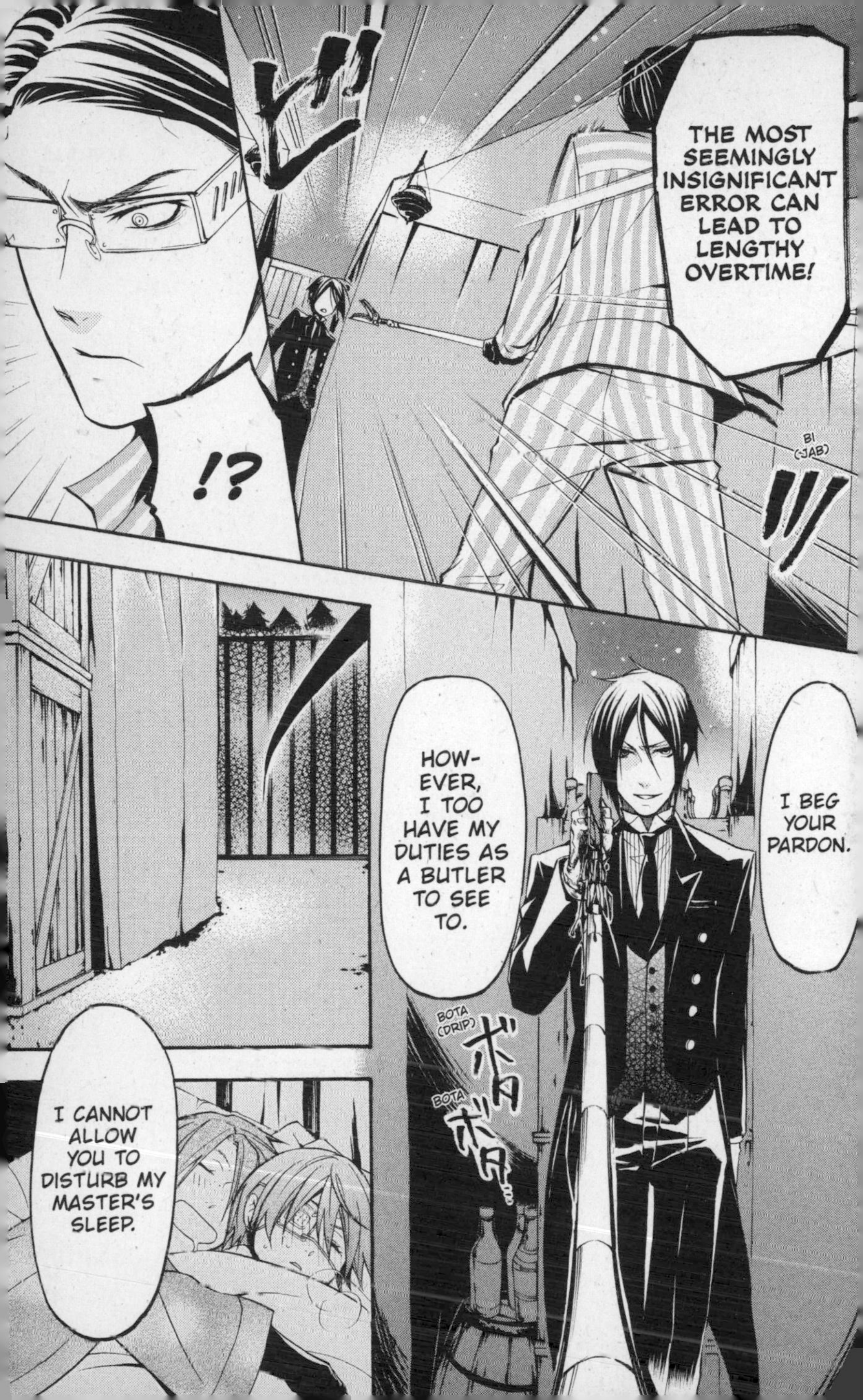
THE MOST SEEMINGLY INSIGNIFICANT ERROR CAN LEAD TO LENGTHY OVERTIME!
BI (JAB)
!?
I BEG YOUR PARDON.
HOW-EVER, I TOO HAVE MY DUTIES AS A BUTLER TO SEE TO.
BOTA (DRIP)
BOTA
I CANNOT ALLOW YOU TO DISTURB MY MASTER'S SLEEP.

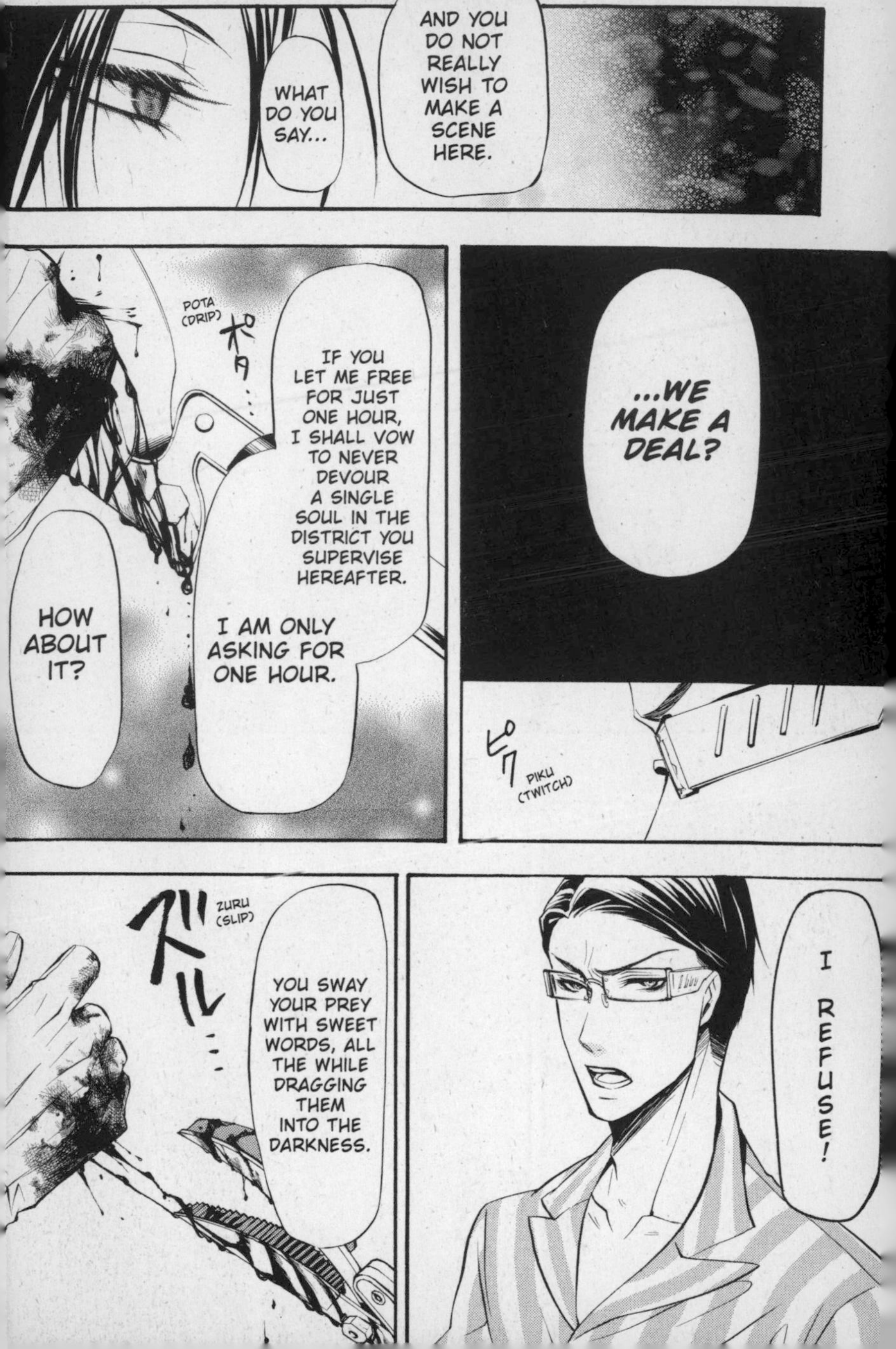
AND YOU DO NOT REALLY WISH TO MAKE A SCENE HERE.
WHAT DO YOU SAY...
...WE MAKE A DEAL?
ピク
PIKU (TWITCH)
ポタ
POTA (DRIP)
IF YOU LET ME FREE FOR JUST ONE HOUR, I SHALL VOW TO NEVER DEVOUR A SINGLE SOUL IN THE DISTRICT YOU SUPERVISE HEREAFTER.
I AM ONLY ASKING FOR ONE HOUR.
HOW ABOUT IT?
I REFUSE!
ズル
ZURU (SLIP)
YOU SWAY YOUR PREY WITH SWEET WORDS, ALL THE WHILE DRAGGING THEM INTO THE DARKNESS.

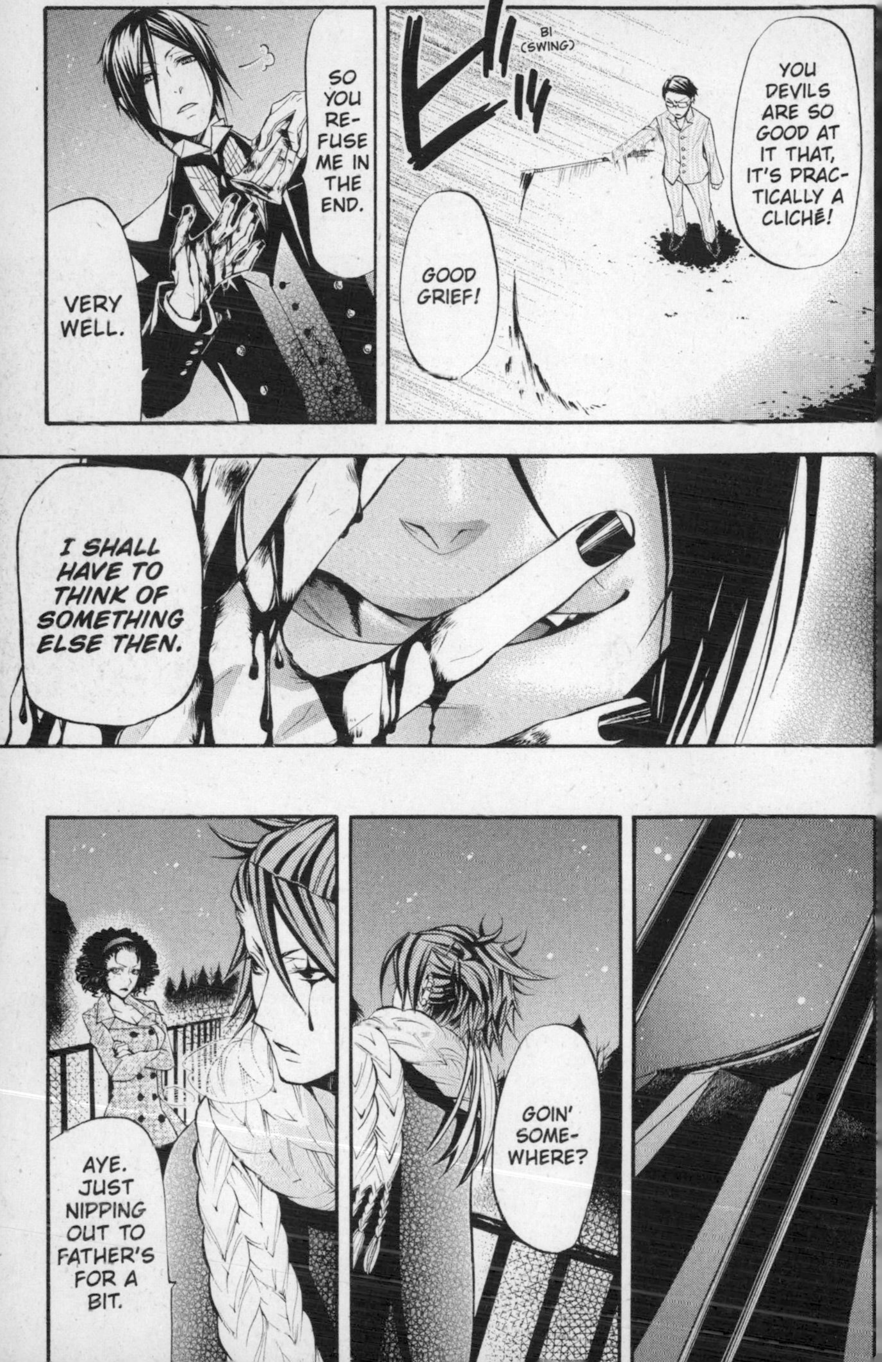
BI (SWING)
YOU DEVILS ARE SO GOOD AT IT THAT, IT'S PRACTICALLY A CLICHÉ!
GOOD GRIEF!
SO YOU REFUSE ME IN THE END.
VERY WELL.
I SHALL HAVE TO THINK OF SOMETHING ELSE THEN.
GOIN' SOMEWHERE?
AYE. JUST NIPPING OUT TO FATHER'S FOR A BIT.

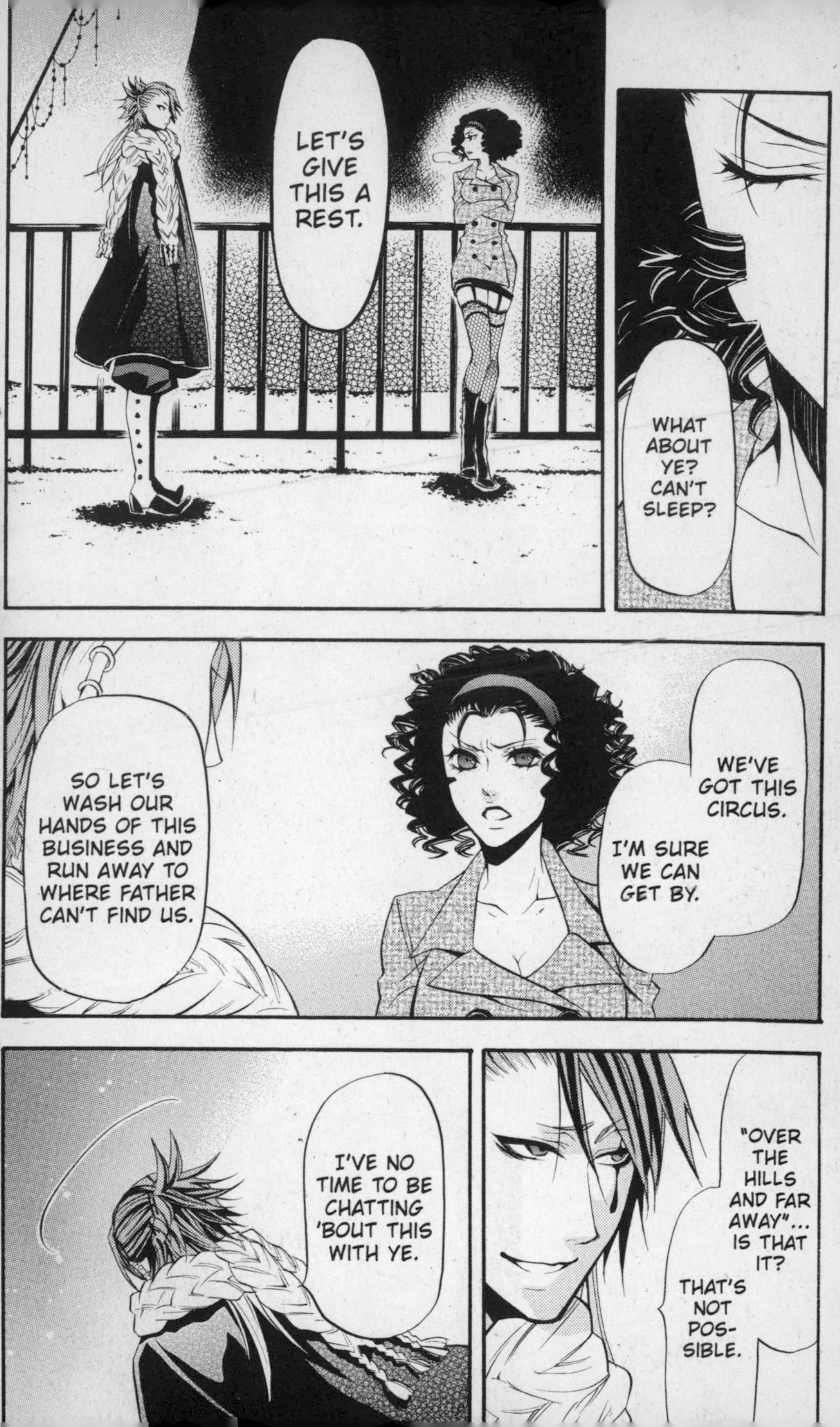
WHAT ABOUT YE? CAN'T SLEEP?
LET'S GIVE THIS A REST.
WE'VE GOT THIS CIRCUS.
I'M SURE WE CAN GET BY.
SO LET'S WASH OUR HANDS OF THIS BUSINESS AND RUN AWAY TO WHERE FATHER CAN'T FIND US.
"OVER THE HILLS AND FAR AWAY"... IS THAT IT?
THAT'S NOT POS-SIBLE.
I'VE NO TIME TO BE CHATTING 'BOUT THIS WITH YE.

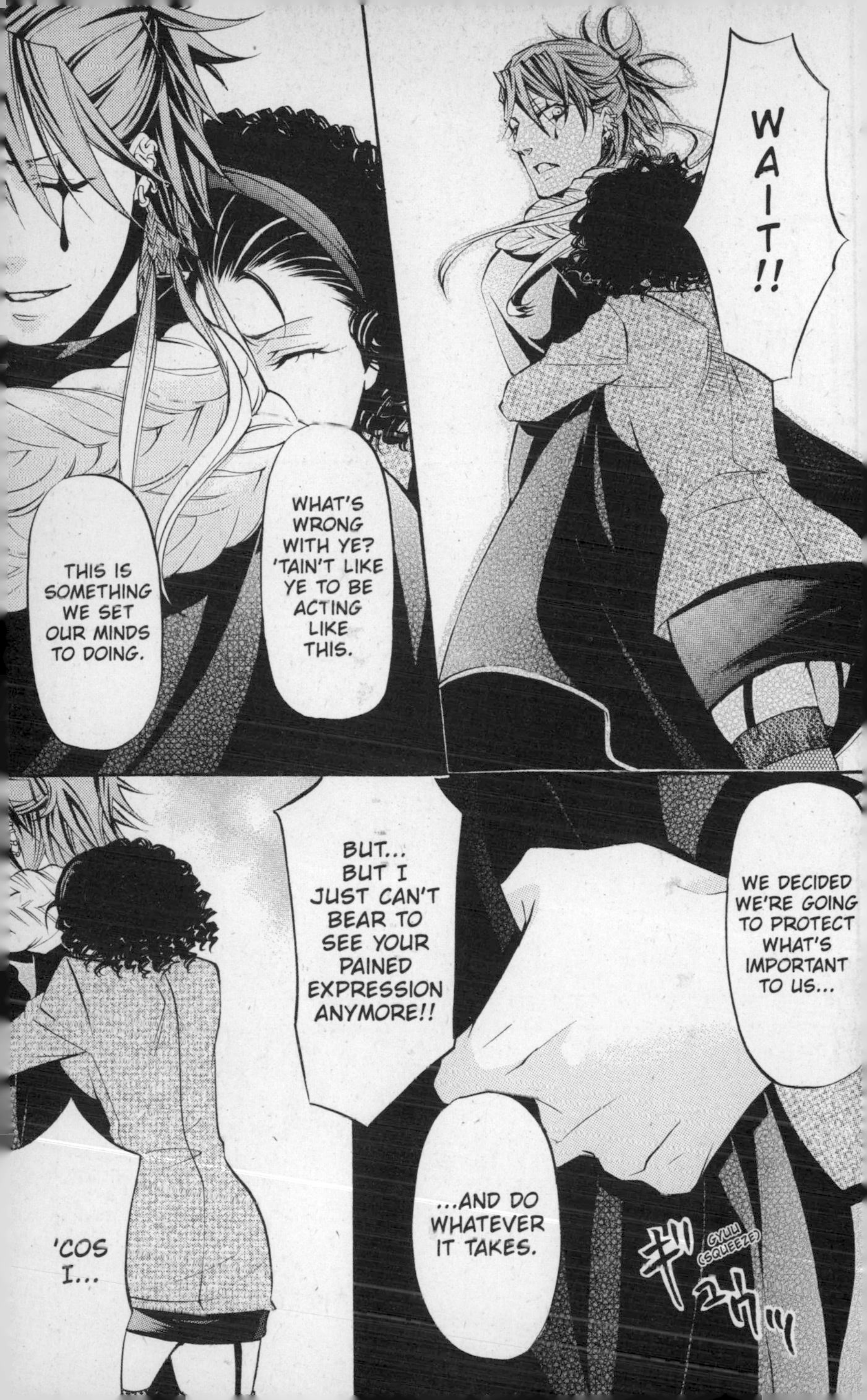
WAIT!!
WHAT'S WRONG WITH YE? 'TAIN'T LIKE YE TO BE ACTING LIKE THIS.
THIS IS SOMETHING WE SET OUR MINDS TO DOING.
WE DECIDED WE'RE GOING TO PROTECT WHAT'S IMPORTANT TO US...
...AND DO WHATEVER IT TAKES.
GYUU (SQUEEZE)
BUT... BUT I JUST CAN'T BEAR TO SEE YOUR PAINED EXPRESSION ANYMORE!!
'COS I...

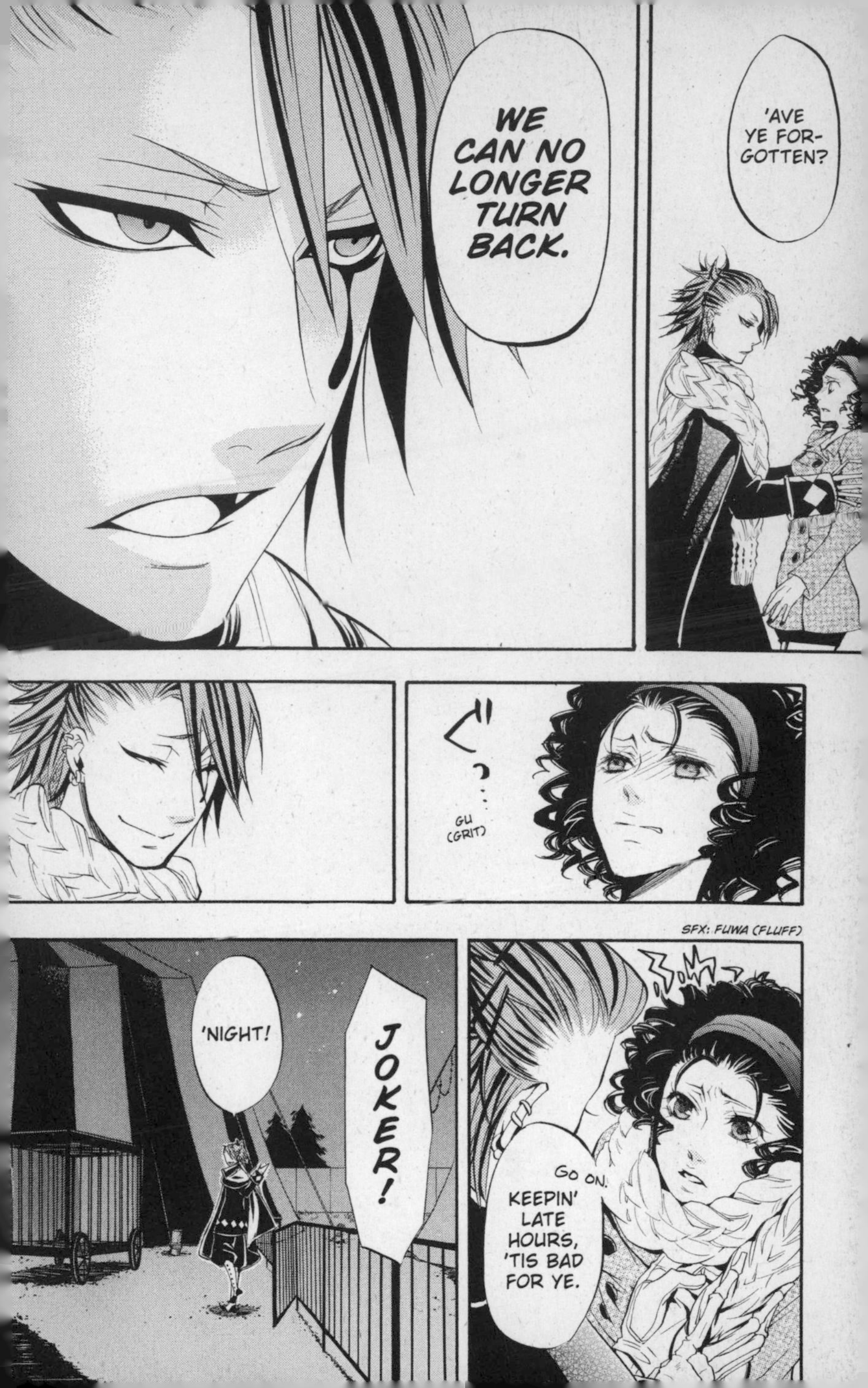
'AVE YE FOR-GOTTEN?
WE CAN NO LONGER TURN BACK.
GU (GRIT)
SFX: FUWA (FLUFF)
GO ON.
KEEPIN' LATE HOURS, 'TIS BAD FOR YE.
JOKER!
'NIGHT!

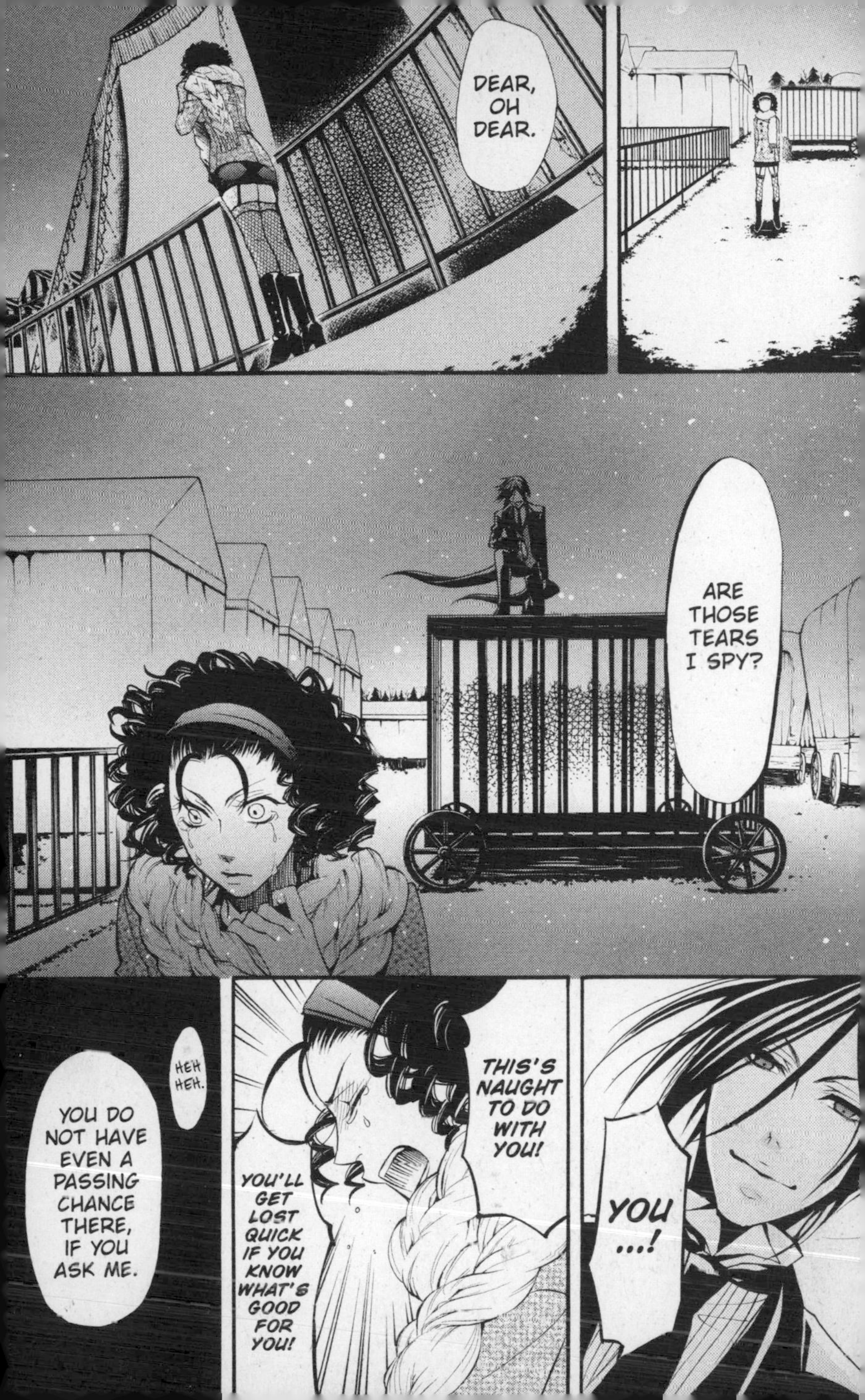
DEAR, OH DEAR.
ARE THOSE TEARS I SPY?
YOU ...!
THIS'S NAUGHT TO DO WITH YOU!
YOU'LL GET LOST QUICK IF YOU KNOW WHAT'S GOOD FOR YOU!
HEH HEH.
YOU DO NOT HAVE EVEN A PASSING CHANCE THERE, IF YOU ASK ME.

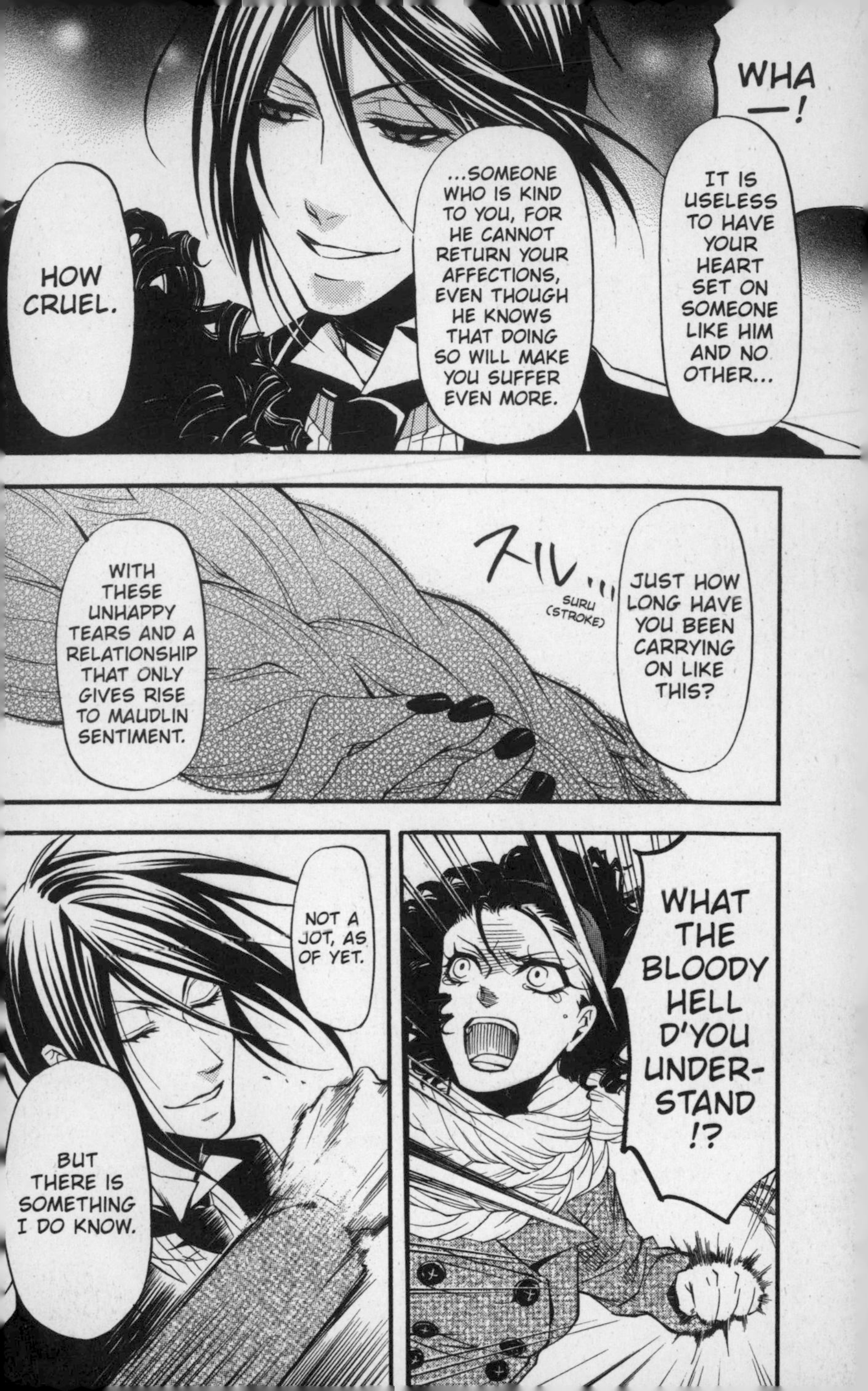
WHA—!
IT IS USELESS TO HAVE YOUR HEART SET ON SOMEONE LIKE HIM AND NO OTHER...
...SOMEONE WHO IS KIND TO YOU, FOR HE CANNOT RETURN YOUR AFFECTIONS, EVEN THOUGH HE KNOWS THAT DOING SO WILL MAKE YOU SUFFER EVEN MORE.
HOW CRUEL.
JUST HOW LONG HAVE YOU BEEN CARRYING ON LIKE THIS?
スル...
SURU (STROKE)
WITH THESE UNHAPPY TEARS AND A RELATIONSHIP THAT ONLY GIVES RISE TO MAUDLIN SENTIMENT.
WHAT THE BLOODY HELL D'YOU UNDER-STAND!?
NOT A JOT, AS OF YET.
BUT THERE IS SOMETHING I DO KNOW.

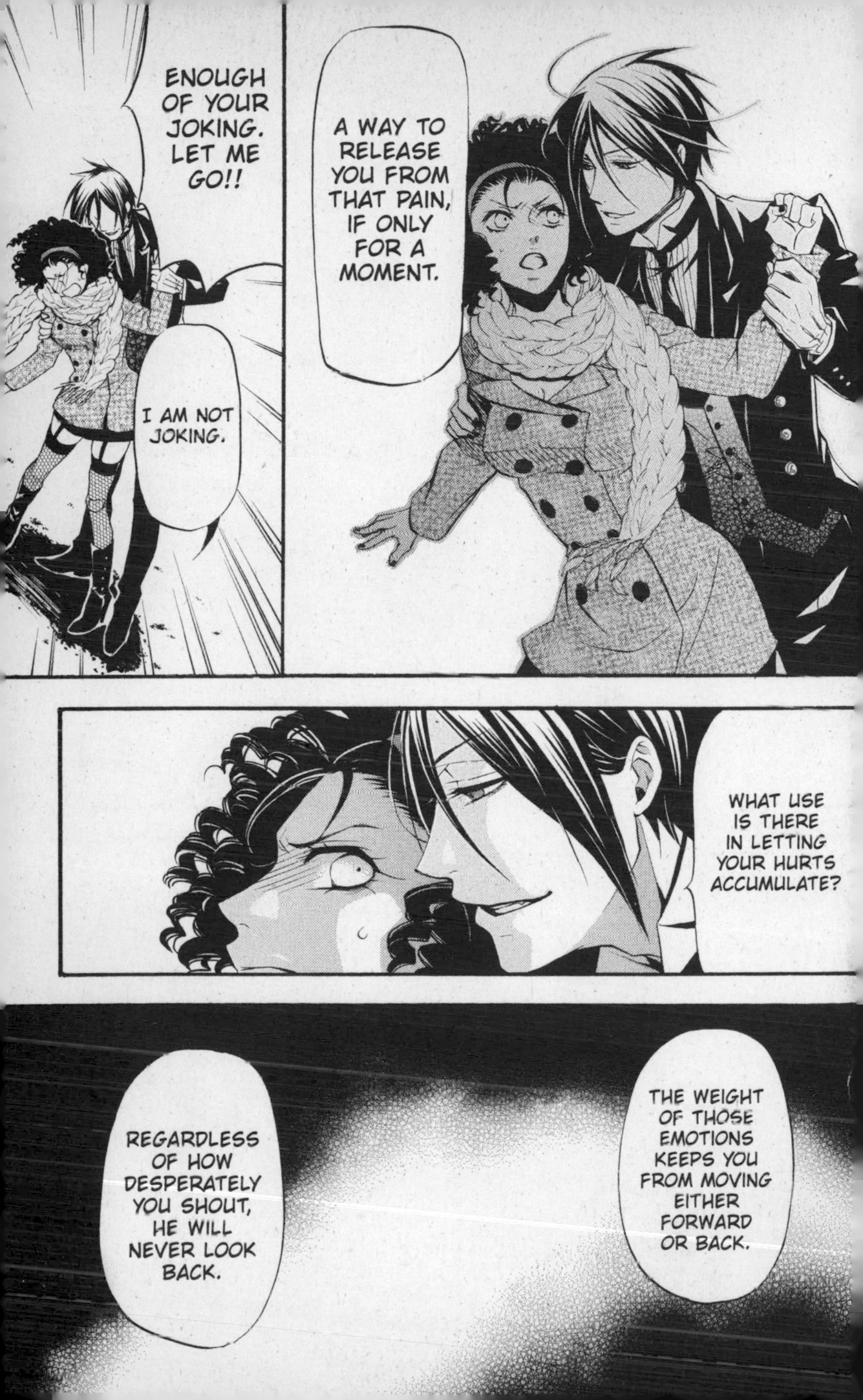
A WAY TO RELEASE YOU FROM THAT PAIN, IF ONLY FOR A MOMENT.
ENOUGH OF YOUR JOKING. LET ME GO!!
I AM NOT JOKING.
WHAT USE IS THERE IN LETTING YOUR HURTS ACCUMULATE?
THE WEIGHT OF THOSE EMOTIONS KEEPS YOU FROM MOVING EITHER FORWARD OR BACK.
REGARDLESS OF HOW DESPERATELY YOU SHOUT, HE WILL NEVER LOOK BACK.

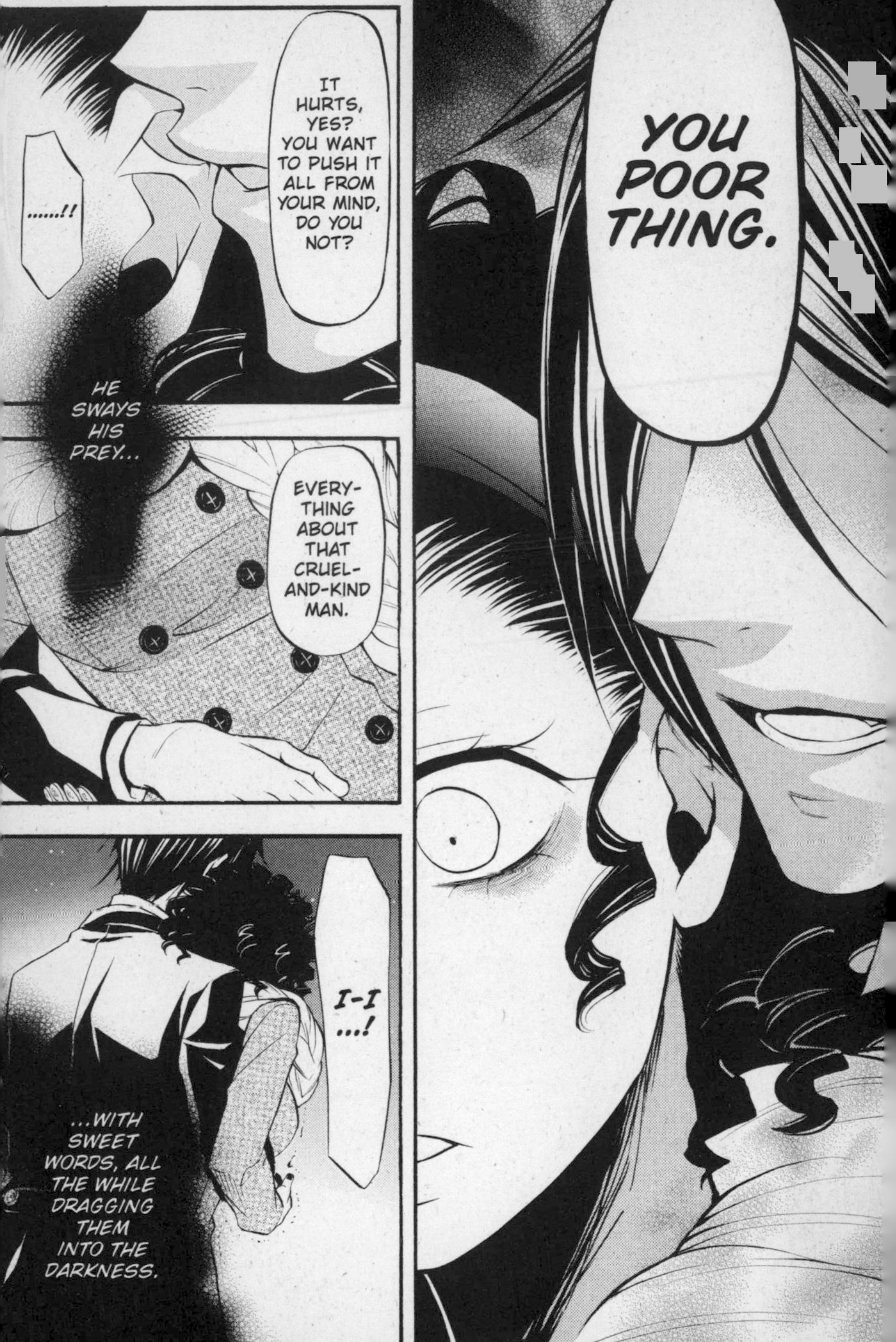
YOU POOR THING.
IT HURTS, YES? YOU WANT TO PUSH IT ALL FROM YOUR MIND, DO YOU NOT?
......!!
HE SWAYS HIS PREY...
EVERY-THING ABOUT THAT CRUEL-AND-KIND MAN.
I-I ...!
...WITH SWEET WORDS, ALL THE WHILE DRAGGING THEM INTO THE DARKNESS.

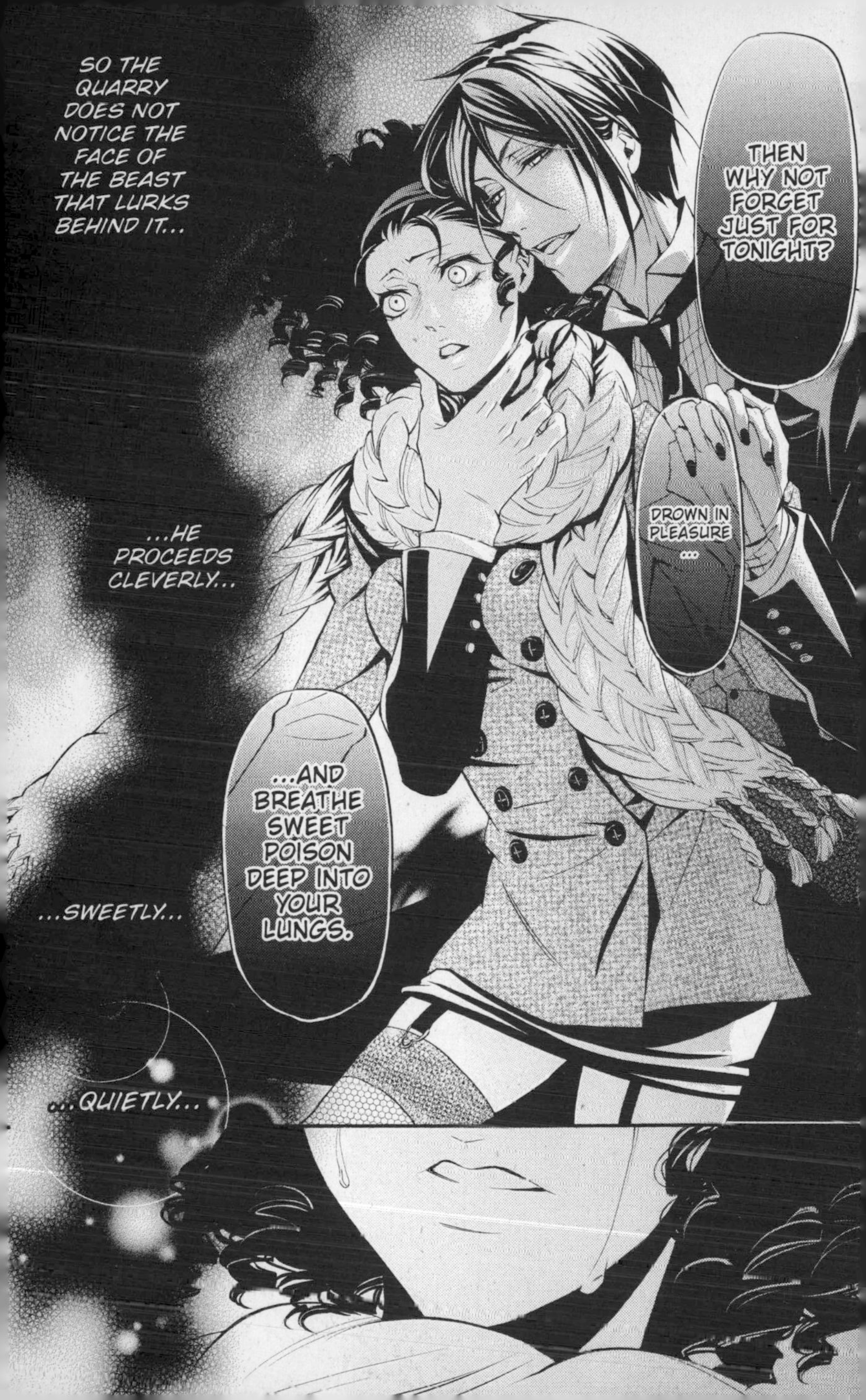
THEN WHY NOT FORGET JUST FOR TONIGHT?
SO THE QUARRY DOES NOT NOTICE THE FACE OF THE BEAST THAT LURKS BEHIND IT...
DROWN IN PLEASURE...
...HE PROCEEDS CLEVERLY...
...AND BREATHE SWEET POISON DEEP INTO YOUR LUNGS.
...SWEETLY...
...QUIETLY...

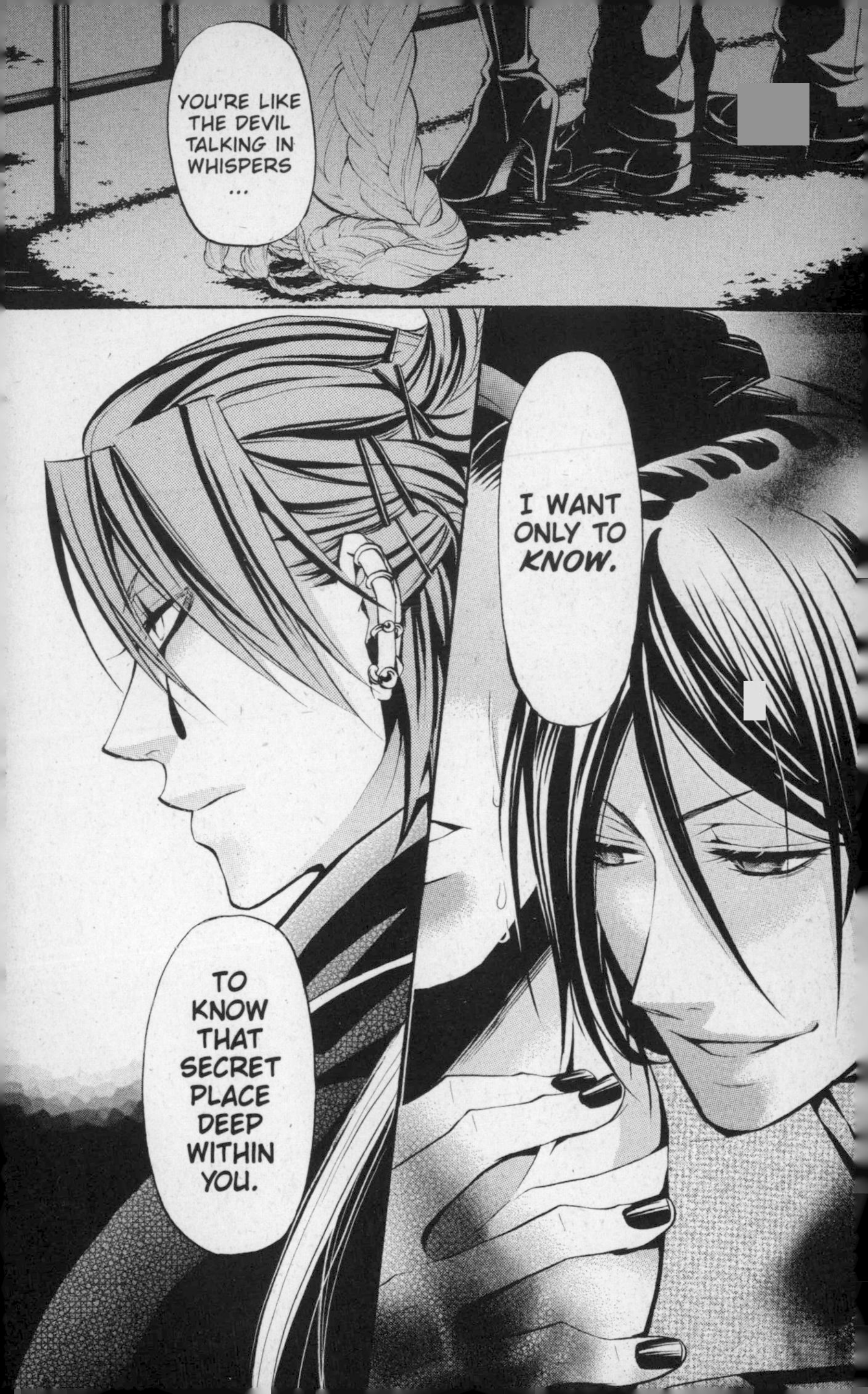
YOU'RE LIKE THE DEVIL TALKING IN WHISPERS ...
I WANT ONLY TO *KNOW.*
TO KNOW THAT SECRET PLACE DEEP WITHIN YOU.

Black Butler

CHAPTER 29

At noon : The Butler, Scandalous

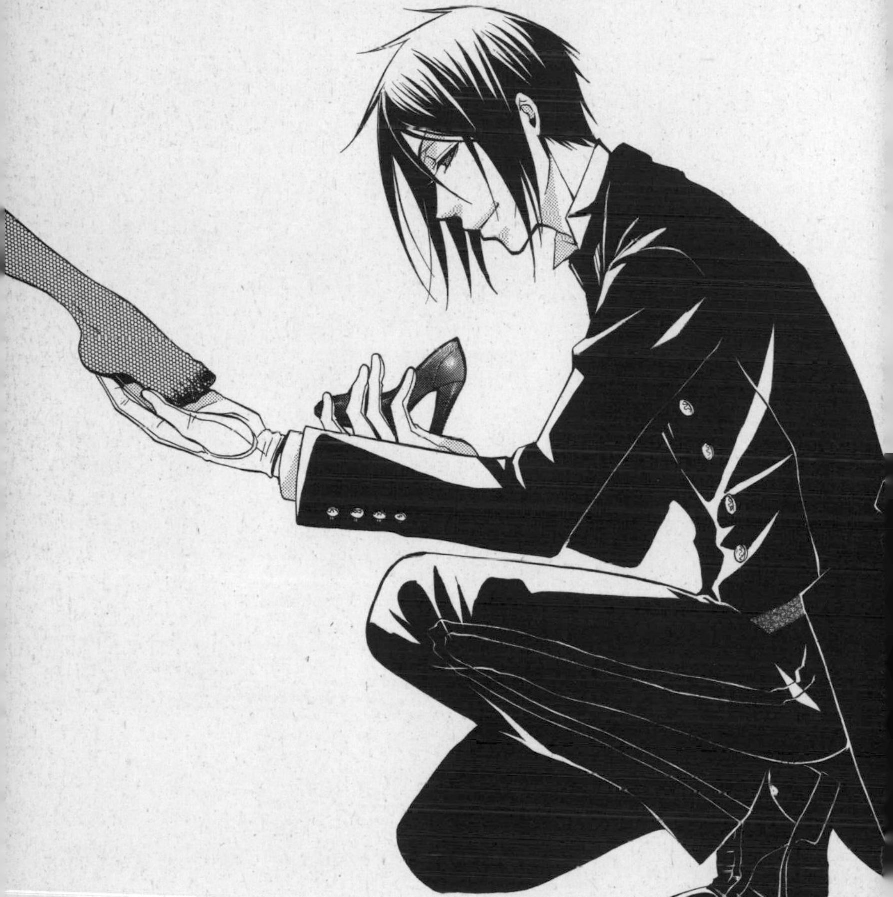

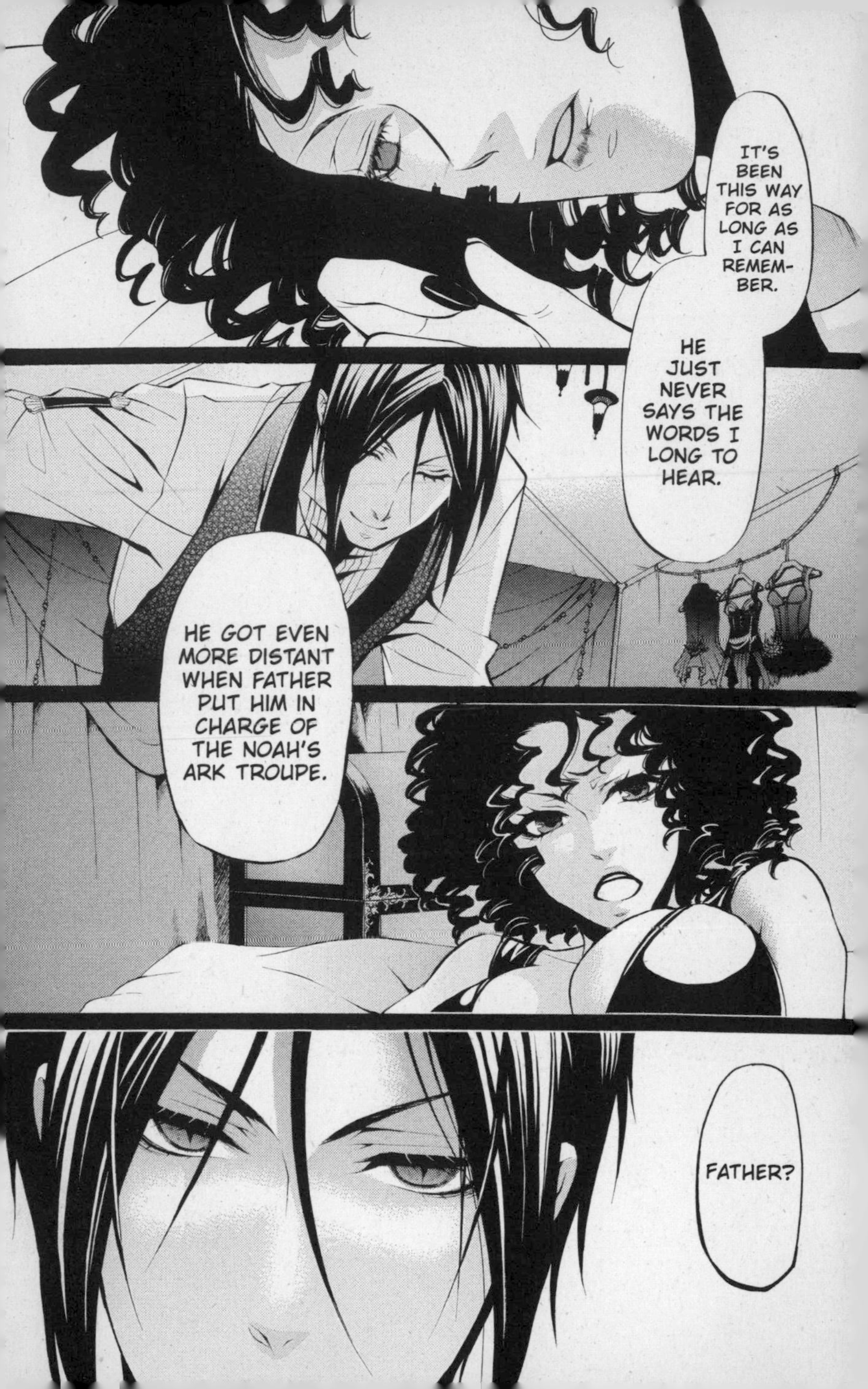
IT'S BEEN THIS WAY FOR AS LONG AS I CAN REMEMBER.
HE JUST NEVER SAYS THE WORDS I LONG TO HEAR.
HE GOT EVEN MORE DISTANT WHEN FATHER PUT HIM IN CHARGE OF THE NOAH'S ARK TROUPE.
FATHER?

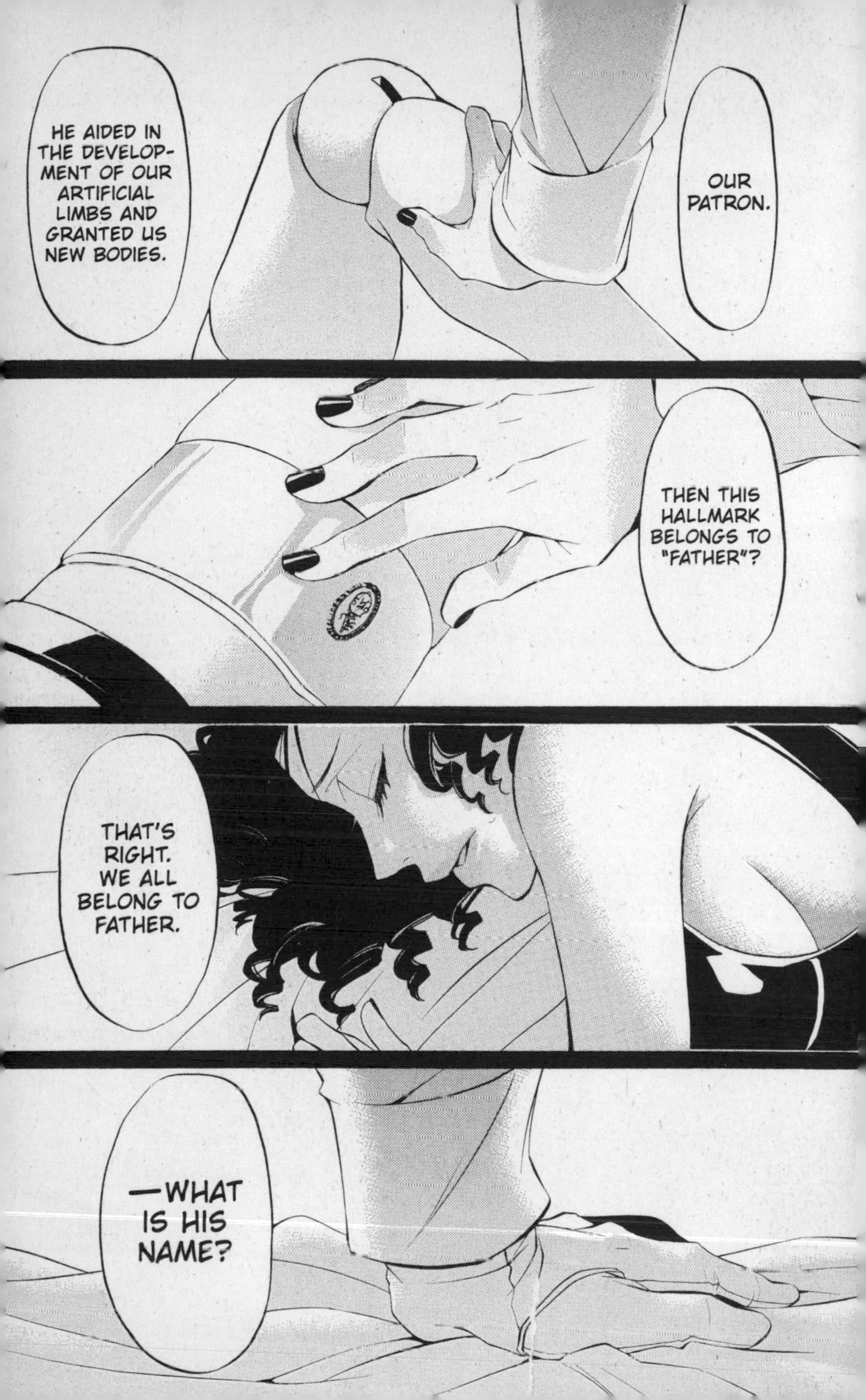
OUR PATRON.
HE AIDED IN THE DEVELOPMENT OF OUR ARTIFICIAL LIMBS AND GRANTED US NEW BODIES.
THEN THIS HALLMARK BELONGS TO "FATHER"?
THAT'S RIGHT. WE ALL BELONG TO FATHER.
—WHAT IS HIS NAME?

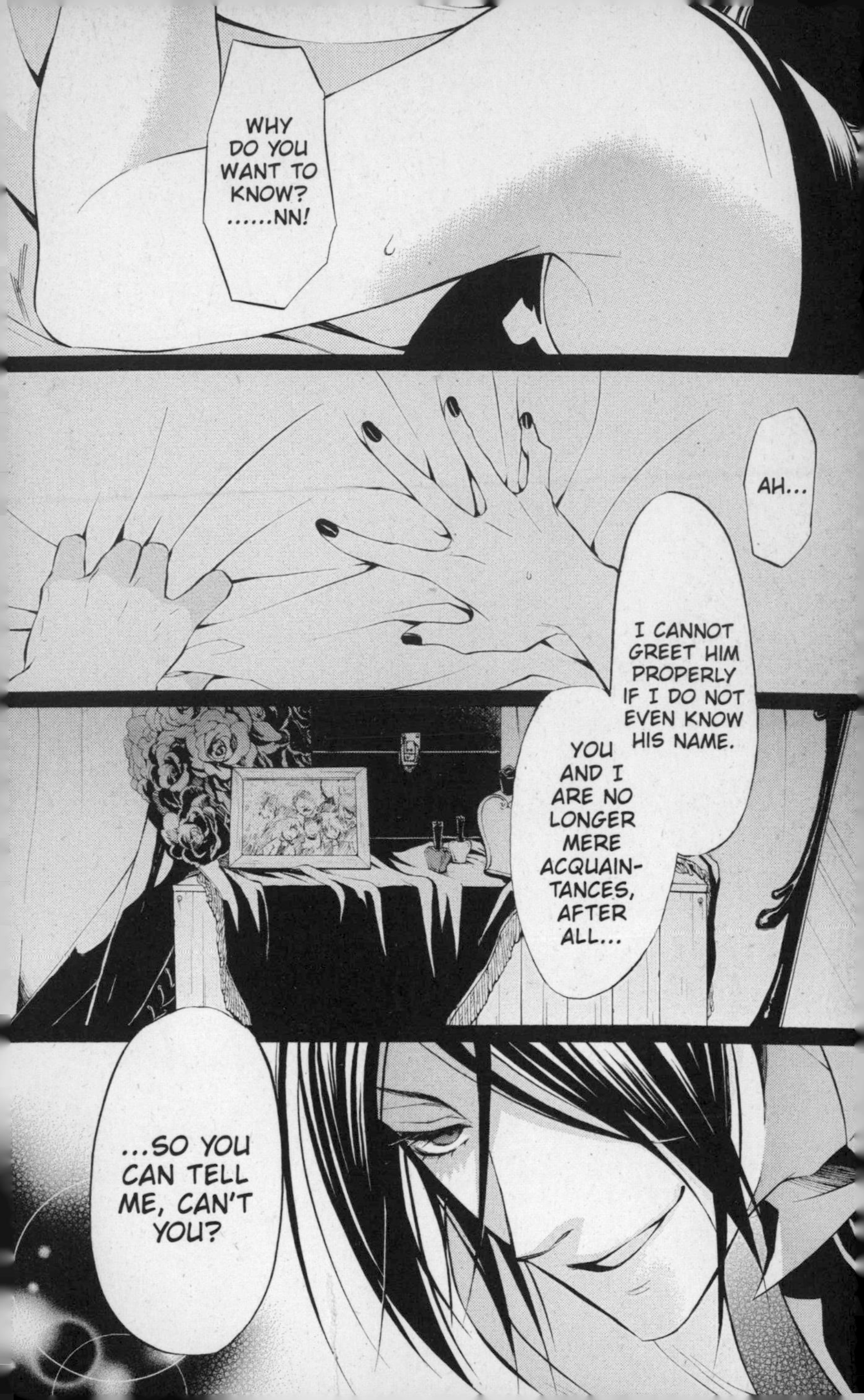
WHY DO YOU WANT TO KNOW? ......NN!
AH...
I CANNOT GREET HIM PROPERLY IF I DO NOT EVEN KNOW HIS NAME.
YOU AND I ARE NO LONGER MERE ACQUAIN-TANCES, AFTER ALL...
...SO YOU CAN TELL ME, CAN'T YOU?

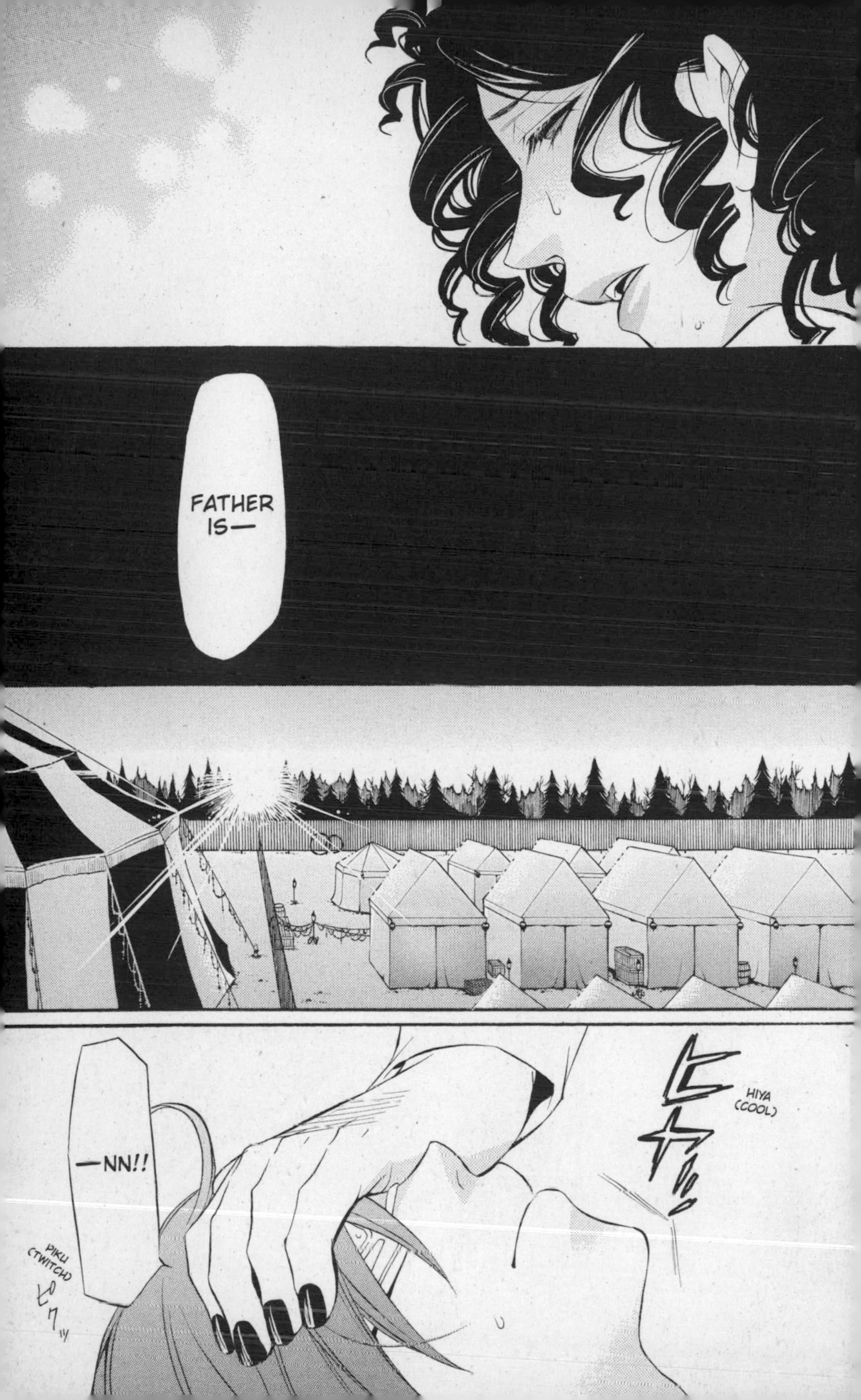
FATHER IS—
HIYA (COOL)
—NN!!
PIKU (TWITCH)

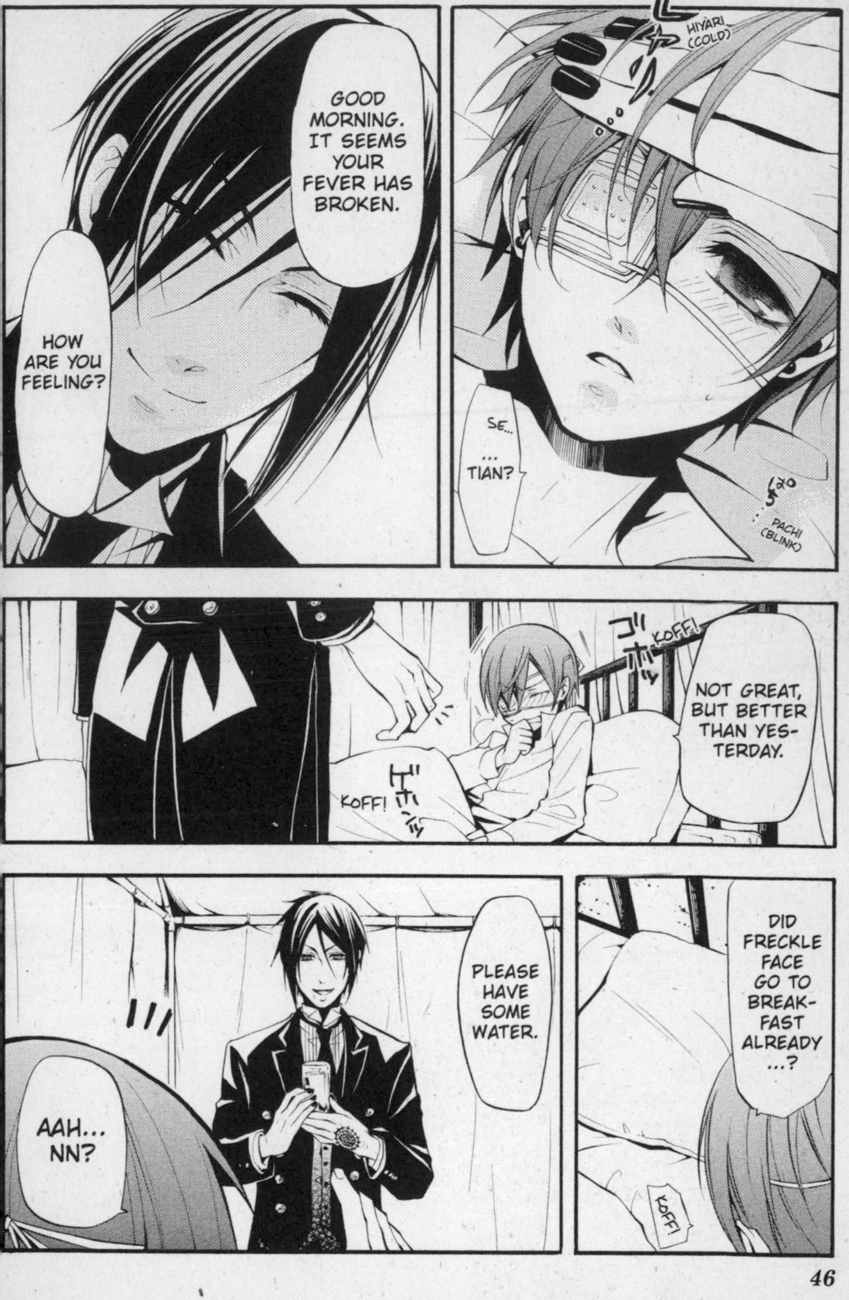
HIYARI (COLD)
SE... ...TIAN?
PACHI (BLINK)
GOOD MORNING. IT SEEMS YOUR FEVER HAS BROKEN.
HOW ARE YOU FEELING?
KOFF!
NOT GREAT, BUT BETTER THAN YES-TERDAY.
KOFF!
DID FRECKLE FACE GO TO BREAK-FAST ALREADY ...?
KOFF!
PLEASE HAVE SOME WATER.
AAH... NN?

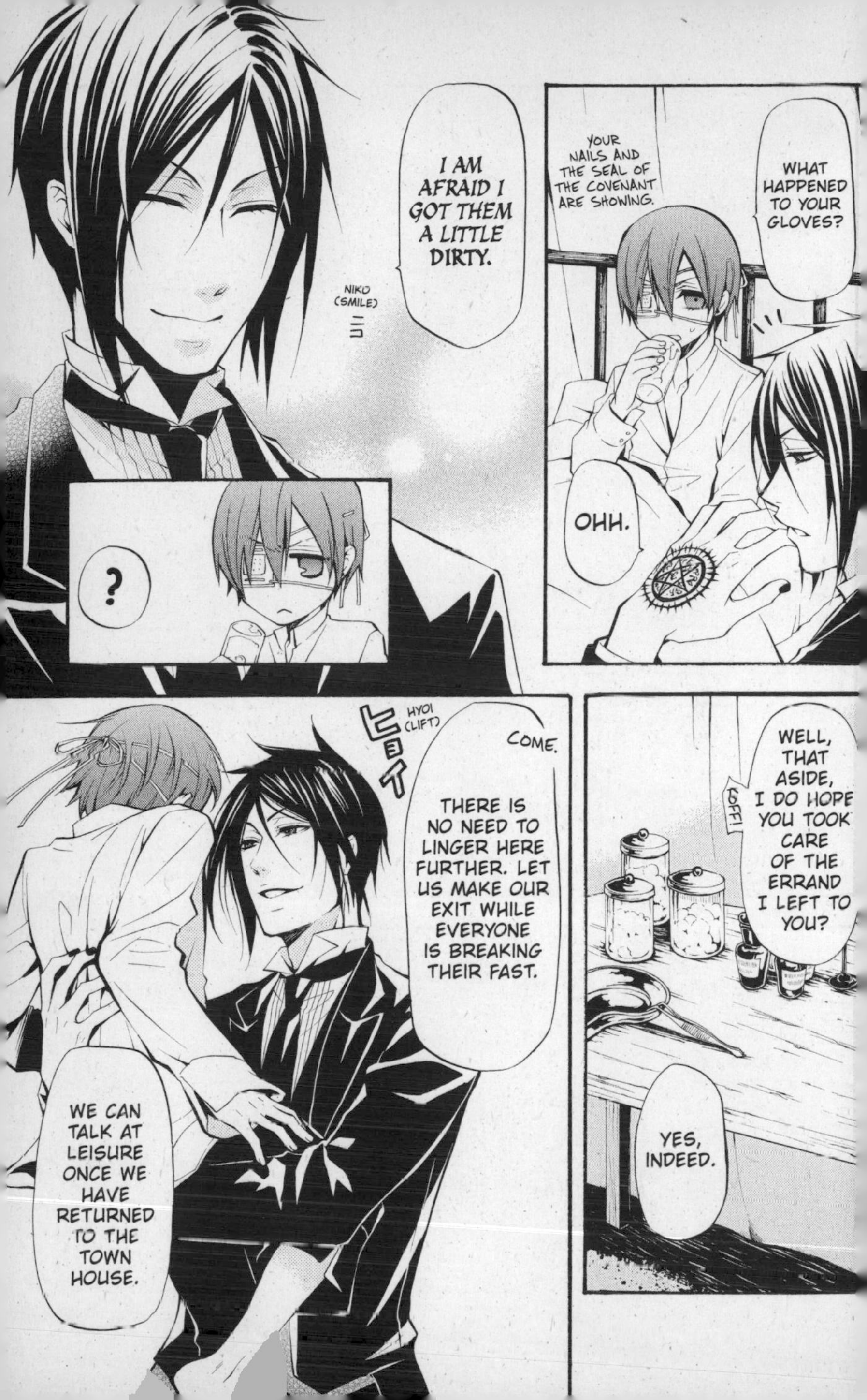
WHAT HAPPENED TO YOUR GLOVES?
YOUR NAILS AND THE SEAL OF THE COVENANT ARE SHOWING.
OHH.
I AM AFRAID I GOT THEM A LITTLE DIRTY.
NIKO (SMILE)
?
KOFF!
WELL, THAT ASIDE, I DO HOPE YOU TOOK CARE OF THE ERRAND I LEFT TO YOU?
YES, INDEED.
HYOI (LIFT)
COME.
THERE IS NO NEED TO LINGER HERE FURTHER. LET US MAKE OUR EXIT WHILE EVERYONE IS BREAKING THEIR FAST.
WE CAN TALK AT LEISURE ONCE WE HAVE RETURNED TO THE TOWN HOUSE.

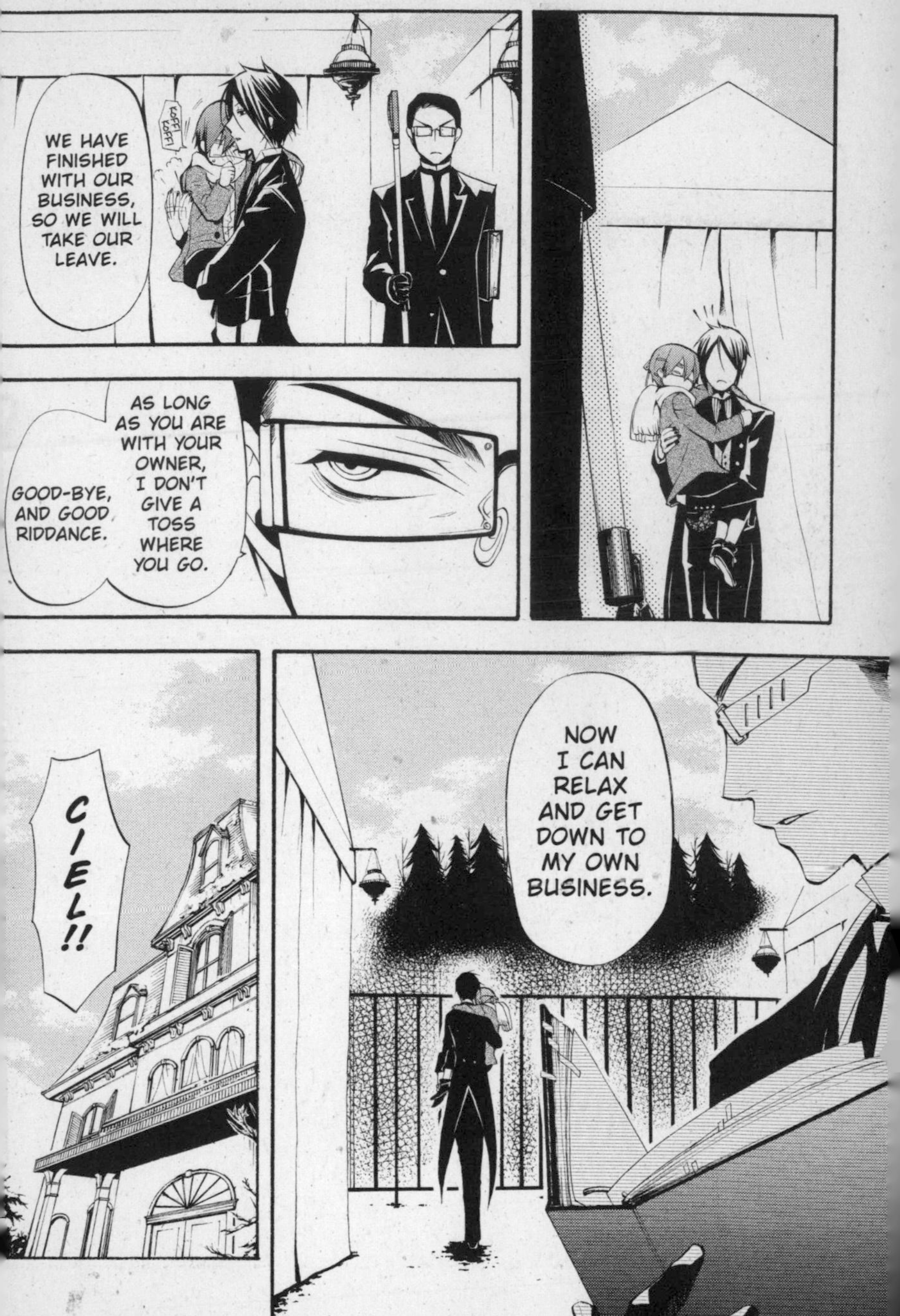
KOFF KOFF
WE HAVE FINISHED WITH OUR BUSINESS, SO WE WILL TAKE OUR LEAVE.
AS LONG AS YOU ARE WITH YOUR OWNER, I DON'T GIVE A TOSS WHERE YOU GO.
GOOD-BYE, AND GOOD RIDDANCE.
NOW I CAN RELAX AND GET DOWN TO MY OWN BUSINESS.
CIEL!!

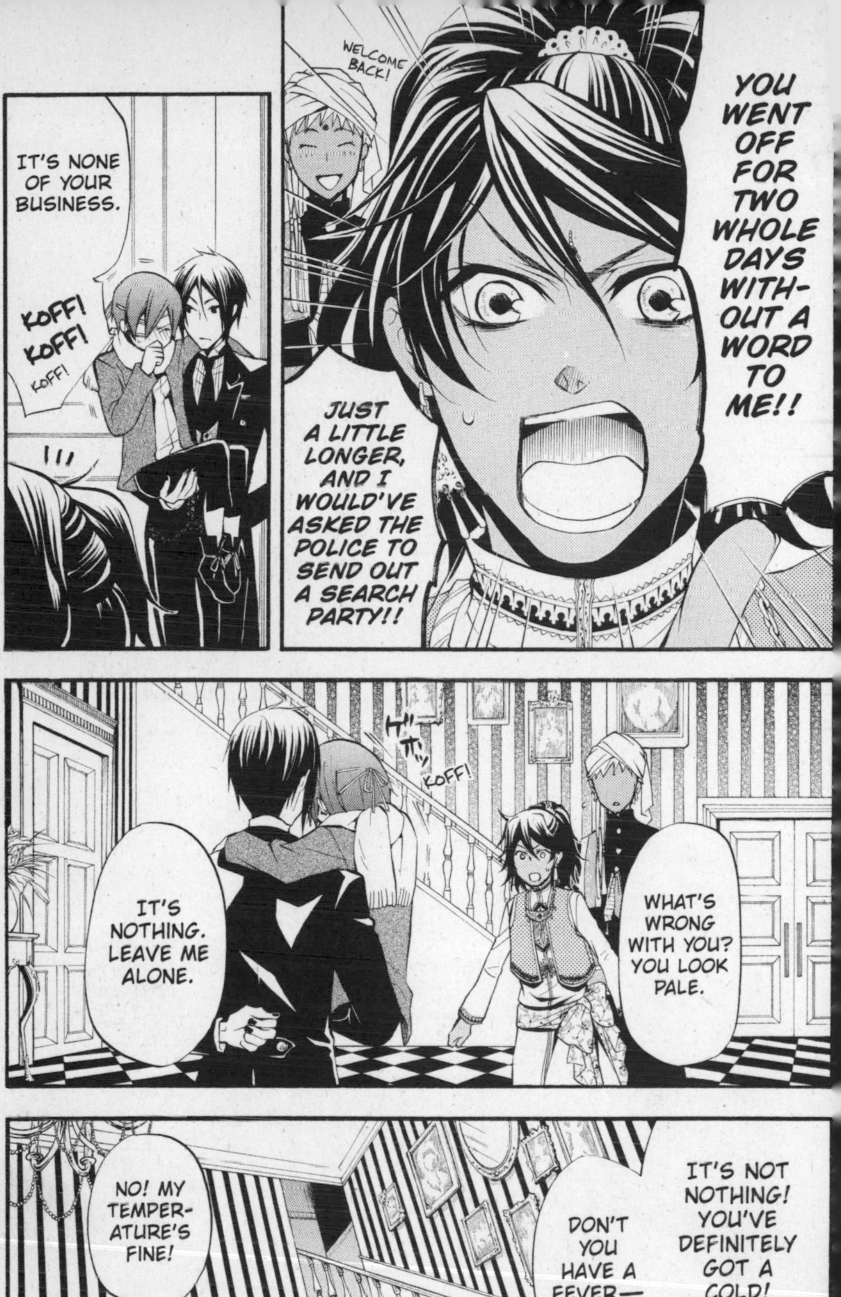
WELCOME BACK!
YOU WENT OFF FOR TWO WHOLE DAYS WITH-OUT A WORD TO ME!!
JUST A LITTLE LONGER, AND I WOULD'VE ASKED THE POLICE TO SEND OUT A SEARCH PARTY!!
IT'S NONE OF YOUR BUSINESS.
KOFF! KOFF!
KOFF!
WHAT'S WRONG WITH YOU? YOU LOOK PALE.
KOFF!
IT'S NOTHING. LEAVE ME ALONE.
IT'S NOT NOTHING! YOU'VE DEFINITELY GOT A COLD!
DON'T YOU HAVE A FEVER—
NO! MY TEMPER-ATURE'S FINE!

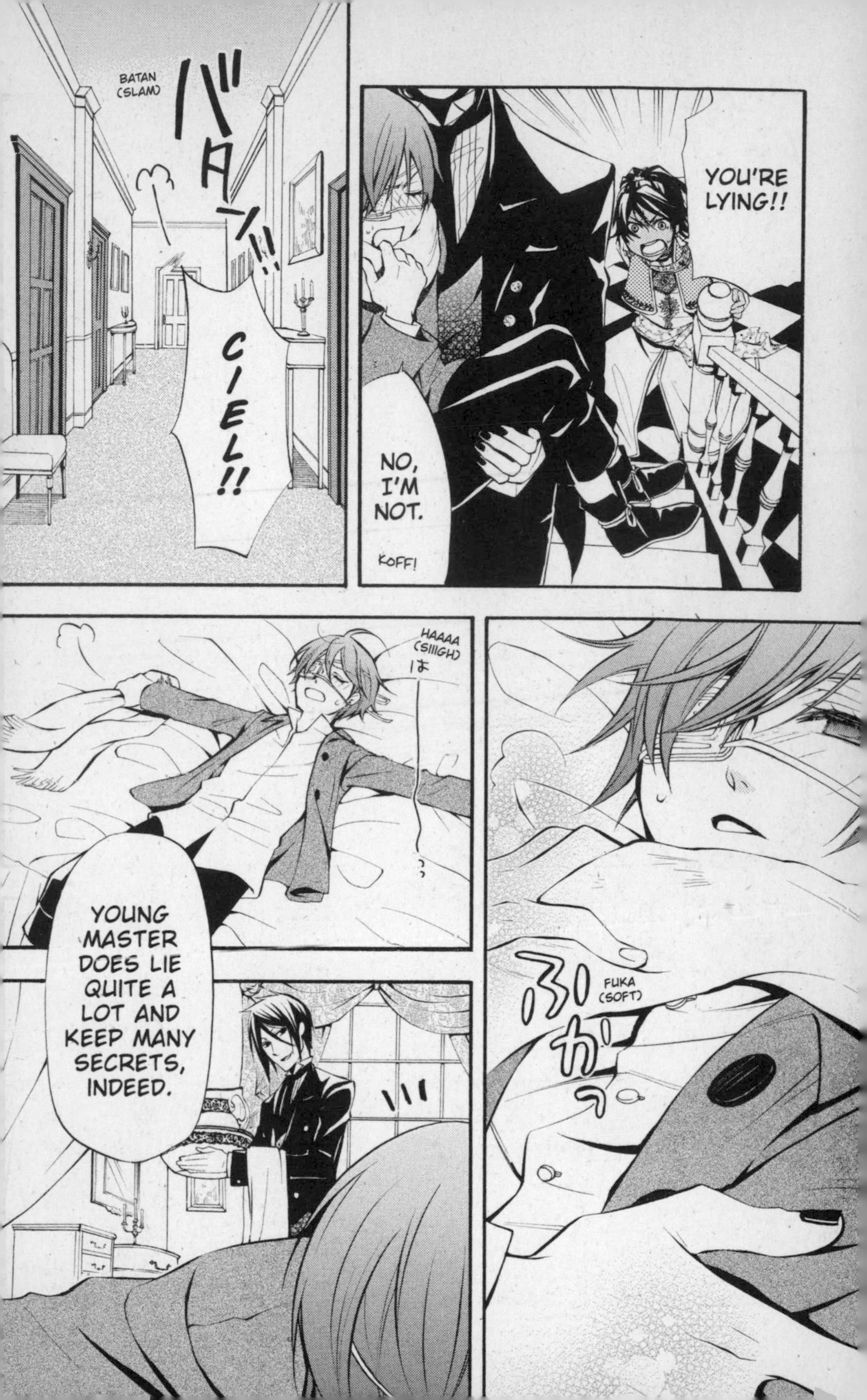
YOU'RE LYING!!
NO, I'M NOT.
KOFF!
BATAN (SLAM)
バターン!!
CIEL!!
ふかっ
FUKA (SOFT)
HAAAA (SIIIGH)
は…っ
YOUNG MASTER DOES LIE QUITE A LOT AND KEEP MANY SECRETS, INDEED.

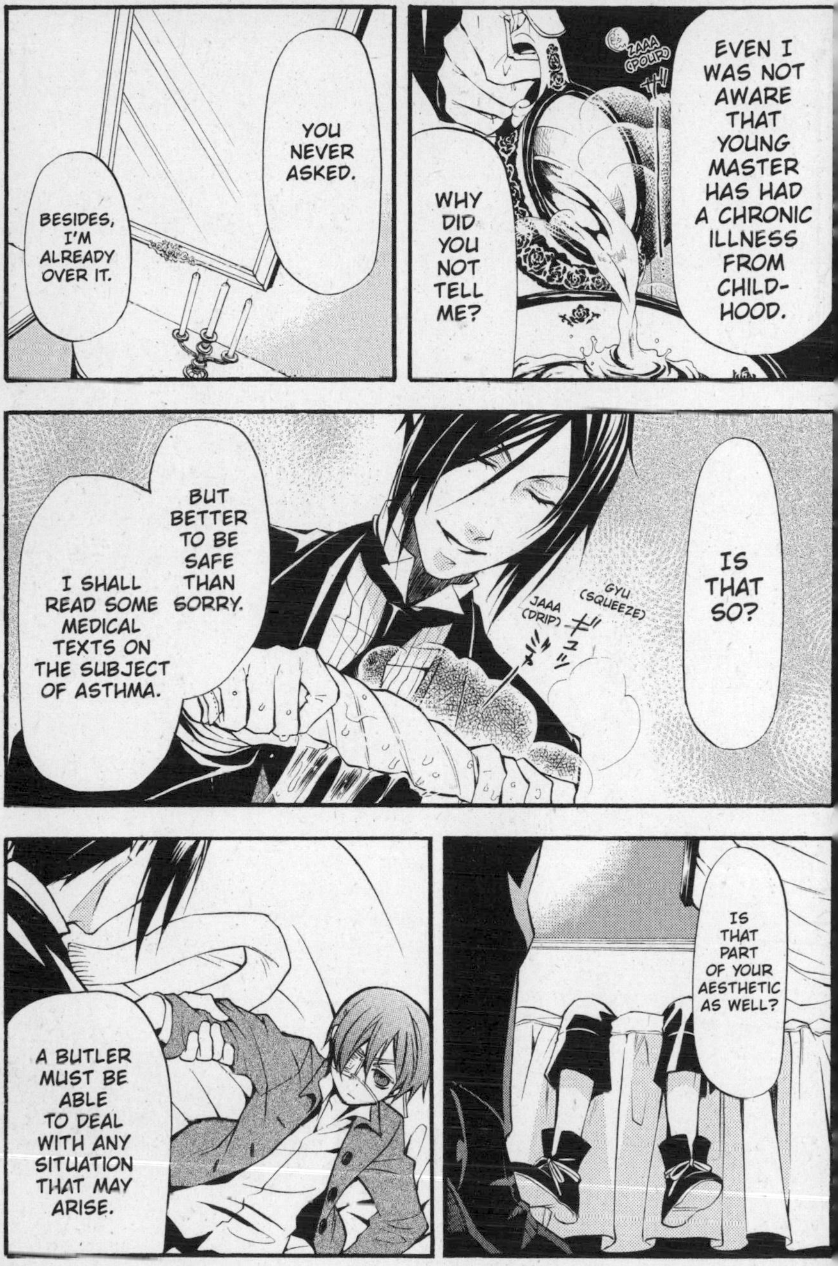
EVEN I WAS NOT AWARE THAT YOUNG MASTER HAS HAD A CHRONIC ILLNESS FROM CHILDHOOD.
ZAAA (POUR)
WHY DID YOU NOT TELL ME?
YOU NEVER ASKED.
BESIDES, I'M ALREADY OVER IT.
IS THAT SO?
GYU (SQUEEZE)
JAAA (DRIP)
BUT BETTER TO BE SAFE THAN SORRY.
I SHALL READ SOME MEDICAL TEXTS ON THE SUBJECT OF ASTHMA.
IS THAT PART OF YOUR AESTHETIC AS WELL?
A BUTLER MUST BE ABLE TO DEAL WITH ANY SITUATION THAT MAY ARISE.

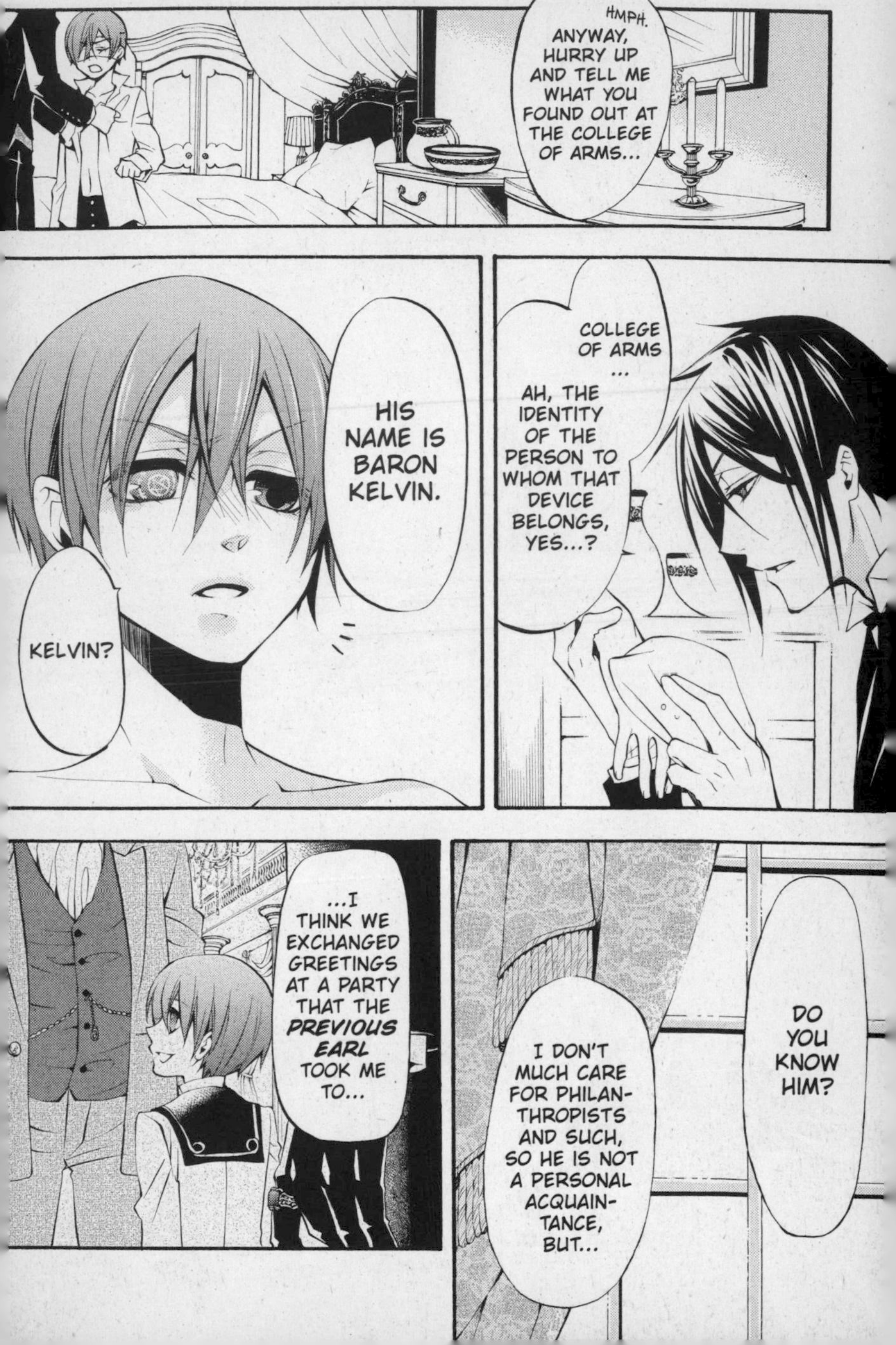
HMPH. ANYWAY, HURRY UP AND TELL ME WHAT YOU FOUND OUT AT THE COLLEGE OF ARMS...
COLLEGE OF ARMS ... AH, THE IDENTITY OF THE PERSON TO WHOM THAT DEVICE BELONGS, YES...?
HIS NAME IS BARON KELVIN.
KELVIN?
DO YOU KNOW HIM?
I DON'T MUCH CARE FOR PHILANTHROPISTS AND SUCH, SO HE IS NOT A PERSONAL ACQUAINTANCE, BUT...
...I THINK WE EXCHANGED GREETINGS AT A PARTY THAT THE *PREVIOUS EARL* TOOK ME TO...

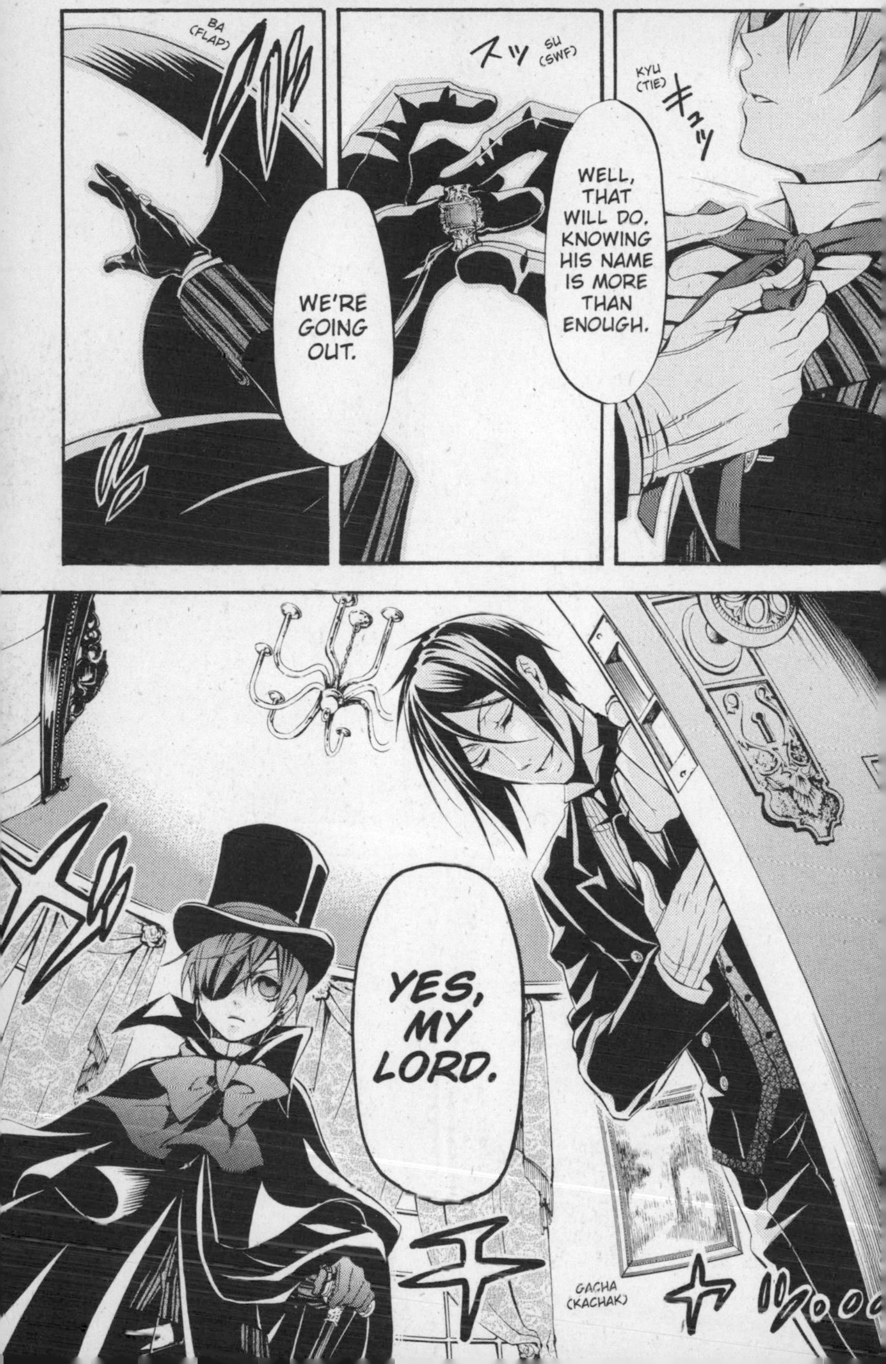
KYU (TIE)
キュッ
WELL, THAT WILL DO. KNOWING HIS NAME IS MORE THAN ENOUGH.
スッ
SU (SWF)
WE'RE GOING OUT.
BA (FLAP)
YES, MY LORD.
GACHA (KACHAK)

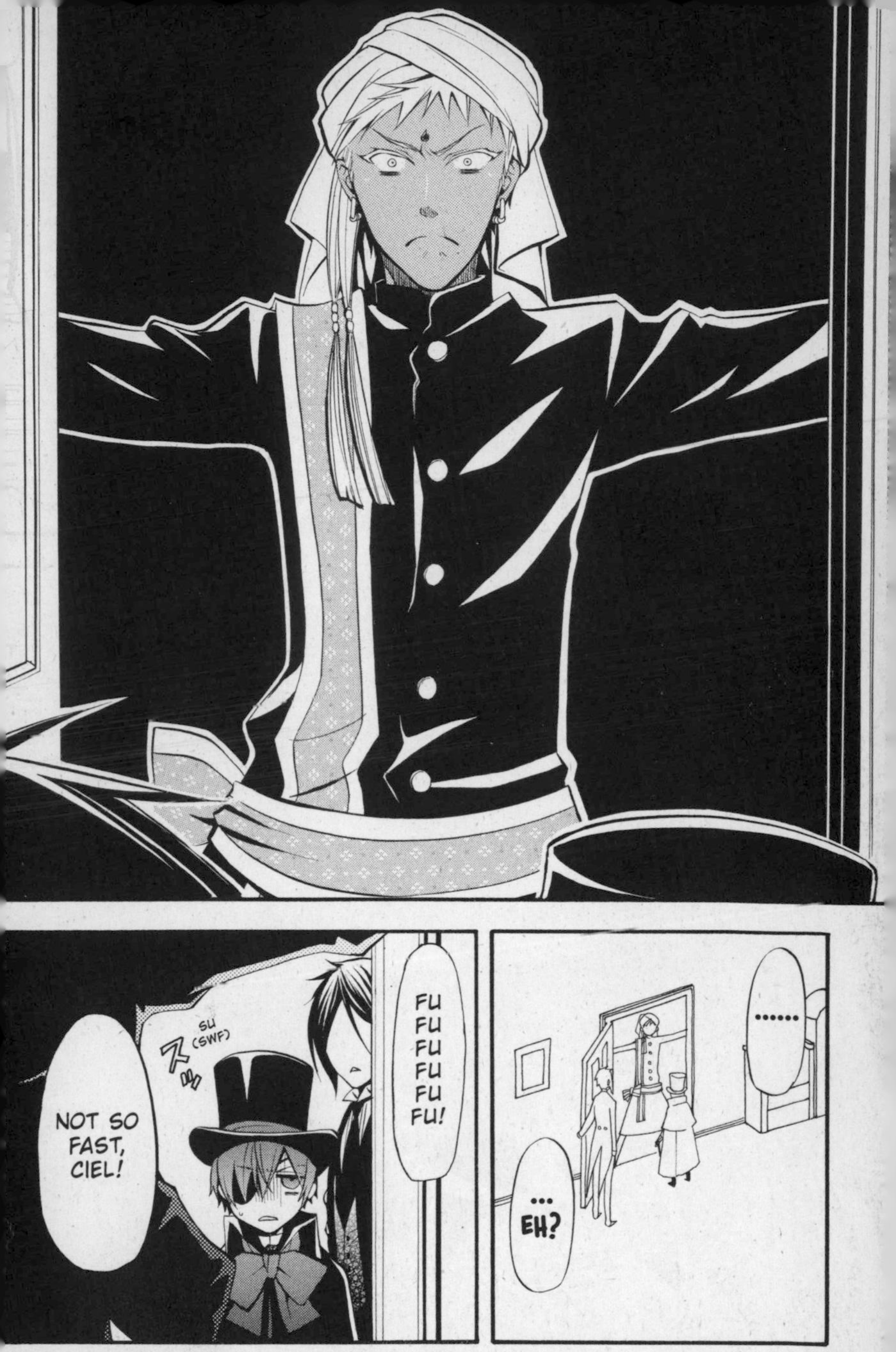
......
... EH?
FU FU FU FU FU FU!
SU (SWF)
NOT SO FAST, CIEL!

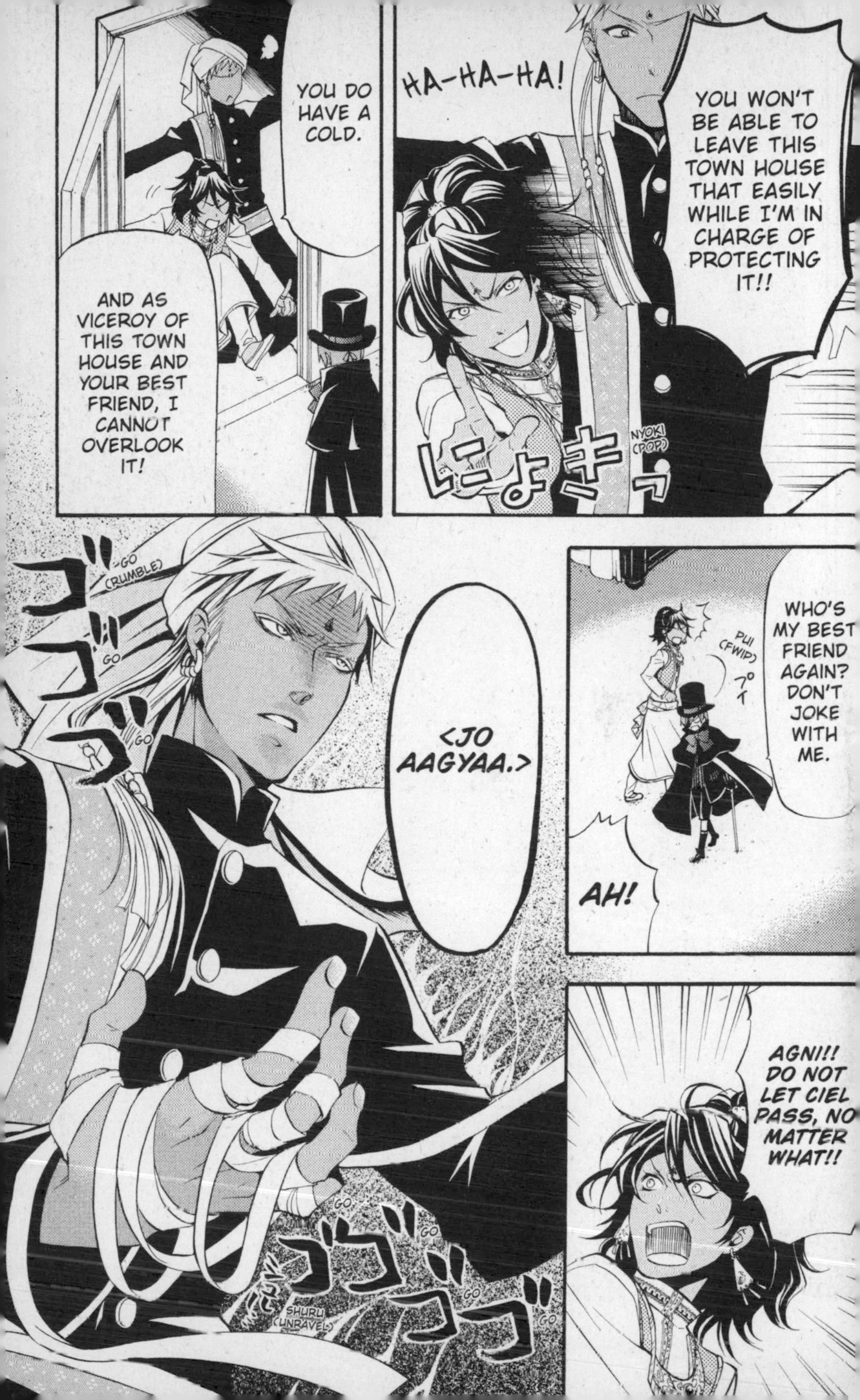
YOU WON'T BE ABLE TO LEAVE THIS TOWN HOUSE THAT EASILY WHILE I'M IN CHARGE OF PROTECTING IT!!
HA-HA-HA!
NYOKI (POP)
YOU DO HAVE A COLD.
AND AS VICEROY OF THIS TOWN HOUSE AND YOUR BEST FRIEND, I CANNOT OVERLOOK IT!
WHO'S MY BEST FRIEND AGAIN? DON'T JOKE WITH ME.
PUI (FWIP)
AH!
AGNI!! DO NOT LET CIEL PASS, NO MATTER WHAT!!
GO (RUMBLE)
GO
GO
<JO AAGYAA.>
GO
GO
GO
GO
SHURU (UNRAVEL)

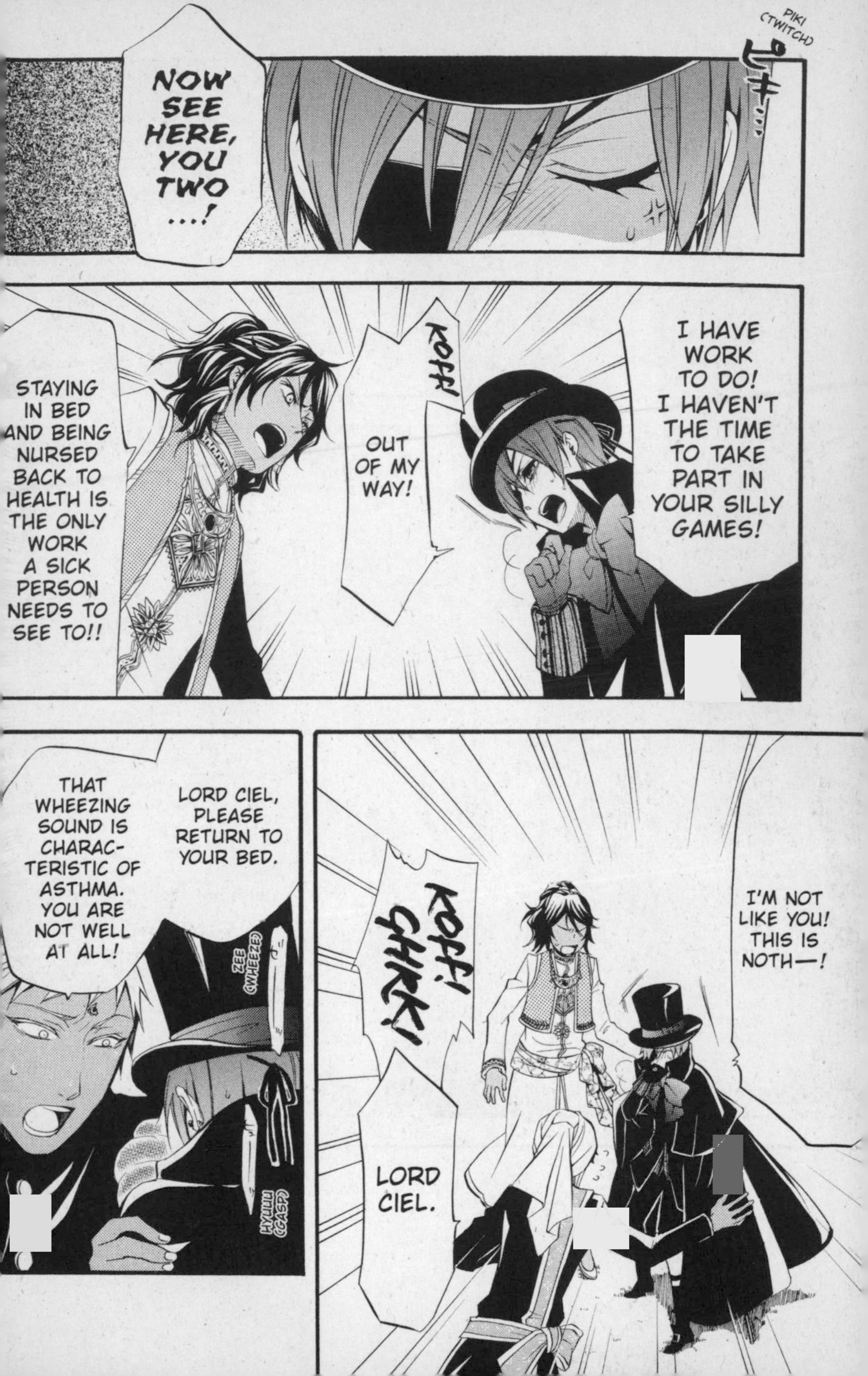
PIKI (TWITCH)
NOW SEE HERE, YOU TWO...!
I HAVE WORK TO DO! I HAVEN'T THE TIME TO TAKE PART IN YOUR SILLY GAMES!
KOFF
OUT OF MY WAY!
STAYING IN BED AND BEING NURSED BACK TO HEALTH IS THE ONLY WORK A SICK PERSON NEEDS TO SEE TO!!
I'M NOT LIKE YOU! THIS IS NOTH—!
KOFF! GHRK!
LORD CIEL.
LORD CIEL, PLEASE RETURN TO YOUR BED.
ZEE (WHEEZE)
THAT WHEEZING SOUND IS CHARAC-TERISTIC OF ASTHMA. YOU ARE NOT WELL AT ALL!
HYUUU (GASP)

SFX: GIRI (CLENCH)

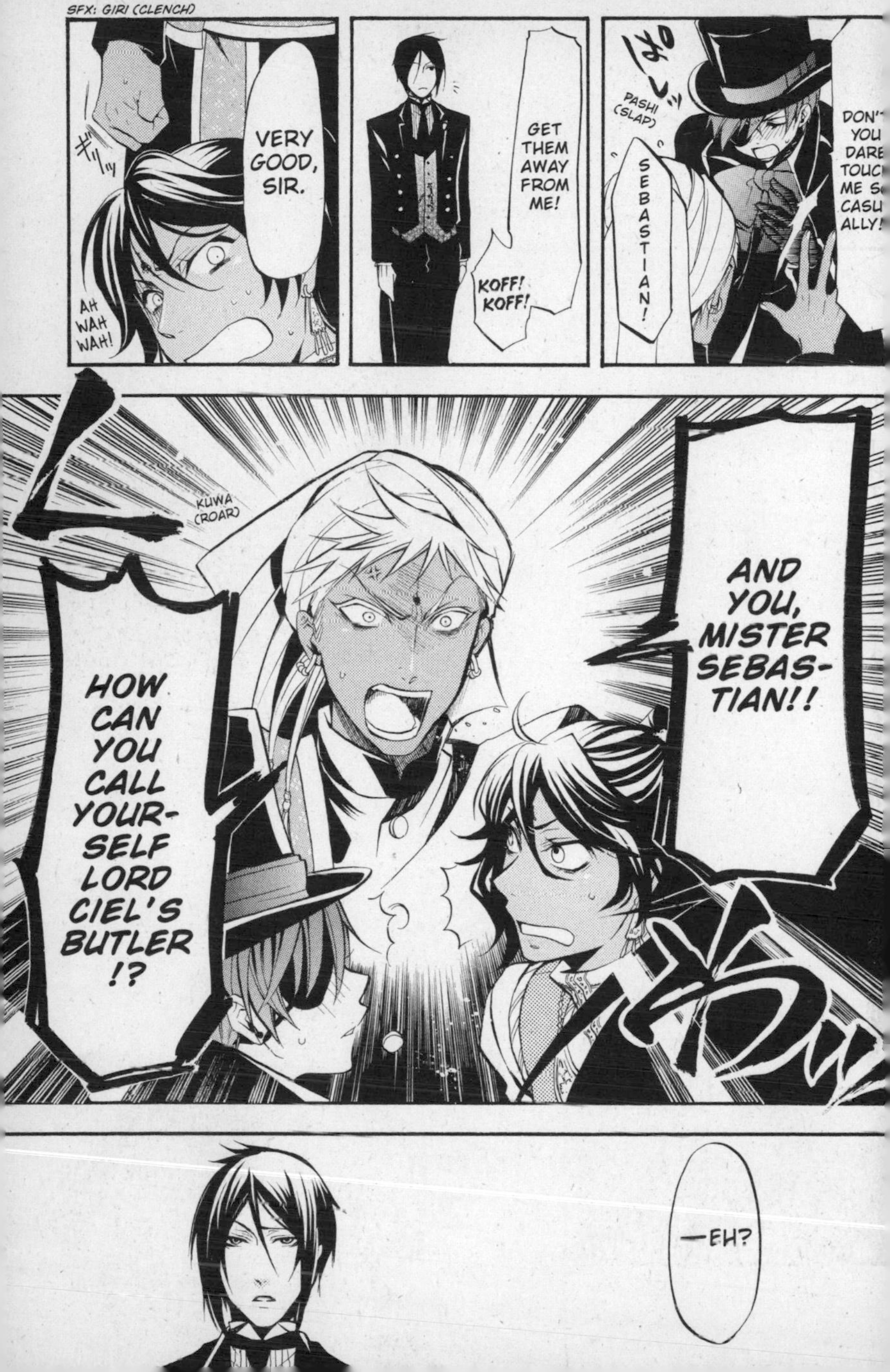
DON'T YOU DARE TOUCH ME SO CASUALLY!
PASHI (SLAP)
SEBASTIAN!
GET THEM AWAY FROM ME!
KOFF! KOFF!
VERY GOOD, SIR.
AH WAH WAH!
AND YOU, MISTER SEBASTIAN!!
KUWA (ROAR)
HOW CAN YOU CALL YOURSELF LORD CIEL'S BUTLER!?
—EH?

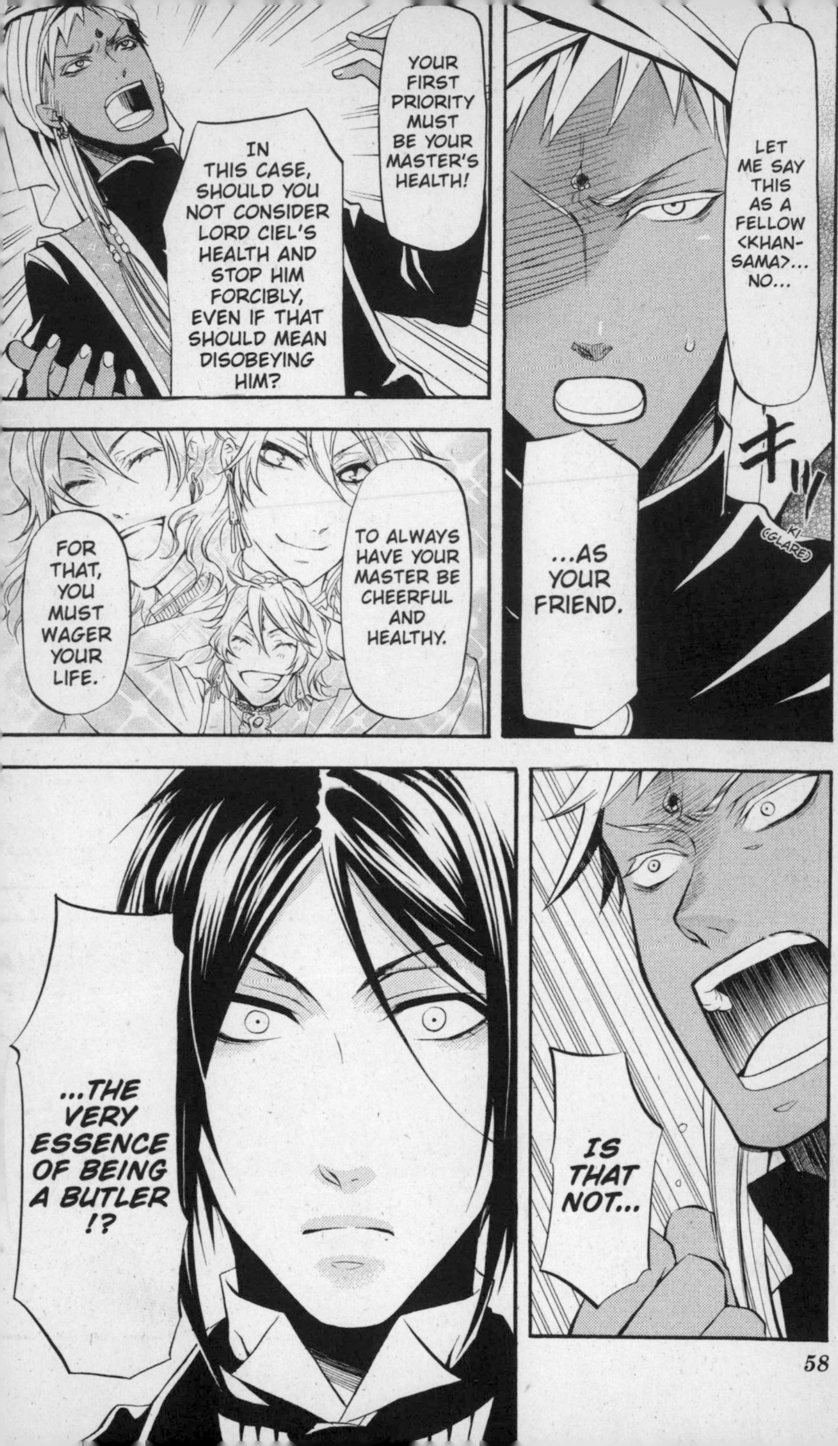
LET ME SAY THIS AS A FELLOW <KHAN-SAMA>... NO...
...AS YOUR FRIEND.
KI (GLARE)
YOUR FIRST PRIORITY MUST BE YOUR MASTER'S HEALTH!
IN THIS CASE, SHOULD YOU NOT CONSIDER LORD CIEL'S HEALTH AND STOP HIM FORCIBLY, EVEN IF THAT SHOULD MEAN DISOBEYING HIM?
TO ALWAYS HAVE YOUR MASTER BE CHEERFUL AND HEALTHY.
FOR THAT, YOU MUST WAGER YOUR LIFE.
IS THAT NOT...
...THE VERY ESSENCE OF BEING A BUTLER !?

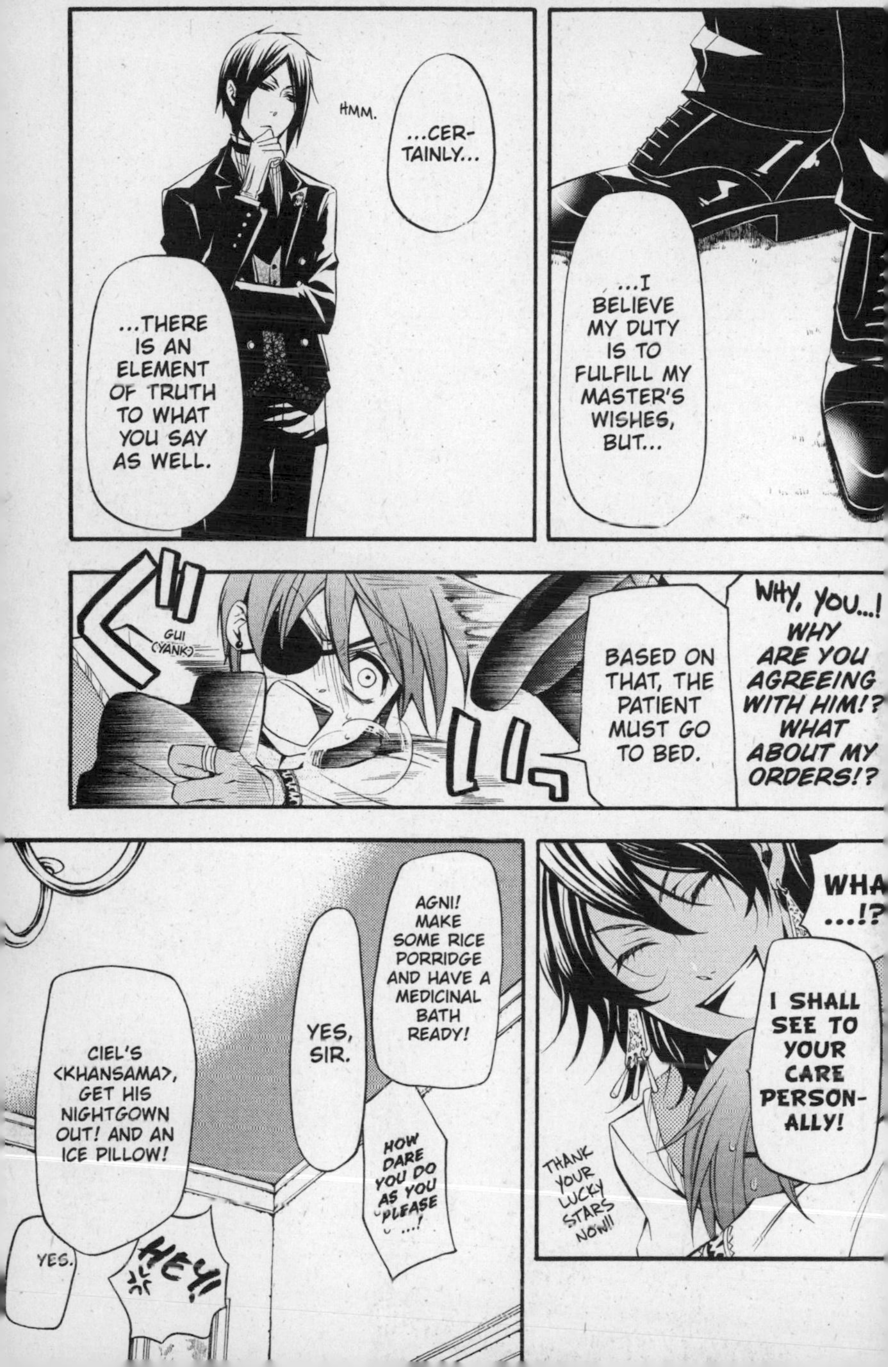
...I BELIEVE MY DUTY IS TO FULFILL MY MASTER'S WISHES, BUT...
HMM.
...CER-TAINLY...
...THERE IS AN ELEMENT OF TRUTH TO WHAT YOU SAY AS WELL.
WHY, YOU...! WHY ARE YOU AGREEING WITH HIM!? WHAT ABOUT MY ORDERS!?
BASED ON THAT, THE PATIENT MUST GO TO BED.
GUI (YANK)
WHA...!?
I SHALL SEE TO YOUR CARE PERSON-ALLY!
THANK YOUR LUCKY STARS NOW!!
AGNI! MAKE SOME RICE PORRIDGE AND HAVE A MEDICINAL BATH READY!
YES, SIR.
HOW DARE YOU DO AS YOU PLEASE ...!
CIEL'S <KHANSAMA>, GET HIS NIGHTGOWN OUT! AND AN ICE PILLOW!
YES.
HEY!!

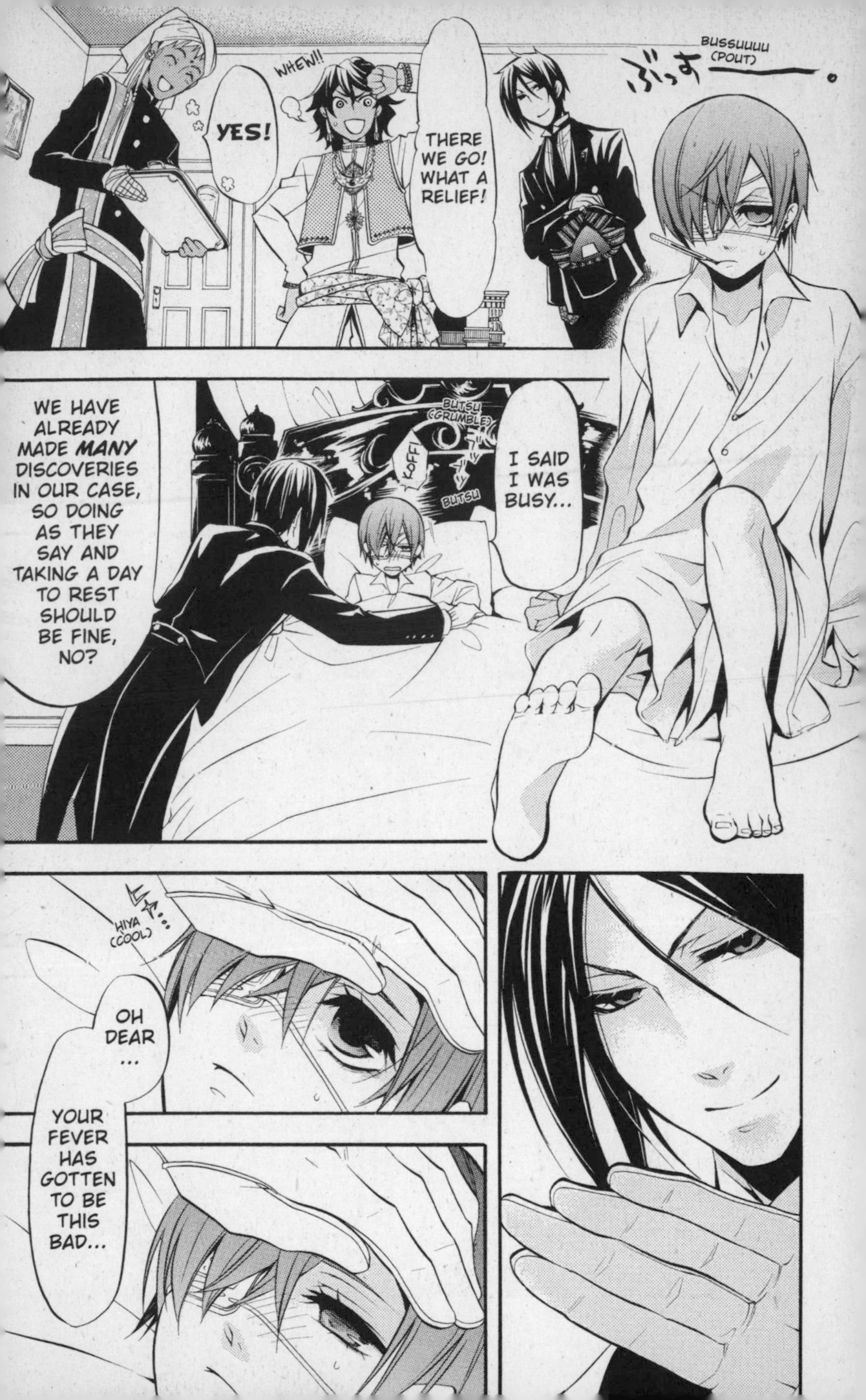
ぶっす
BUSSUUUU (POUT)
THERE WE GO! WHAT A RELIEF!
WHEW!!
YES!
I SAID I WAS BUSY...
BUTSU (GRUMBLE)
KOFF!
BUTSU
WE HAVE ALREADY MADE MANY DISCOVERIES IN OUR CASE, SO DOING AS THEY SAY AND TAKING A DAY TO REST SHOULD BE FINE, NO?
HIYA (COOL)
OH DEAR ...
YOUR FEVER HAS GOTTEN TO BE THIS BAD...

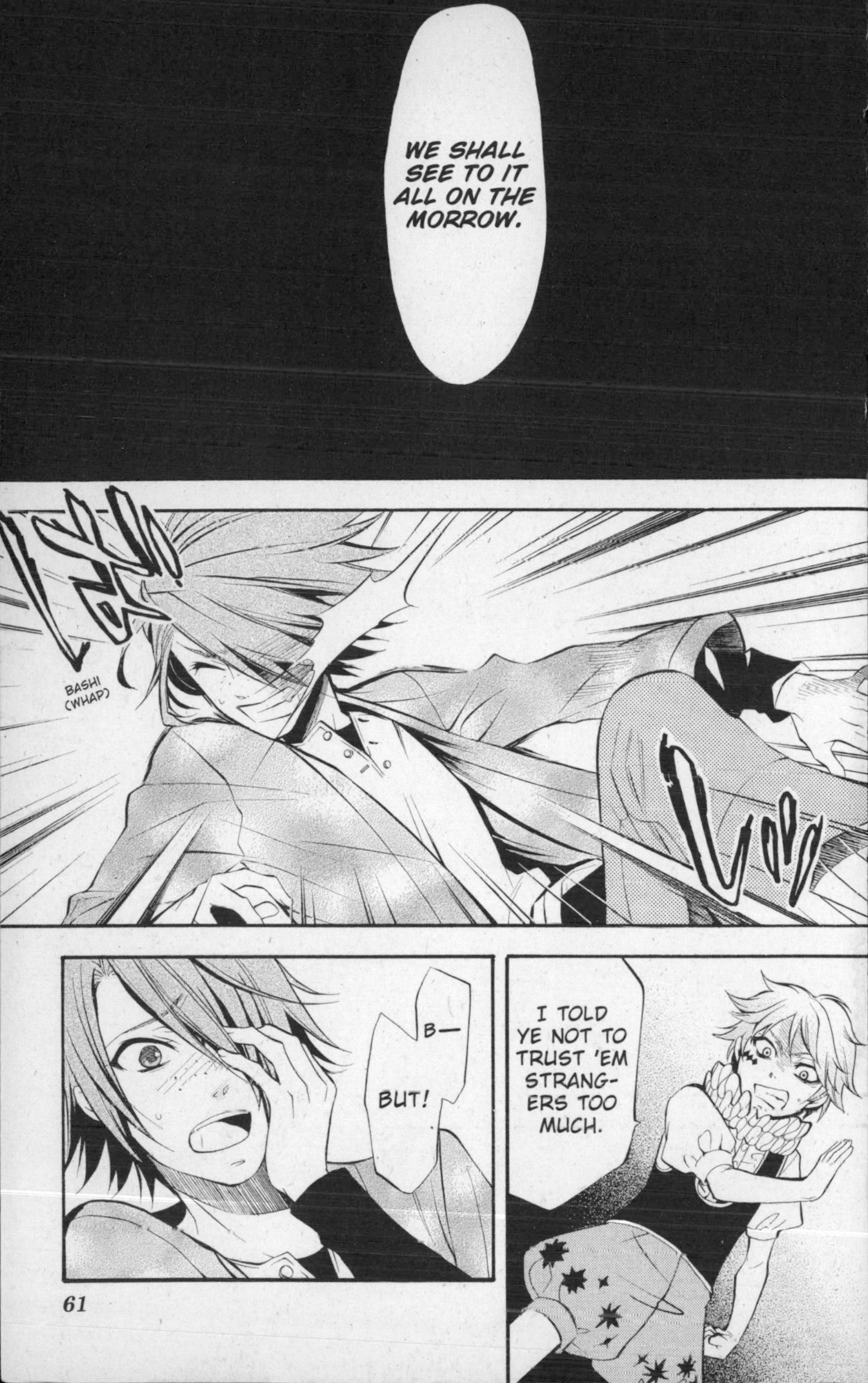
WE SHALL SEE TO IT ALL ON THE MORROW.
BASHI (WHAP)
I TOLD YE NOT TO TRUST 'EM STRANGERS TOO MUCH.
B—
BUT!

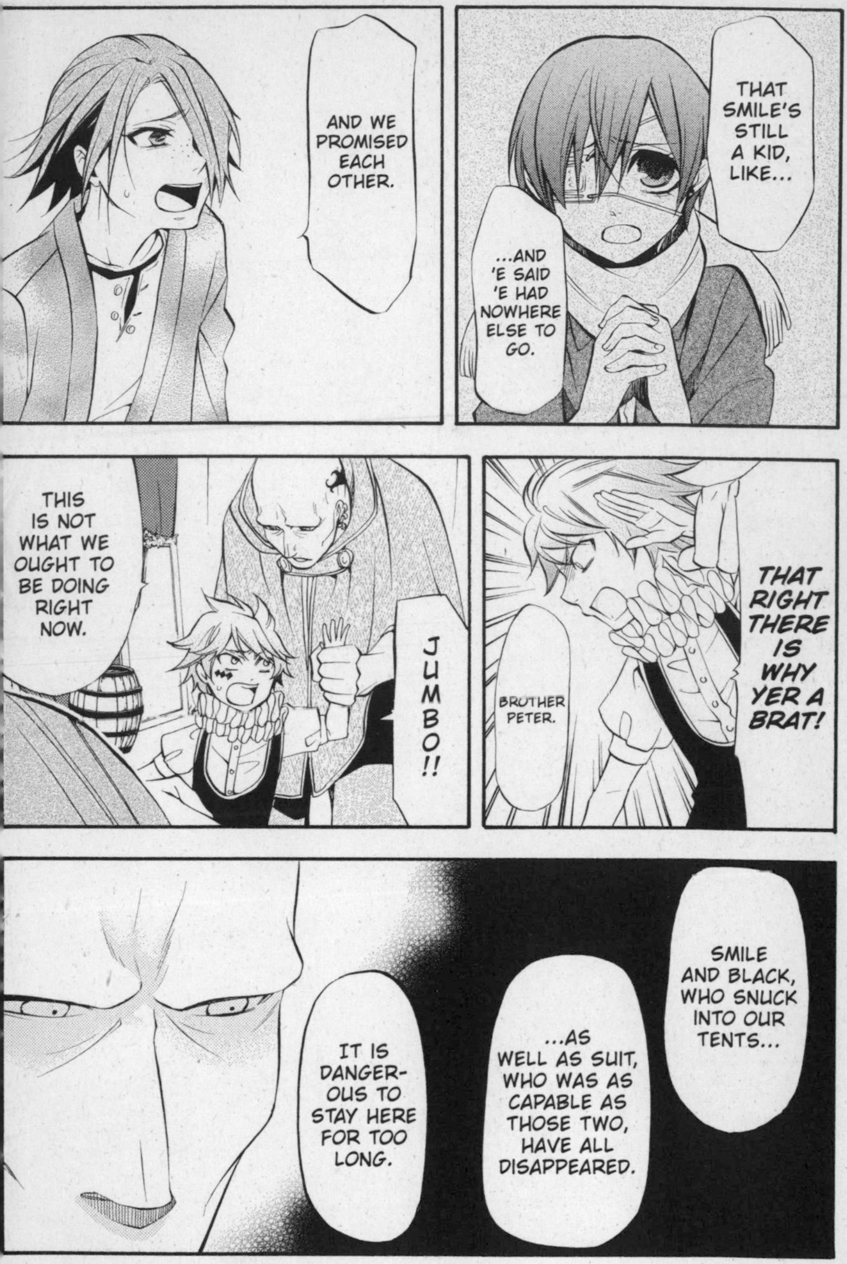
THAT SMILE'S STILL A KID, LIKE...
...AND 'E SAID 'E HAD NOWHERE ELSE TO GO.
AND WE PROMISED EACH OTHER.
THAT RIGHT THERE IS WHY YER A BRAT!
BROTHER PETER.
JUMBO!!
THIS IS NOT WHAT WE OUGHT TO BE DOING RIGHT NOW.
SMILE AND BLACK, WHO SNUCK INTO OUR TENTS...
...AS WELL AS SUIT, WHO WAS AS CAPABLE AS THOSE TWO, HAVE ALL DISAPPEARED.
IT IS DANGEROUS TO STAY HERE FOR TOO LONG.

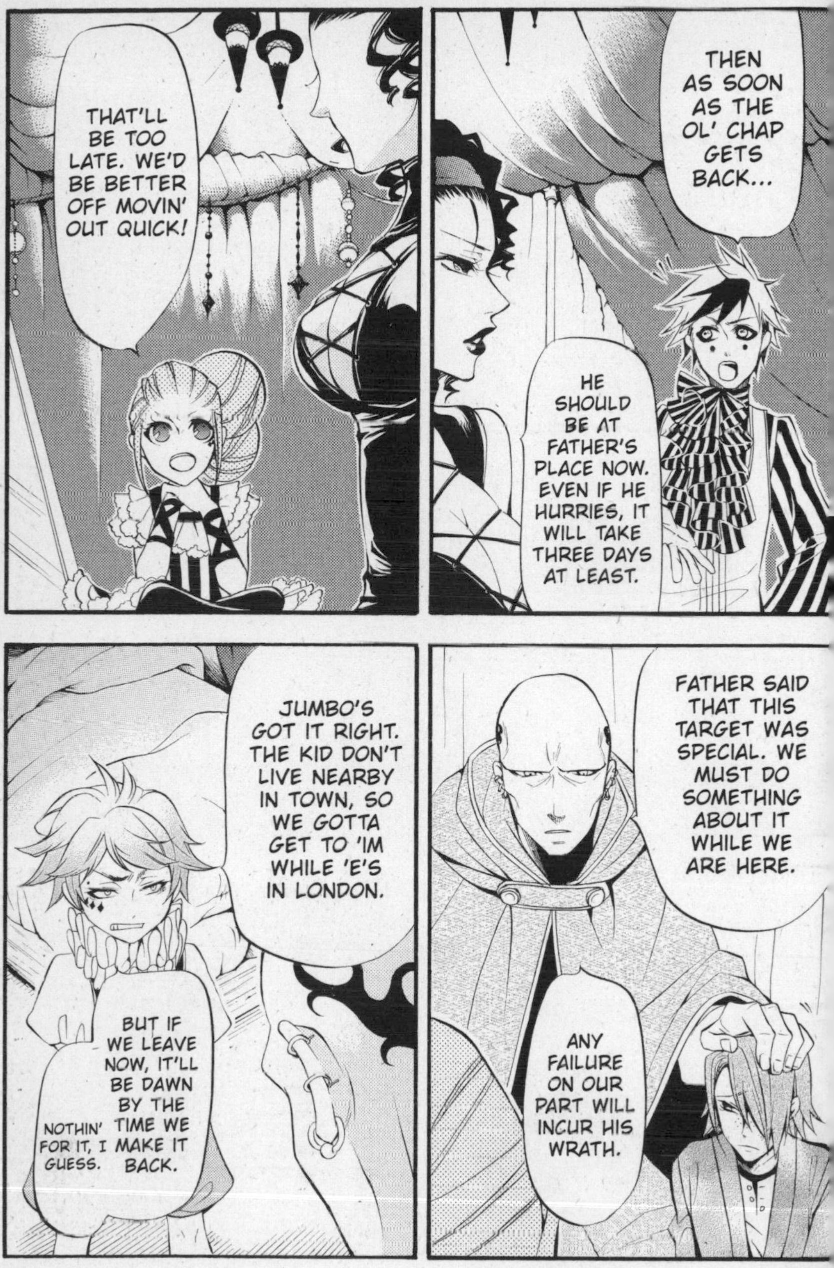
THEN AS SOON AS THE OL' CHAP GETS BACK...
HE SHOULD BE AT FATHER'S PLACE NOW. EVEN IF HE HURRIES, IT WILL TAKE THREE DAYS AT LEAST.
THAT'LL BE TOO LATE. WE'D BE BETTER OFF MOVIN' OUT QUICK!
FATHER SAID THAT THIS TARGET WAS SPECIAL. WE MUST DO SOMETHING ABOUT IT WHILE WE ARE HERE.
ANY FAILURE ON OUR PART WILL INCUR HIS WRATH.
JUMBO'S GOT IT RIGHT. THE KID DON'T LIVE NEARBY IN TOWN, SO WE GOTTA GET TO 'IM WHILE 'E'S IN LONDON.
BUT IF WE LEAVE NOW, IT'LL BE DAWN BY THE TIME WE MAKE IT BACK.
NOTHIN' FOR IT, I GUESS.

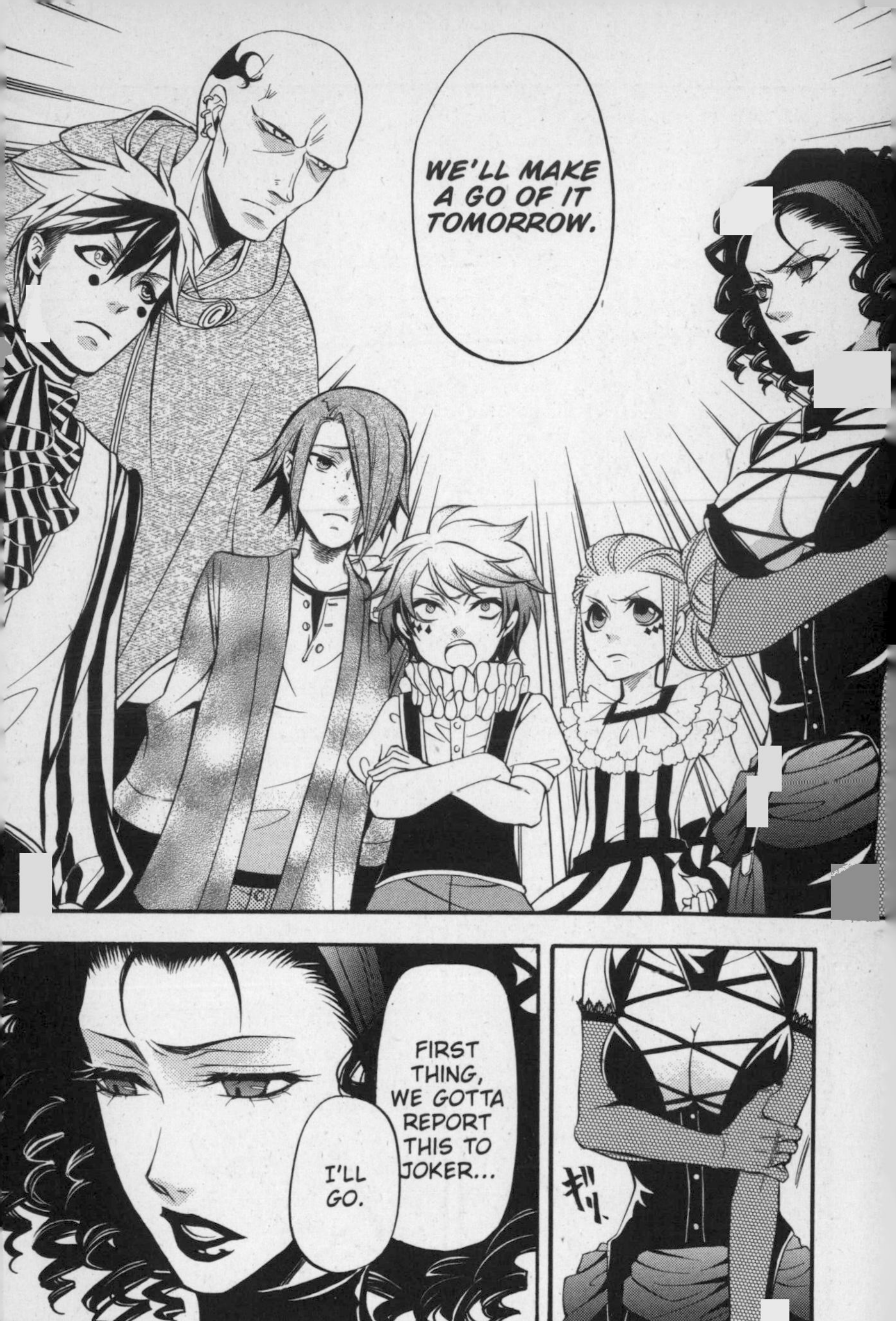
WE'LL MAKE A GO OF IT TOMORROW.
FIRST THING, WE GOTTA REPORT THIS TO JOKER...
I'LL GO.
ギリ

SFX: GIRI (CLUTCH)

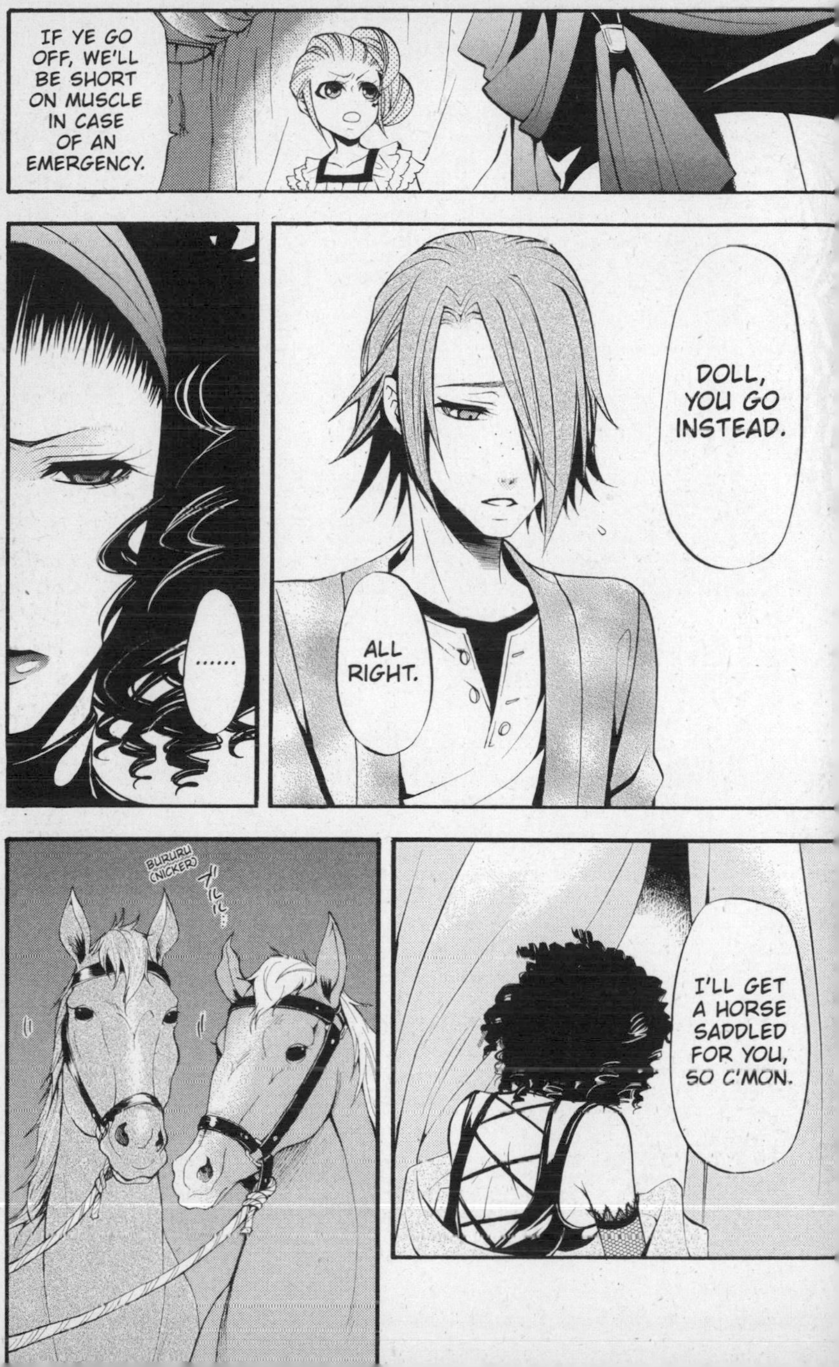
IF YE GO OFF, WE'LL BE SHORT ON MUSCLE IN CASE OF AN EMERGENCY.
DOLL, YOU GO INSTEAD.
ALL RIGHT.
......
I'LL GET A HORSE SADDLED FOR YOU, SO C'MON.
BURURU (NICKER)
ブルル…

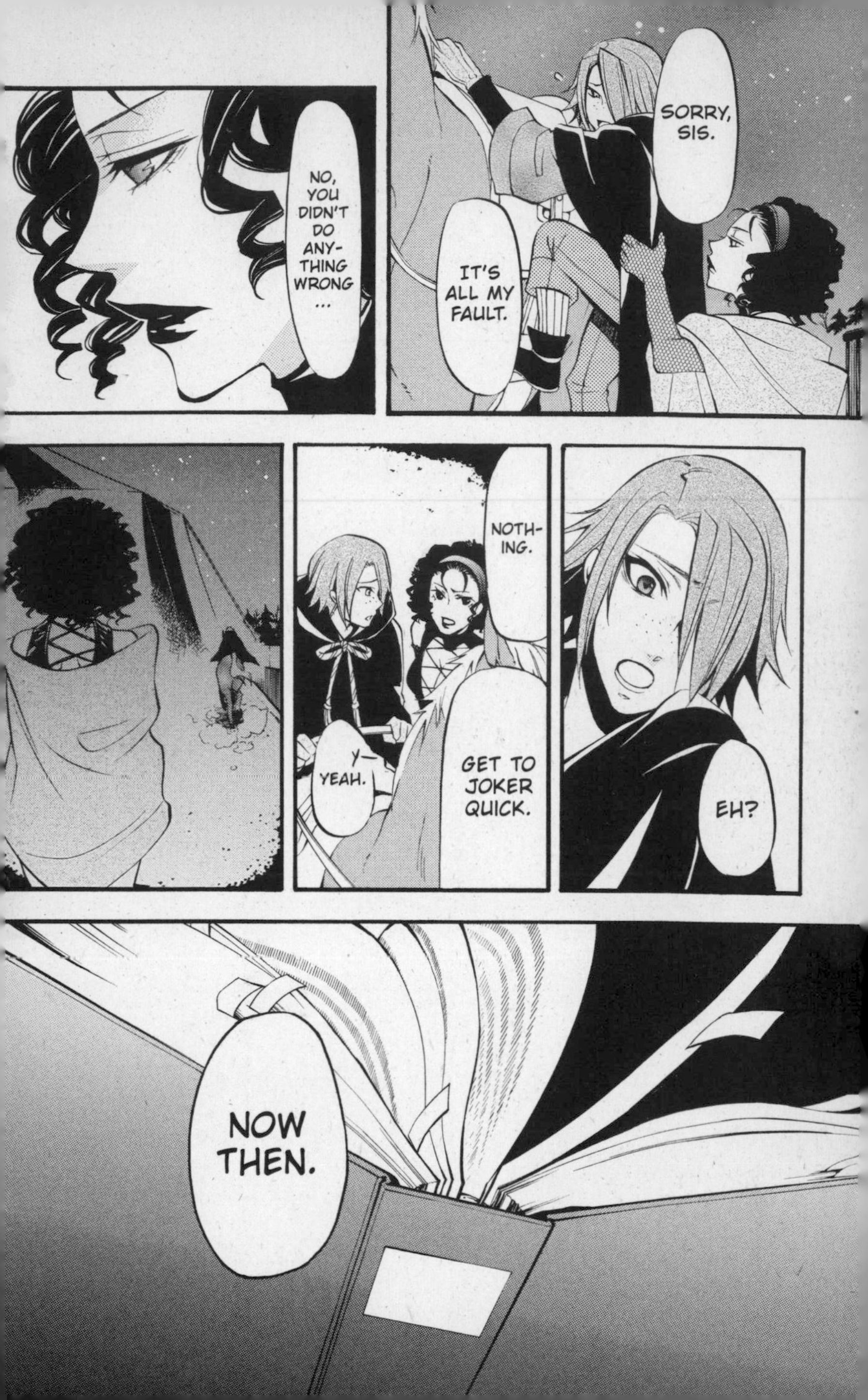
SORRY, SIS.
IT'S ALL MY FAULT.
NO, YOU DIDN'T DO ANY-THING WRONG ...
EH?
NOTH-ING.
GET TO JOKER QUICK.
Y— YEAH.
NOW THEN.

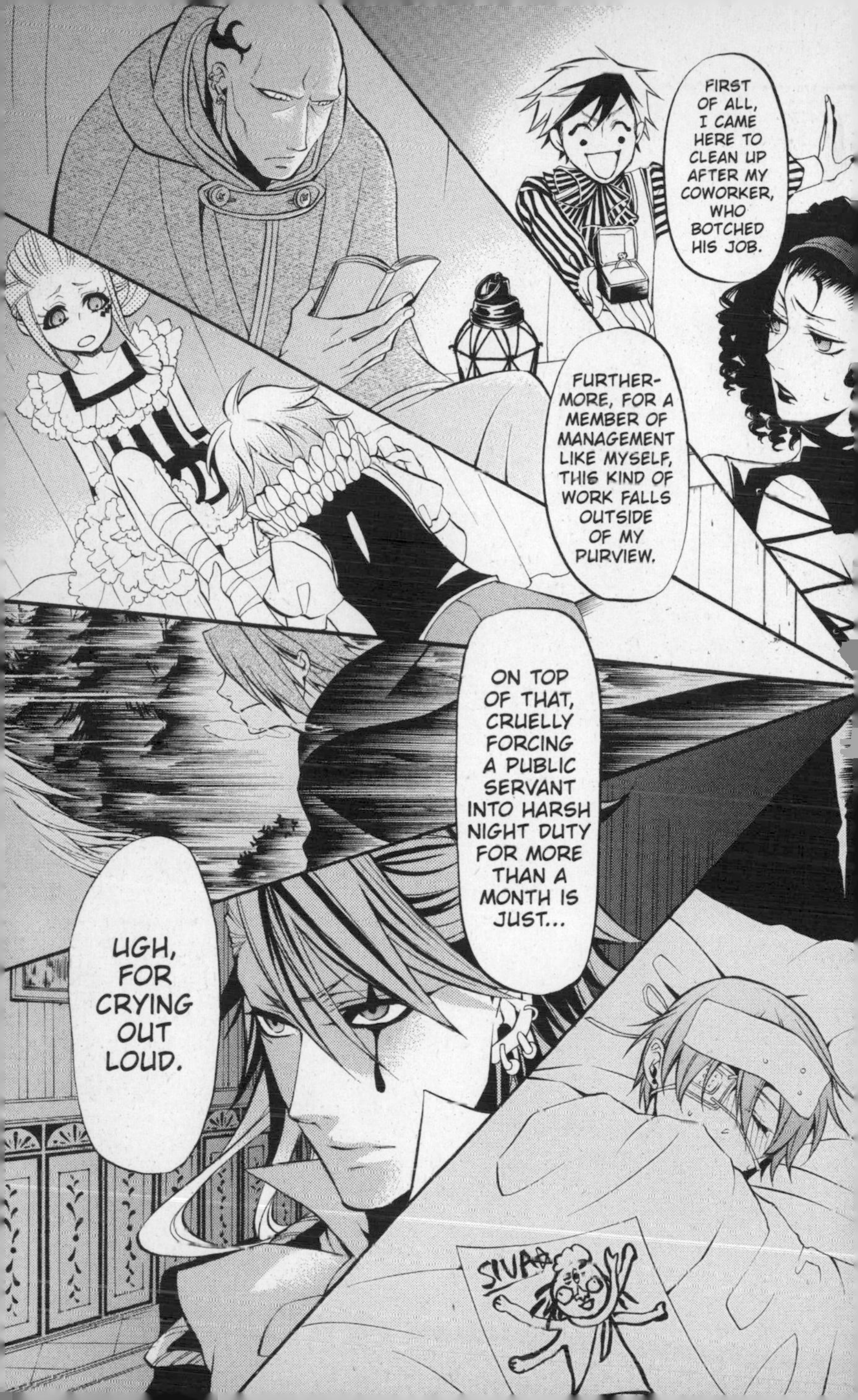
FIRST OF ALL, I CAME HERE TO CLEAN UP AFTER MY COWORKER, WHO BOTCHED HIS JOB.
FURTHER-MORE, FOR A MEMBER OF MANAGEMENT LIKE MYSELF, THIS KIND OF WORK FALLS OUTSIDE OF MY PURVIEW.
ON TOP OF THAT, CRUELLY FORCING A PUBLIC SERVANT INTO HARSH NIGHT DUTY FOR MORE THAN A MONTH IS JUST...
UGH, FOR CRYING OUT LOUD.

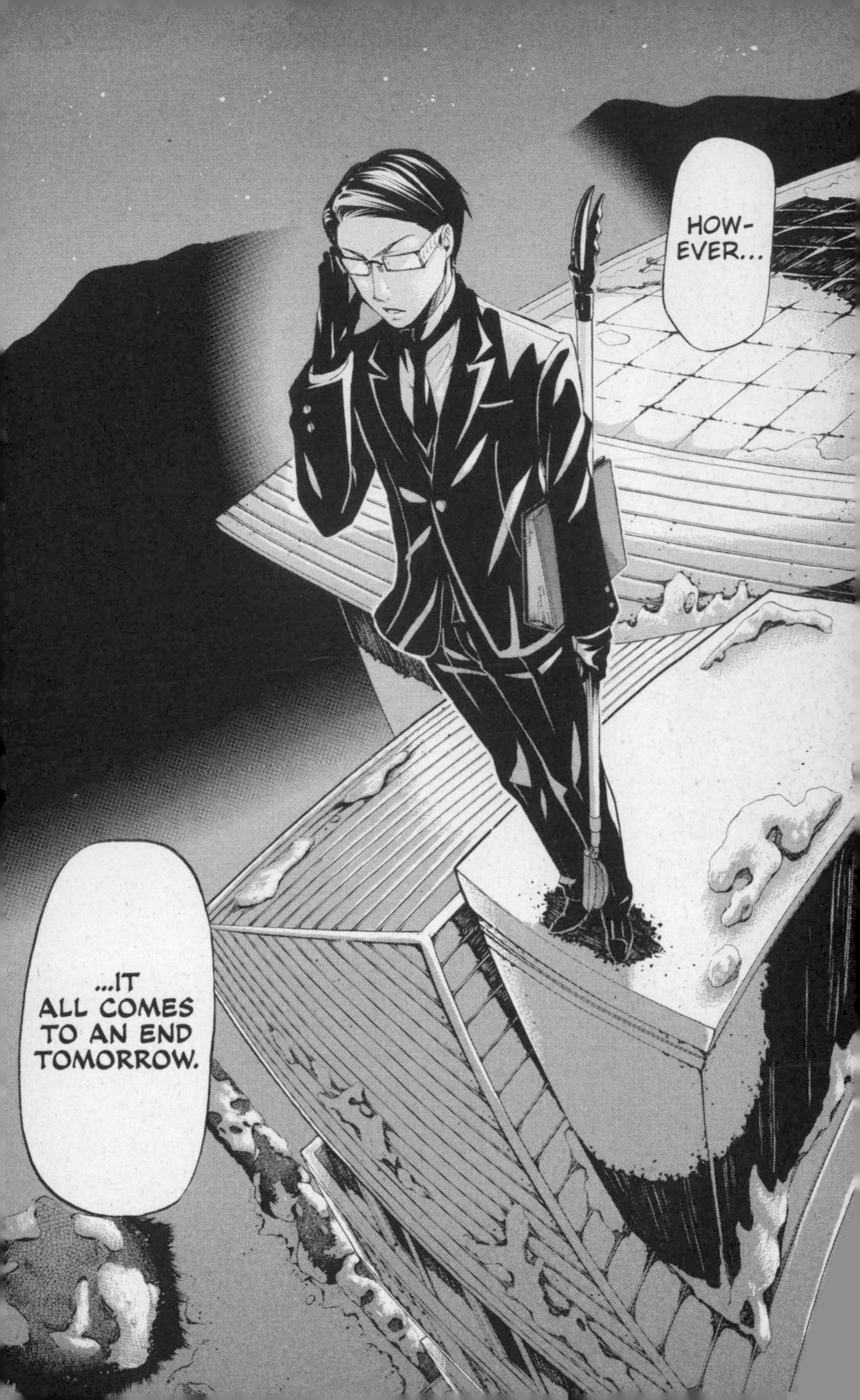
HOW-EVER...
...IT ALL COMES TO AN END TOMORROW.

Black Butler

Chapter 30

In the afternoon : The Butler, Nurturing

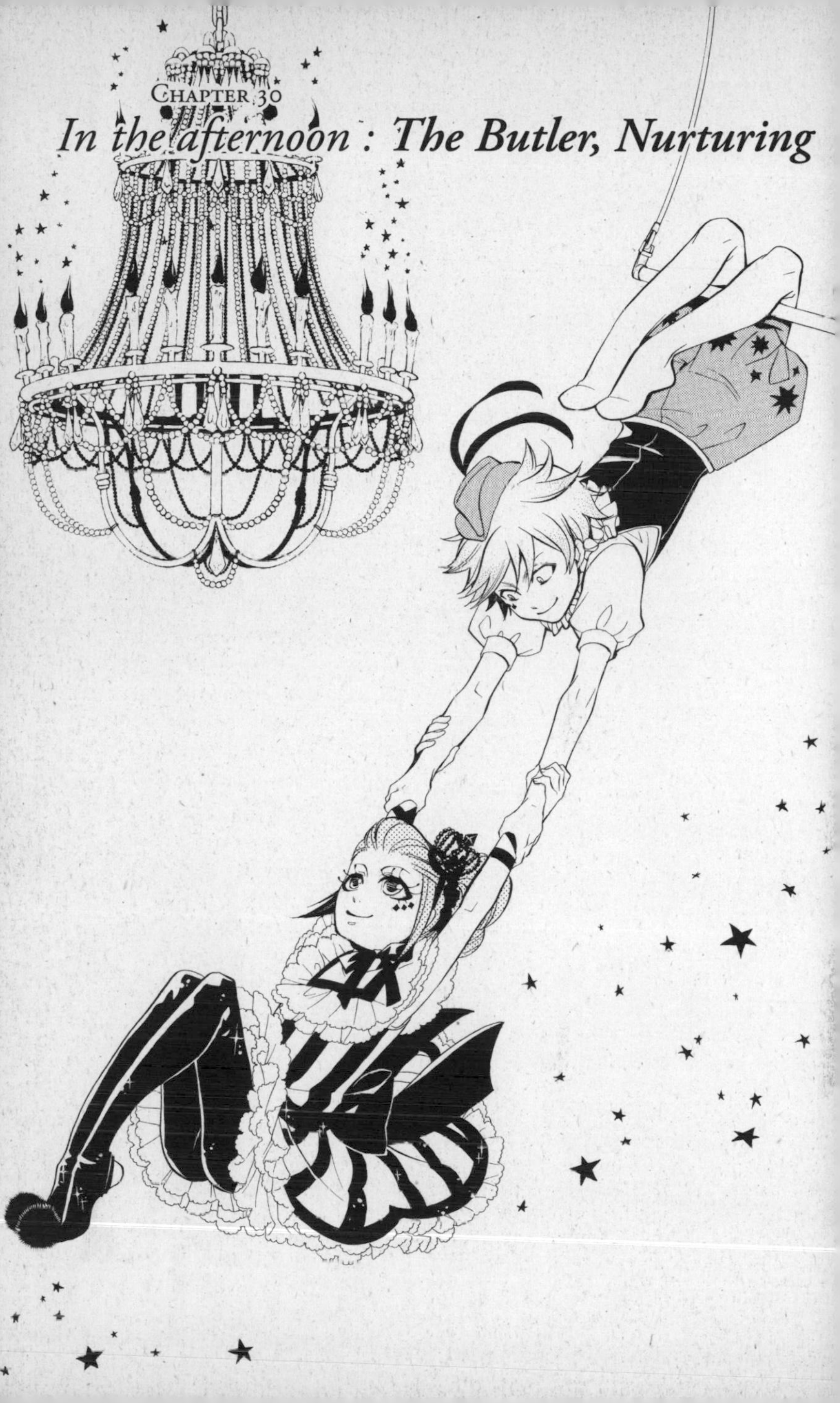

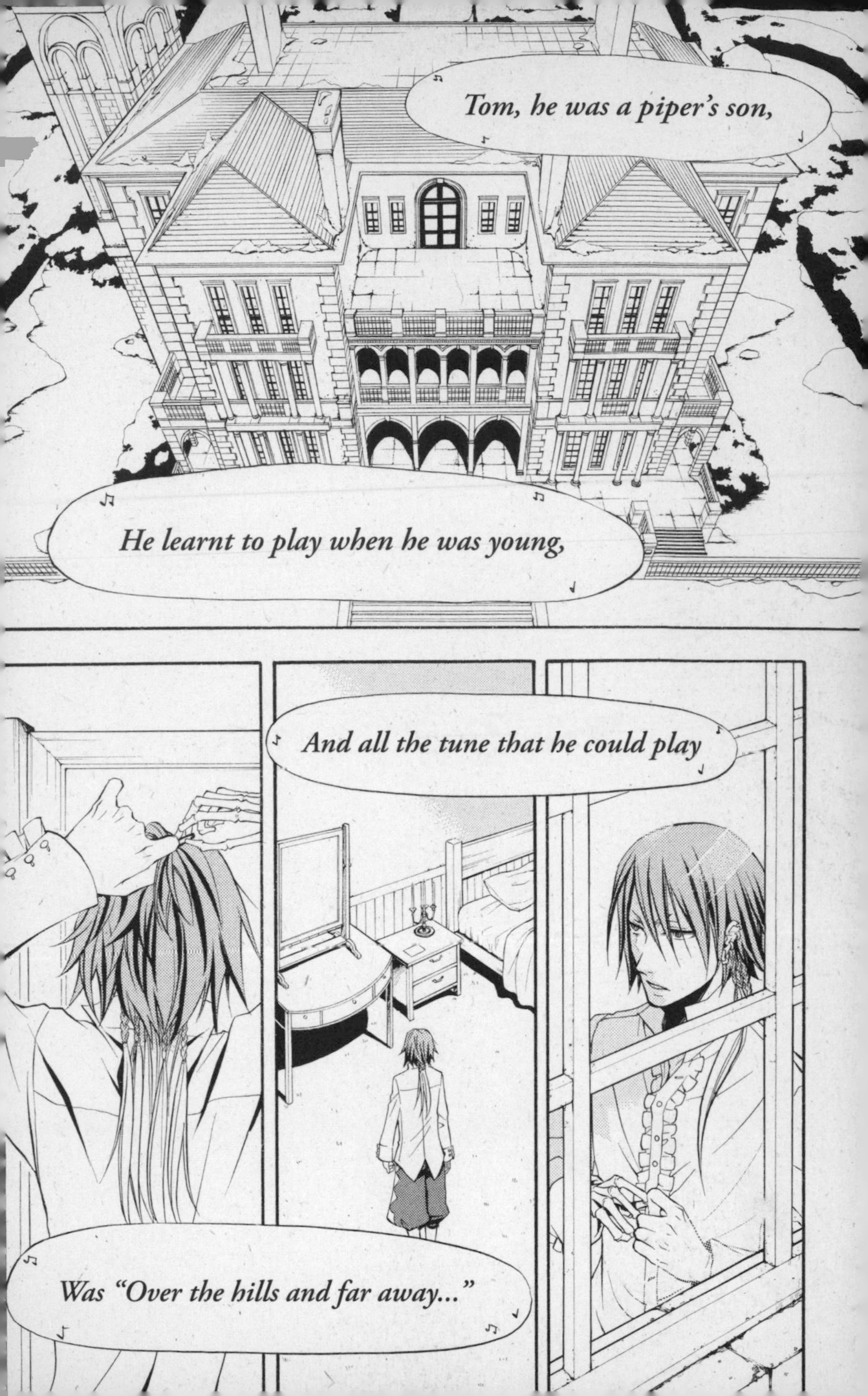
Tom, he was a piper's son,
He learnt to play when he was young,
And all the tune that he could play
Was "Over the hills and far away..."

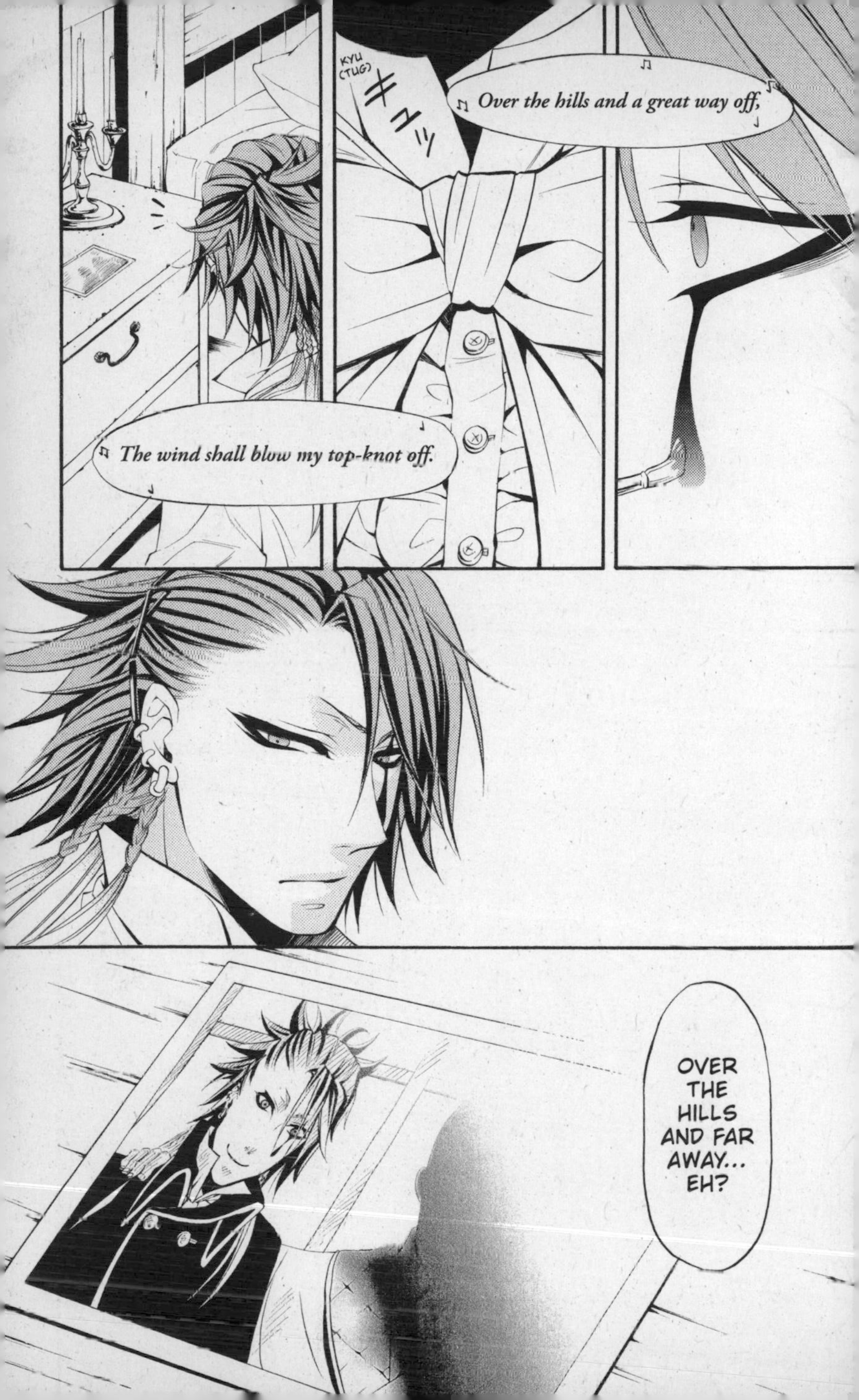

Over the hills and a great way off,
KYU (TUG)
キュッ
The wind shall blow my top-knot off.
OVER THE HILLS AND FAR AWAY... EH?

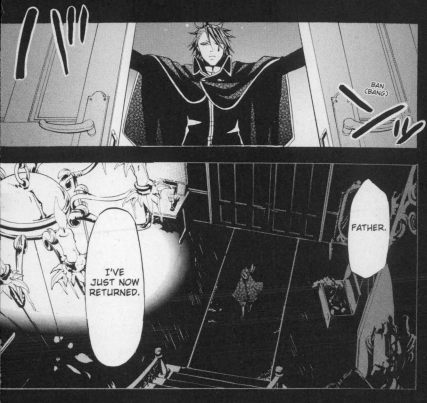

BAN (BANG)

FATHER.

I'VE JUST NOW RETURNED.

KON (KNOCK)

KON

FATHER, MAY I COME IN?

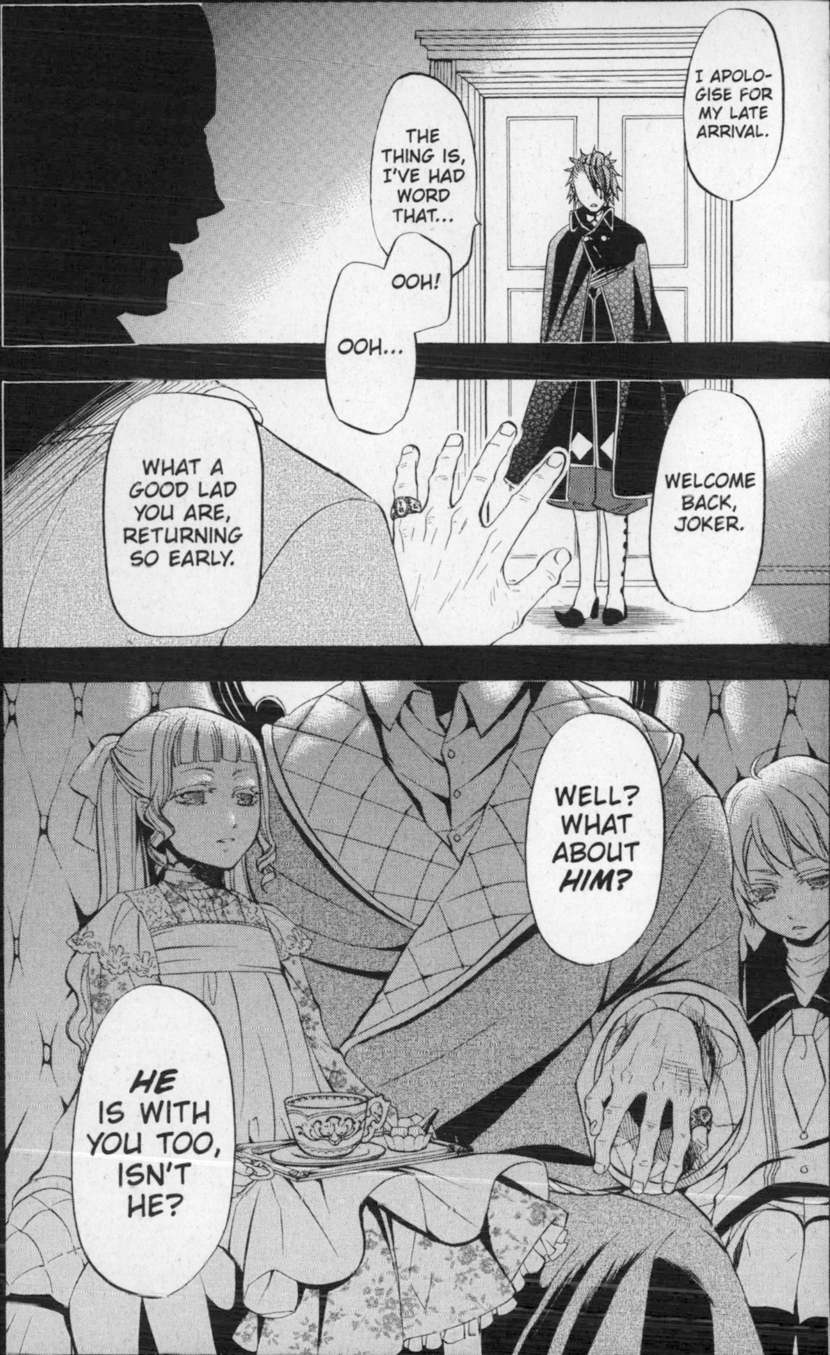
I APOLOGISE FOR MY LATE ARRIVAL.
THE THING IS, I'VE HAD WORD THAT...
OOH!
OOH...
WELCOME BACK, JOKER.
WHAT A GOOD LAD YOU ARE, RETURNING SO EARLY.
WELL? WHAT ABOUT *HIM*?
HE IS WITH YOU TOO, ISN'T HE?

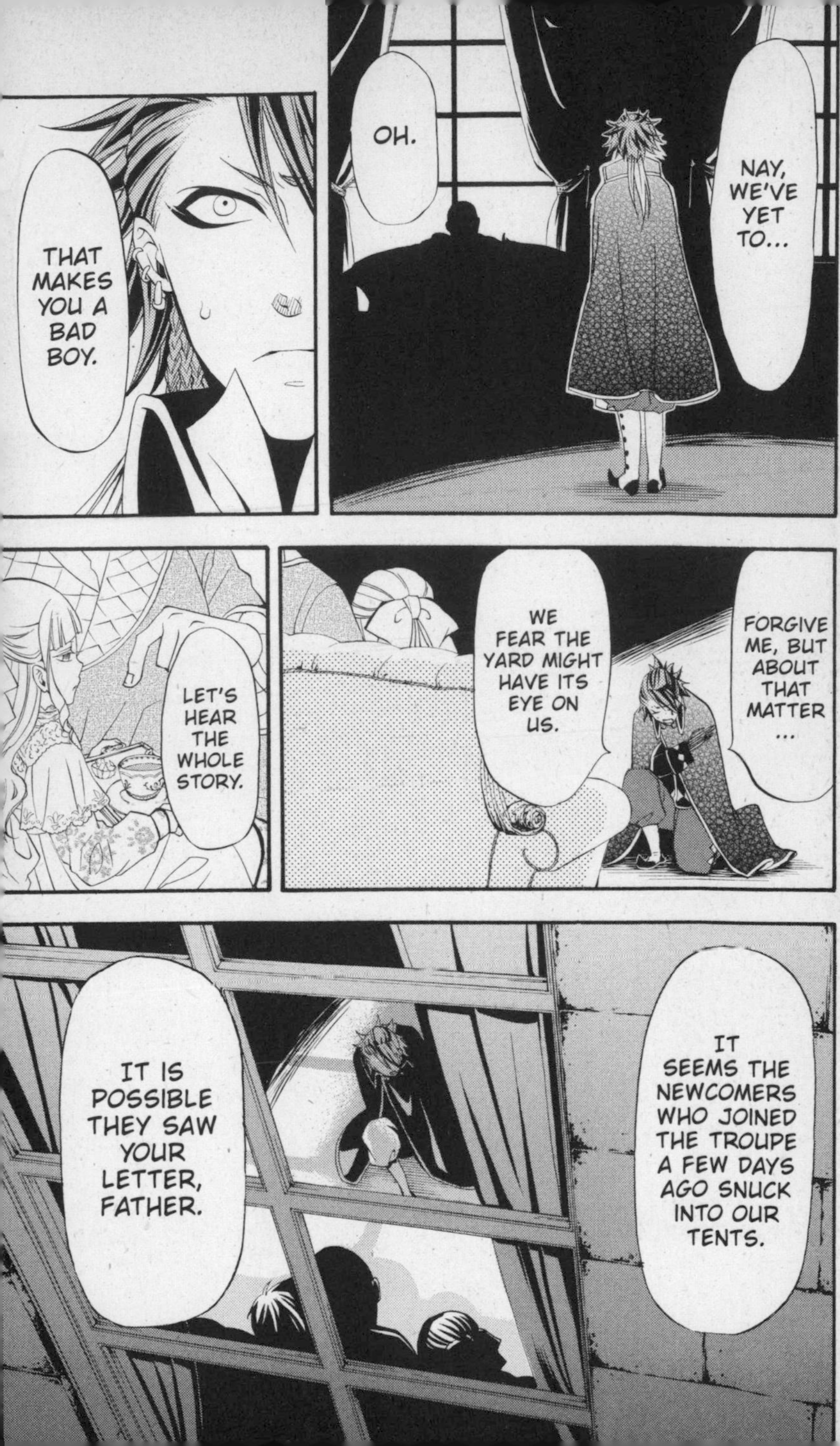
NAY, WE'VE YET TO...
OH.
THAT MAKES YOU A BAD BOY.
FORGIVE ME, BUT ABOUT THAT MATTER...
WE FEAR THE YARD MIGHT HAVE ITS EYE ON US.
LET'S HEAR THE WHOLE STORY.
IT SEEMS THE NEWCOMERS WHO JOINED THE TROUPE A FEW DAYS AGO SNUCK INTO OUR TENTS.
IT IS POSSIBLE THEY SAW YOUR LETTER, FATHER.

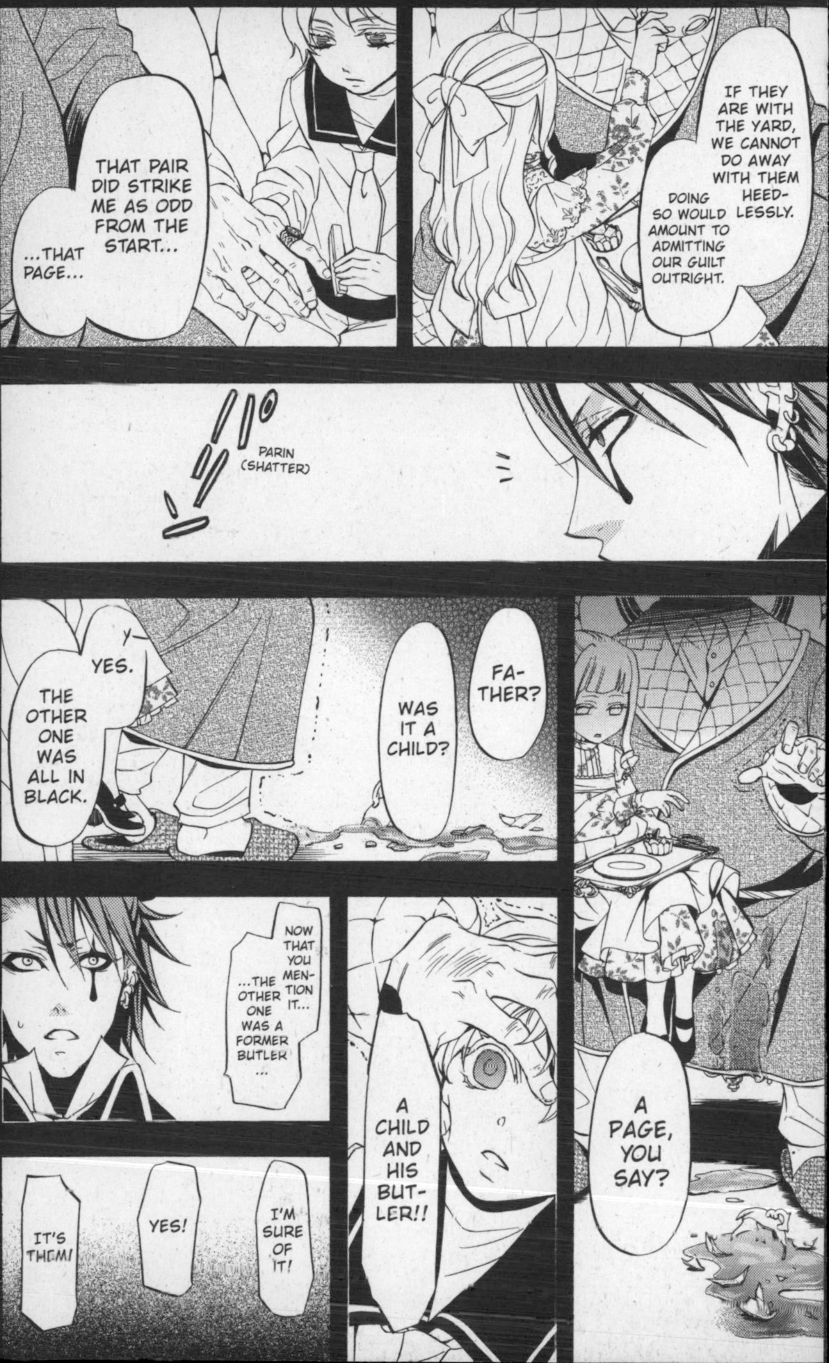
IF THEY ARE WITH THE YARD, WE CANNOT DO AWAY WITH THEM HEEDLESSLY.
DOING SO WOULD AMOUNT TO ADMITTING OUR GUILT OUTRIGHT.
THAT PAIR DID STRIKE ME AS ODD FROM THE START...
...THAT PAGE...
PARIN (SHATTER)
A PAGE, YOU SAY?
FATHER?
WAS IT A CHILD?
Y-YES.
THE OTHER ONE WAS ALL IN BLACK.
A CHILD AND HIS BUTLER!!
NOW THAT YOU MENTION IT...
...THE OTHER ONE WAS A FORMER BUTLER...
I'M SURE OF IT!
YES!
IT'S THEM!

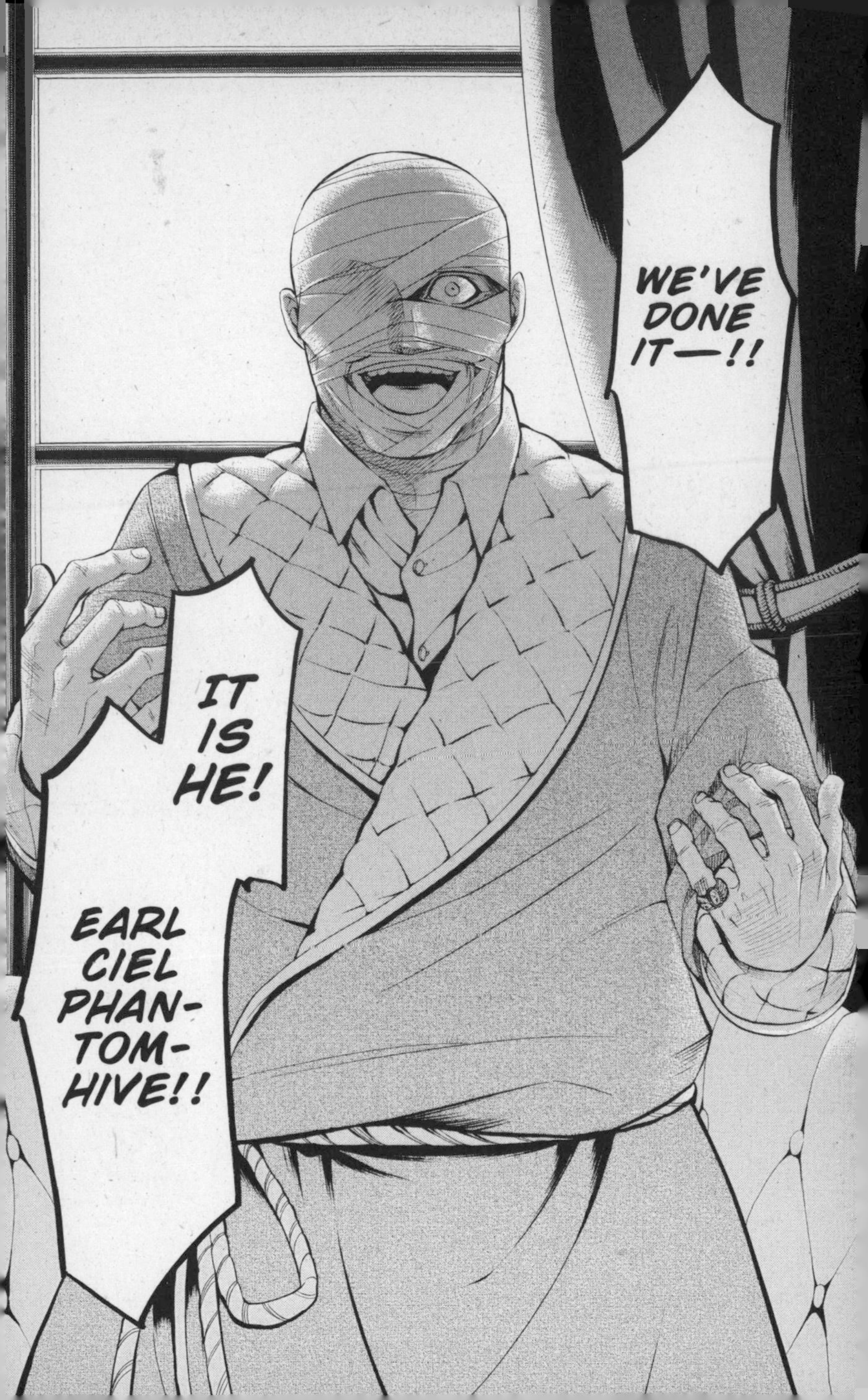
WE'VE DONE IT—!!
IT IS HE!
EARL CIEL PHAN-TOM-HIVE!!

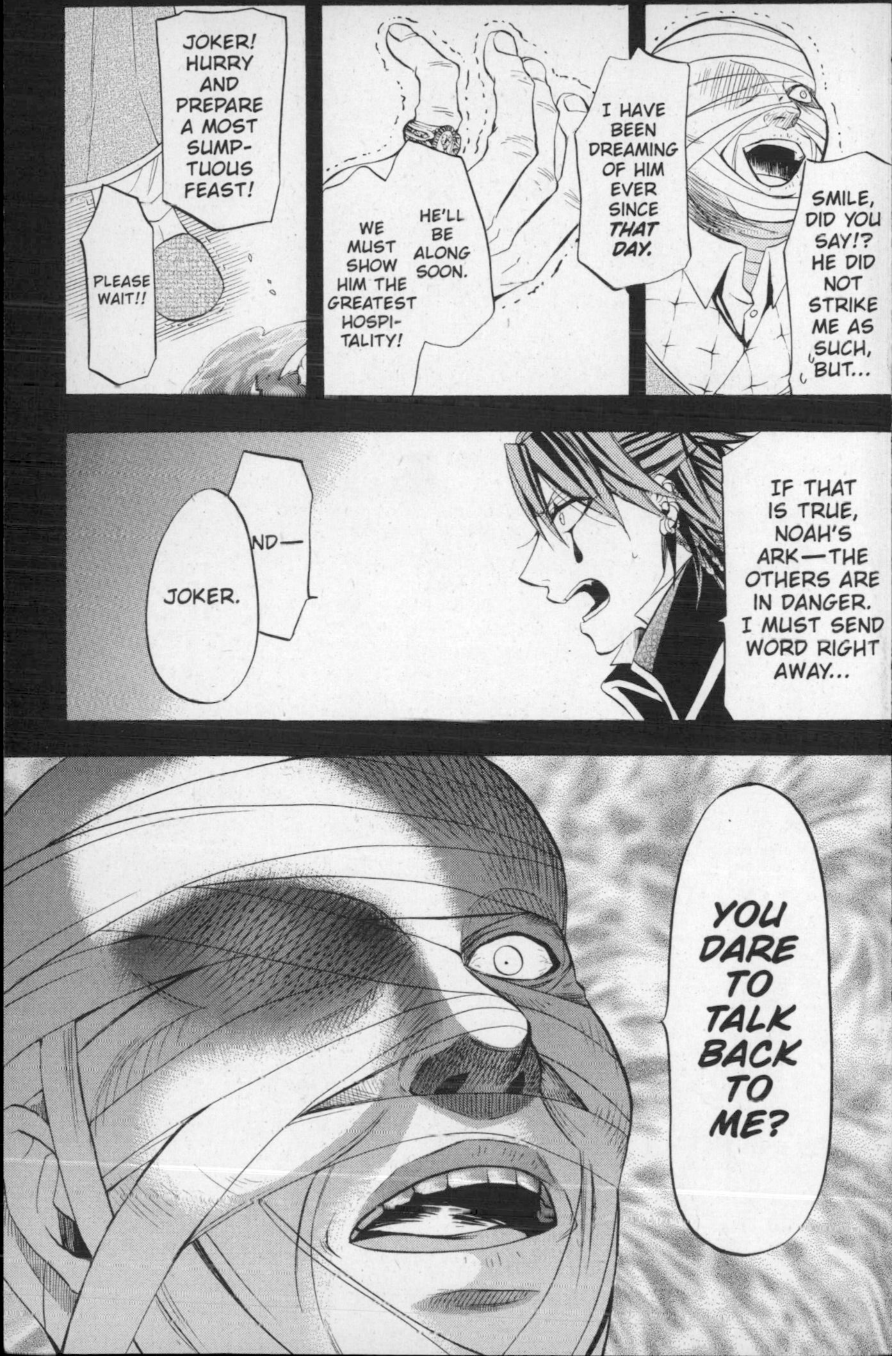
SMILE, DID YOU SAY!? HE DID NOT STRIKE ME AS SUCH, BUT...
I HAVE BEEN DREAMING OF HIM EVER SINCE *THAT DAY.*
HE'LL BE ALONG SOON.
WE MUST SHOW HIM THE GREATEST HOSPI-TALITY!
JOKER! HURRY AND PREPARE A MOST SUMP-TUOUS FEAST!
PLEASE WAIT!!
IF THAT IS TRUE, NOAH'S ARK—THE OTHERS ARE IN DANGER. I MUST SEND WORD RIGHT AWAY...
ND—
JOKER.
YOU DARE TO TALK BACK TO ME?

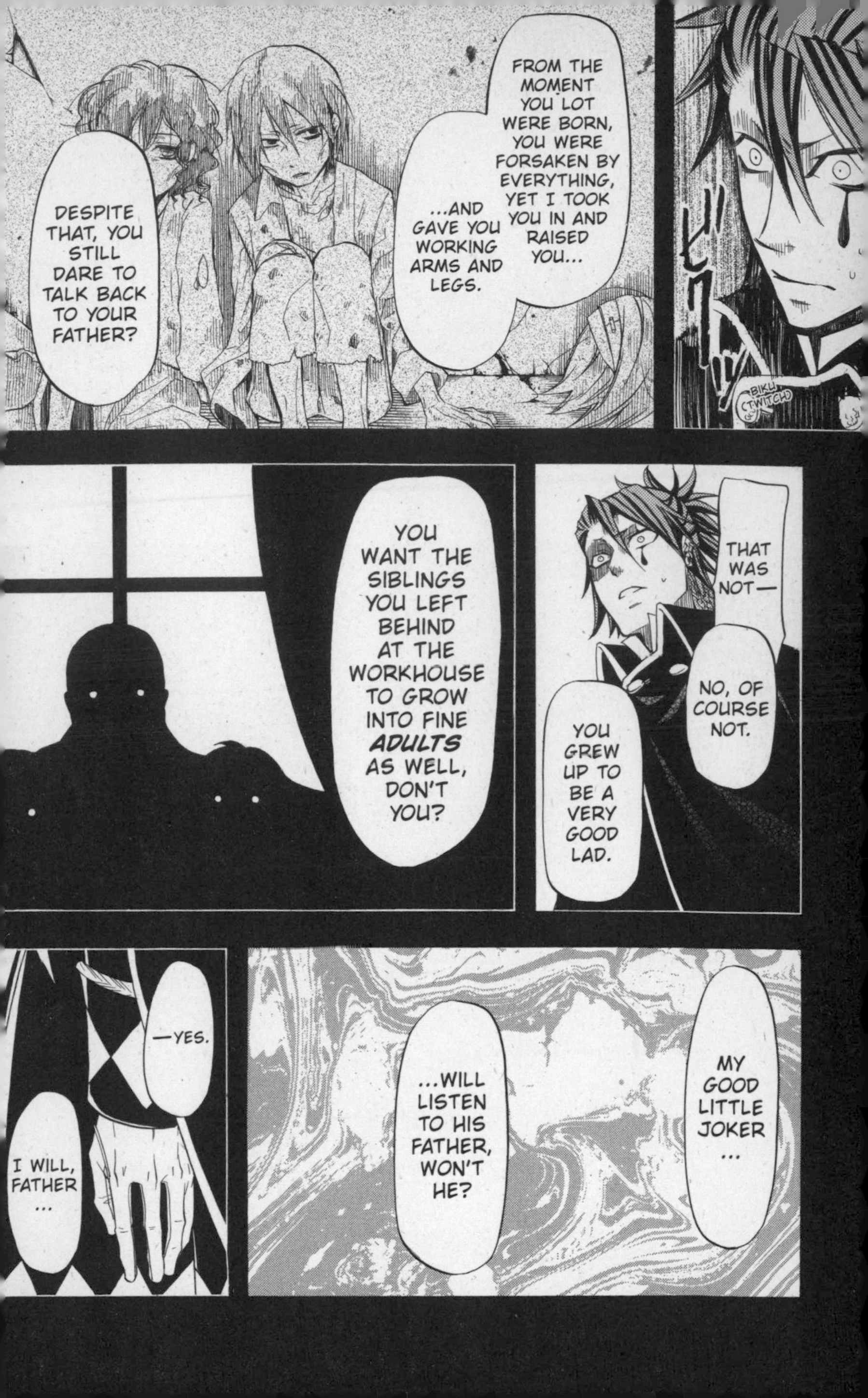
BIKU (TWITCH)
FROM THE MOMENT YOU LOT WERE BORN, YOU WERE FORSAKEN BY EVERYTHING, YET I TOOK YOU IN AND RAISED YOU...
...AND GAVE YOU WORKING ARMS AND LEGS.
DESPITE THAT, YOU STILL DARE TO TALK BACK TO YOUR FATHER?
THAT WAS NOT—
NO, OF COURSE NOT.
YOU GREW UP TO BE A VERY GOOD LAD.
YOU WANT THE SIBLINGS YOU LEFT BEHIND AT THE WORKHOUSE TO GROW INTO FINE ***ADULTS*** AS WELL, DON'T YOU?
MY GOOD LITTLE JOKER ...
...WILL LISTEN TO HIS FATHER, WON'T HE?
—YES.
I WILL, FATHER ...

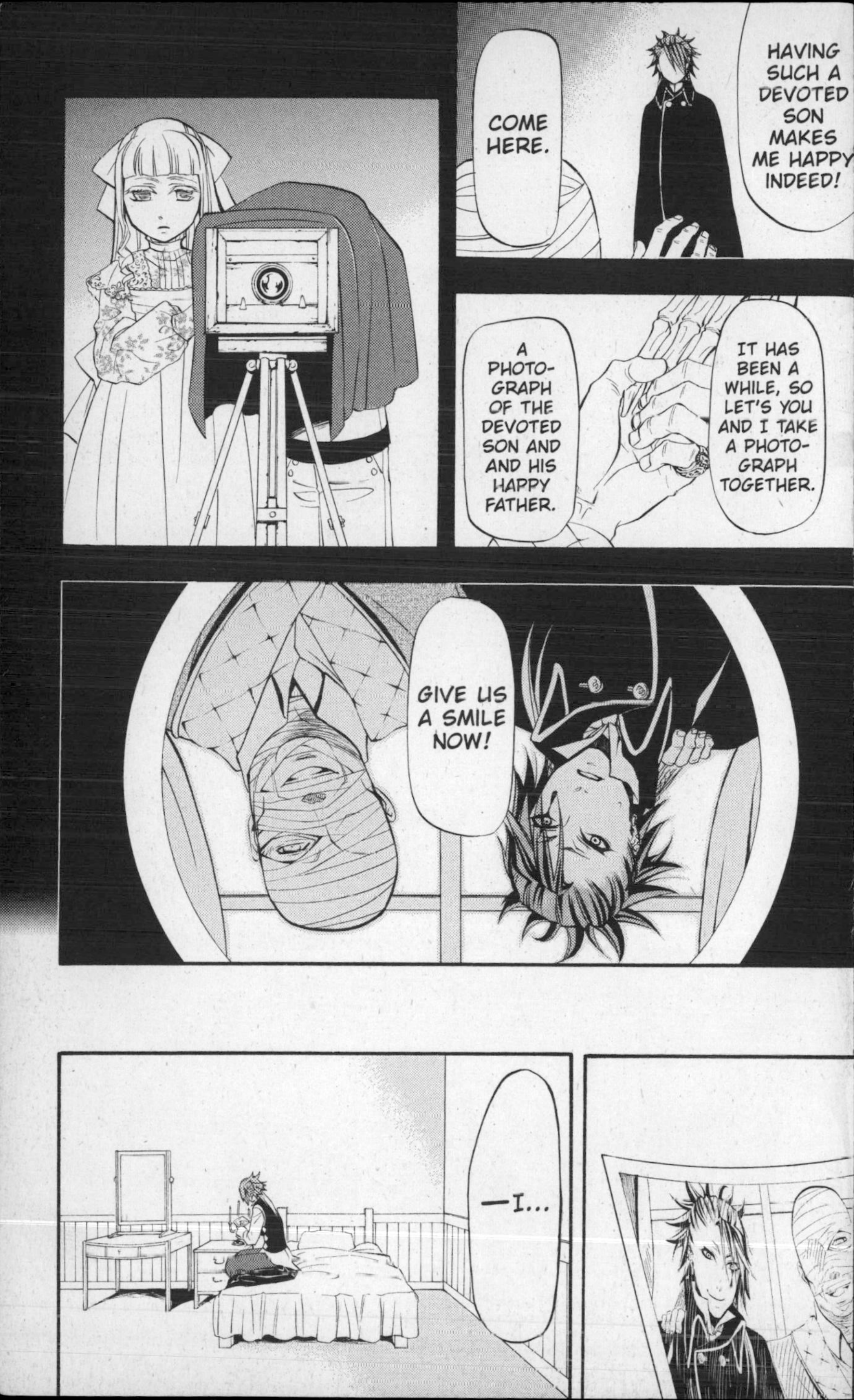
HAVING SUCH A DEVOTED SON MAKES ME HAPPY INDEED!
COME HERE.
IT HAS BEEN A WHILE, SO LET'S YOU AND I TAKE A PHOTOGRAPH TOGETHER.
A PHOTOGRAPH OF THE DEVOTED SON AND AND HIS HAPPY FATHER.
GIVE US A SMILE NOW!
—I...

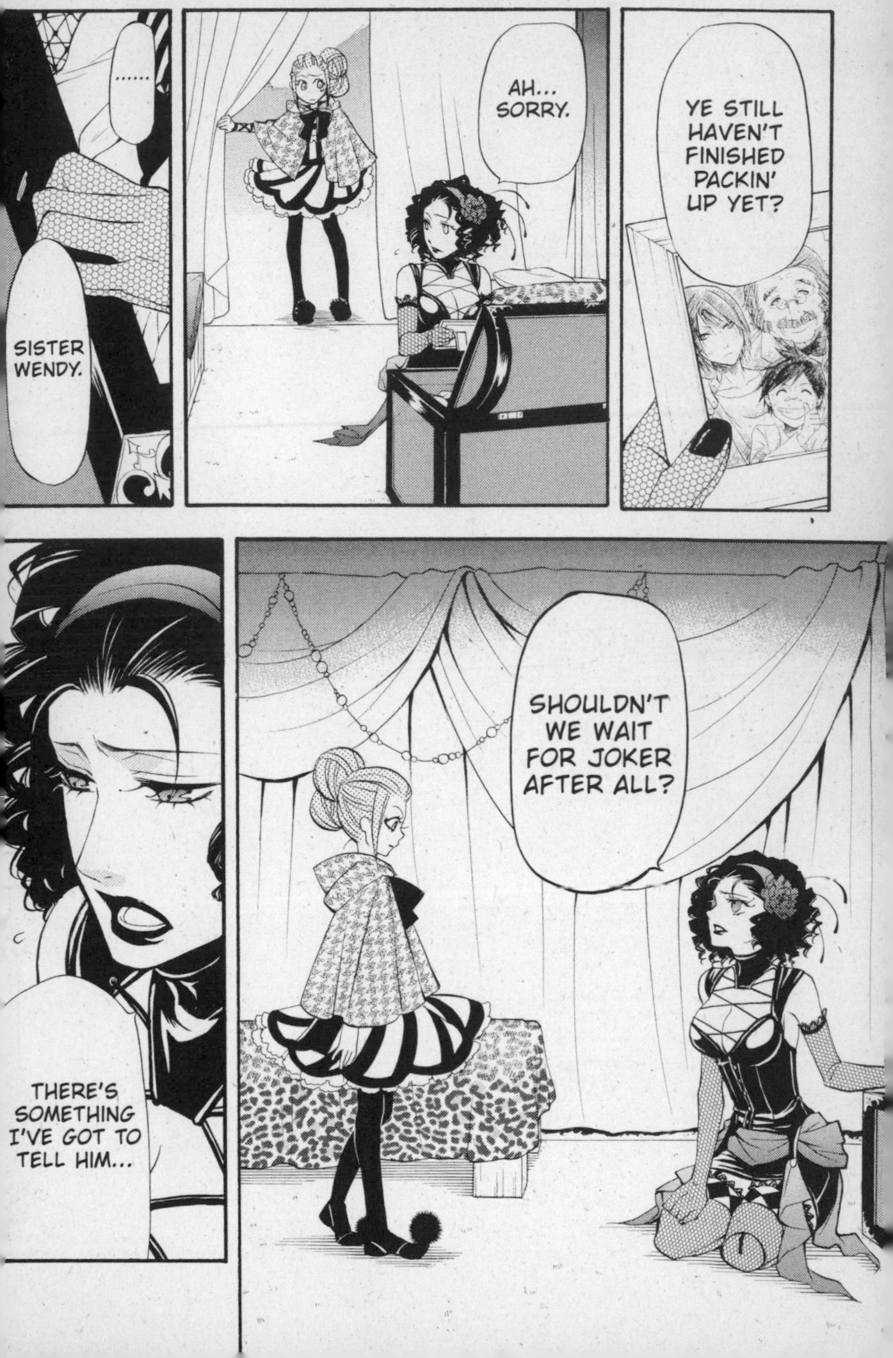
YE STILL HAVEN'T FINISHED PACKIN' UP YET?
AH... SORRY.
......
SISTER WENDY.
SHOULDN'T WE WAIT FOR JOKER AFTER ALL?
THERE'S SOMETHING I'VE GOT TO TELL HIM...

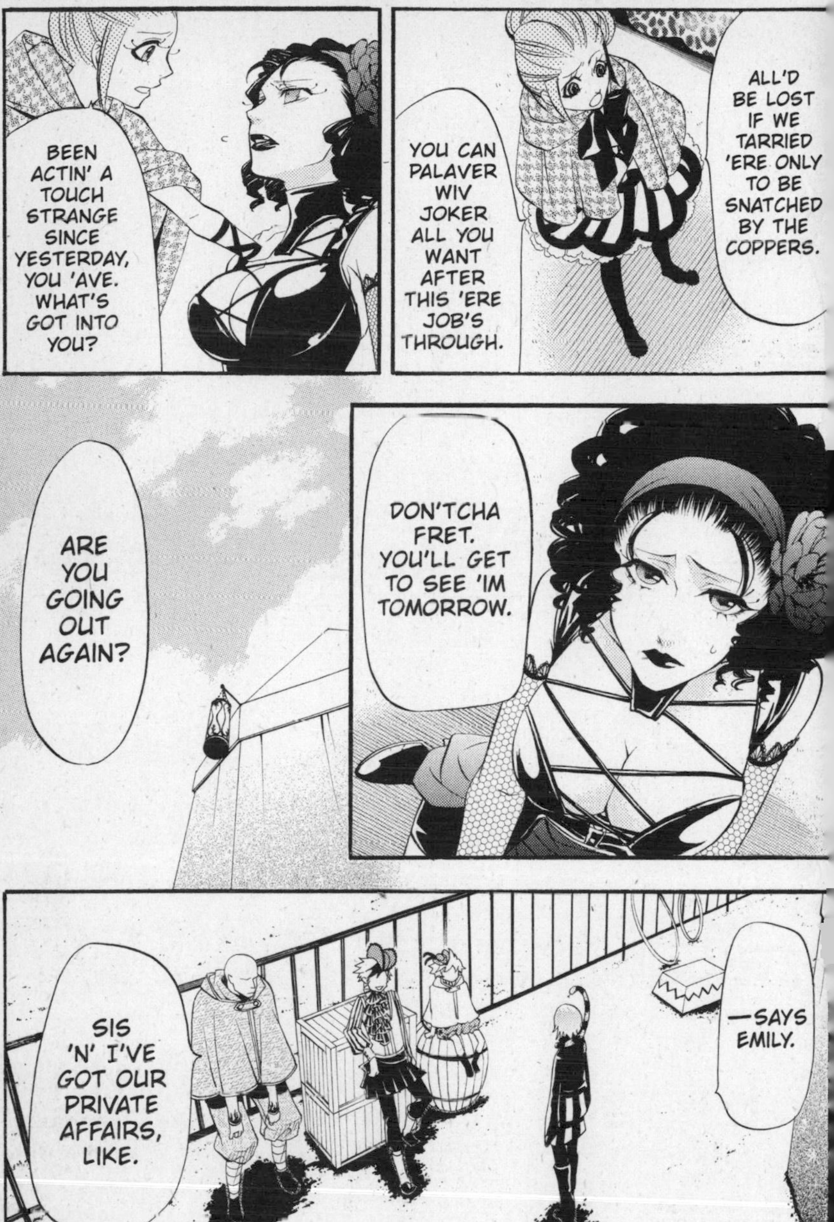
ALL'D BE LOST IF WE TARRIED 'ERE ONLY TO BE SNATCHED BY THE COPPERS.
YOU CAN PALAVER WIV JOKER ALL YOU WANT AFTER THIS 'ERE JOB'S THROUGH.
BEEN ACTIN' A TOUCH STRANGE SINCE YESTERDAY, YOU 'AVE. WHAT'S GOT INTO YOU?
DON'TCHA FRET. YOU'LL GET TO SEE 'IM TOMORROW.
ARE YOU GOING OUT AGAIN?
—SAYS EMILY.
SIS 'N' I'VE GOT OUR PRIVATE AFFAIRS, LIKE.

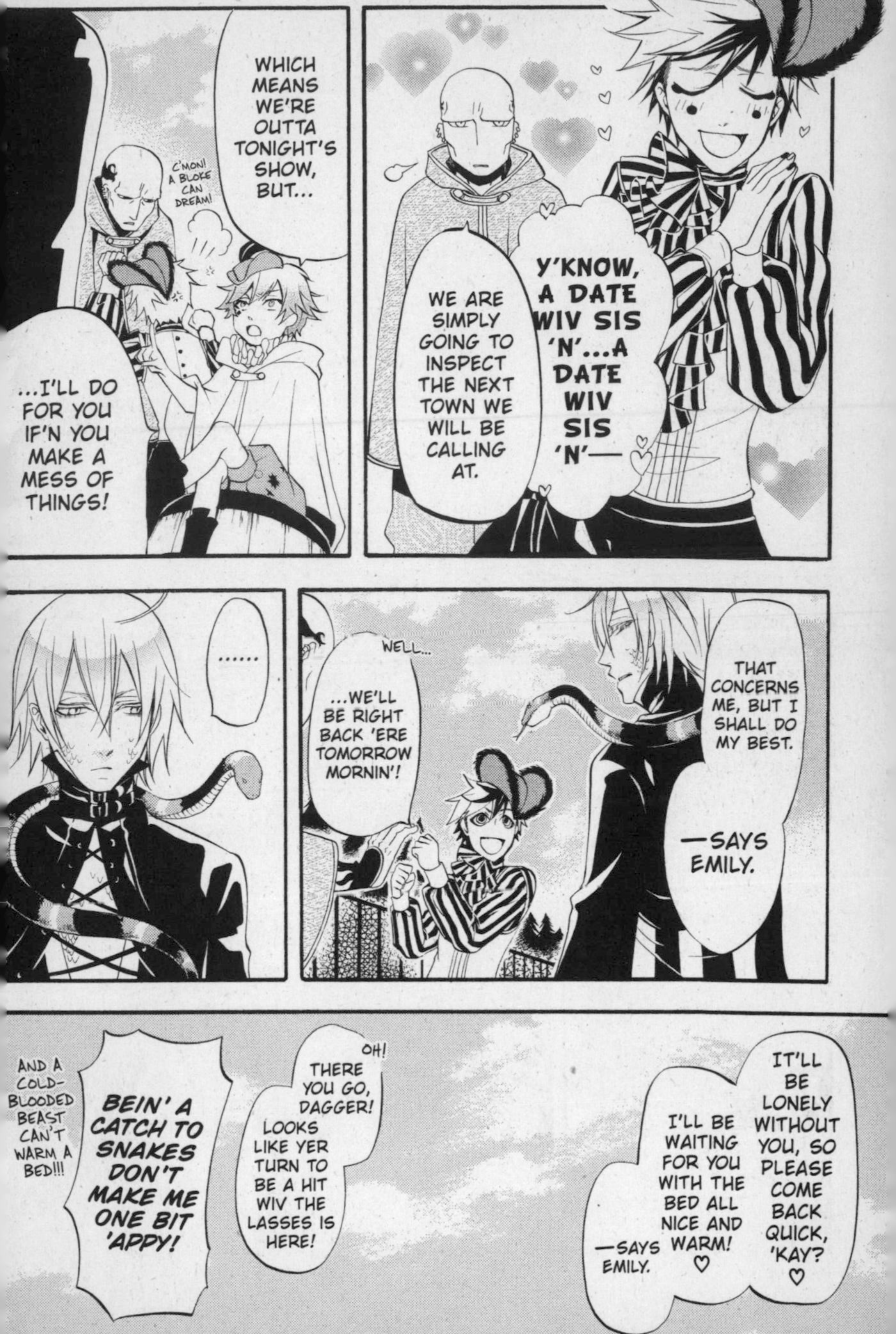
Y'KNOW, A DATE WIV SIS 'N'...A DATE WIV SIS 'N'—
WE ARE SIMPLY GOING TO INSPECT THE NEXT TOWN WE WILL BE CALLING AT.
WHICH MEANS WE'RE OUTTA TONIGHT'S SHOW, BUT...
C'MON! A BLOKE CAN DREAM!
...I'LL DO FOR YOU IF'N YOU MAKE A MESS OF THINGS!
THAT CONCERNS ME, BUT I SHALL DO MY BEST.
—SAYS EMILY.
WELL...
...WE'LL BE RIGHT BACK 'ERE TOMORROW MORNIN'!
......
IT'LL BE LONELY WITHOUT YOU, SO PLEASE COME BACK QUICK, 'KAY? ♡
I'LL BE WAITING FOR YOU WITH THE BED ALL NICE AND WARM! ♡
—SAYS EMILY.
OH!
THERE YOU GO, DAGGER!
LOOKS LIKE YER TURN TO BE A HIT WIV THE LASSES IS HERE!
BEIN' A CATCH TO SNAKES DON'T MAKE ME ONE BIT 'APPY!
AND A COLD-BLOODED BEAST CAN'T WARM A BED!!!

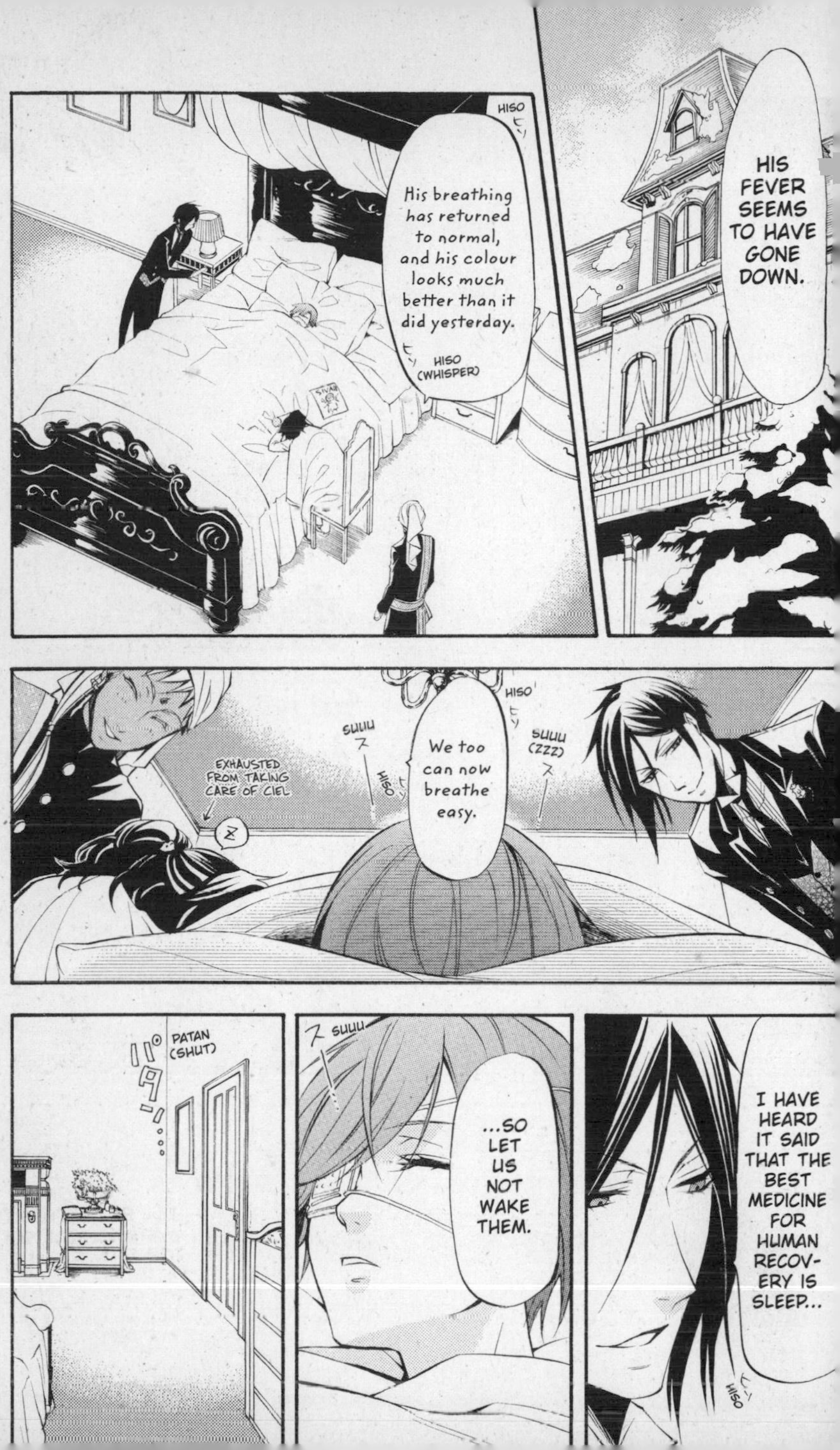
HIS FEVER SEEMS TO HAVE GONE DOWN.
HISO
His breathing has returned to normal, and his colour looks much better than it did yesterday.
HISO (WHISPER)
HISO
SUUU (ZZZ)
We too can now breathe easy.
HISO
SUUU
EXHAUSTED FROM TAKING CARE OF CIEL
Z
I HAVE HEARD IT SAID THAT THE BEST MEDICINE FOR HUMAN RECOV-ERY IS SLEEP...
HISO
SUUU
...SO LET US NOT WAKE THEM.
PATAN (SHUT)

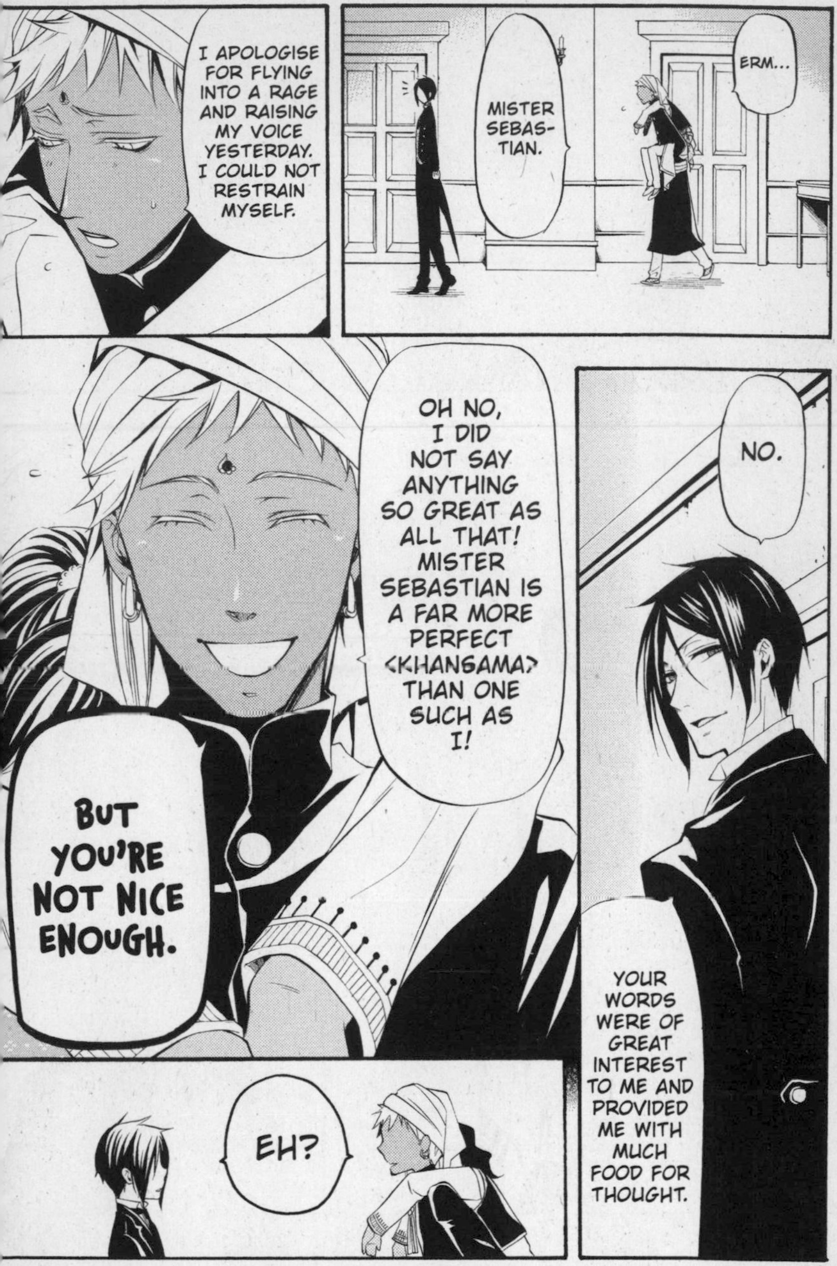
ERM...
MISTER SEBAS-TIAN.
I APOLOGISE FOR FLYING INTO A RAGE AND RAISING MY VOICE YESTERDAY. I COULD NOT RESTRAIN MYSELF.
NO.
YOUR WORDS WERE OF GREAT INTEREST TO ME AND PROVIDED ME WITH MUCH FOOD FOR THOUGHT.
OH NO, I DID NOT SAY ANYTHING SO GREAT AS ALL THAT! MISTER SEBASTIAN IS A FAR MORE PERFECT <KHANSAMA> THAN ONE SUCH AS I!
BUT YOU'RE NOT NICE ENOUGH.
EH?

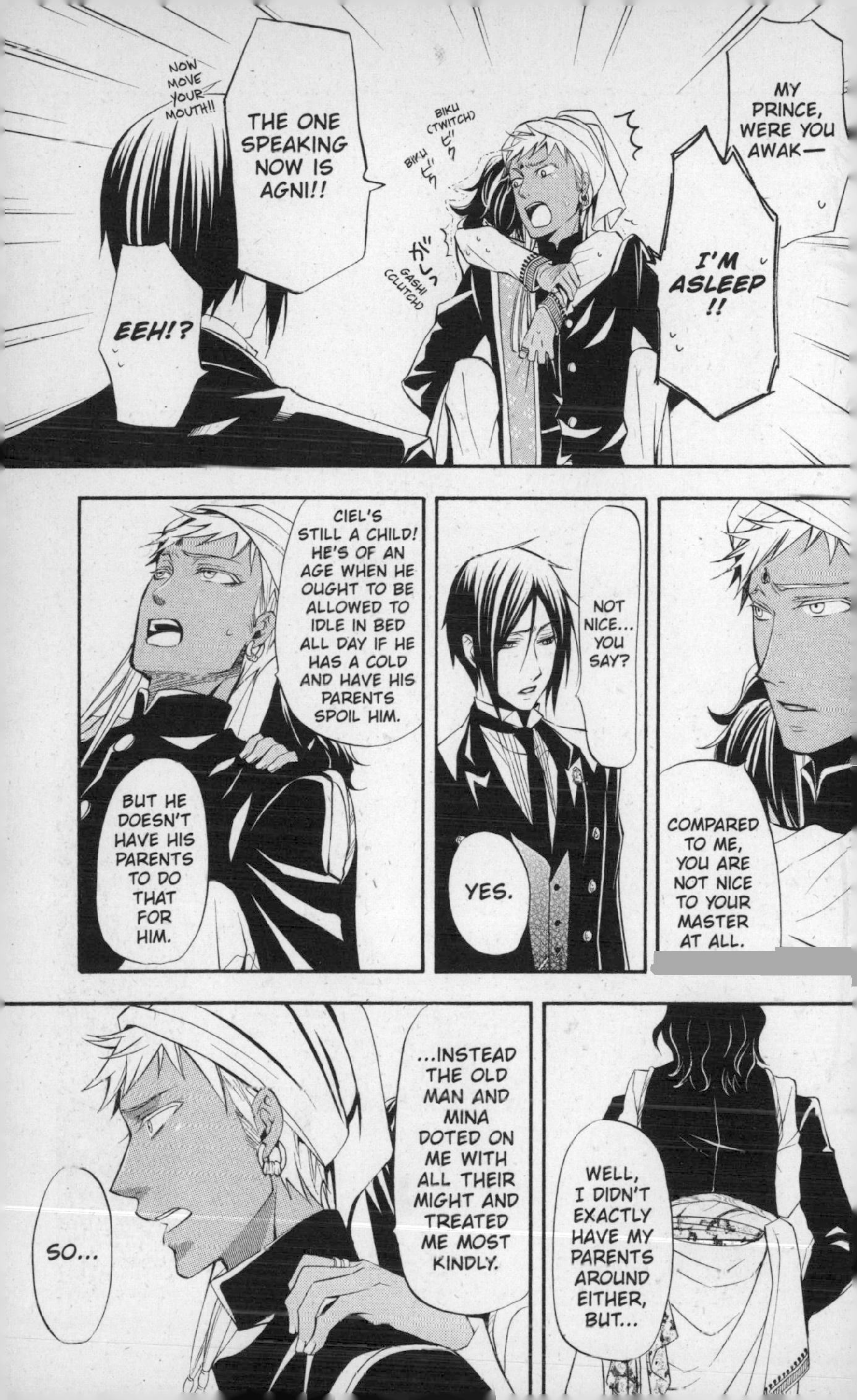
MY PRINCE, WERE YOU AWAK—
I'M ASLEEP!!
BIKU (TWITCH)
BIKU
GASHI (CLUTCH)
THE ONE SPEAKING NOW IS AGNI!!
NOW MOVE YOUR MOUTH!!
EEH!?
COMPARED TO ME, YOU ARE NOT NICE TO YOUR MASTER AT ALL.
NOT NICE... YOU SAY?
YES.
CIEL'S STILL A CHILD! HE'S OF AN AGE WHEN HE OUGHT TO BE ALLOWED TO IDLE IN BED ALL DAY IF HE HAS A COLD AND HAVE HIS PARENTS SPOIL HIM.
BUT HE DOESN'T HAVE HIS PARENTS TO DO THAT FOR HIM.
WELL, I DIDN'T EXACTLY HAVE MY PARENTS AROUND EITHER, BUT...
...INSTEAD THE OLD MAN AND MINA DOTED ON ME WITH ALL THEIR MIGHT AND TREATED ME MOST KINDLY.
SO...

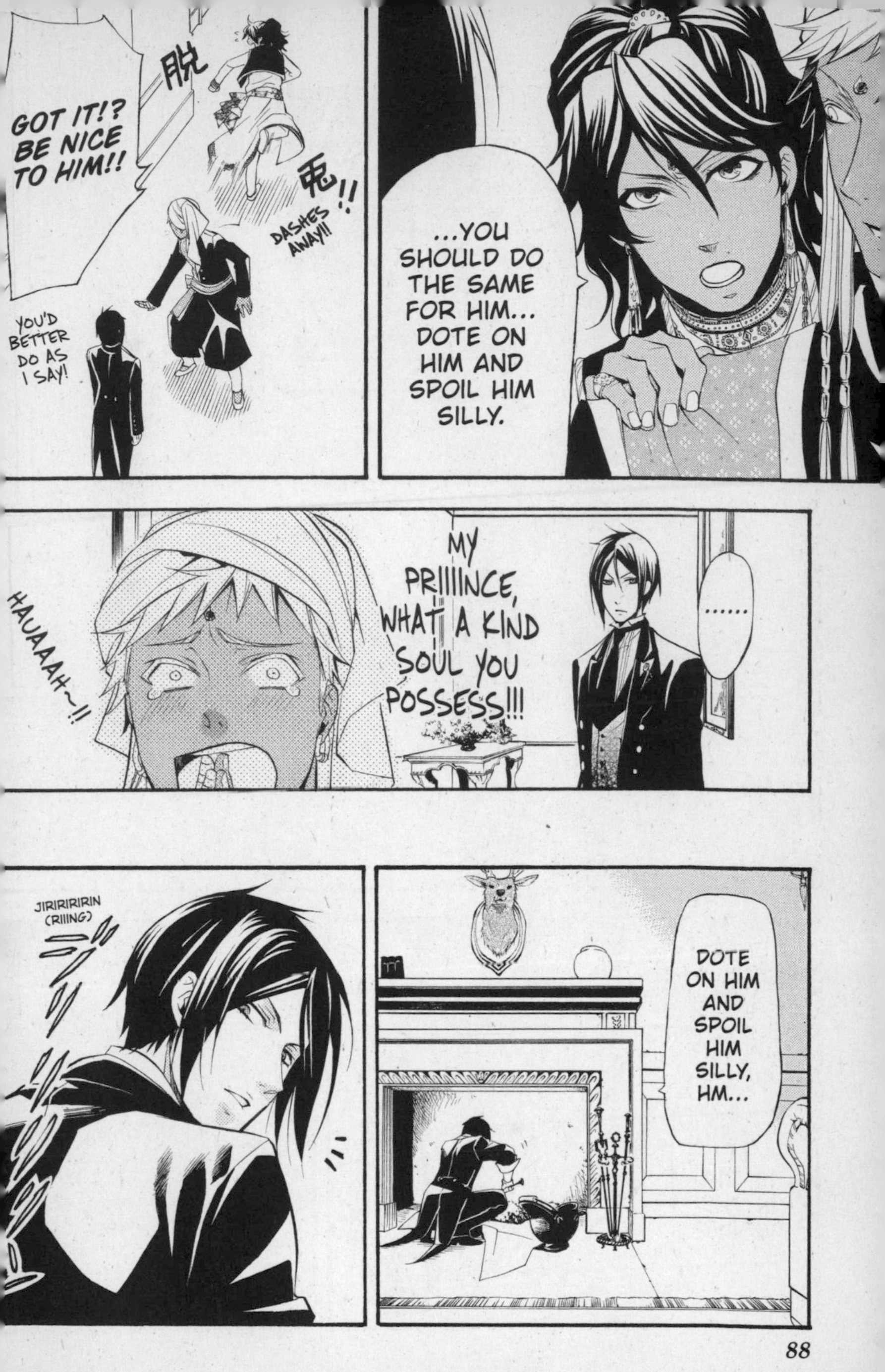
...YOU SHOULD DO THE SAME FOR HIM... DOTE ON HIM AND SPOIL HIM SILLY.
GOT IT!? BE NICE TO HIM!!
脱兎!!
DASHES AWAY!!
YOU'D BETTER DO AS I SAY!
......
MY PRIIIINCE, WHAT A KIND SOUL YOU POSSESS!!!
HAUAAAH~!!
DOTE ON HIM AND SPOIL HIM SILLY, HM...
JIRIRIRIRIN (RIIING)

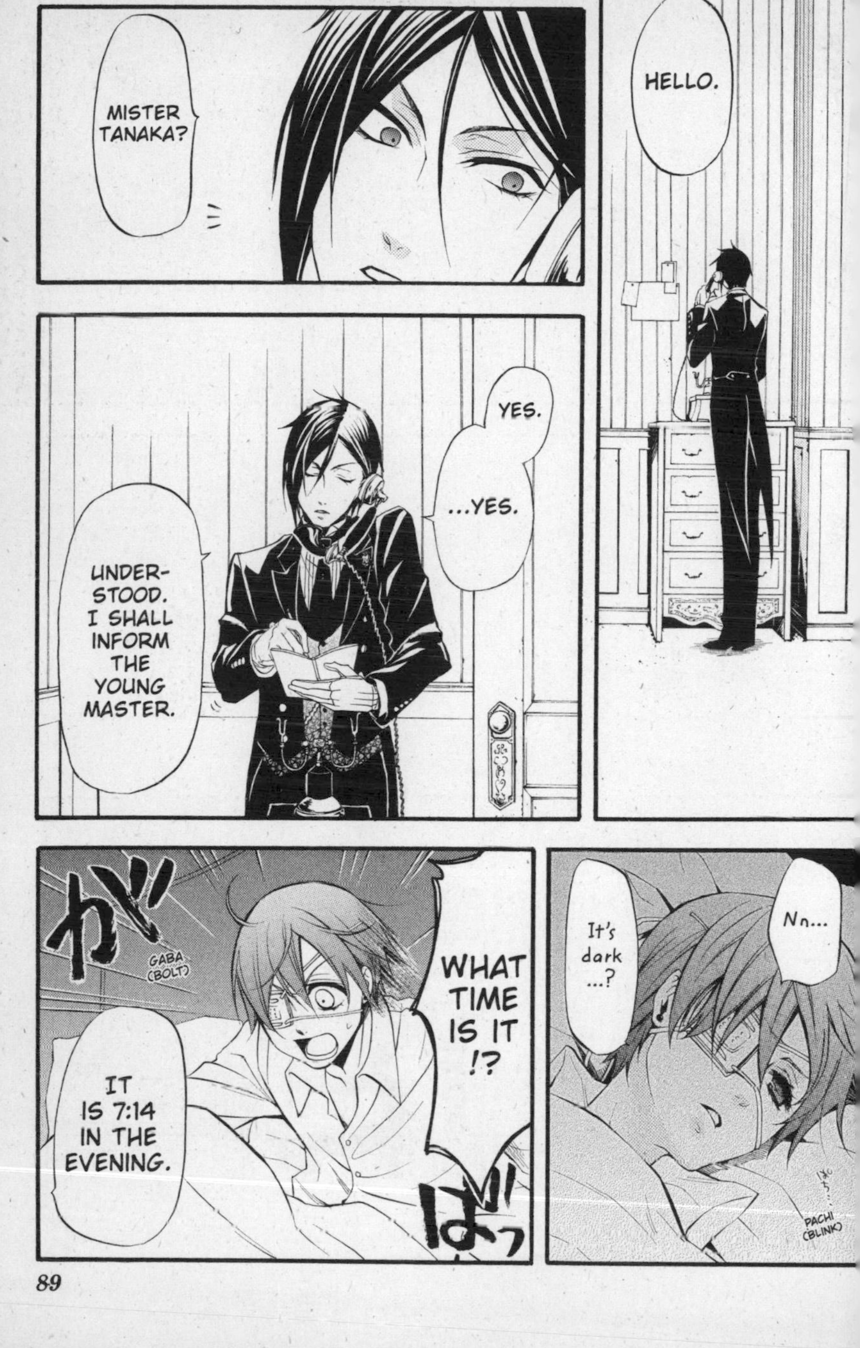
HELLO.
MISTER TANAKA?
YES.
...YES.
UNDER-STOOD. I SHALL INFORM THE YOUNG MASTER.
Nn...
It's dark ...?
PACHI (BLINK)
GABA (BOLT)
WHAT TIME IS IT !?
IT IS 7:14 IN THE EVENING.

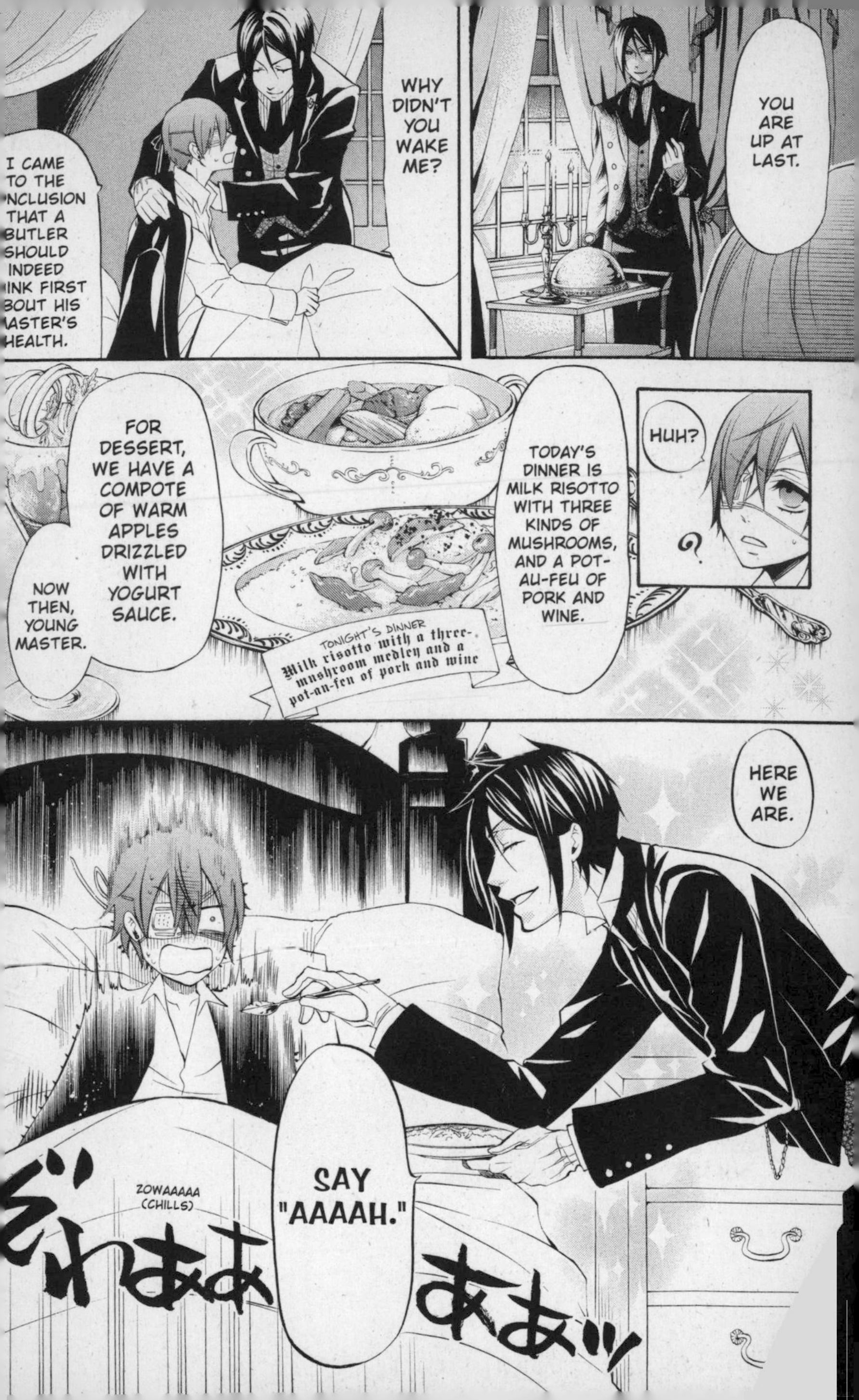
YOU ARE UP AT LAST.
WHY DIDN'T YOU WAKE ME?
I CAME TO THE NCLUSION THAT A BUTLER SHOULD INDEED INK FIRST BOUT HIS ASTER'S HEALTH.
HUH?
TODAY'S DINNER IS MILK RISOTTO WITH THREE KINDS OF MUSHROOMS, AND A POT-AU-FEU OF PORK AND WINE.
TONIGHT'S DINNER
Milk risotto with a three-mushroom medley and a pot-au-feu of pork and wine
FOR DESSERT, WE HAVE A COMPOTE OF WARM APPLES DRIZZLED WITH YOGURT SAUCE.
NOW THEN, YOUNG MASTER.
HERE WE ARE.
SAY "AAAAH."
ぞわあああっ
ZOWAAAAA (CHILLS)

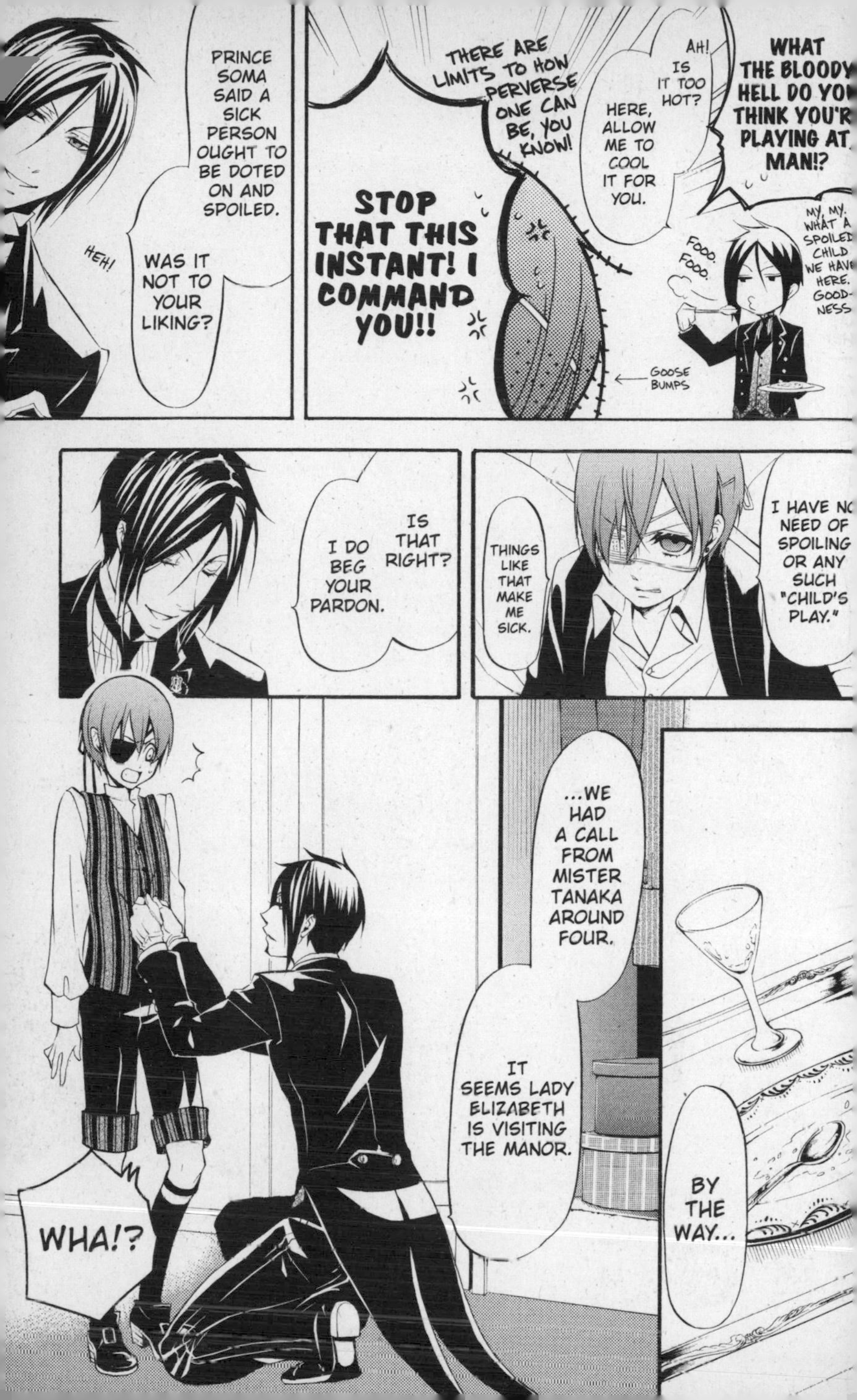
WHAT THE BLOODY HELL DO YO THINK YOU'R PLAYING AT, MAN!?
AH! IS IT TOO HOT?
HERE, ALLOW ME TO COOL IT FOR YOU.
MY, MY. WHAT A SPOILED CHILD WE HAVE HERE. GOOD-NESS
FOOO. FOOO.
THERE ARE LIMITS TO HOW PERVERSE ONE CAN BE, YOU KNOW!
STOP THAT THIS INSTANT! I COMMAND YOU!!
GOOSE BUMPS
PRINCE SOMA SAID A SICK PERSON OUGHT TO BE DOTED ON AND SPOILED.
HEH!
WAS IT NOT TO YOUR LIKING?
I HAVE NO NEED OF SPOILING OR ANY SUCH "CHILD'S PLAY."
THINGS LIKE THAT MAKE ME SICK.
IS THAT RIGHT?
I DO BEG YOUR PARDON.
BY THE WAY...
...WE HAD A CALL FROM MISTER TANAKA AROUND FOUR.
IT SEEMS LADY ELIZABETH IS VISITING THE MANOR.
WHA!?

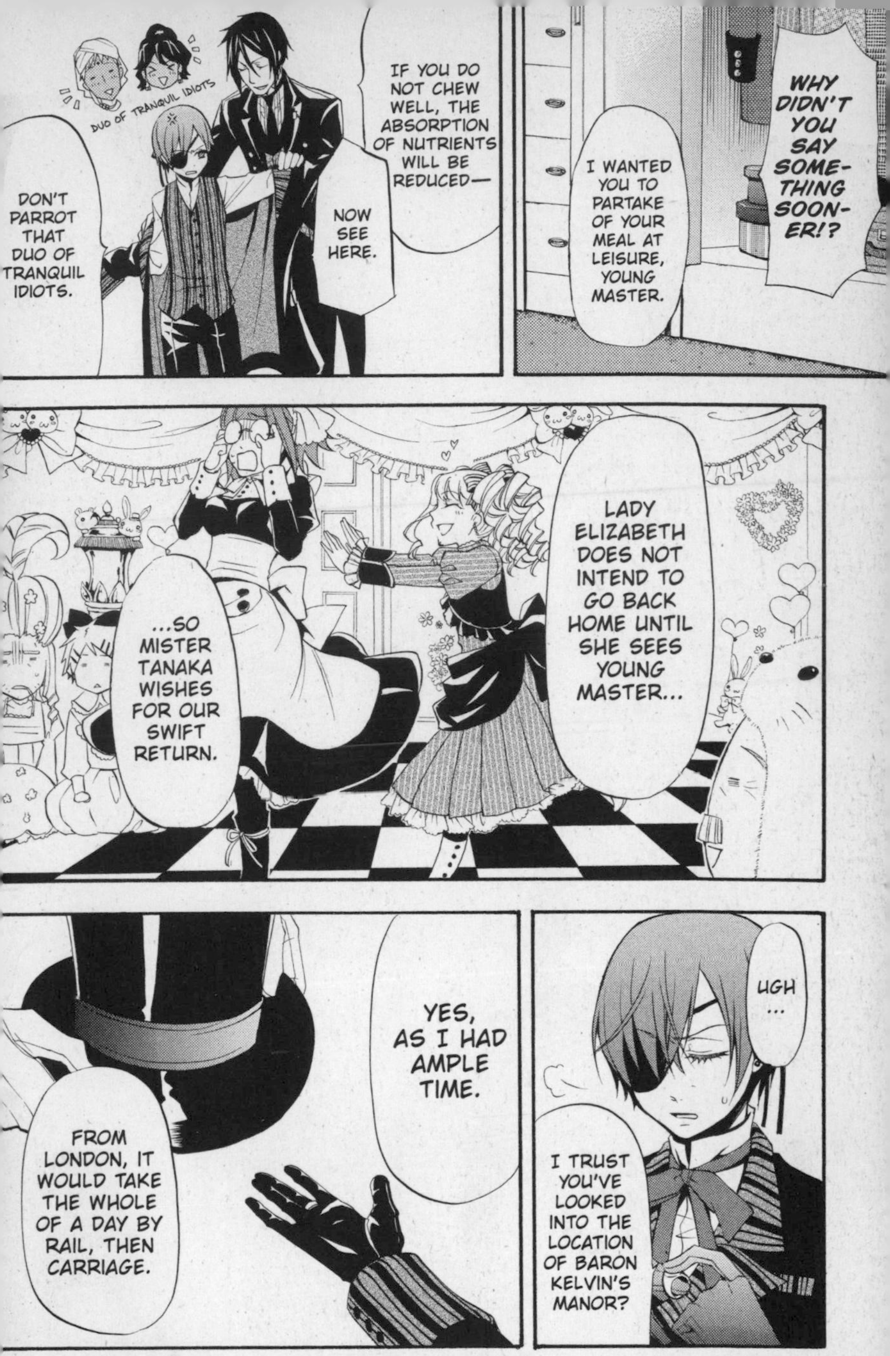
WHY DIDN'T YOU SAY SOMETHING SOONER!?
I WANTED YOU TO PARTAKE OF YOUR MEAL AT LEISURE, YOUNG MASTER.
IF YOU DO NOT CHEW WELL, THE ABSORPTION OF NUTRIENTS WILL BE REDUCED—
NOW SEE HERE.
DUO OF TRANQUIL IDIOTS
DON'T PARROT THAT DUO OF TRANQUIL IDIOTS.
LADY ELIZABETH DOES NOT INTEND TO GO BACK HOME UNTIL SHE SEES YOUNG MASTER...
...SO MISTER TANAKA WISHES FOR OUR SWIFT RETURN.
UGH...
I TRUST YOU'VE LOOKED INTO THE LOCATION OF BARON KELVIN'S MANOR?
YES, AS I HAD AMPLE TIME.
FROM LONDON, IT WOULD TAKE THE WHOLE OF A DAY BY RAIL, THEN CARRIAGE.

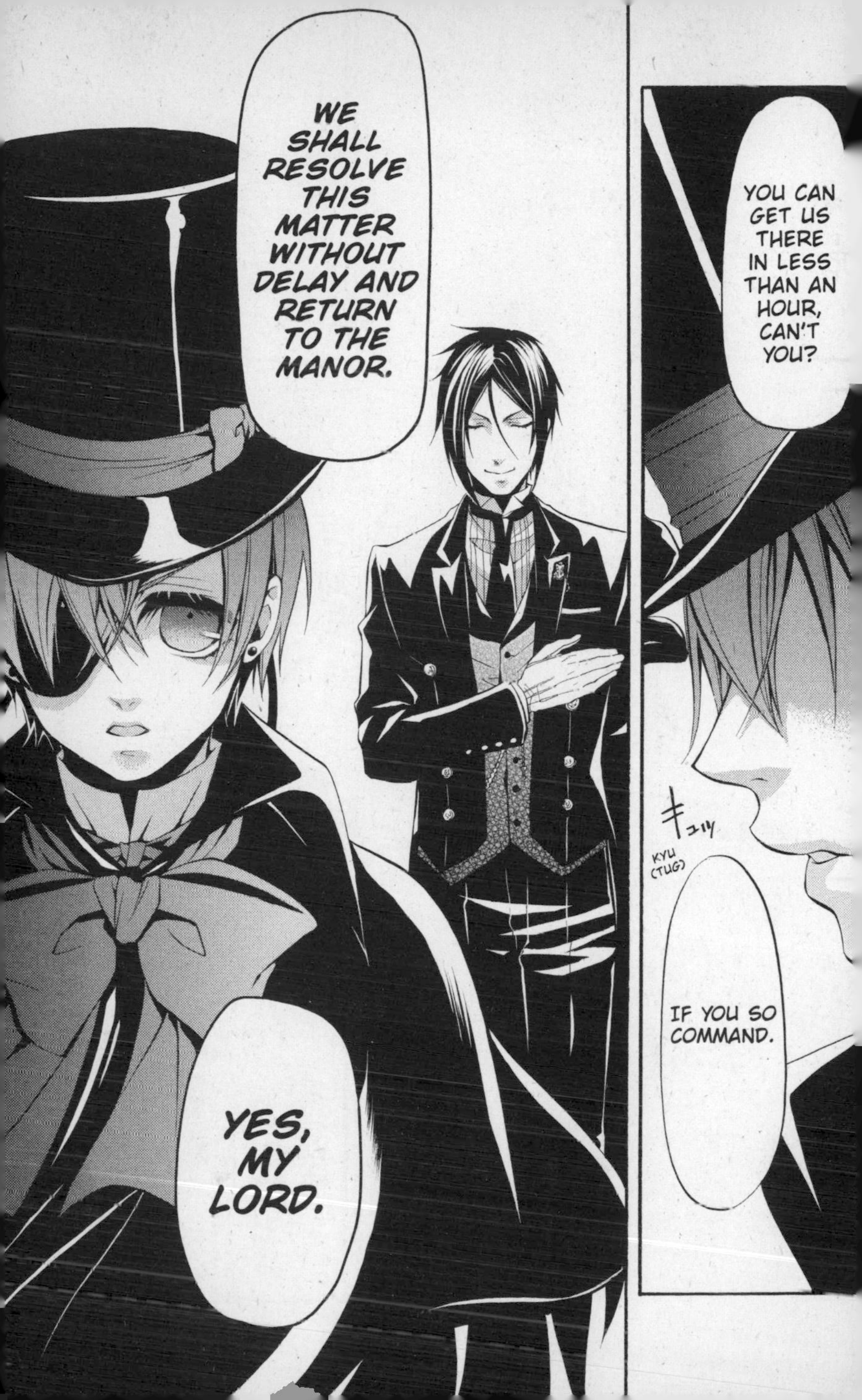
YOU CAN GET US THERE IN LESS THAN AN HOUR, CAN'T YOU?
KYU (TUG)
IF YOU SO COMMAND.
WE SHALL RESOLVE THIS MATTER WITHOUT DELAY AND RETURN TO THE MANOR.
YES, MY LORD.

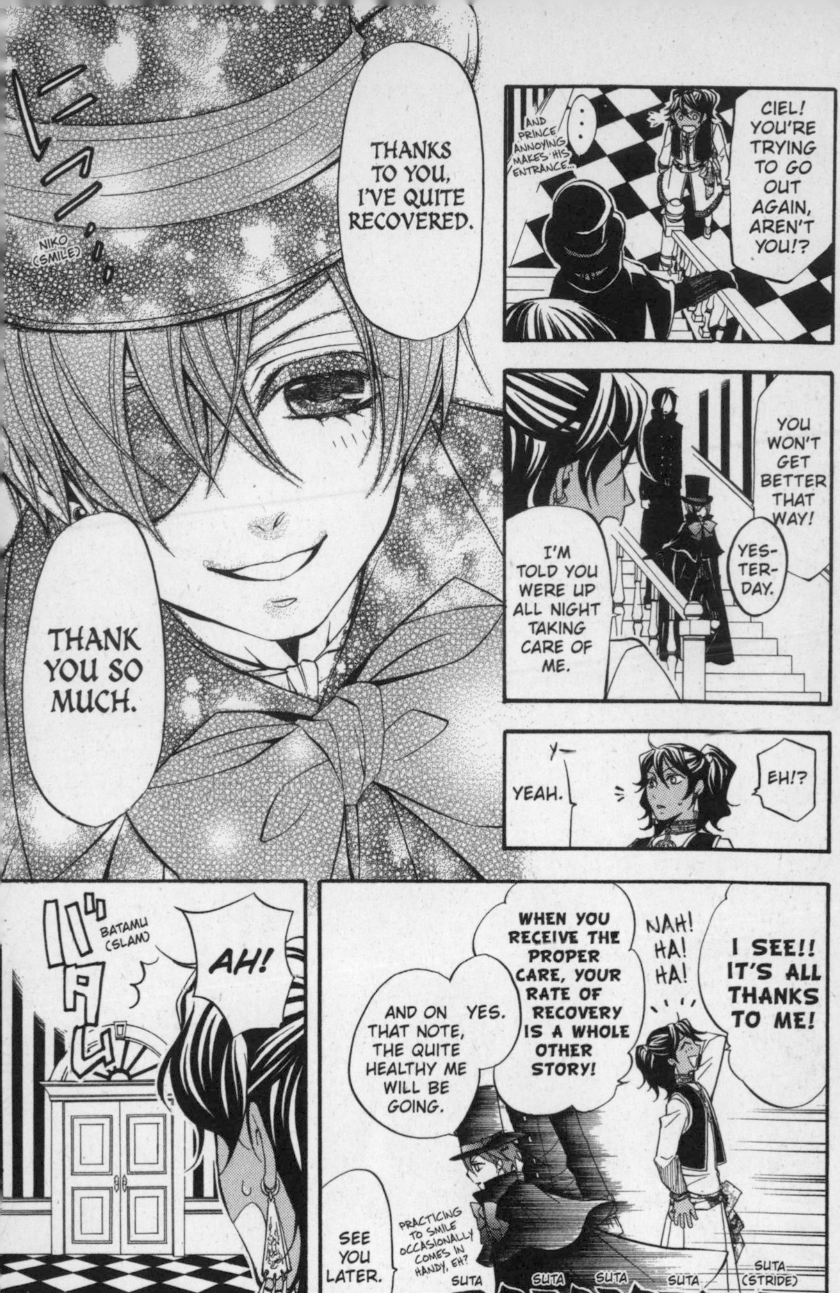
CIEL! YOU'RE TRYING TO GO OUT AGAIN, AREN'T YOU!?
...
AND PRINCE ANNOYING MAKES HIS ENTRANCE...
YOU WON'T GET BETTER THAT WAY!
YES-TER-DAY.
I'M TOLD YOU WERE UP ALL NIGHT TAKING CARE OF ME.
EH!?
Y— YEAH.
THANKS TO YOU, I'VE QUITE RECOVERED.
NIKO (SMILE)
THANK YOU SO MUCH.
I SEE!! IT'S ALL THANKS TO ME!
NAH! HA! HA!
WHEN YOU RECEIVE THE PROPER CARE, YOUR RATE OF RECOVERY IS A WHOLE OTHER STORY!
YES.
AND ON THAT NOTE, THE QUITE HEALTHY ME WILL BE GOING.
PRACTICING TO SMILE OCCASIONALLY COMES IN HANDY, EH?
SEE YOU LATER.
SUTA SUTA SUTA SUTA SUTA (STRIDE)
スタスタスタスタスタ
AH!
BATAMU (SLAM)
バタム

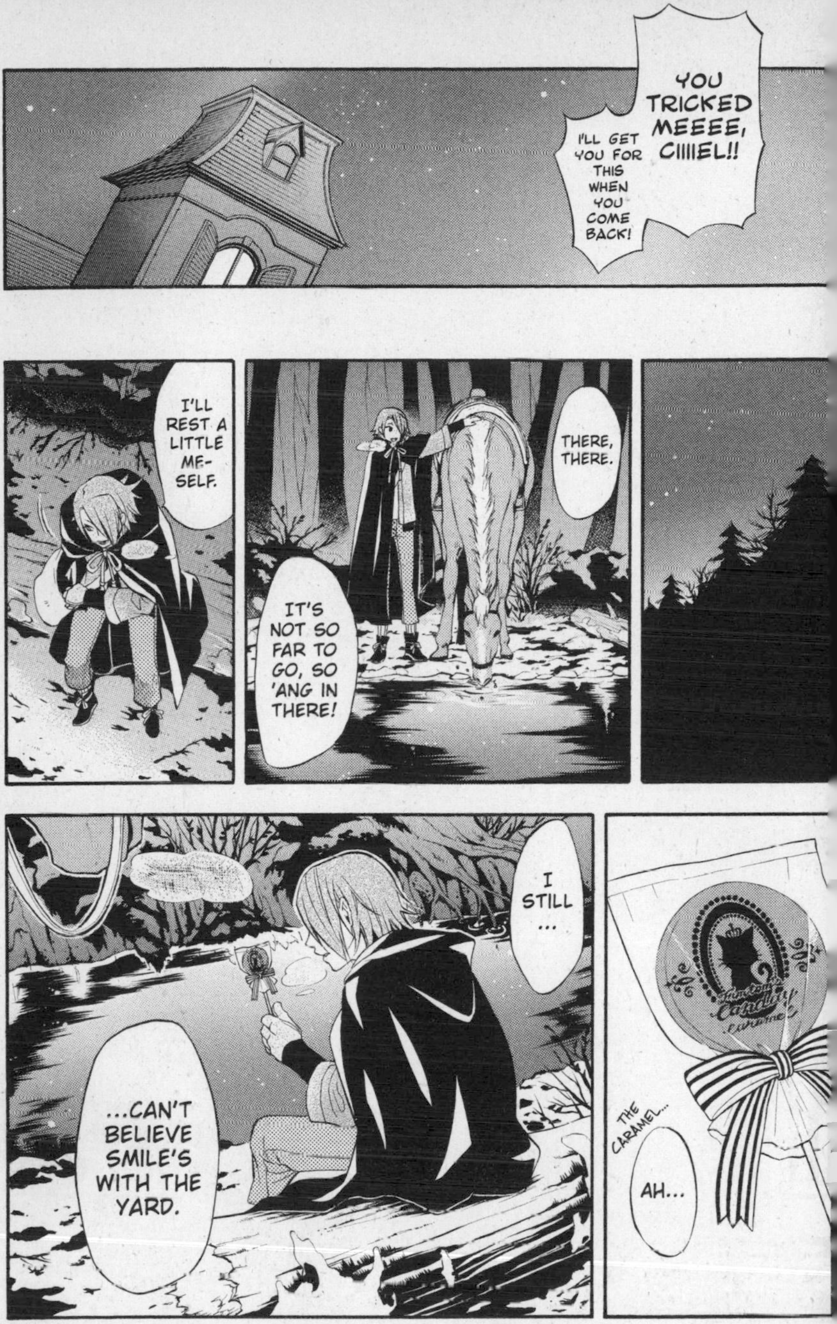
YOU TRICKED MEEEE, CIIIIEL!!
I'LL GET YOU FOR THIS WHEN YOU COME BACK!
THERE, THERE.
IT'S NOT SO FAR TO GO, SO 'ANG IN THERE!
I'LL REST A LITTLE ME-SELF.
THE CARAMEL...
AH...
I STILL ...
...CAN'T BELIEVE SMILE'S WITH THE YARD.

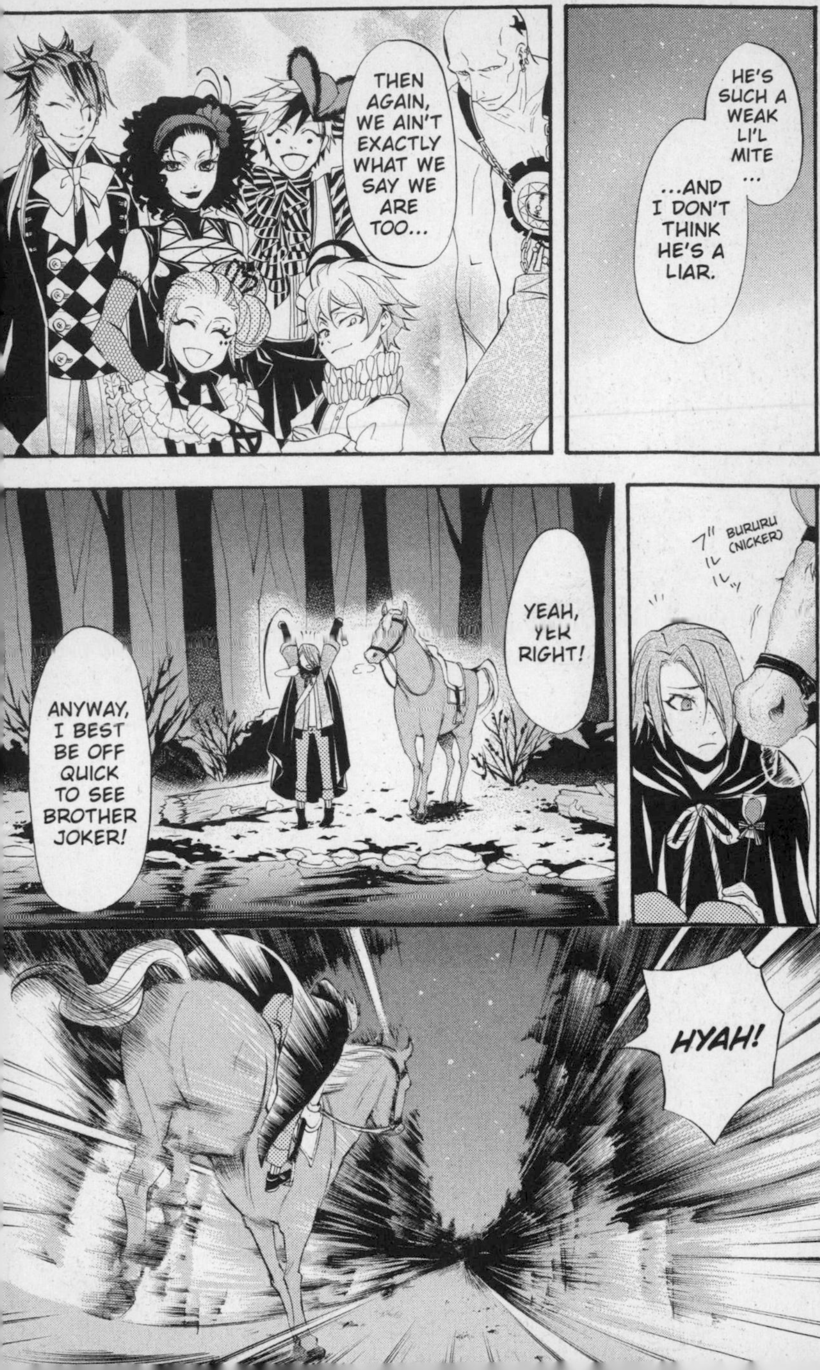
HE'S SUCH A WEAK LI'L MITE...
...AND I DON'T THINK HE'S A LIAR.
THEN AGAIN, WE AIN'T EXACTLY WHAT WE SAY WE ARE TOO...
ブルルルッ
BURURU (NICKER)
YEAH, YER RIGHT!
ANYWAY, I BEST BE OFF QUICK TO SEE BROTHER JOKER!
HYAH!

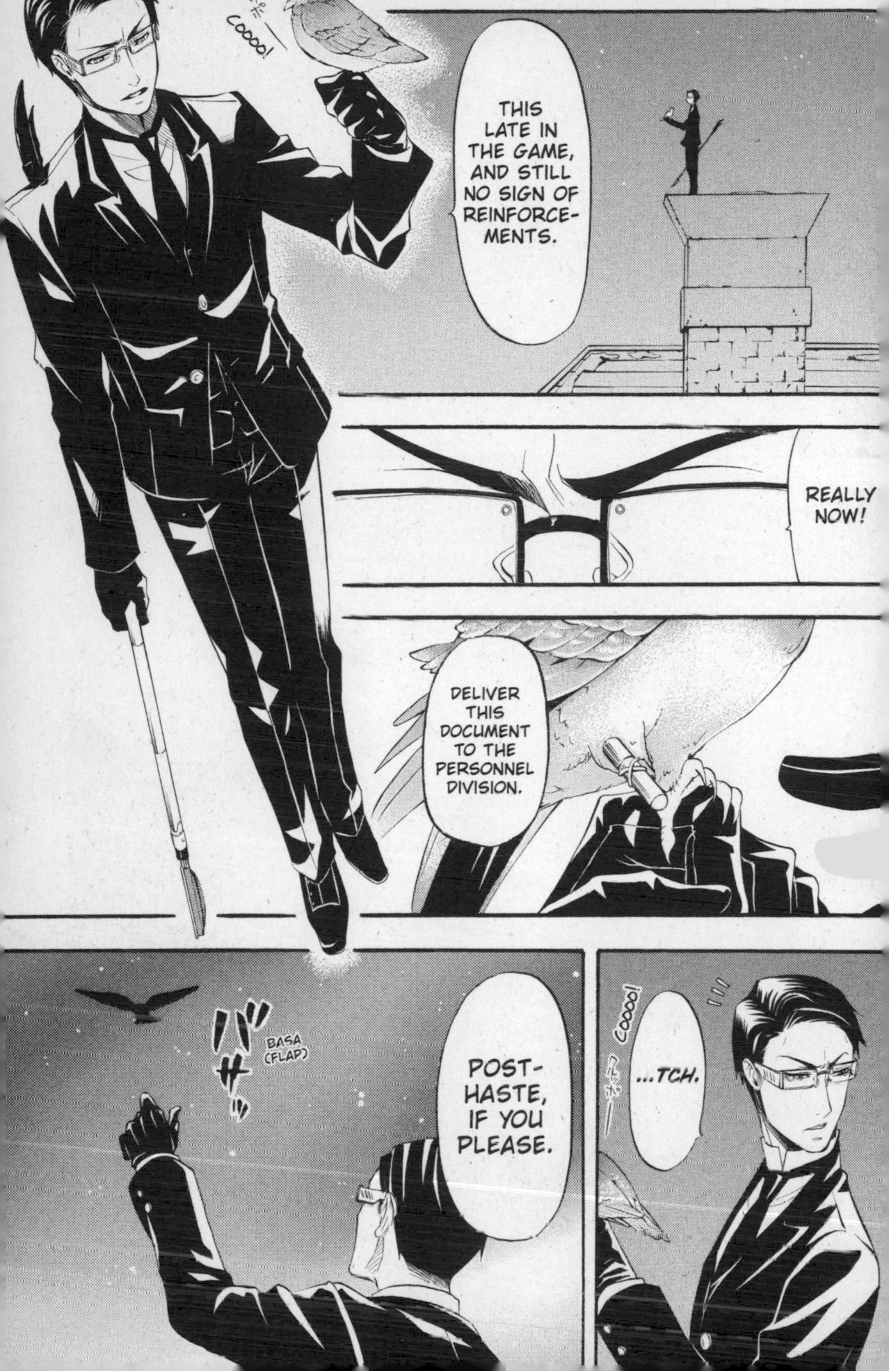
THIS LATE IN THE GAME, AND STILL NO SIGN OF REINFORCE-MENTS.
REALLY NOW!
DELIVER THIS DOCUMENT TO THE PERSONNEL DIVISION.
COOOO!
...TCH.
COOOO!
POST-HASTE, IF YOU PLEASE.
BASA (FLAP)

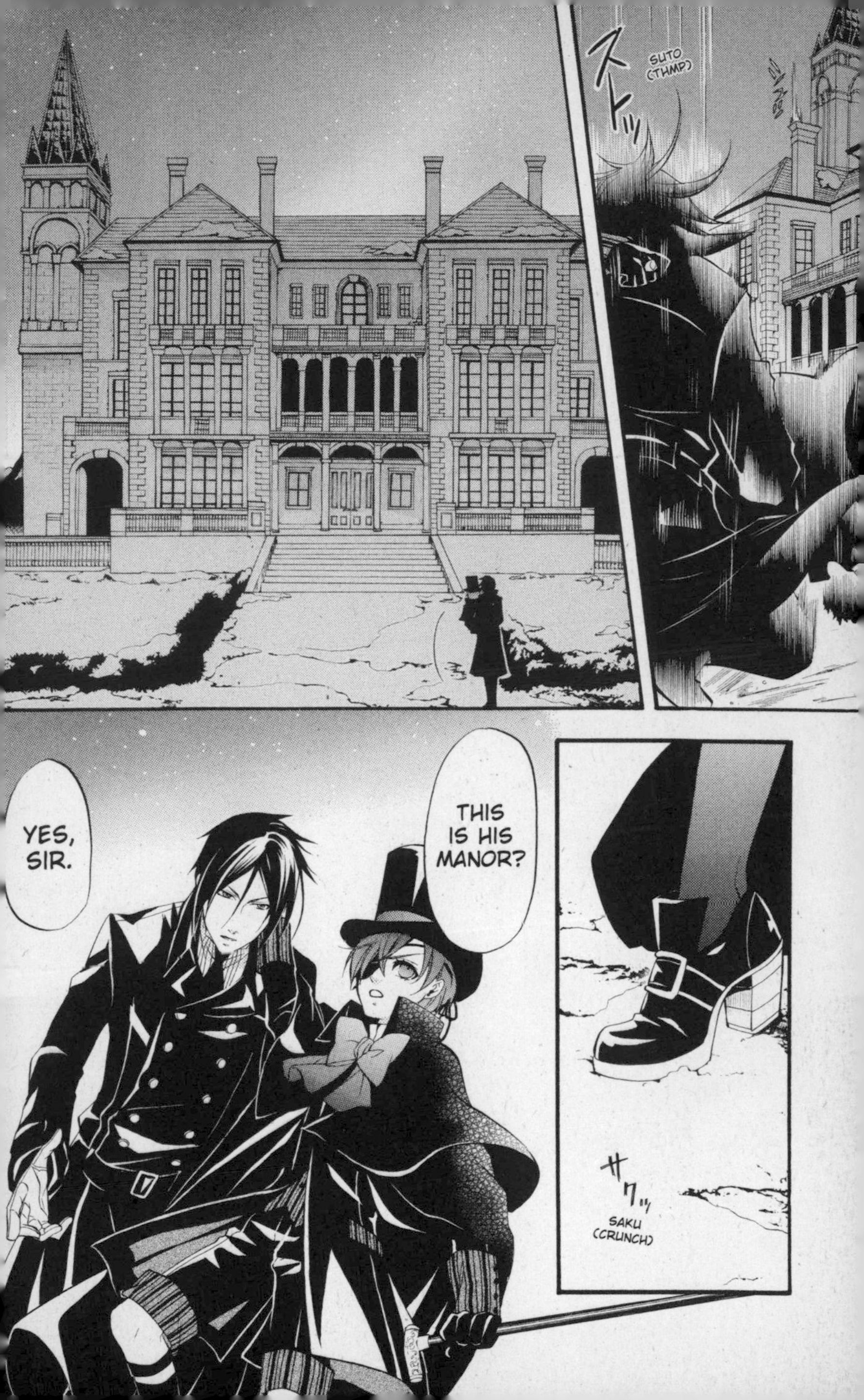

SUTO (THMP)
SAKU (CRUNCH)
THIS IS HIS MANOR?
YES, SIR.

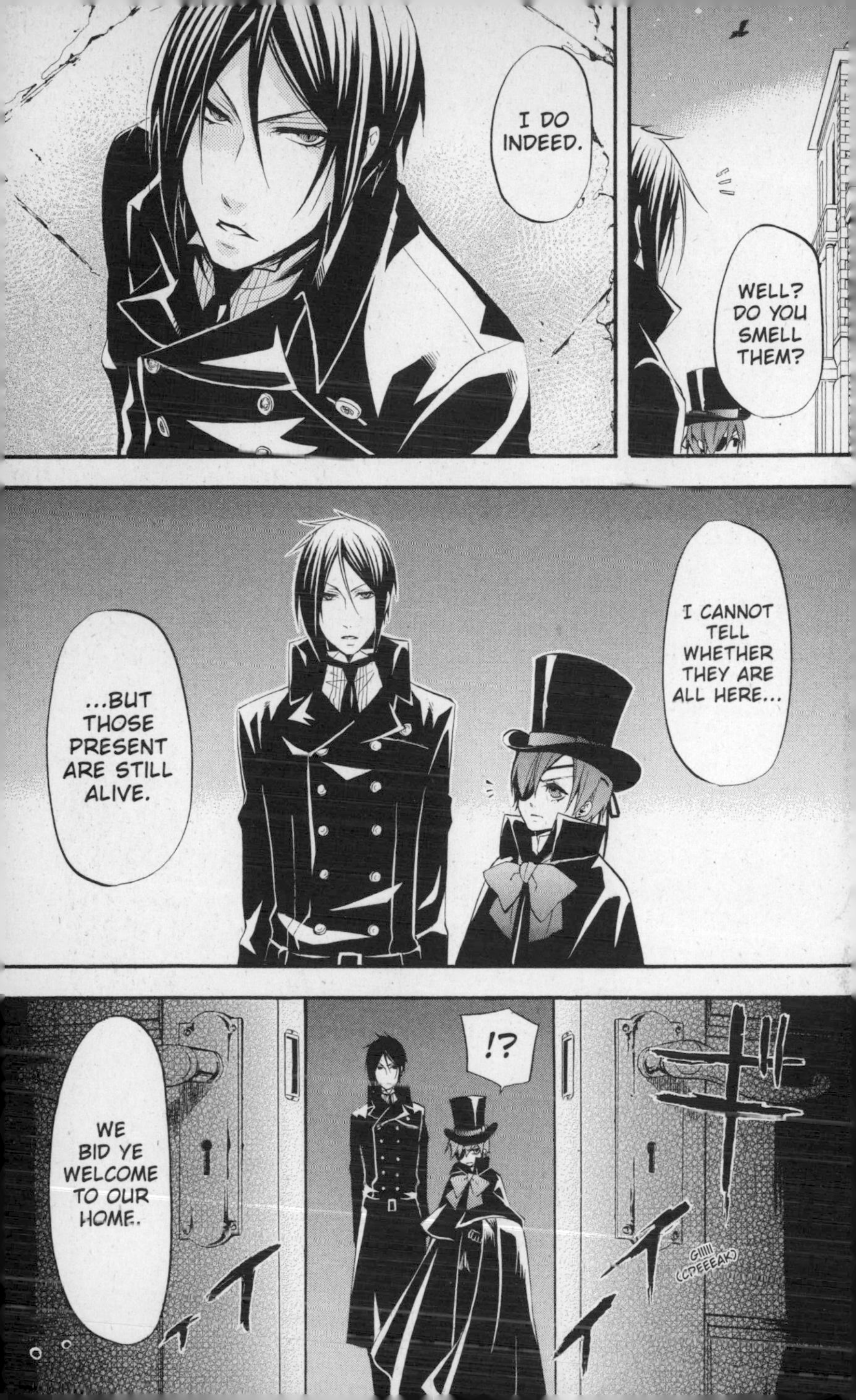
WELL? DO YOU SMELL THEM?
I DO INDEED.
I CANNOT TELL WHETHER THEY ARE ALL HERE...
...BUT THOSE PRESENT ARE STILL ALIVE.
!?
GIIIII (CREEEAK)
WE BID YE WELCOME TO OUR HOME.

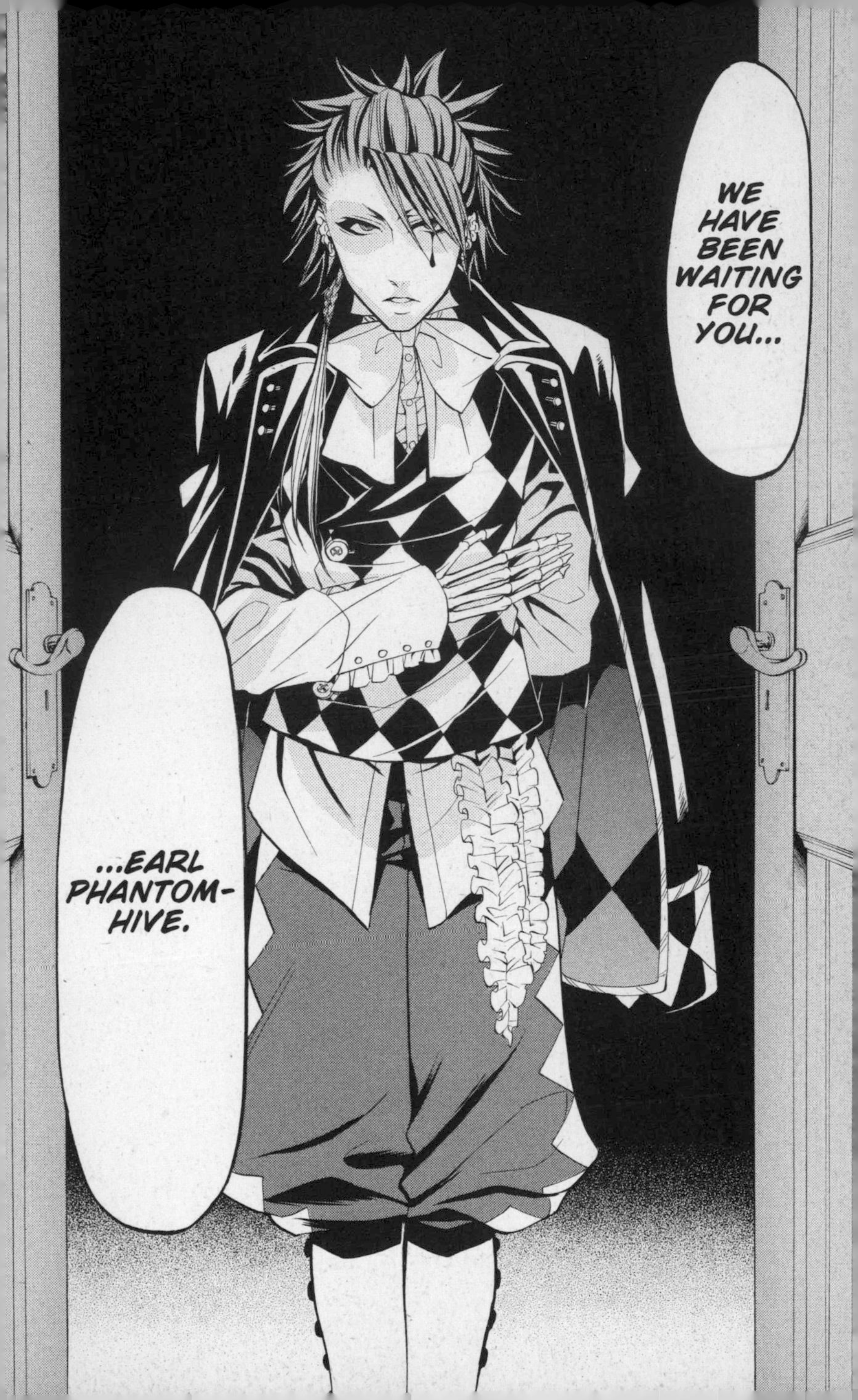
WE HAVE BEEN WAITING FOR YOU...
...EARL PHANTOM-HIVE.

Black Butler

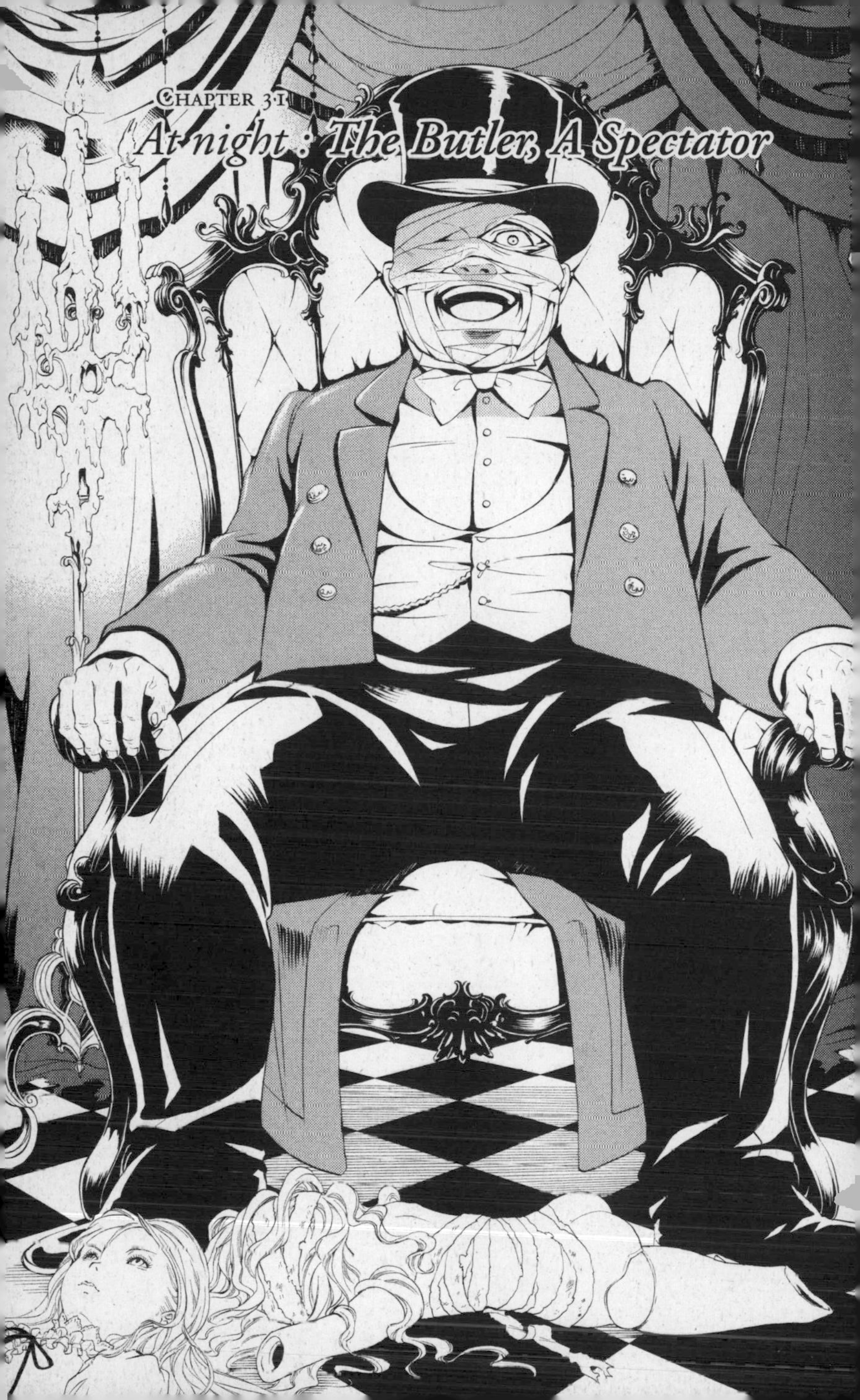
Chapter 31
At night : The Butler, A Spectator

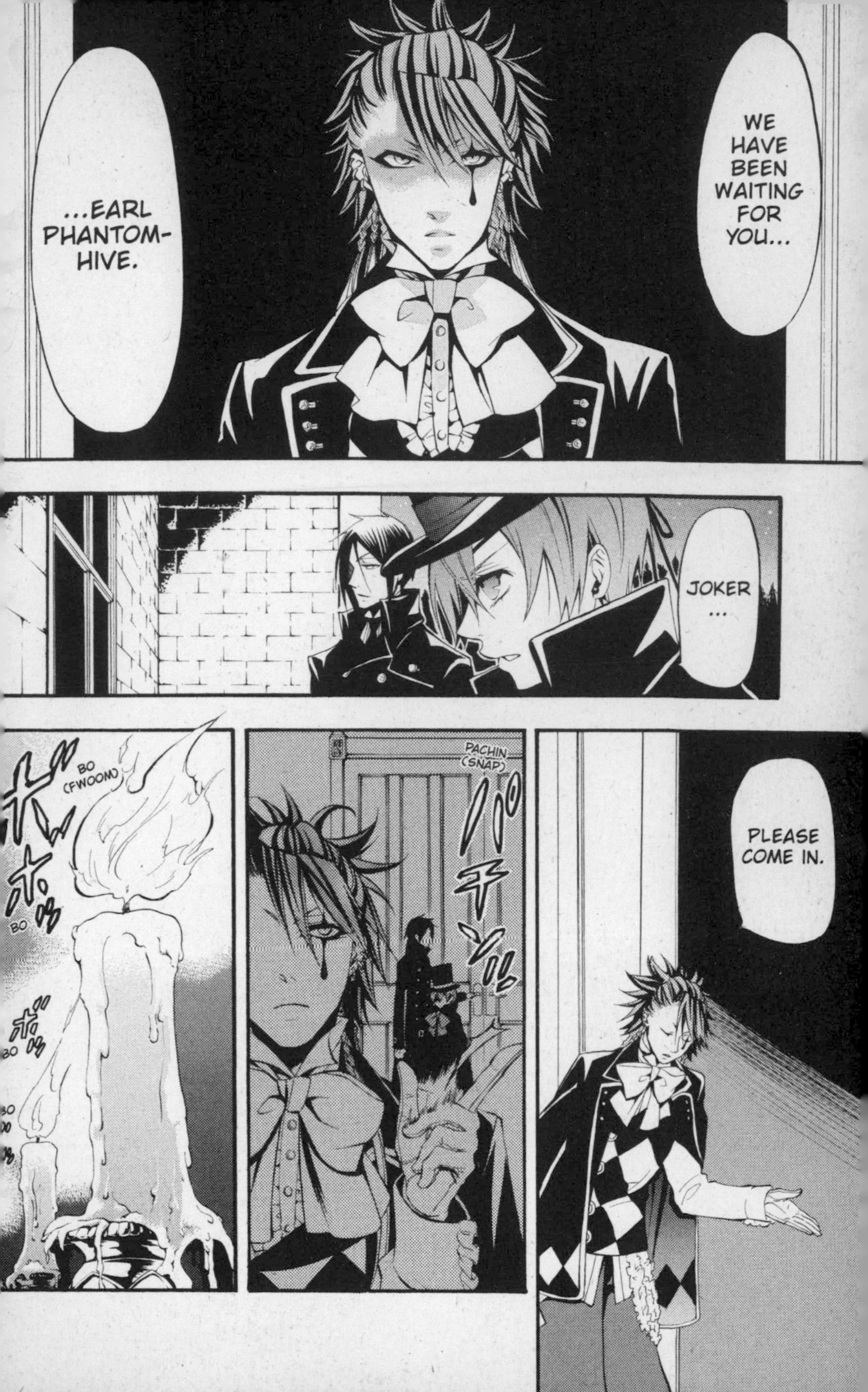
WE HAVE BEEN WAITING FOR YOU...
...EARL PHANTOM-HIVE.
JOKER ...
PLEASE COME IN.
PACHIN (SNAP)
BO (FWOOM)
BO
BO

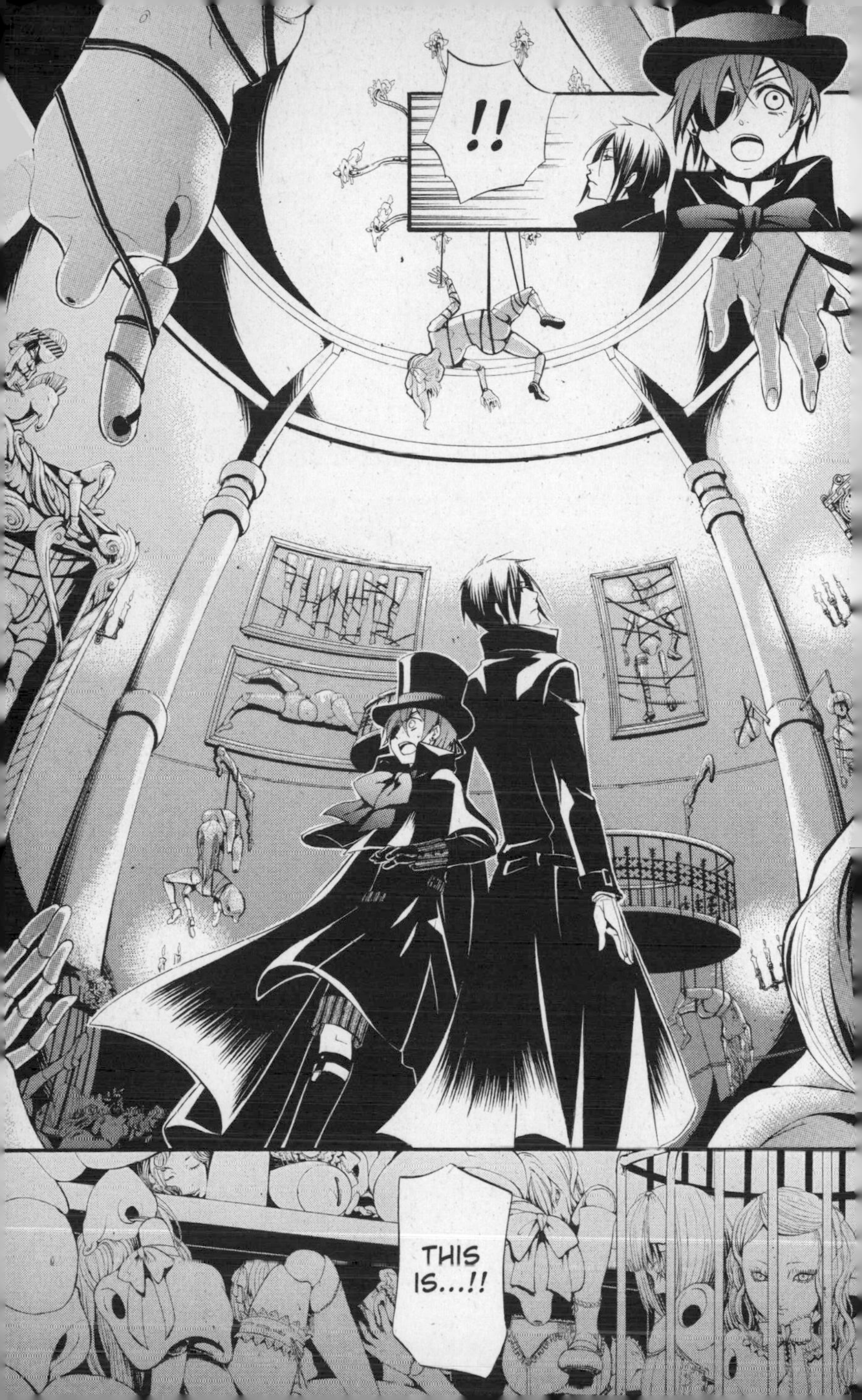
!!
THIS IS...!!

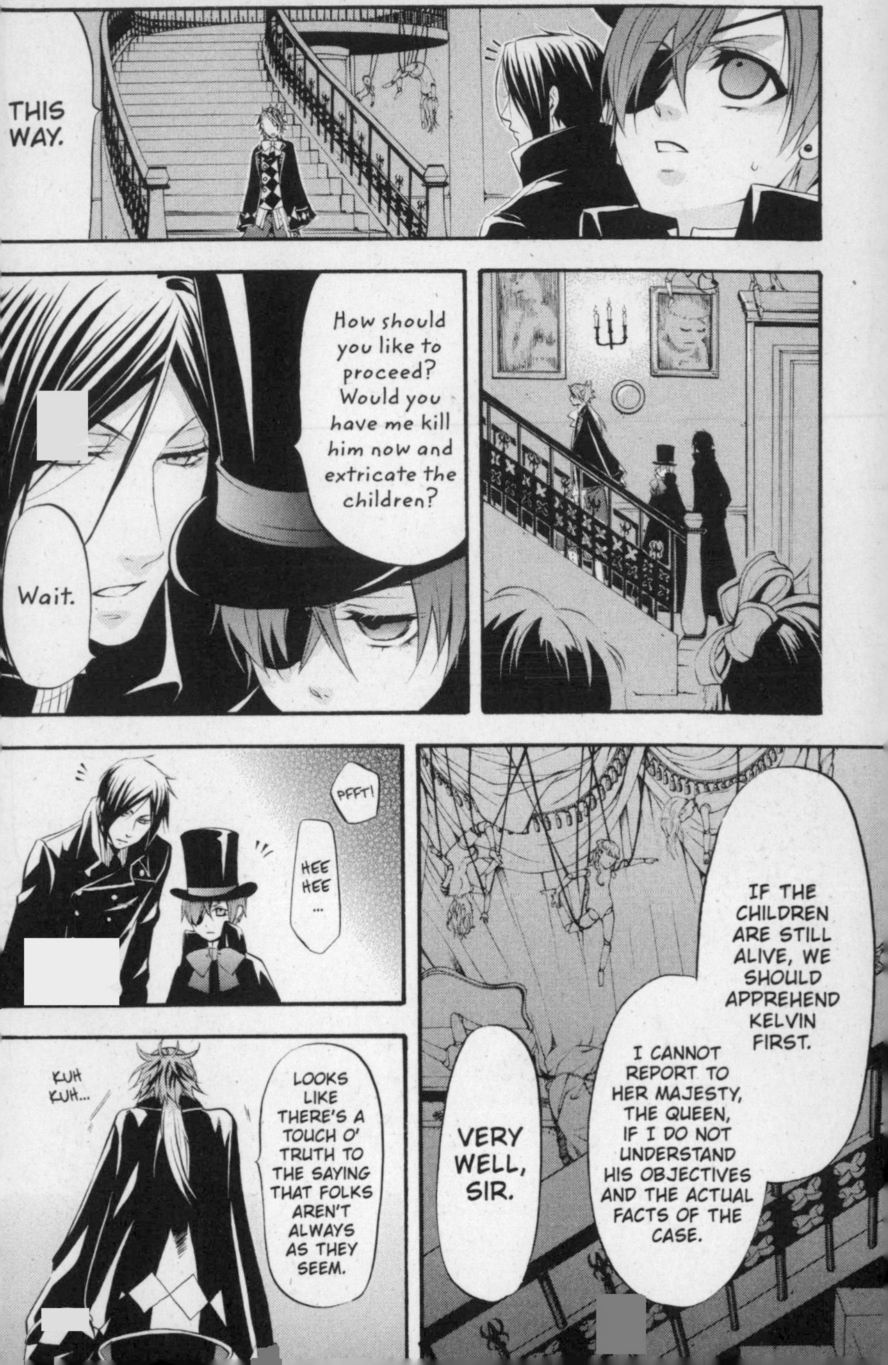
THIS WAY.
How should you like to proceed? Would you have me kill him now and extricate the children?
Wait.
IF THE CHILDREN ARE STILL ALIVE, WE SHOULD APPREHEND KELVIN FIRST.
I CANNOT REPORT TO HER MAJESTY, THE QUEEN, IF I DO NOT UNDERSTAND HIS OBJECTIVES AND THE ACTUAL FACTS OF THE CASE.
VERY WELL, SIR.
PFFT!
HEE HEE ...
LOOKS LIKE THERE'S A TOUCH O' TRUTH TO THE SAYING THAT FOLKS AREN'T ALWAYS AS THEY SEEM.
KUH KUH...

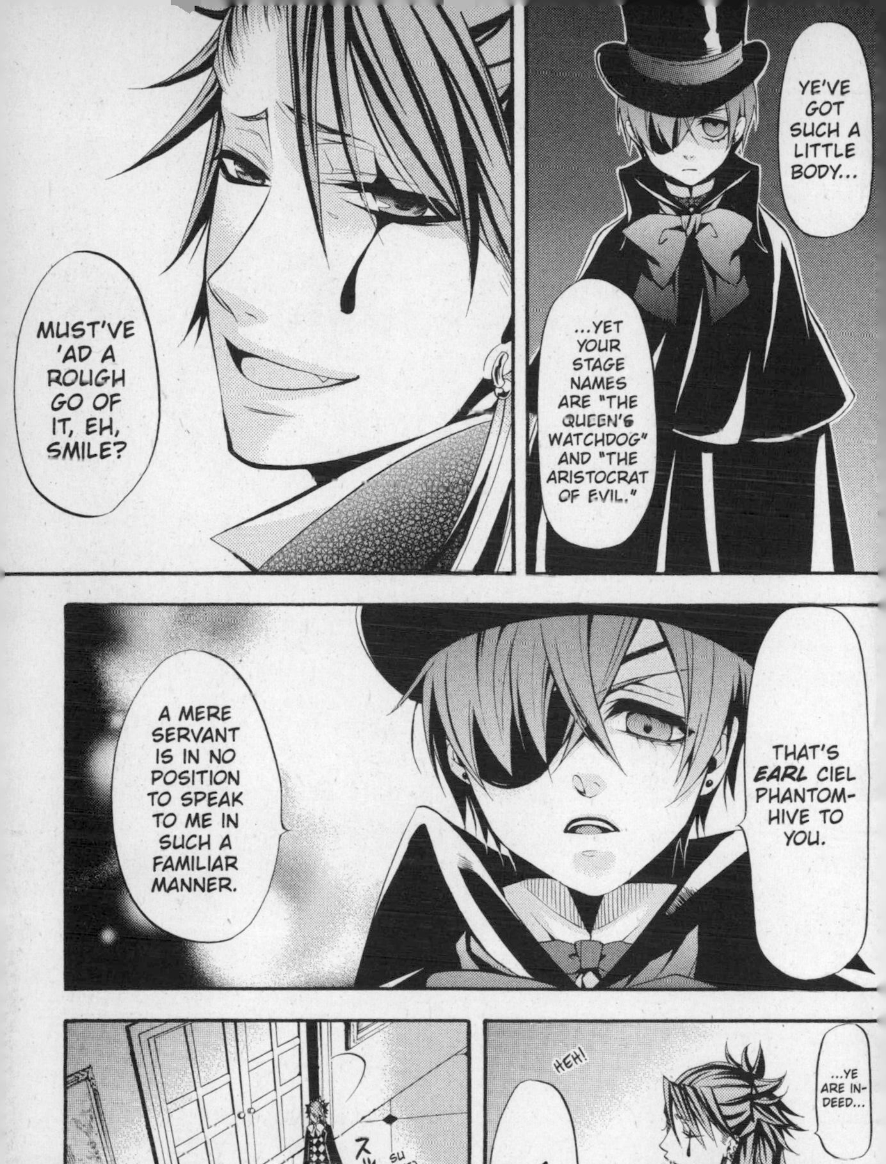
YE'VE GOT SUCH A LITTLE BODY...
...YET YOUR STAGE NAMES ARE "THE QUEEN'S WATCHDOG" AND "THE ARISTOCRAT OF EVIL."
MUST'VE 'AD A ROUGH GO OF IT, EH, SMILE?
THAT'S EARL CIEL PHANTOM-HIVE TO YOU.
A MERE SERVANT IS IN NO POSITION TO SPEAK TO ME IN SUCH A FAMILIAR MANNER.
...YE ARE IN-DEED...
HEH!
...A NOBLE ARISTO-CRAT.
スッ
SU (SWF)

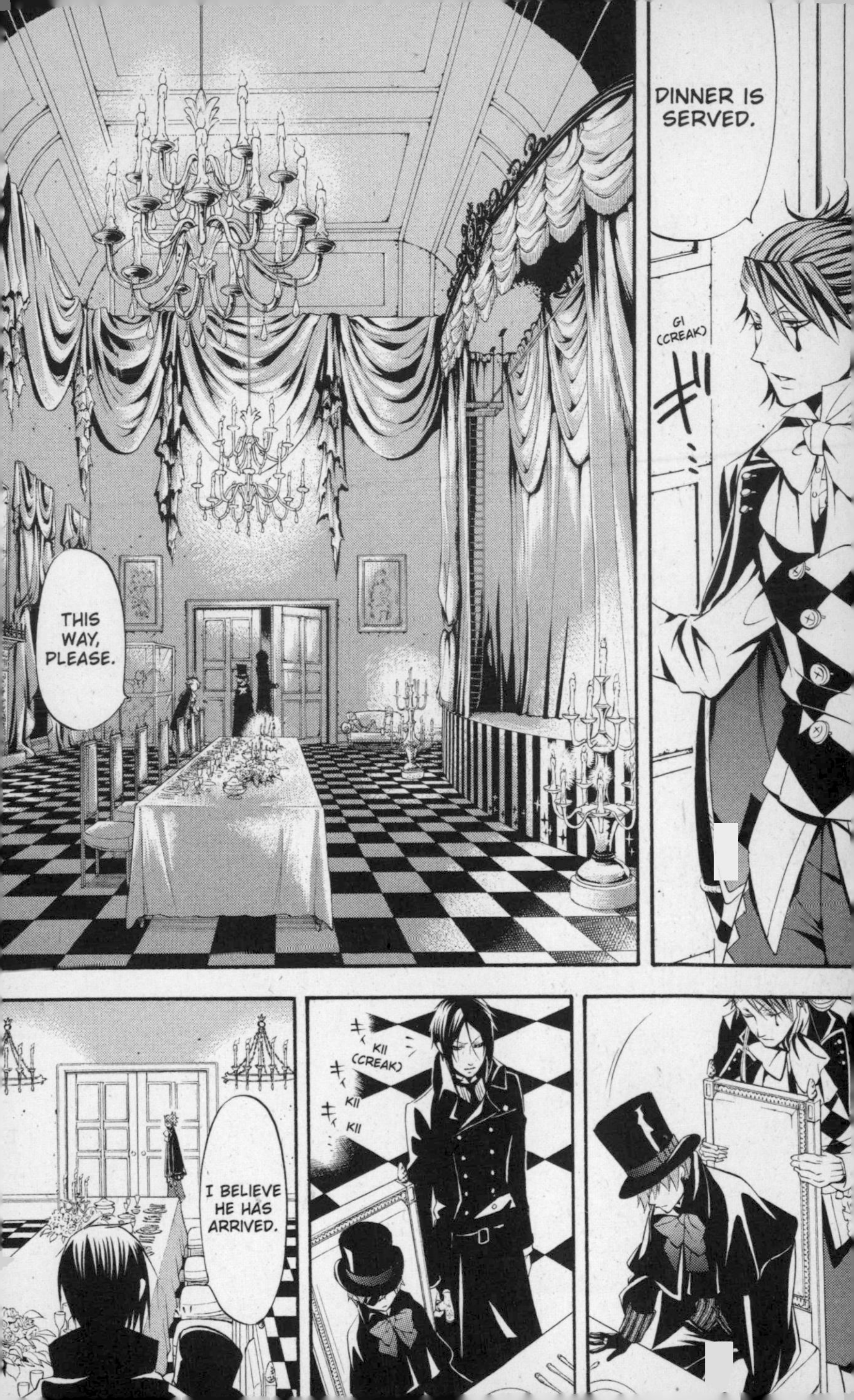
DINNER IS SERVED.
GI (CREAK)
THIS WAY, PLEASE.
KII (CREAK)
KII
KII
I BELIEVE HE HAS ARRIVED.

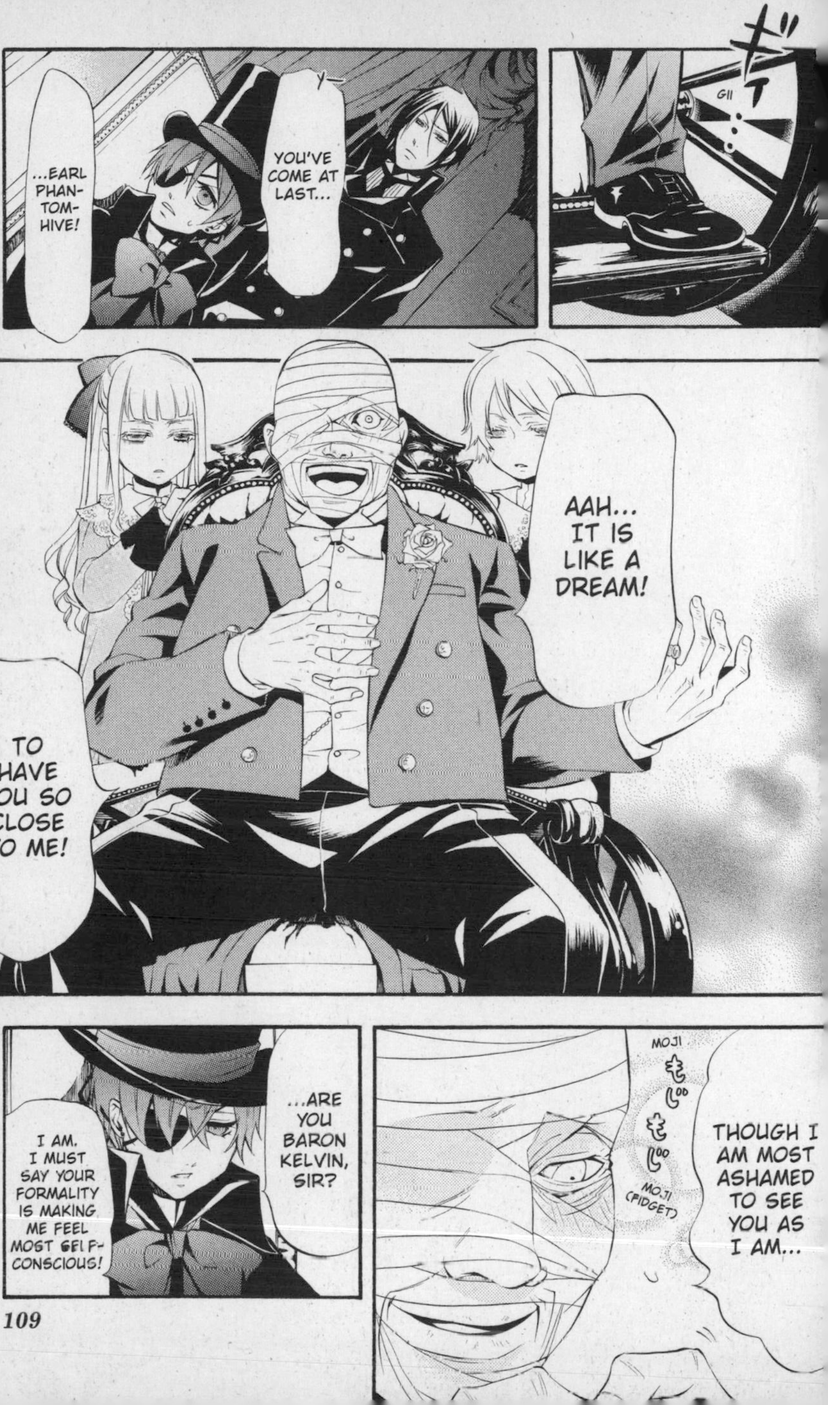
GII
YOU'VE COME AT LAST...
...EARL PHANTOMHIVE!
AAH... IT IS LIKE A DREAM!
TO HAVE YOU SO CLOSE TO ME!
THOUGH I AM MOST ASHAMED TO SEE YOU AS I AM...
MOJI
MOJI (FIDGET)
...ARE YOU BARON KELVIN, SIR?
I AM. I MUST SAY YOUR FORMALITY IS MAKING ME FEEL MOST SELF-CONSCIOUS!

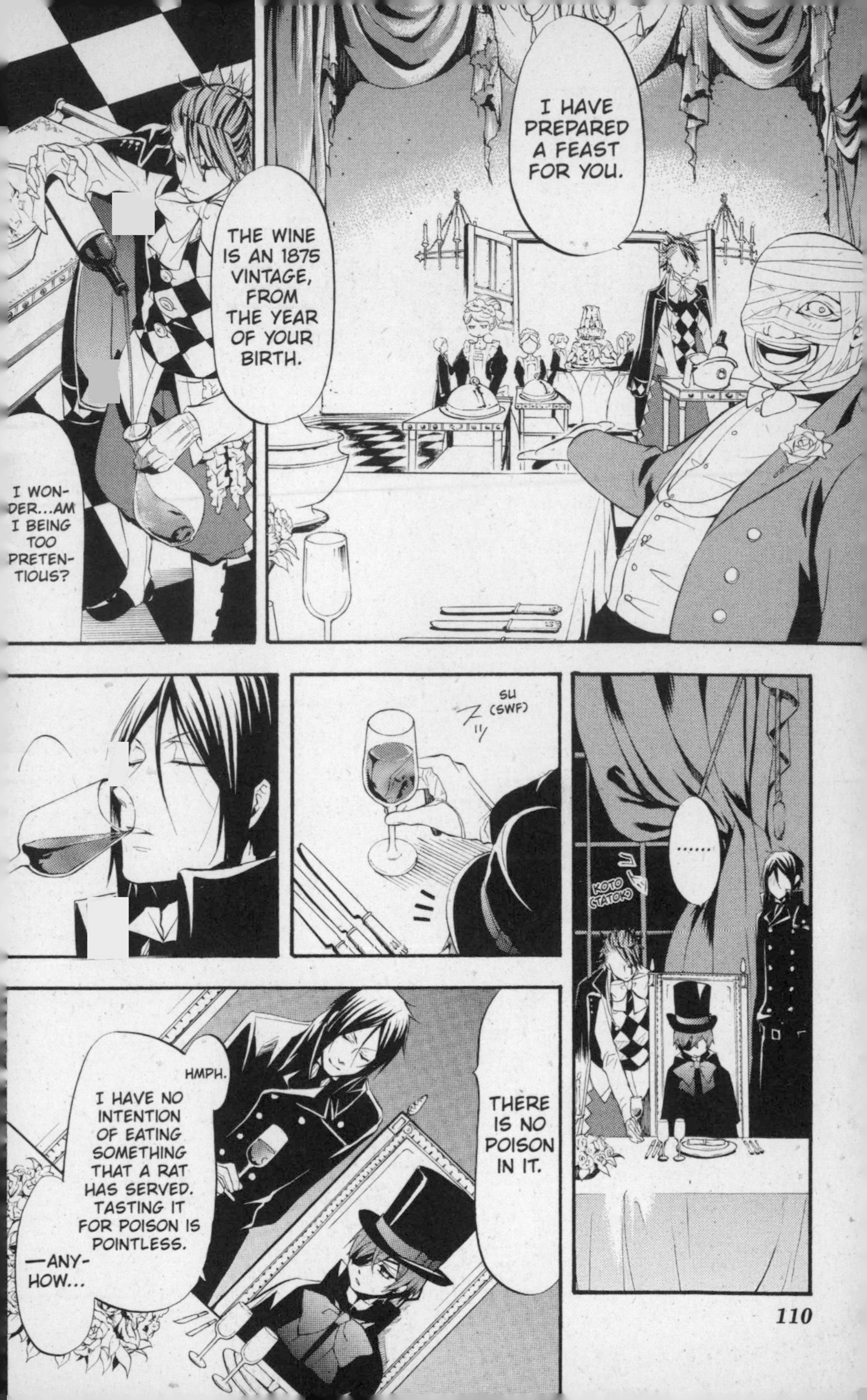
I HAVE PREPARED A FEAST FOR YOU.
THE WINE IS AN 1875 VINTAGE, FROM THE YEAR OF YOUR BIRTH.
I WONDER...AM I BEING TOO PRETENTIOUS?
KOTO (TATOK)
......
SU (SWF)
THERE IS NO POISON IN IT.
HMPH.
I HAVE NO INTENTION OF EATING SOMETHING THAT A RAT HAS SERVED. TASTING IT FOR POISON IS POINTLESS.
—ANYHOW...

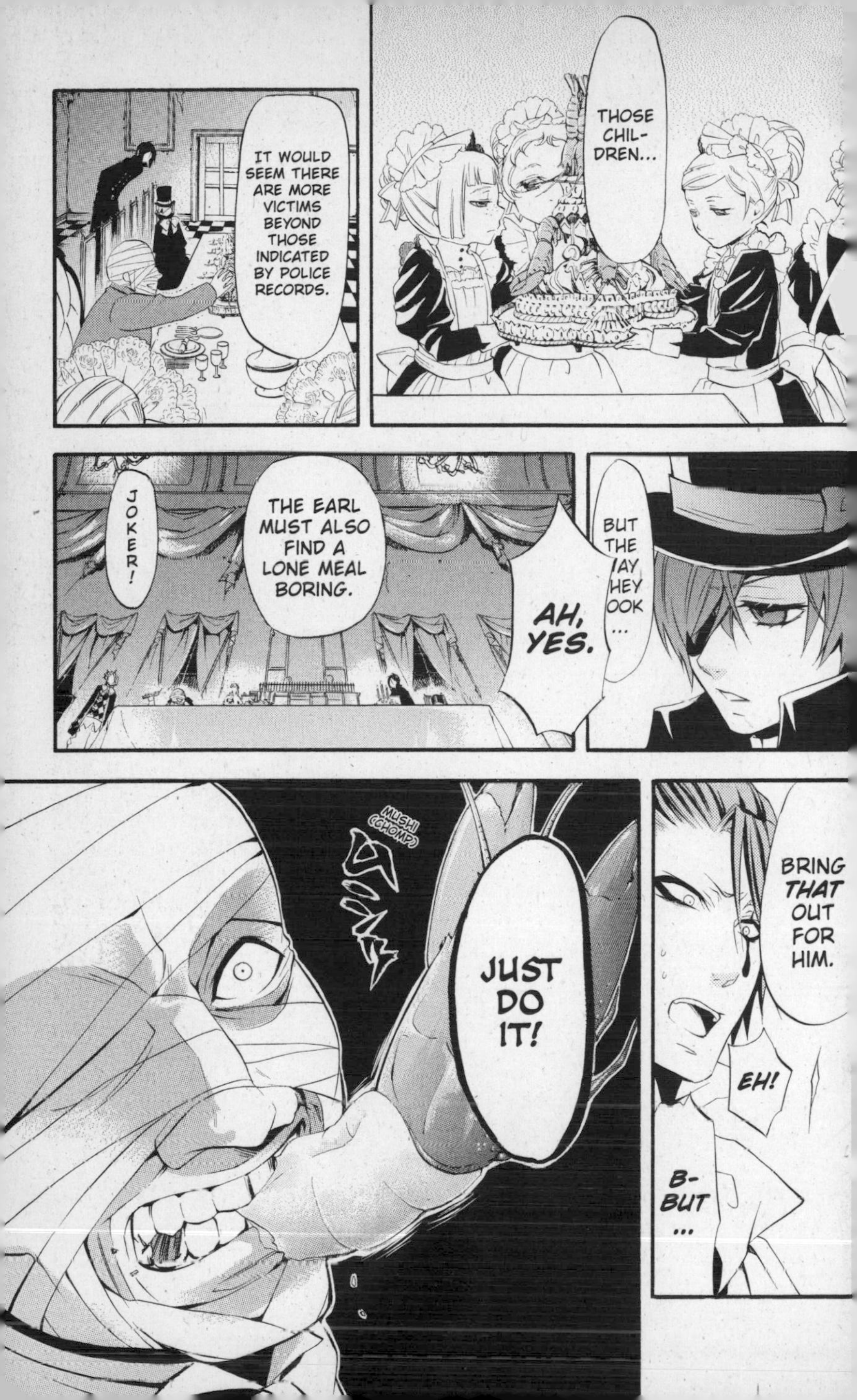
THOSE CHIL-DREN...
IT WOULD SEEM THERE ARE MORE VICTIMS BEYOND THOSE INDICATED BY POLICE RECORDS.
BUT THE AY HEY OOK ...
AH, YES.
THE EARL MUST ALSO FIND A LONE MEAL BORING.
JOKER!
BRING THAT OUT FOR HIM.
EH!
B-BUT ...
JUST DO IT!
MUSHI (CHOMP)

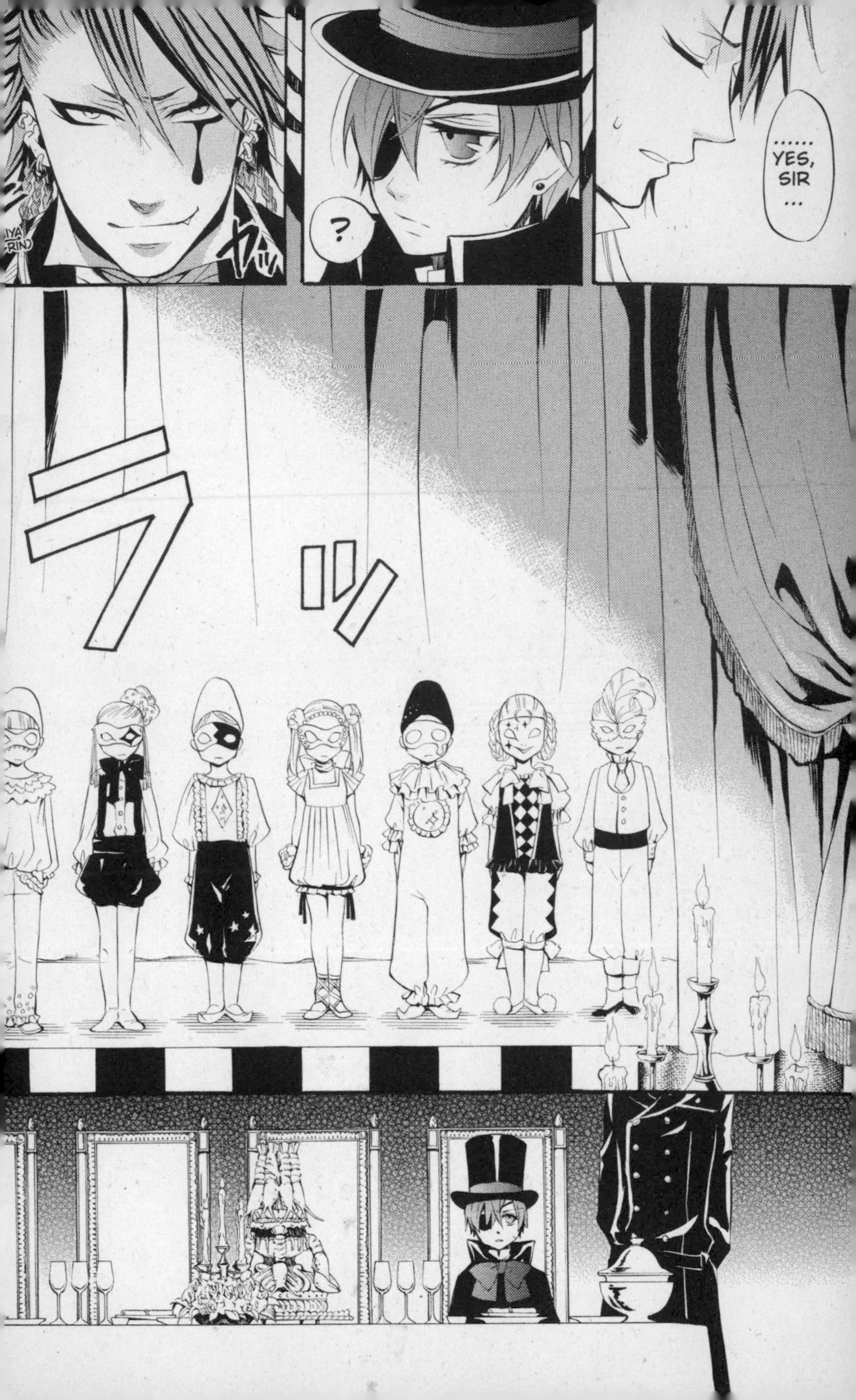
......
YES, SIR
...
?

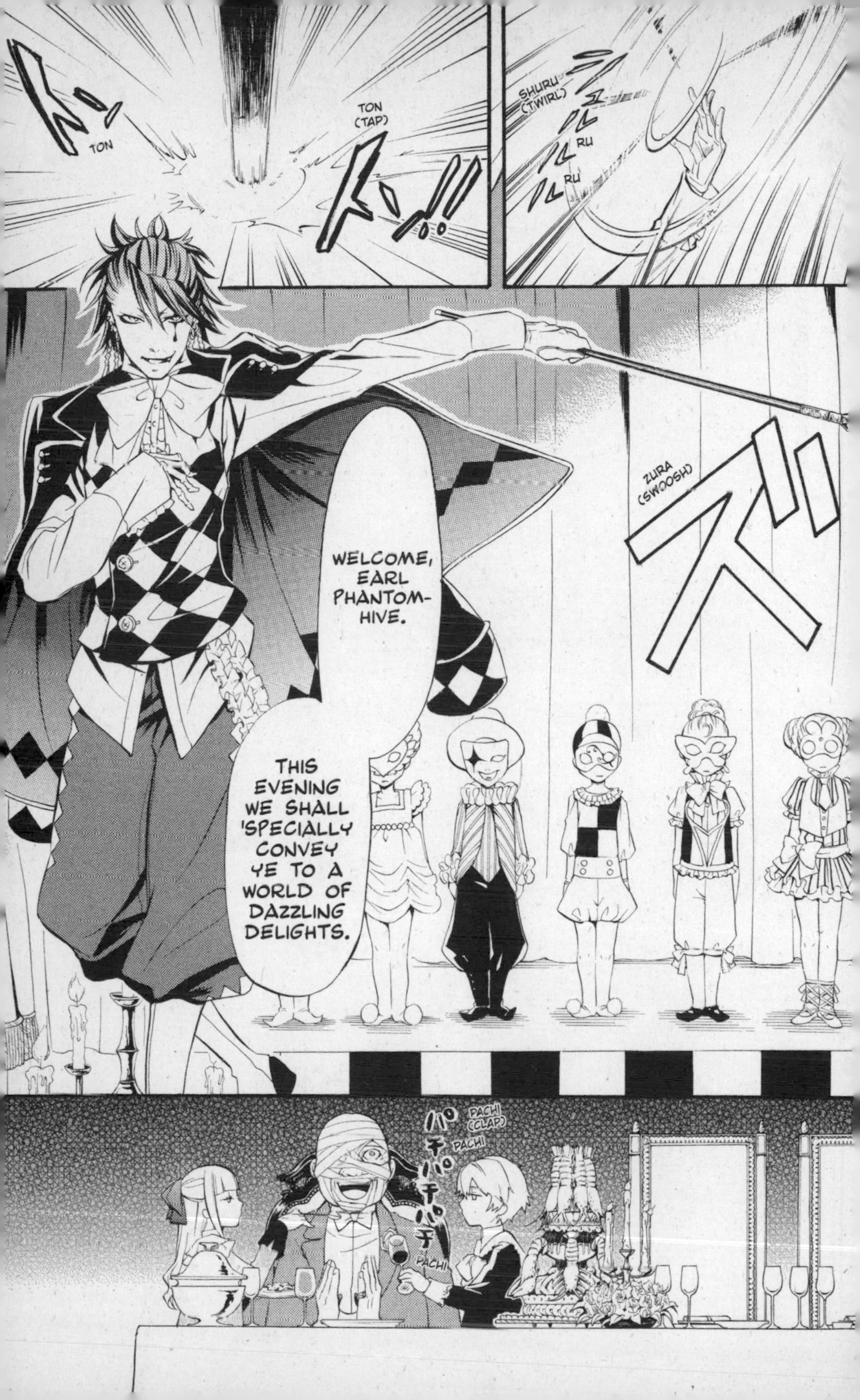
SHURU (TWIRL)
RU
RU
TON (TAP)
TON
ZURA (SWOOSH)
WELCOME, EARL PHANTOMHIVE.
THIS EVENING WE SHALL 'SPECIALLY CONVEY YE TO A WORLD OF DAZZLING DELIGHTS.
PACHI (CLAP)
PACHI
PACHI

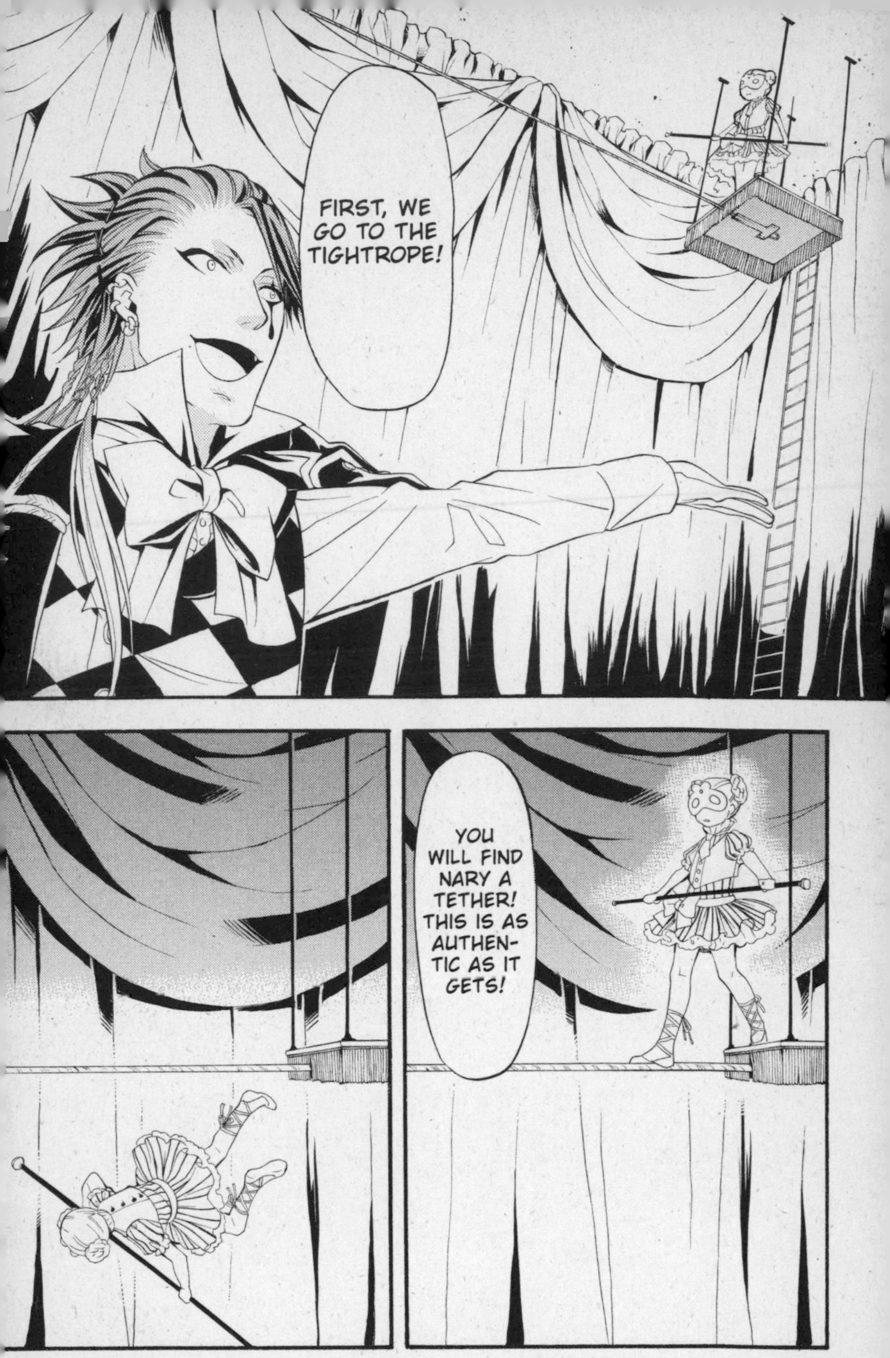
FIRST, WE GO TO THE TIGHTROPE!
YOU WILL FIND NARY A TETHER! THIS IS AS AUTHENTIC AS IT GETS!

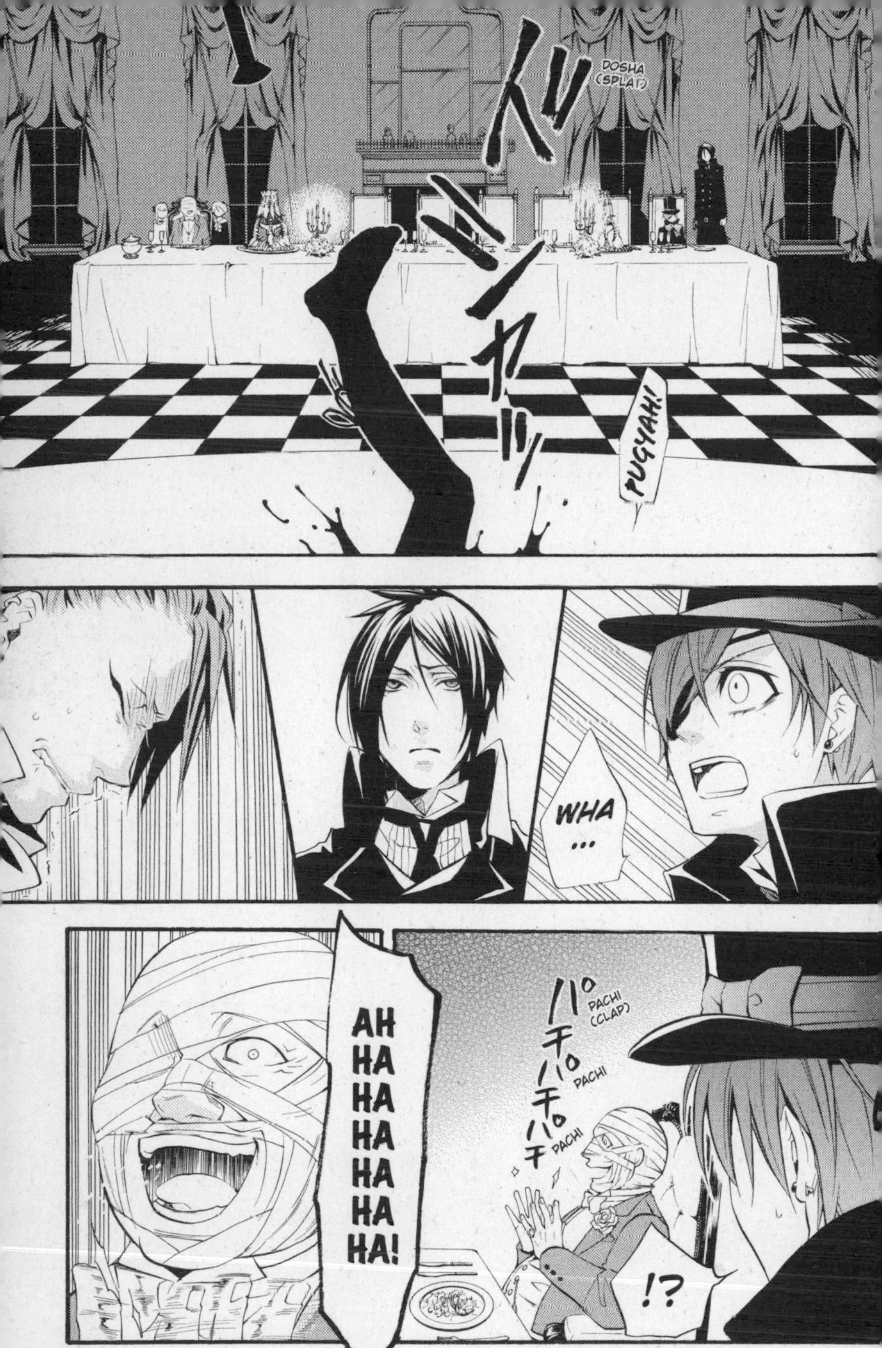
DOSHA (SPLAT!)
PUGYAH!
WHA ...
PACHI (CLAP)
PACHI
PACHI
!?
AH HA HA HA HA HA HA HA HA!

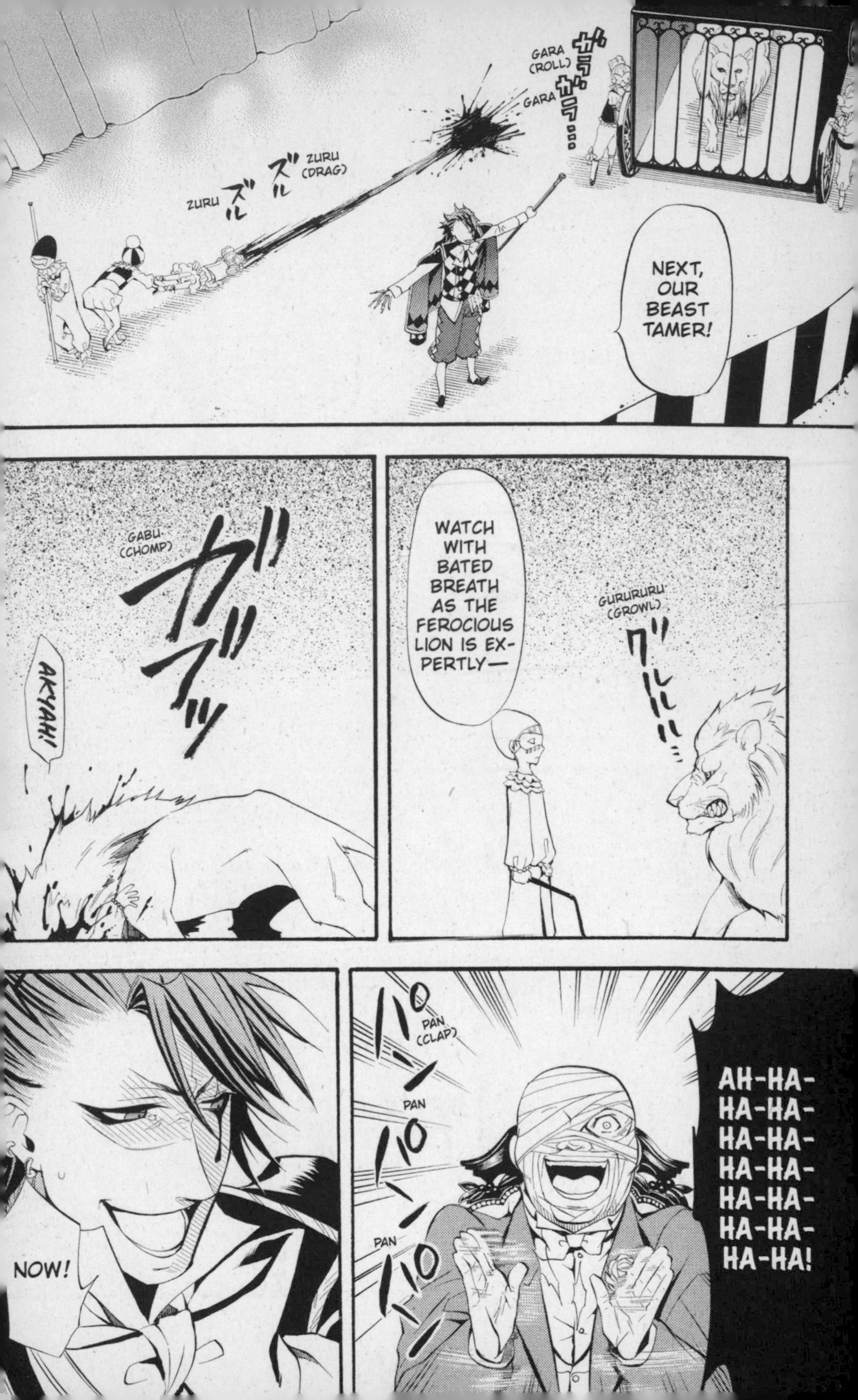

GARA (ROLL)
GARA
NEXT, OUR BEAST TAMER!
ZURU (DRAG)
ZURU
WATCH WITH BATED BREATH AS THE FEROCIOUS LION IS EXPERTLY—
GURURURU (GROWL)
GABU (CHOMP)
AKYAH!
PAN (CLAP)
PAN
PAN
AH-HA-HA-HA-HA-HA-HA-HA-HA-HA-HA-HA-HA-HA!
NOW!

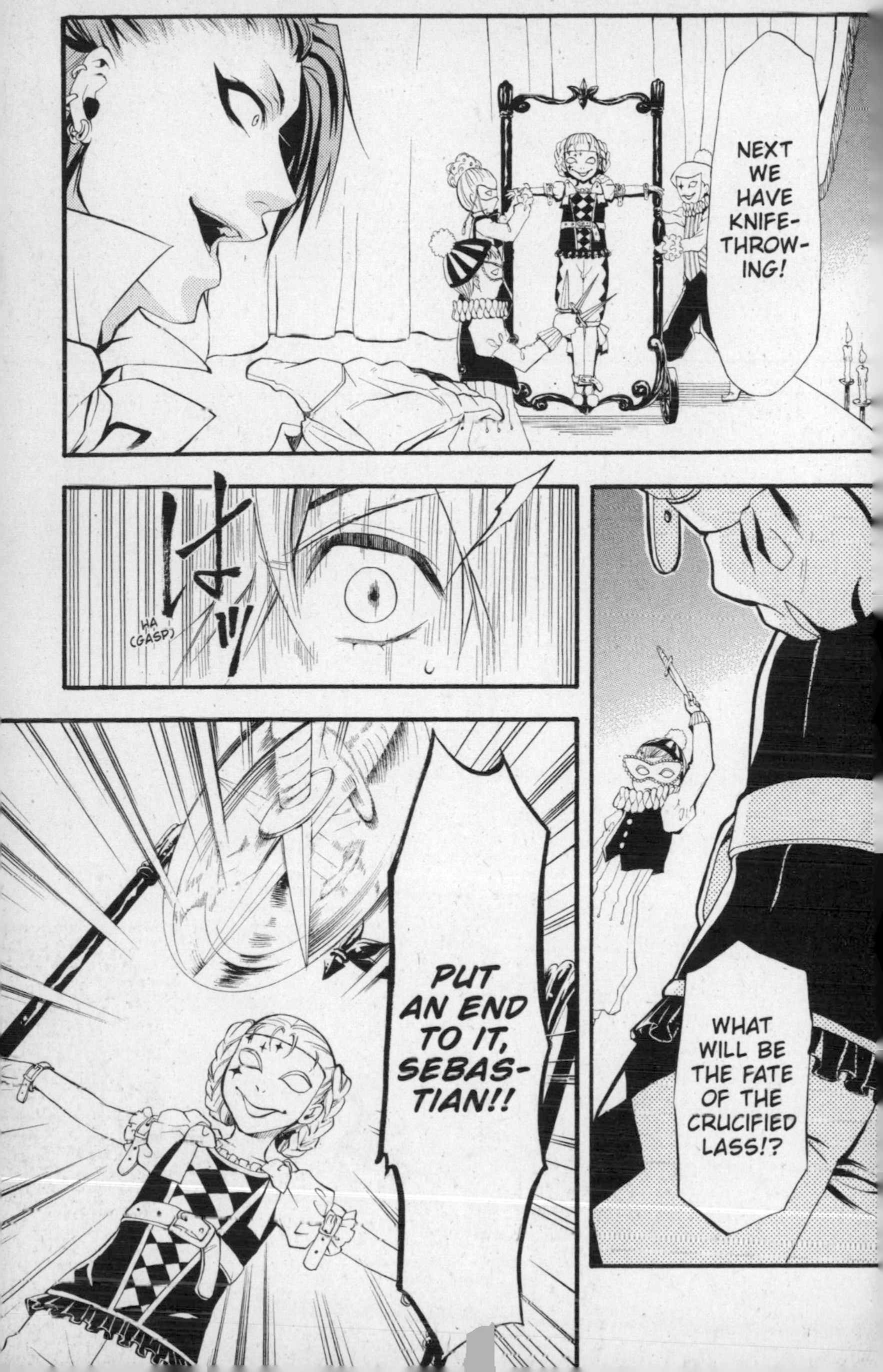
NEXT WE HAVE KNIFE-THROWING!
WHAT WILL BE THE FATE OF THE CRUCIFIED LASS!?
はッ
HA (GASP)
PUT AN END TO IT, SEBASTIAN!!

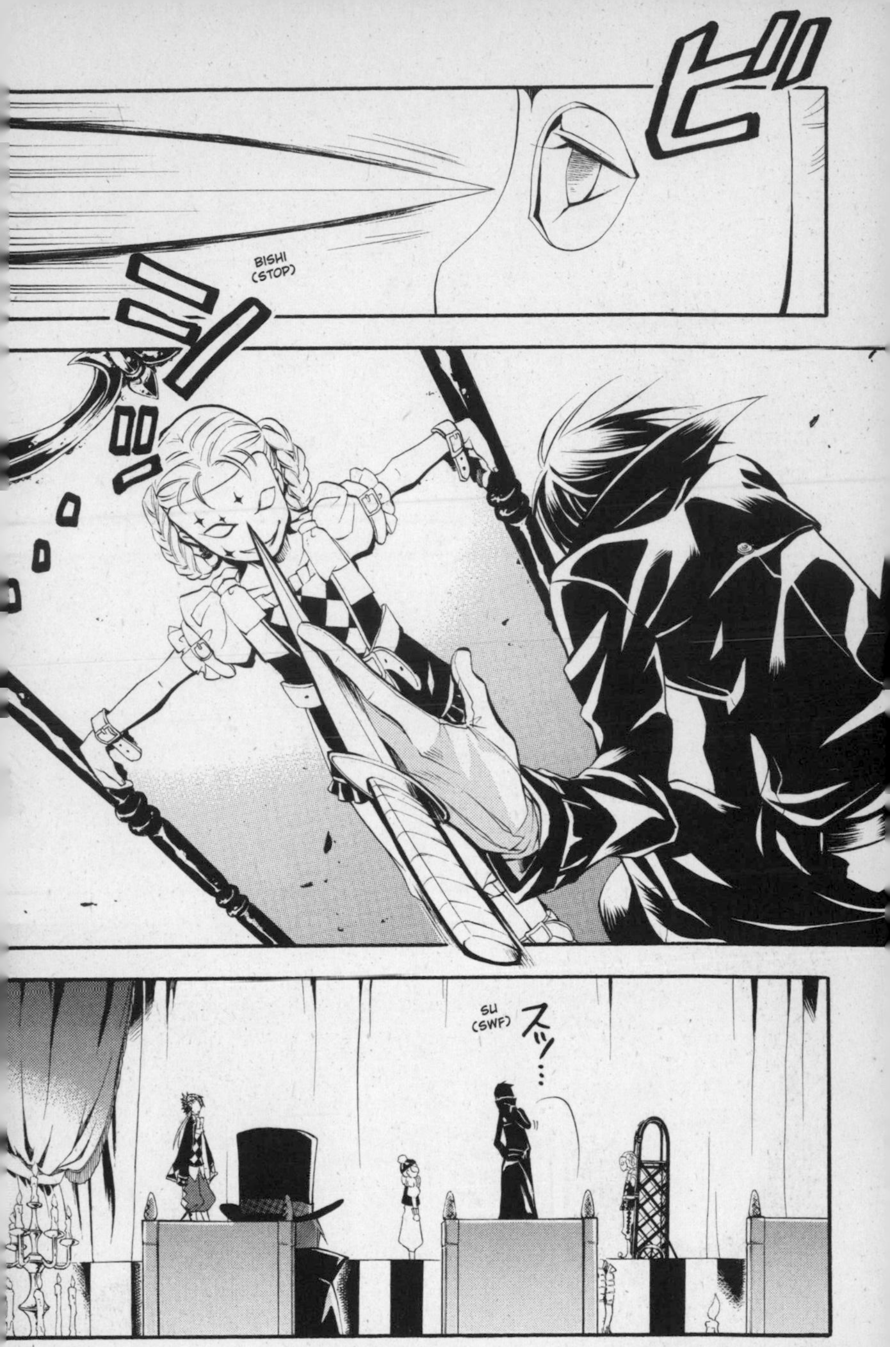
BISHI
(STOP)
SU
(SWF)
ズッ…

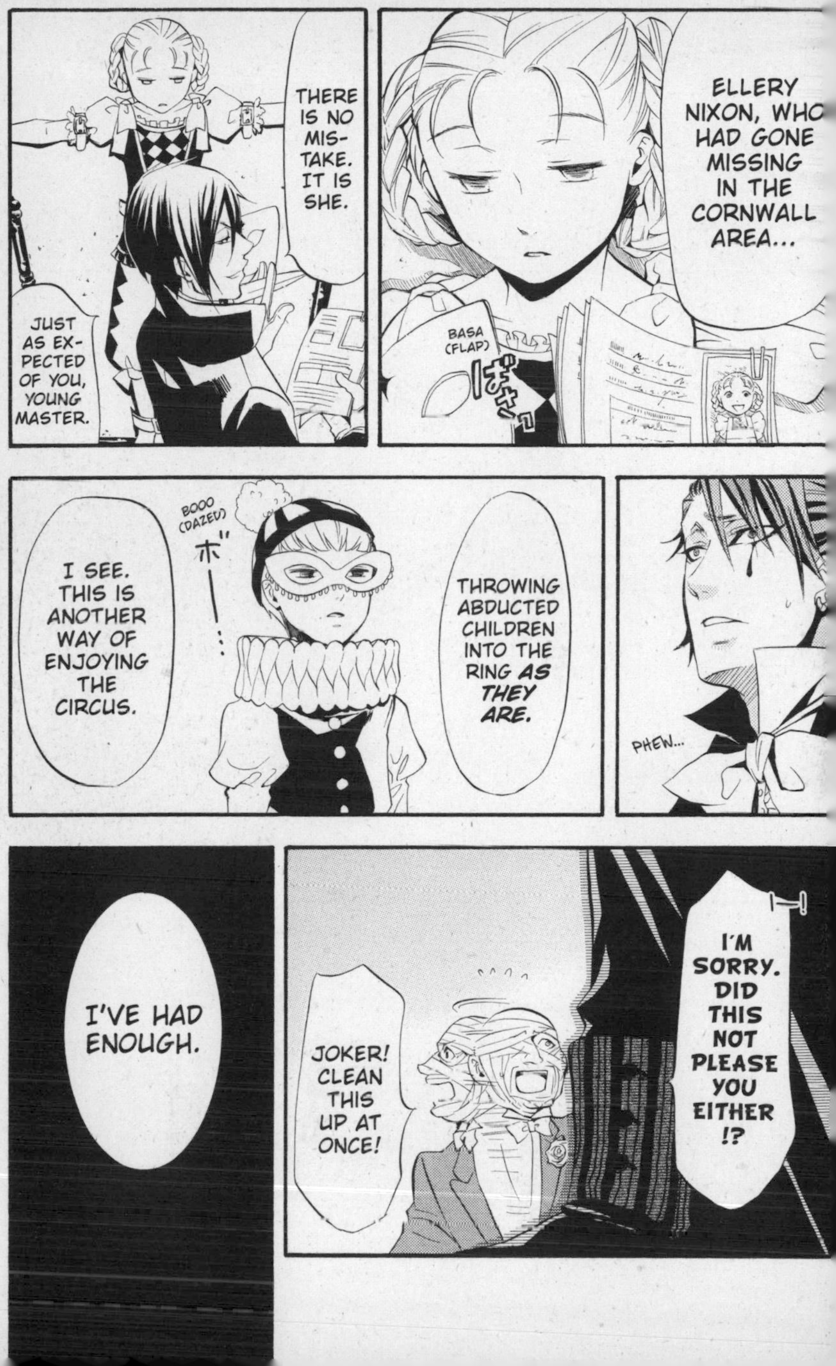
ELLERY NIXON, WHO HAD GONE MISSING IN THE CORNWALL AREA...
BASA (FLAP)
THERE IS NO MIS-TAKE. IT IS SHE.
JUST AS EX-PECTED OF YOU, YOUNG MASTER.
PHEW...
THROWING ABDUCTED CHILDREN INTO THE RING *AS THEY ARE.*
BOOO (DAZED)
I SEE. THIS IS ANOTHER WAY OF ENJOYING THE CIRCUS.
I'M SORRY. DID THIS NOT PLEASE YOU EITHER !?
JOKER! CLEAN THIS UP AT ONCE!
I'VE HAD ENOUGH.

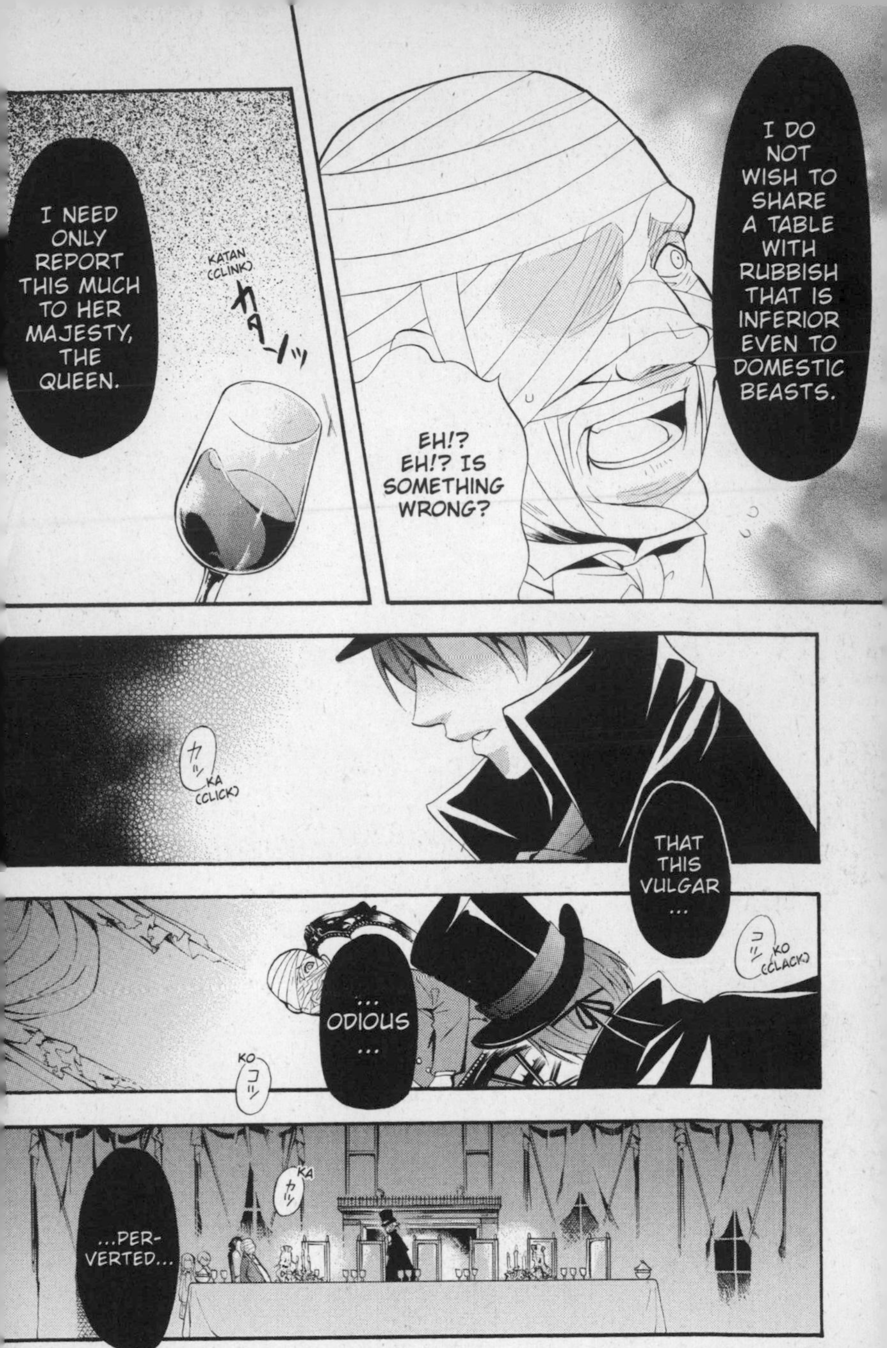
I DO NOT WISH TO SHARE A TABLE WITH RUBBISH THAT IS INFERIOR EVEN TO DOMESTIC BEASTS.
EH!? EH!? IS SOMETHING WRONG?
カターンッ
KATAN (CLINK)
I NEED ONLY REPORT THIS MUCH TO HER MAJESTY, THE QUEEN.
カッ
KA (CLICK)
THAT THIS VULGAR ...
コッ
KO (CLACK)
... ODIOUS ...
コッ
KO
カッ
KA
...PER-VERTED...

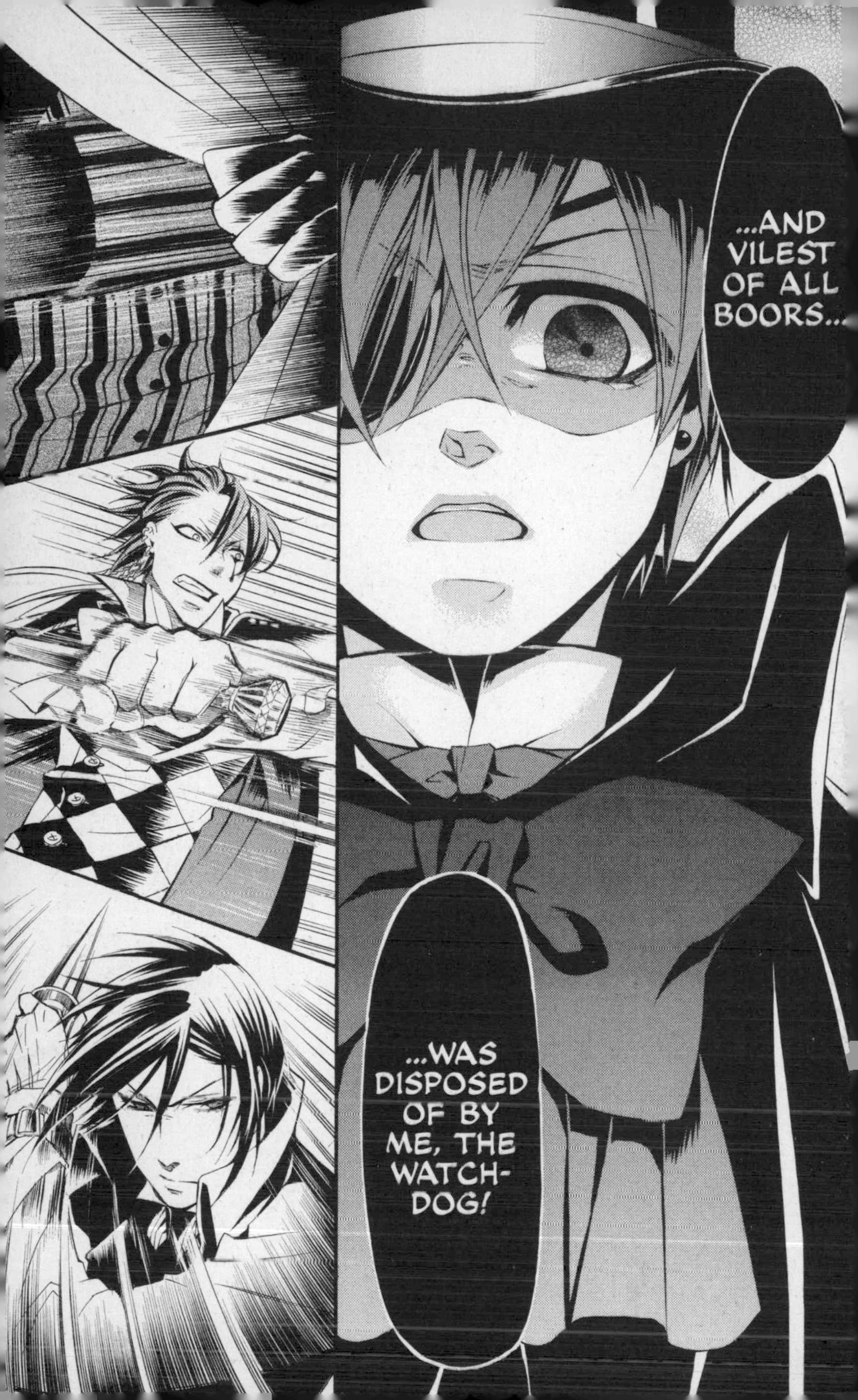
...AND VILEST OF ALL BOORS...
...WAS DISPOSED OF BY ME, THE WATCH-DOG!

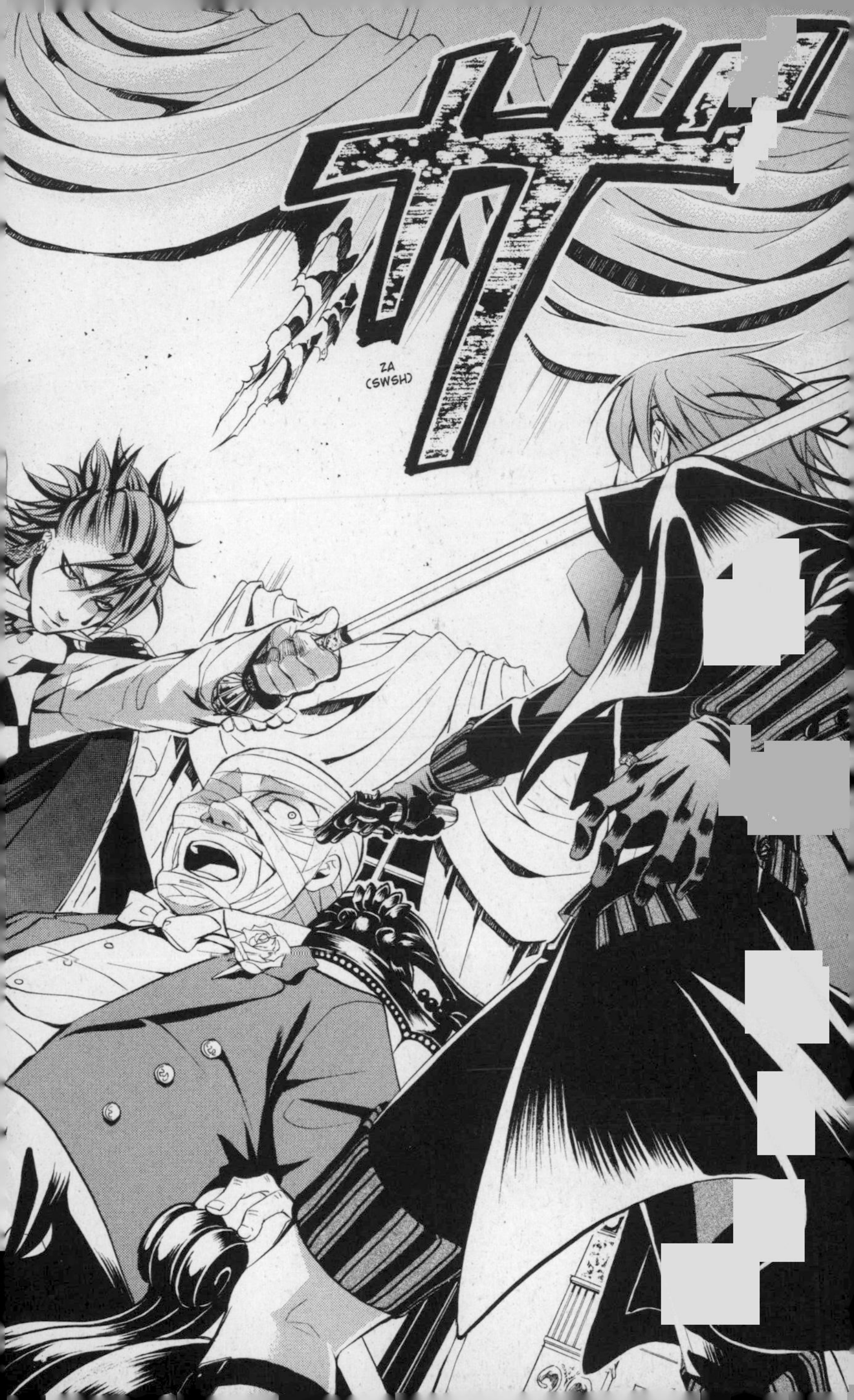
ZA
(SWSH)

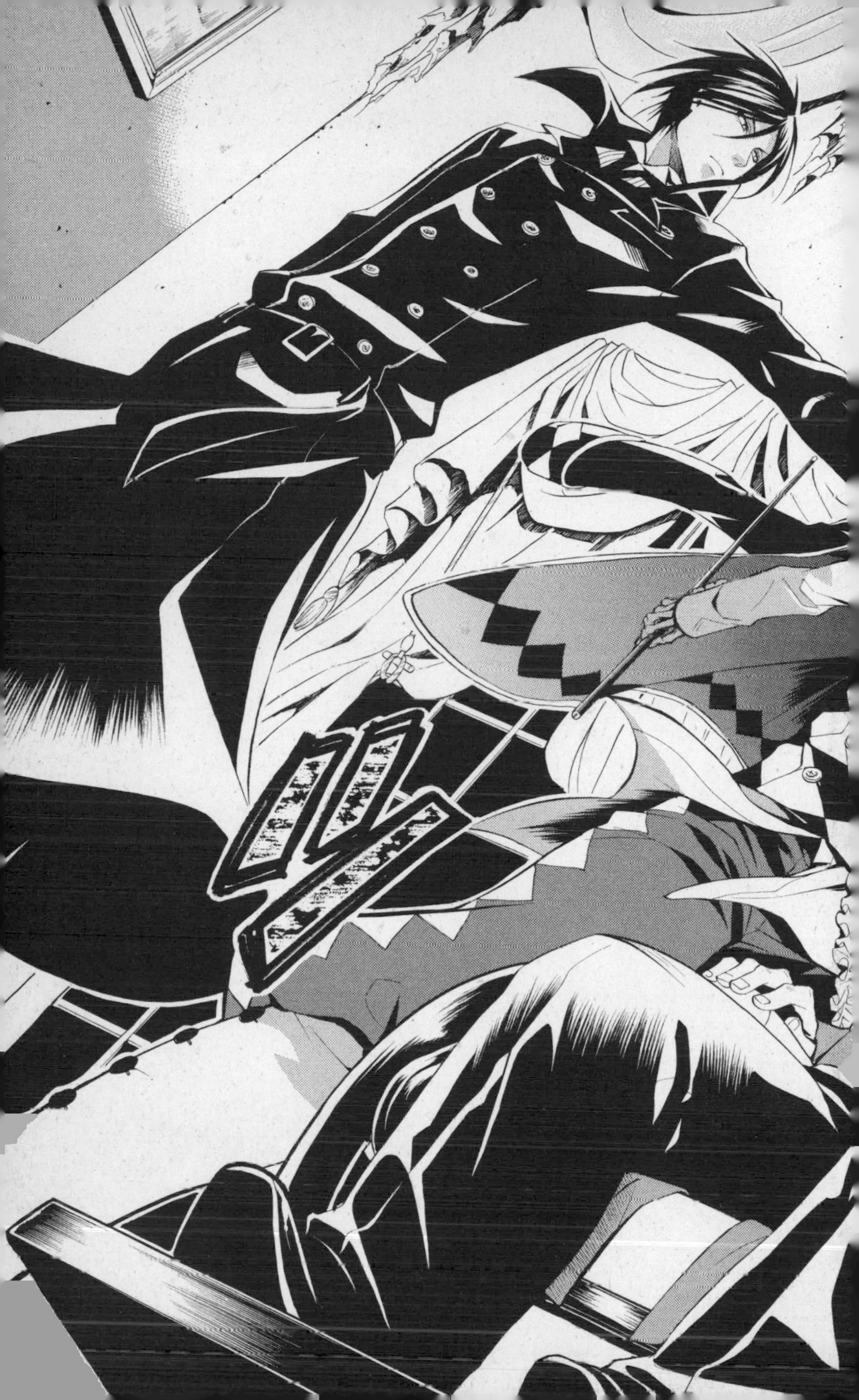

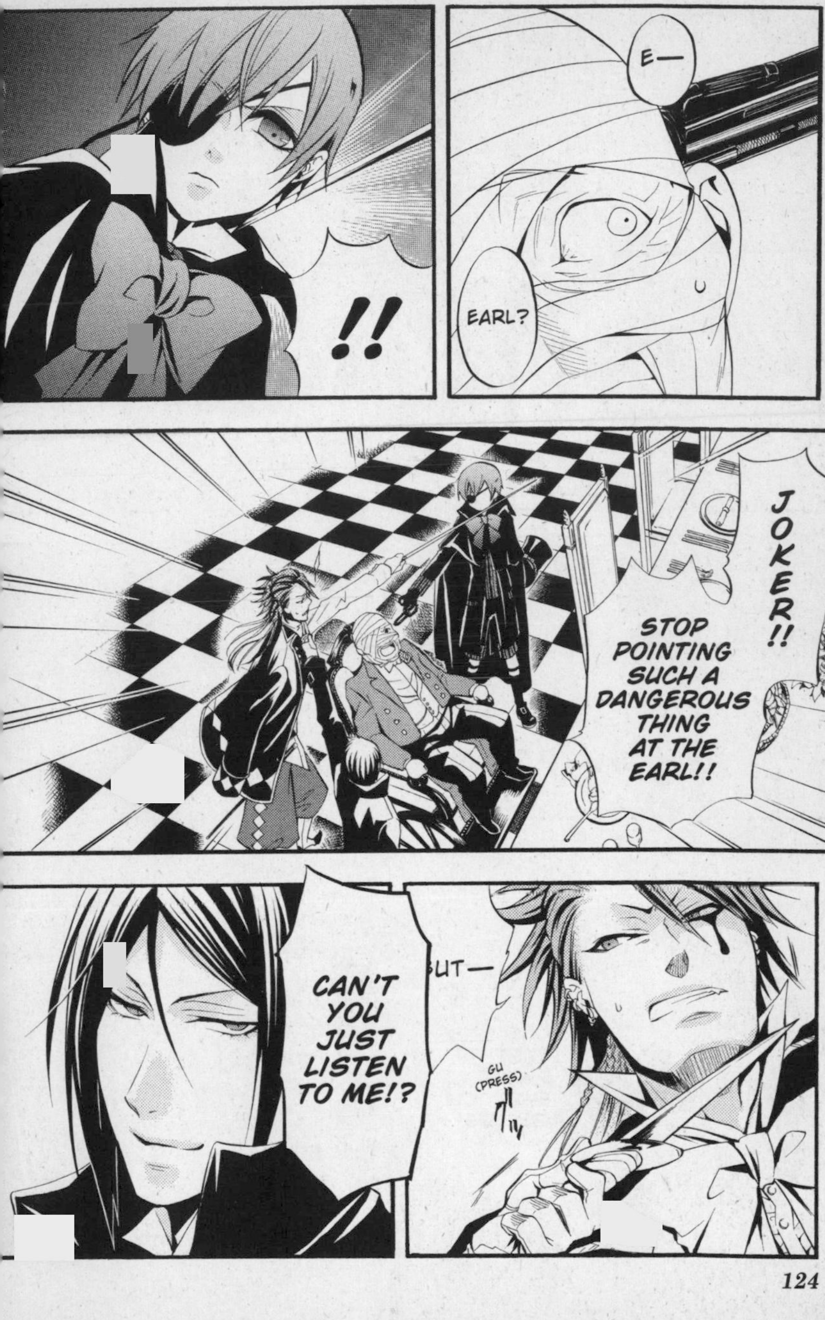
E—
EARL?
!!
JOKER!!
STOP POINTING SUCH A DANGEROUS THING AT THE EARL!!
BUT—
GU (PRESS)
CAN'T YOU JUST LISTEN TO ME!?

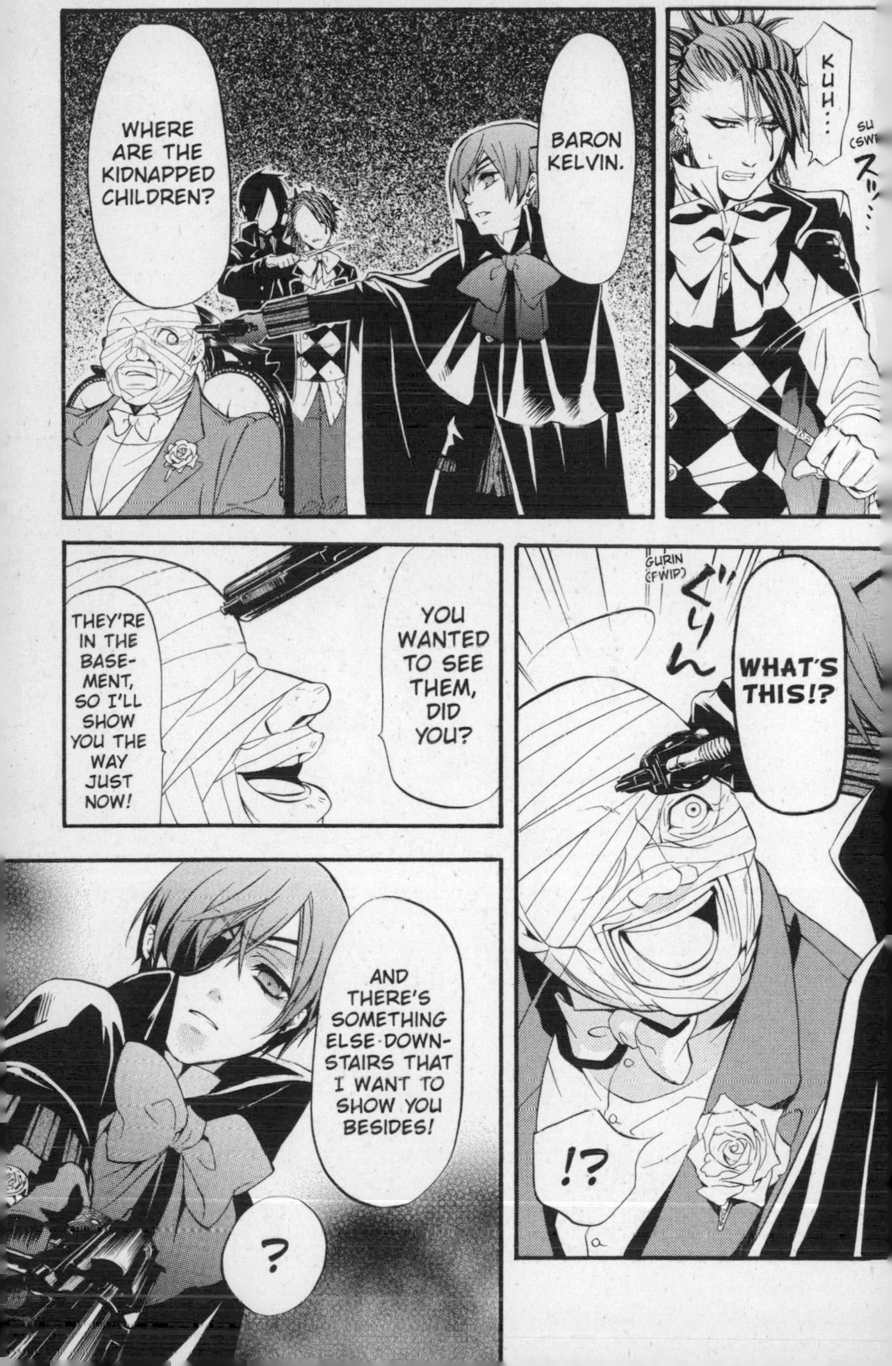
KUH...
SU (SWI
スッ…
BARON KELVIN.
WHERE ARE THE KIDNAPPED CHILDREN?
GURIN (FWIP)
ぐりん
WHAT'S THIS!?
!?
YOU WANTED TO SEE THEM, DID YOU?
THEY'RE IN THE BASEMENT, SO I'LL SHOW YOU THE WAY JUST NOW!
AND THERE'S SOMETHING ELSE DOWNSTAIRS THAT I WANT TO SHOW YOU BESIDES!
?

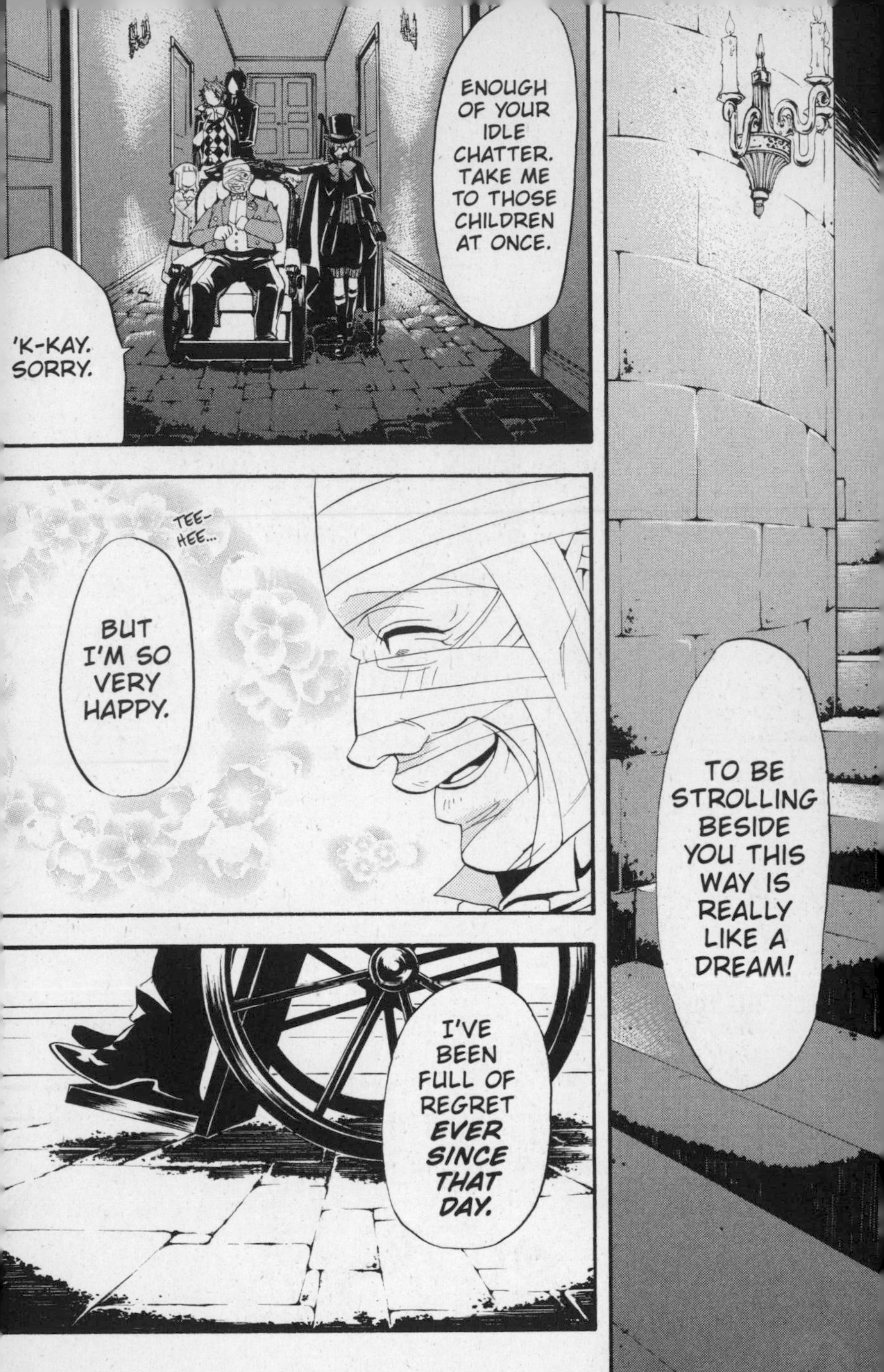
TO BE STROLLING BESIDE YOU THIS WAY IS REALLY LIKE A DREAM!
ENOUGH OF YOUR IDLE CHATTER. TAKE ME TO THOSE CHILDREN AT ONCE.
'K-KAY. SORRY.
TEE-HEE...
BUT I'M SO VERY HAPPY.
I'VE BEEN FULL OF REGRET EVER SINCE THAT DAY.

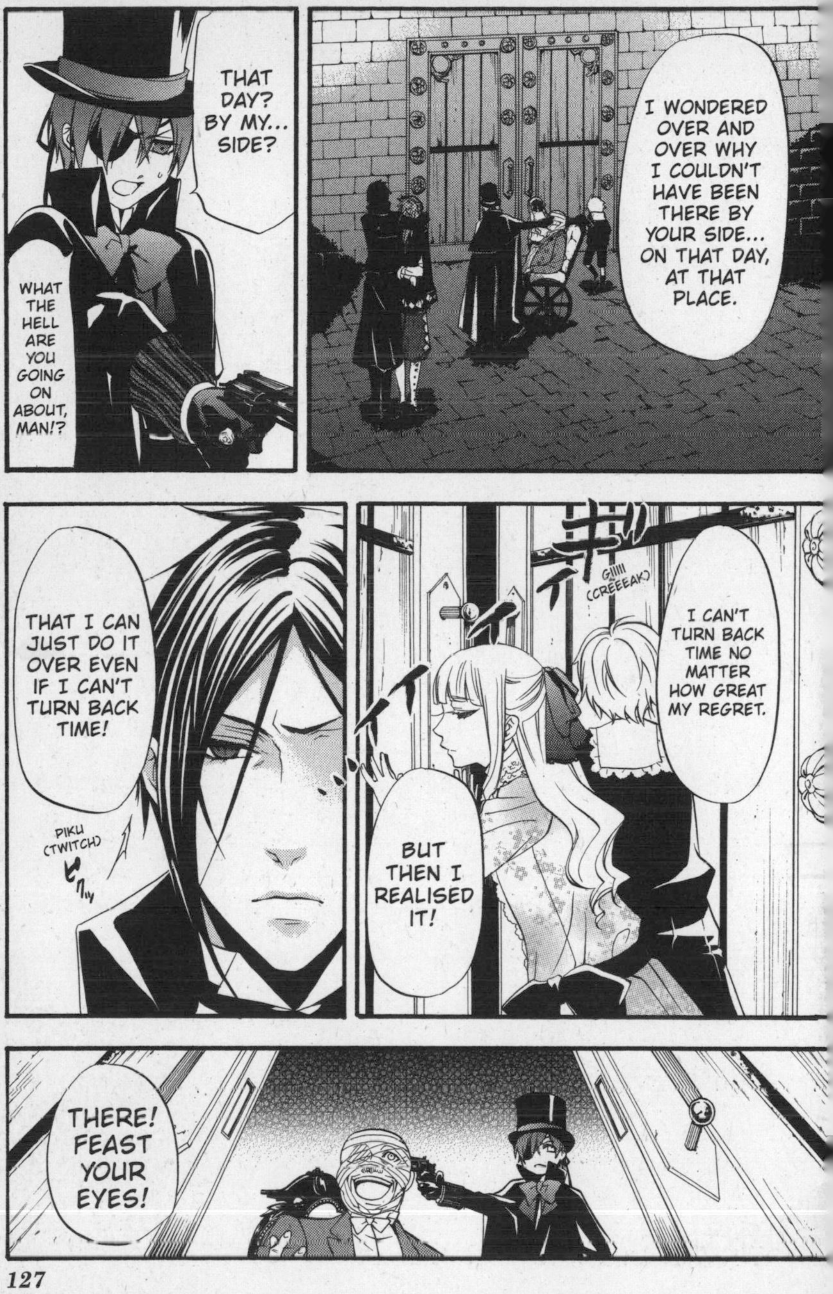
I WONDERED OVER AND OVER WHY I COULDN'T HAVE BEEN THERE BY YOUR SIDE... ON THAT DAY, AT THAT PLACE.
THAT DAY? BY MY... SIDE?
WHAT THE HELL ARE YOU GOING ON ABOUT, MAN!?
GIIII (CREEEAK)
I CAN'T TURN BACK TIME NO MATTER HOW GREAT MY REGRET.
BUT THEN I REALISED IT!
THAT I CAN JUST DO IT OVER EVEN IF I CAN'T TURN BACK TIME!
PIKU (TWITCH)
THERE! FEAST YOUR EYES!

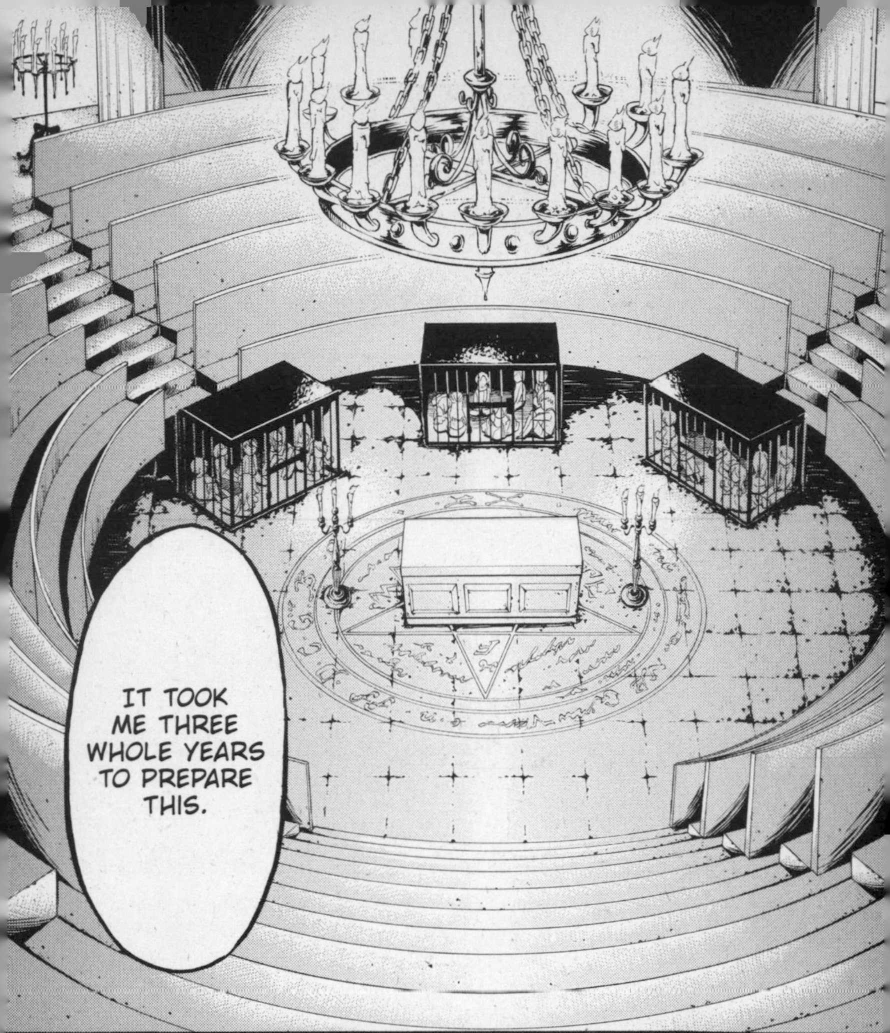
IT TOOK ME THREE WHOLE YEARS TO PREPARE THIS.

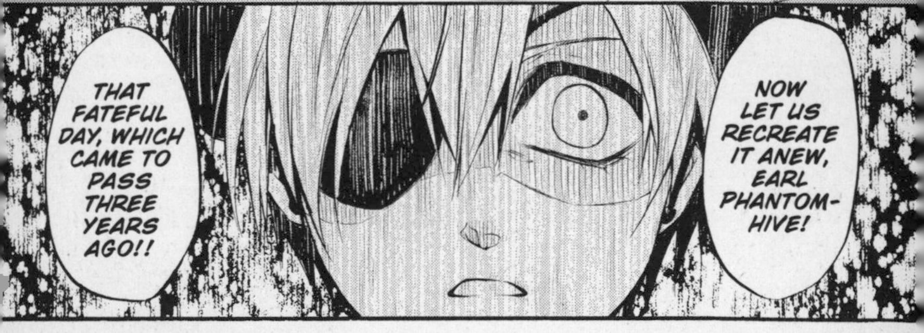
NOW LET US RECREATE IT ANEW, EARL PHANTOM-HIVE!
THAT FATEFUL DAY, WHICH CAME TO PASS THREE YEARS AGO!!

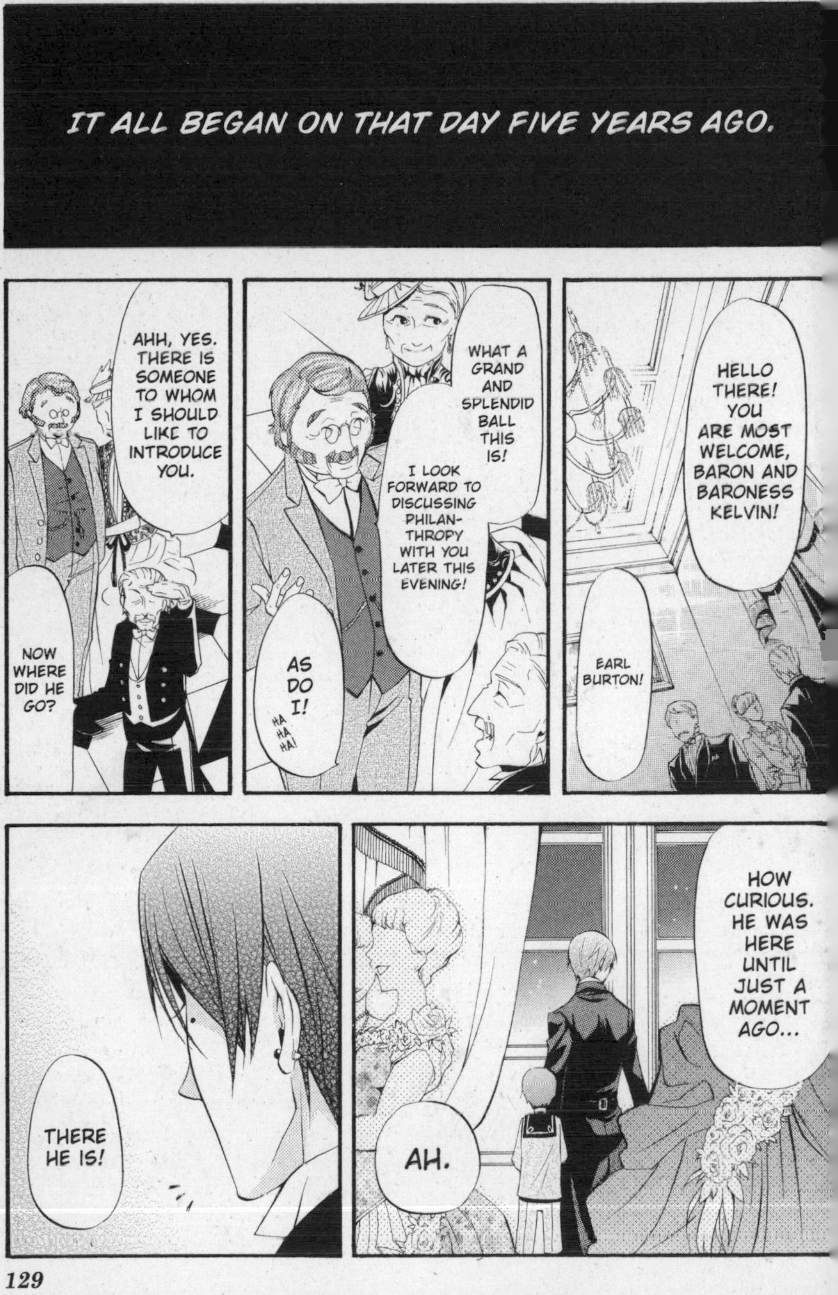
IT ALL BEGAN ON THAT DAY FIVE YEARS AGO.
HELLO THERE! YOU ARE MOST WELCOME, BARON AND BARONESS KELVIN!
EARL BURTON!
WHAT A GRAND AND SPLENDID BALL THIS IS!
I LOOK FORWARD TO DISCUSSING PHILAN-THROPY WITH YOU LATER THIS EVENING!
AS DO I!
HA HA HA!
AHH, YES. THERE IS SOMEONE TO WHOM I SHOULD LIKE TO INTRODUCE YOU.
NOW WHERE DID HE GO?
HOW CURIOUS. HE WAS HERE UNTIL JUST A MOMENT AGO...
AH.
THERE HE IS!

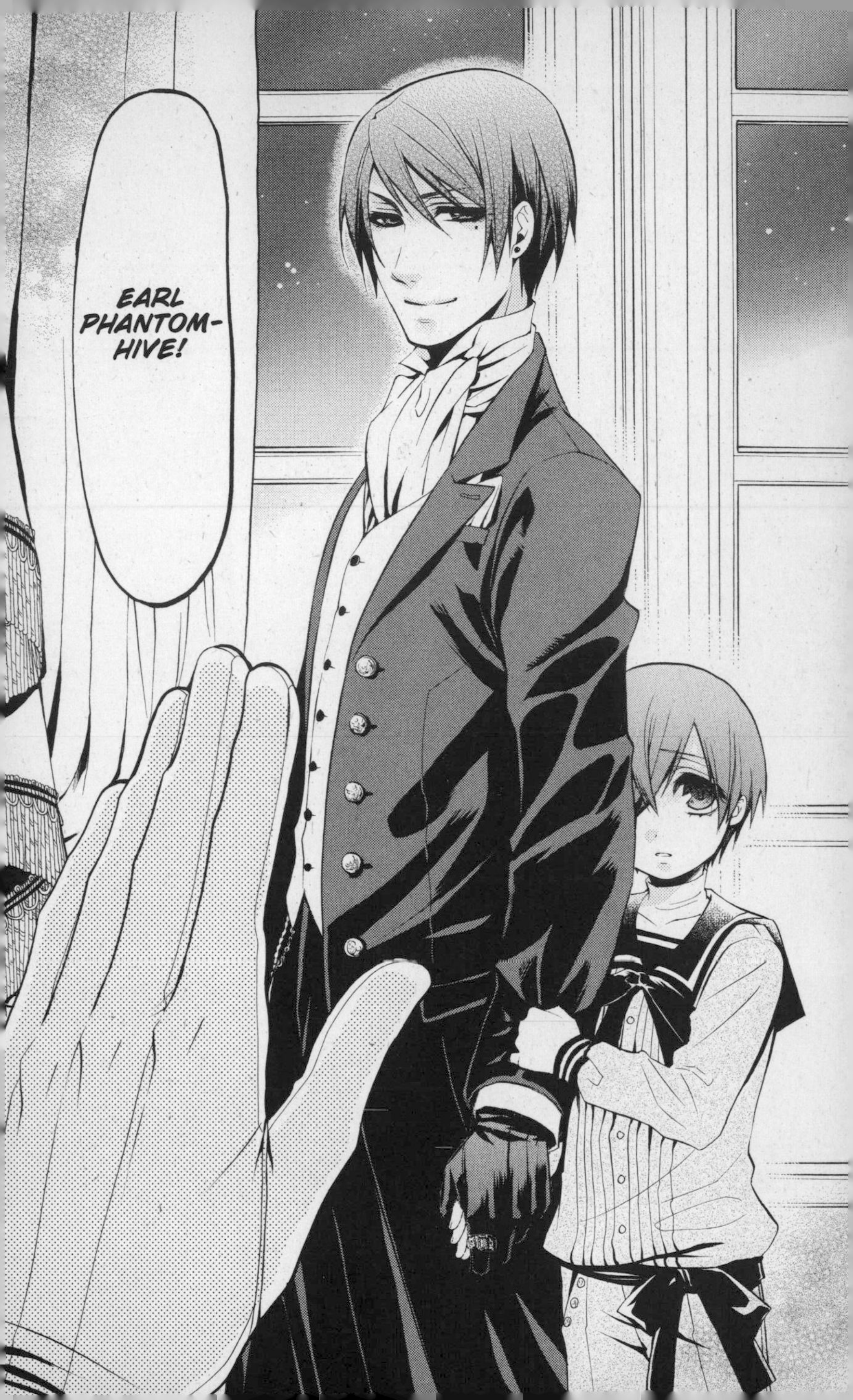
EARL PHANTOM-HIVE!

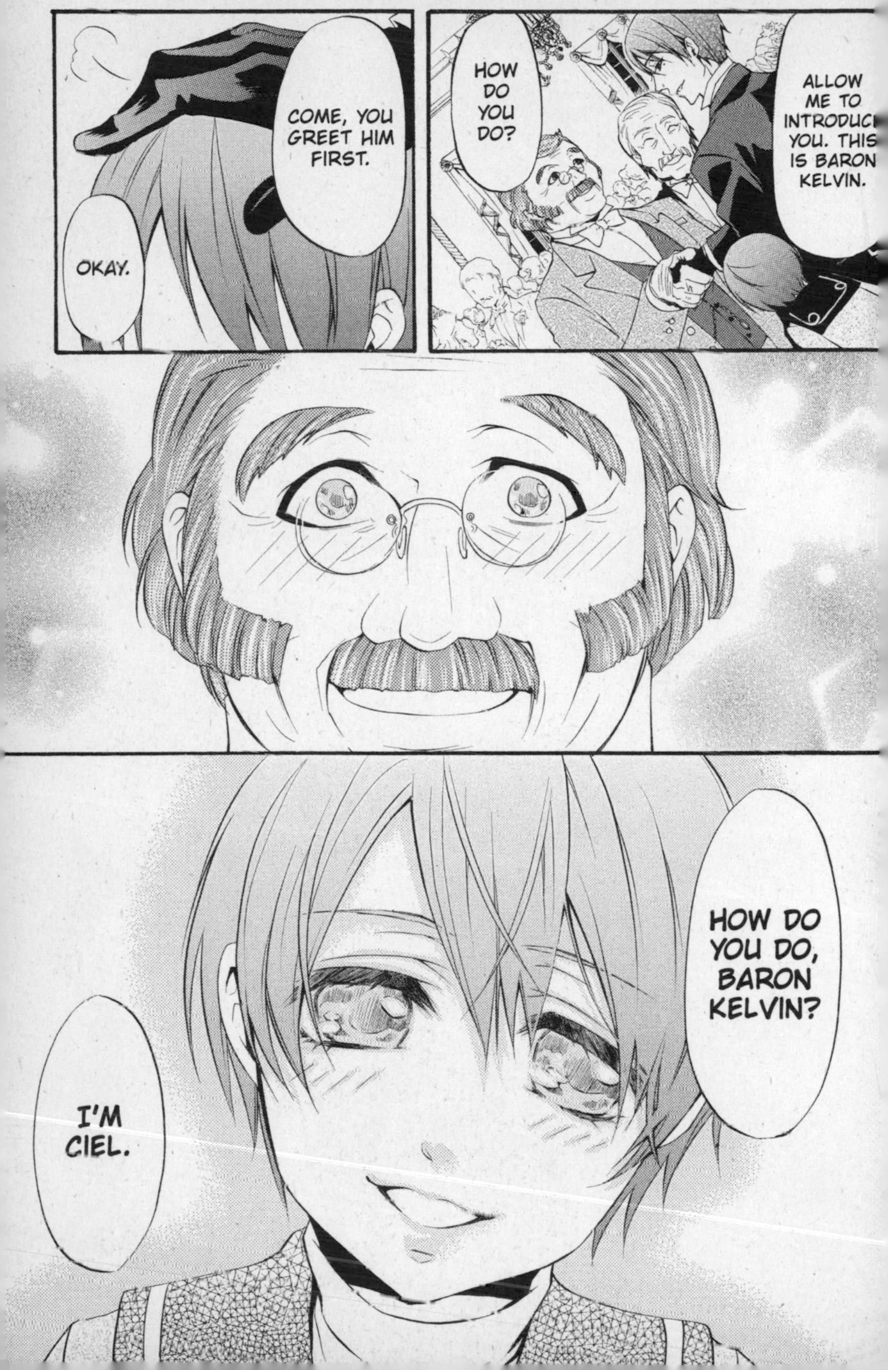
ALLOW ME TO INTRODUC YOU. THIS IS BARON KELVIN.
HOW DO YOU DO?
COME, YOU GREET HIM FIRST.
OKAY.
HOW DO YOU DO, BARON KELVIN?
I'M CIEL.

Black Butler

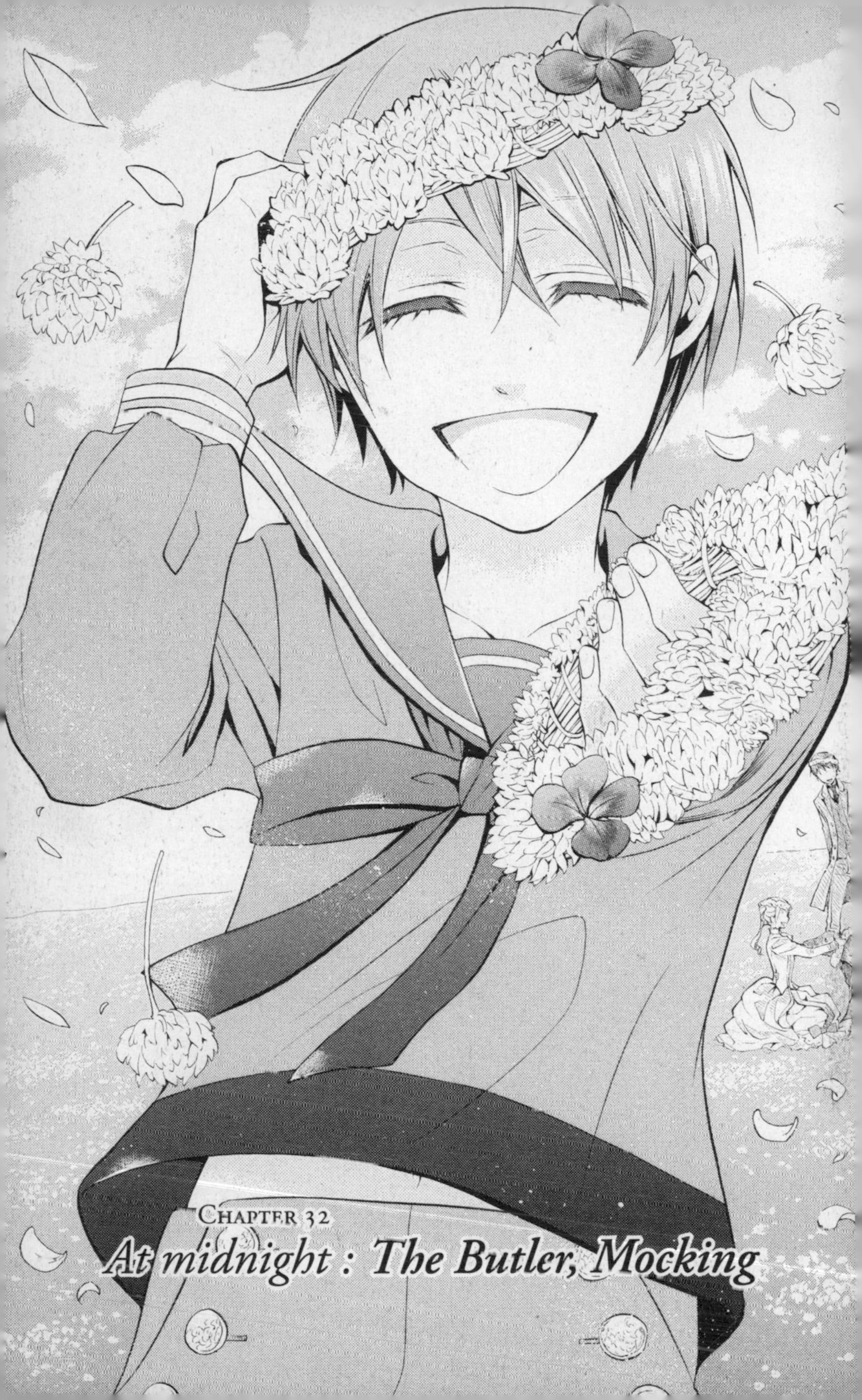
Chapter 32
At midnight : The Butler, Mocking

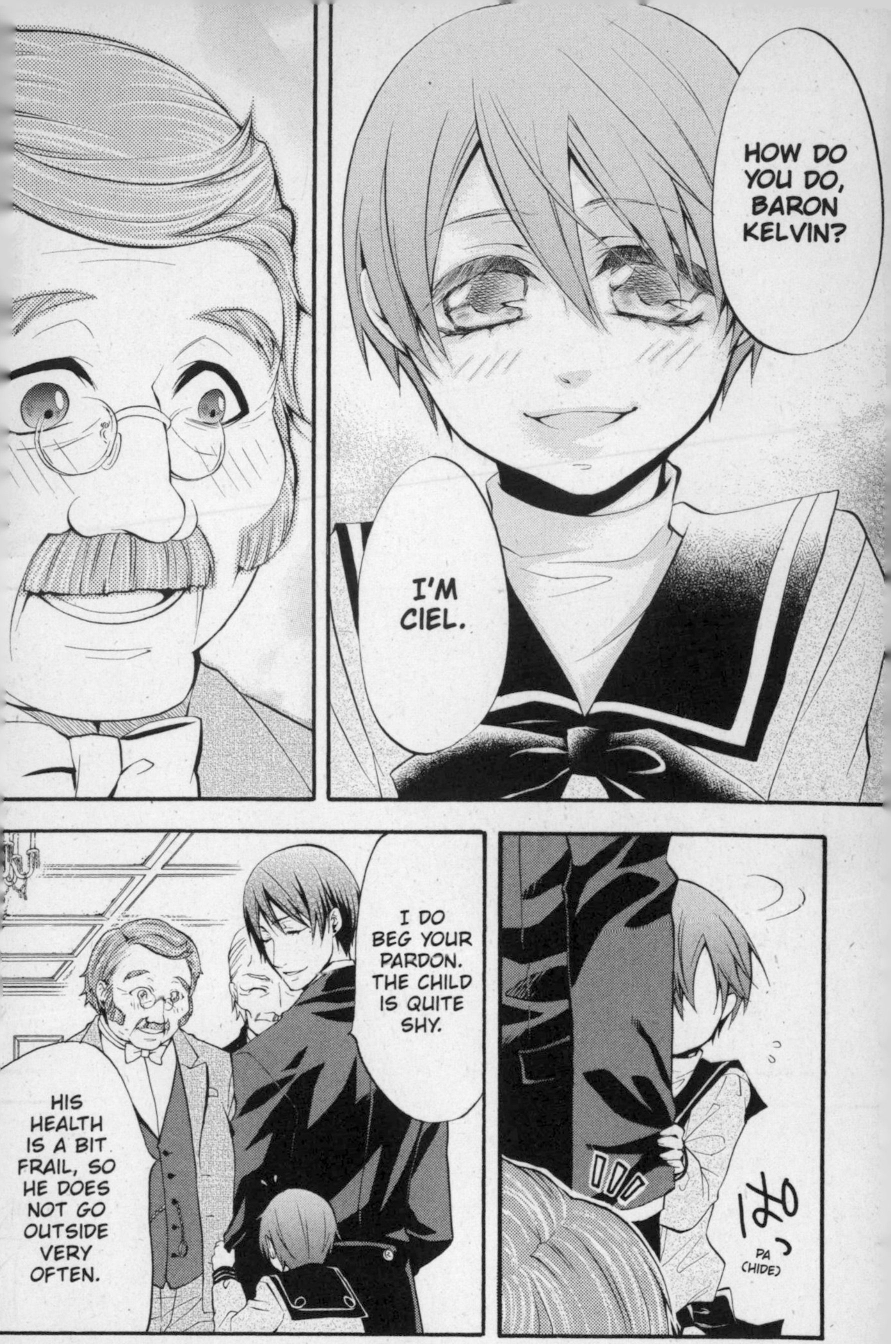
HOW DO YOU DO, BARON KELVIN?
I'M CIEL.
はっ
PA (HIDE)
I DO BEG YOUR PARDON. THE CHILD IS QUITE SHY.
HIS HEALTH IS A BIT FRAIL, SO HE DOES NOT GO OUTSIDE VERY OFTEN.

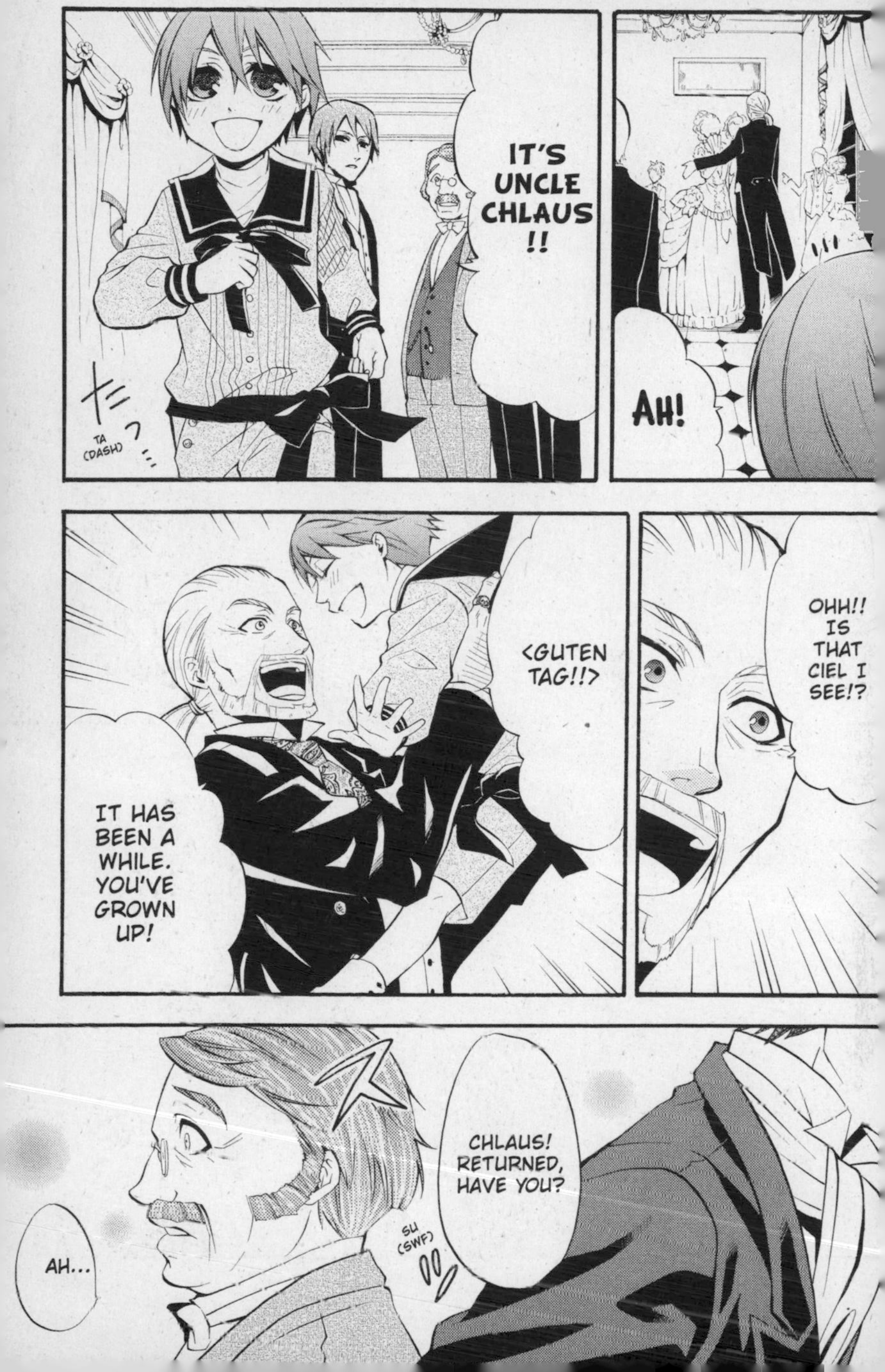
AH!
IT'S UNCLE CHLAUS!!
TA (DASH)
OHH!! IS THAT CIEL I SEE!?
<GUTEN TAG!!>
IT HAS BEEN A WHILE. YOU'VE GROWN UP!
CHLAUS! RETURNED, HAVE YOU?
SU (SWF)
AH...

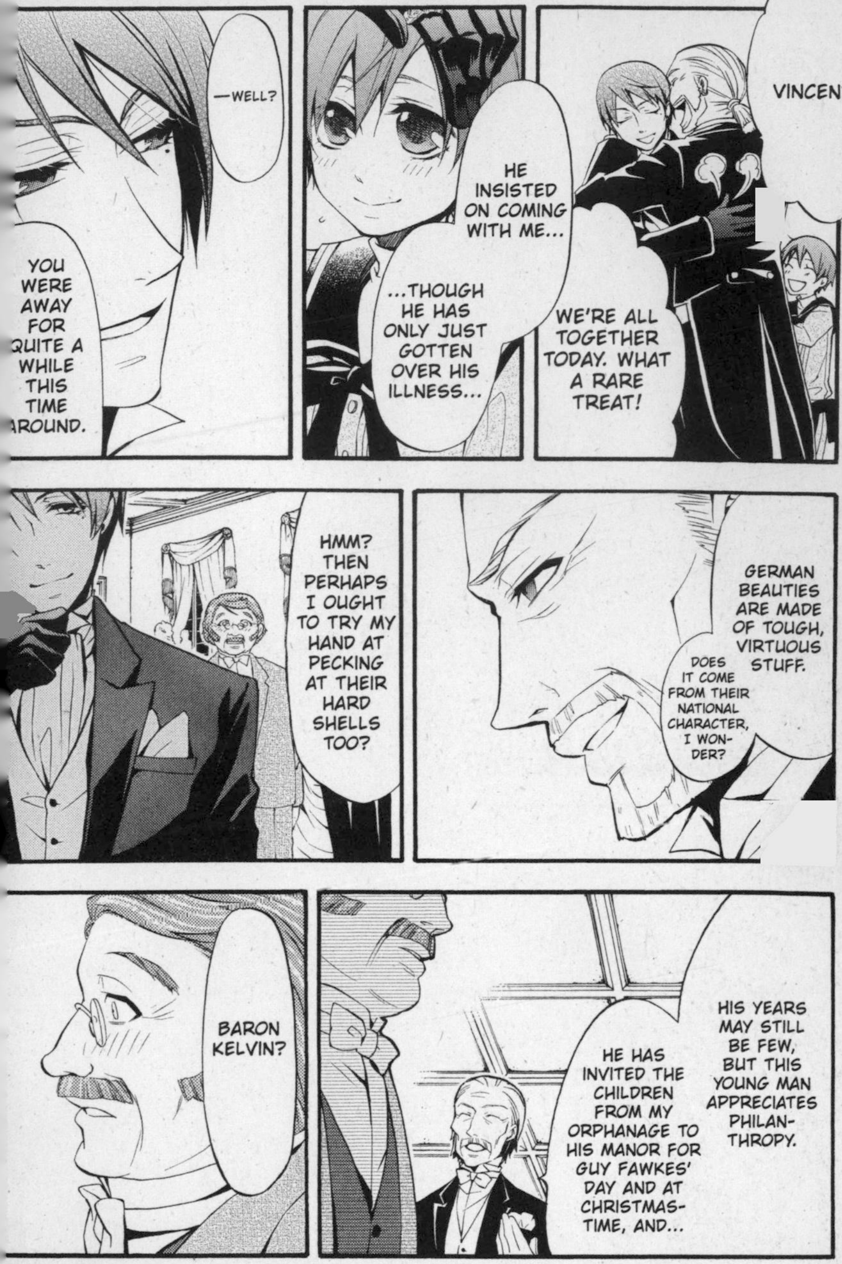
VINCENT.
WE'RE ALL TOGETHER TODAY. WHAT A RARE TREAT!
HE INSISTED ON COMING WITH ME...
...THOUGH HE HAS ONLY JUST GOTTEN OVER HIS ILLNESS...
—WELL?
YOU WERE AWAY FOR QUITE A WHILE THIS TIME AROUND.
GERMAN BEAUTIES ARE MADE OF TOUGH, VIRTUOUS STUFF.
DOES IT COME FROM THEIR NATIONAL CHARACTER, I WONDER?
HMM? THEN PERHAPS I OUGHT TO TRY MY HAND AT PECKING AT THEIR HARD SHELLS TOO?
HIS YEARS MAY STILL BE FEW, BUT THIS YOUNG MAN APPRECIATES PHILANTHROPY.
HE HAS INVITED THE CHILDREN FROM MY ORPHANAGE TO HIS MANOR FOR GUY FAWKES' DAY AND AT CHRISTMASTIME, AND...
BARON KELVIN?

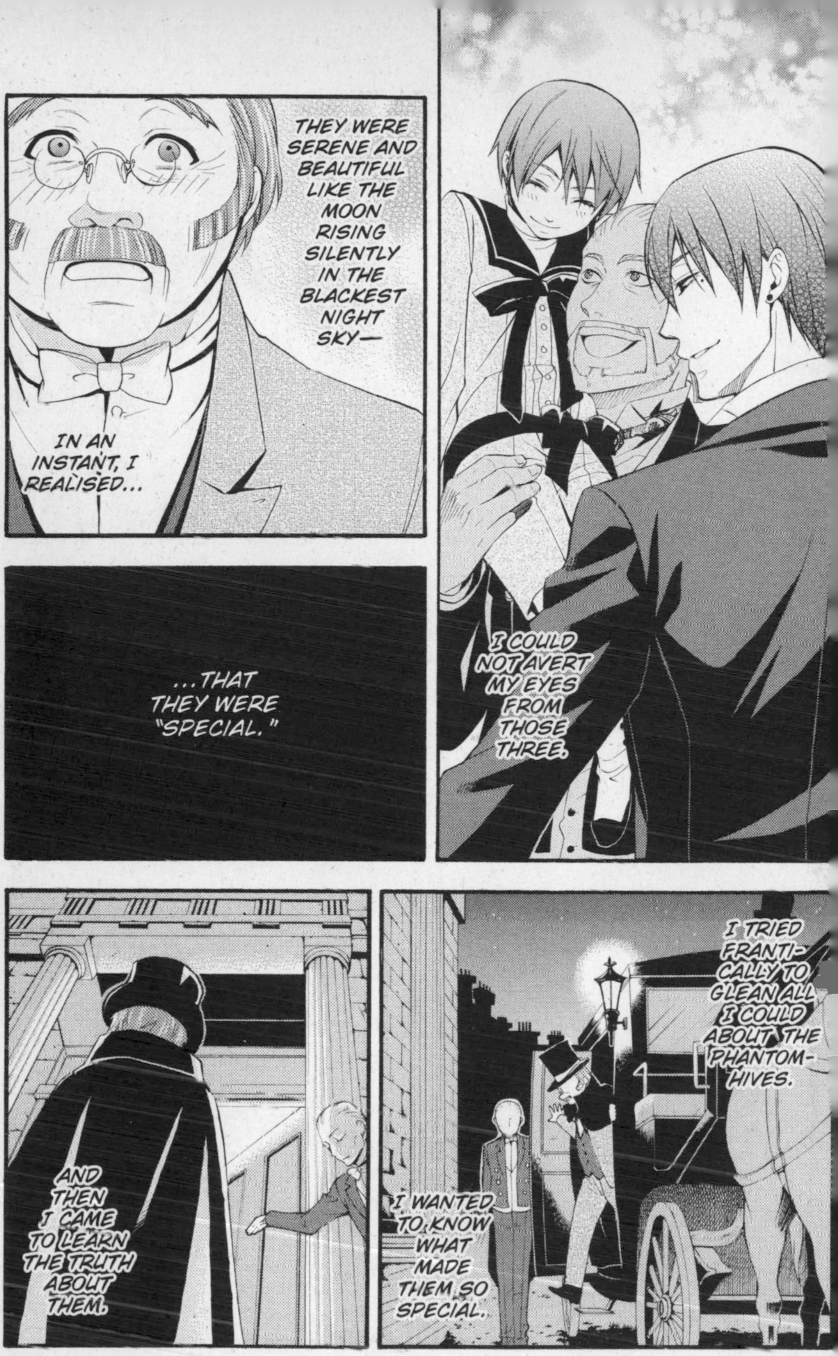
I COULD NOT AVERT MY EYES FROM THOSE THREE.
THEY WERE SERENE AND BEAUTIFUL LIKE THE MOON RISING SILENTLY IN THE BLACKEST NIGHT SKY—
IN AN INSTANT, I REALISED...
...THAT THEY WERE "SPECIAL."
I TRIED FRANTI-CALLY TO GLEAN ALL I COULD ABOUT THE PHANTOM-HIVES.
I WANTED TO KNOW WHAT MADE THEM SO SPECIAL.
AND THEN I CAME TO LEARN THE TRUTH ABOUT THEM.

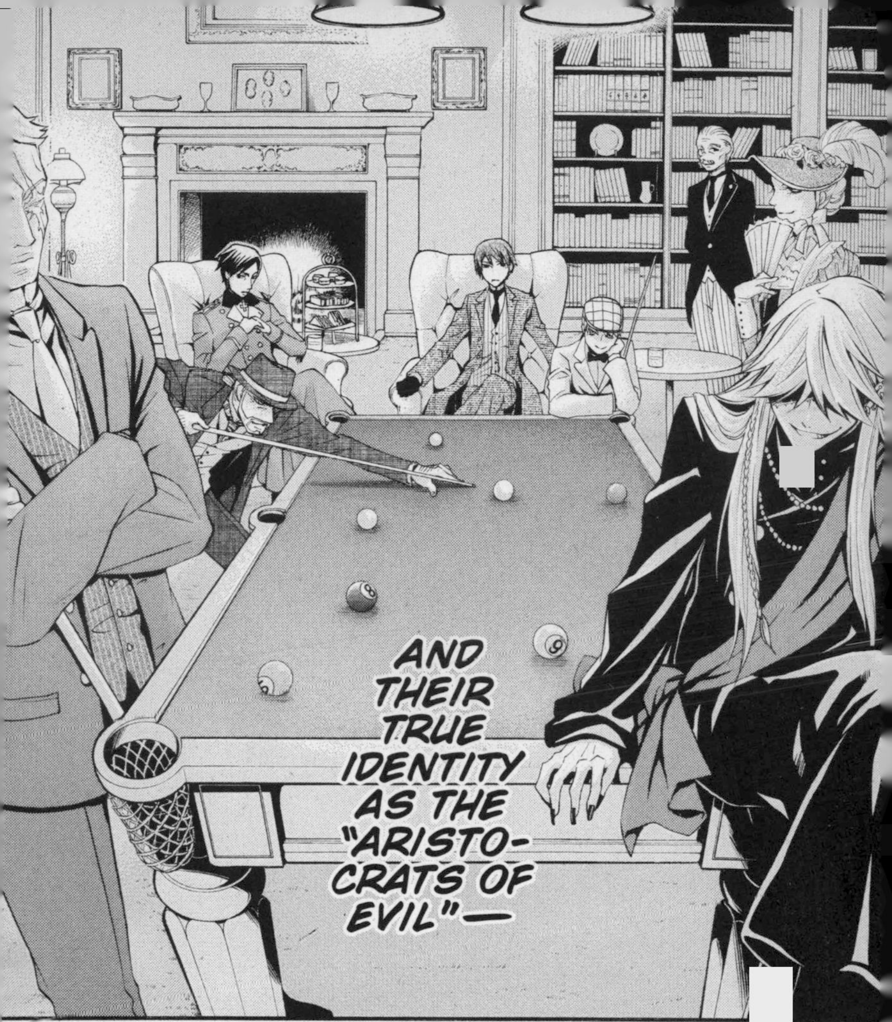
AND THEIR TRUE IDENTITY AS THE "ARISTO-CRATS OF EVIL"—
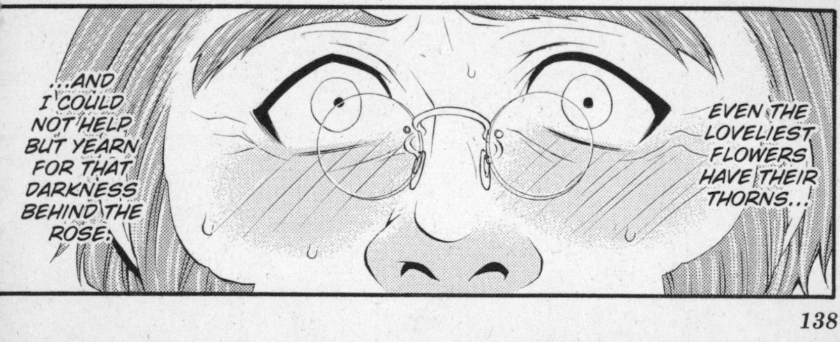
EVEN THE LOVELIEST FLOWERS HAVE THEIR THORNS...
...AND I COULD NOT HELP BUT YEARN FOR THAT DARKNESS BEHIND THE ROSE.

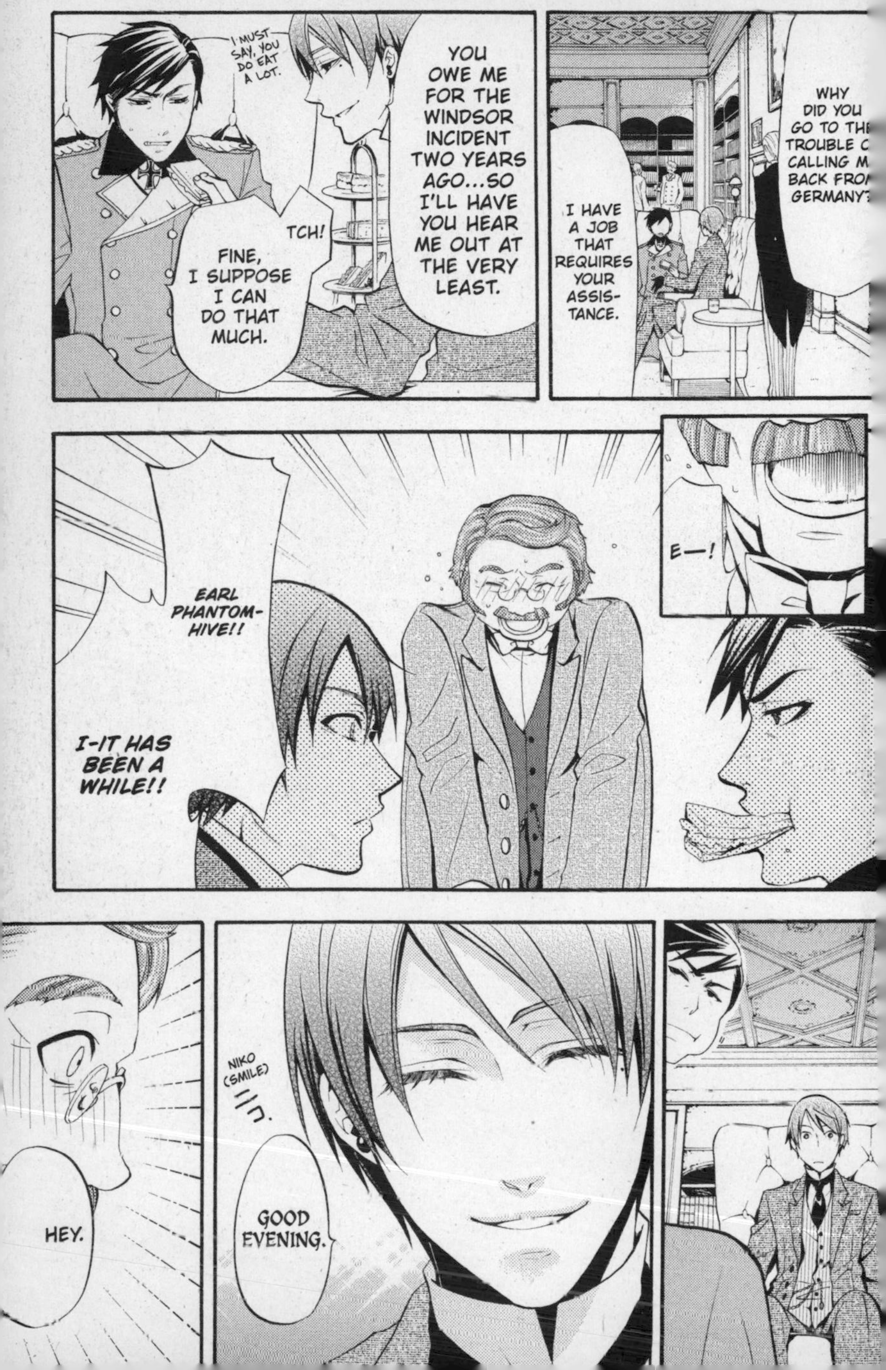
WHY DID YOU GO TO THE TROUBLE C CALLING M BACK FROM GERMANY?
I HAVE A JOB THAT REQUIRES YOUR ASSISTANCE.
YOU OWE ME FOR THE WINDSOR INCIDENT TWO YEARS AGO...SO I'LL HAVE YOU HEAR ME OUT AT THE VERY LEAST.
I MUST SAY, YOU DO EAT A LOT.
TCH!
FINE, I SUPPOSE I CAN DO THAT MUCH.
E—!
EARL PHANTOMHIVE!!
I-IT HAS BEEN A WHILE!!
NIKO (SMILE)
ニコ
GOOD EVENING.
HEY.

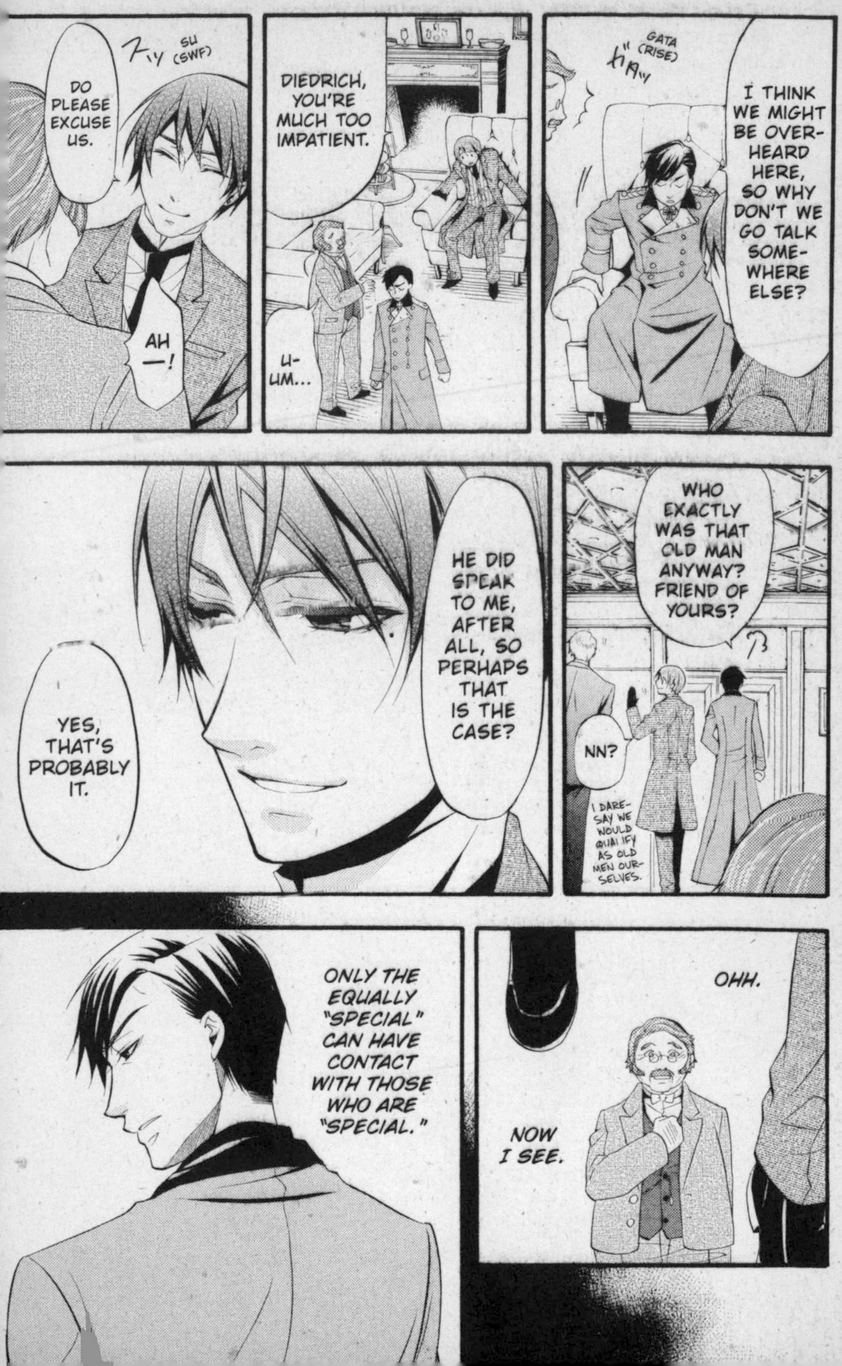
GATA (RISE)
I THINK WE MIGHT BE OVER-HEARD HERE, SO WHY DON'T WE GO TALK SOME-WHERE ELSE?
DIEDRICH, YOU'RE MUCH TOO IMPATIENT.
U-UM...
SU (SWF)
DO PLEASE EXCUSE US.
AH—!
WHO EXACTLY WAS THAT OLD MAN ANYWAY? FRIEND OF YOURS?
NN?
I DARE-SAY WE WOULD QUALIFY AS OLD MEN OUR-SELVES.
HE DID SPEAK TO ME, AFTER ALL, SO PERHAPS THAT IS THE CASE?
YES, THAT'S PROBABLY IT.
OHH.
NOW I SEE.
ONLY THE EQUALLY "SPECIAL" CAN HAVE CONTACT WITH THOSE WHO ARE "SPECIAL."

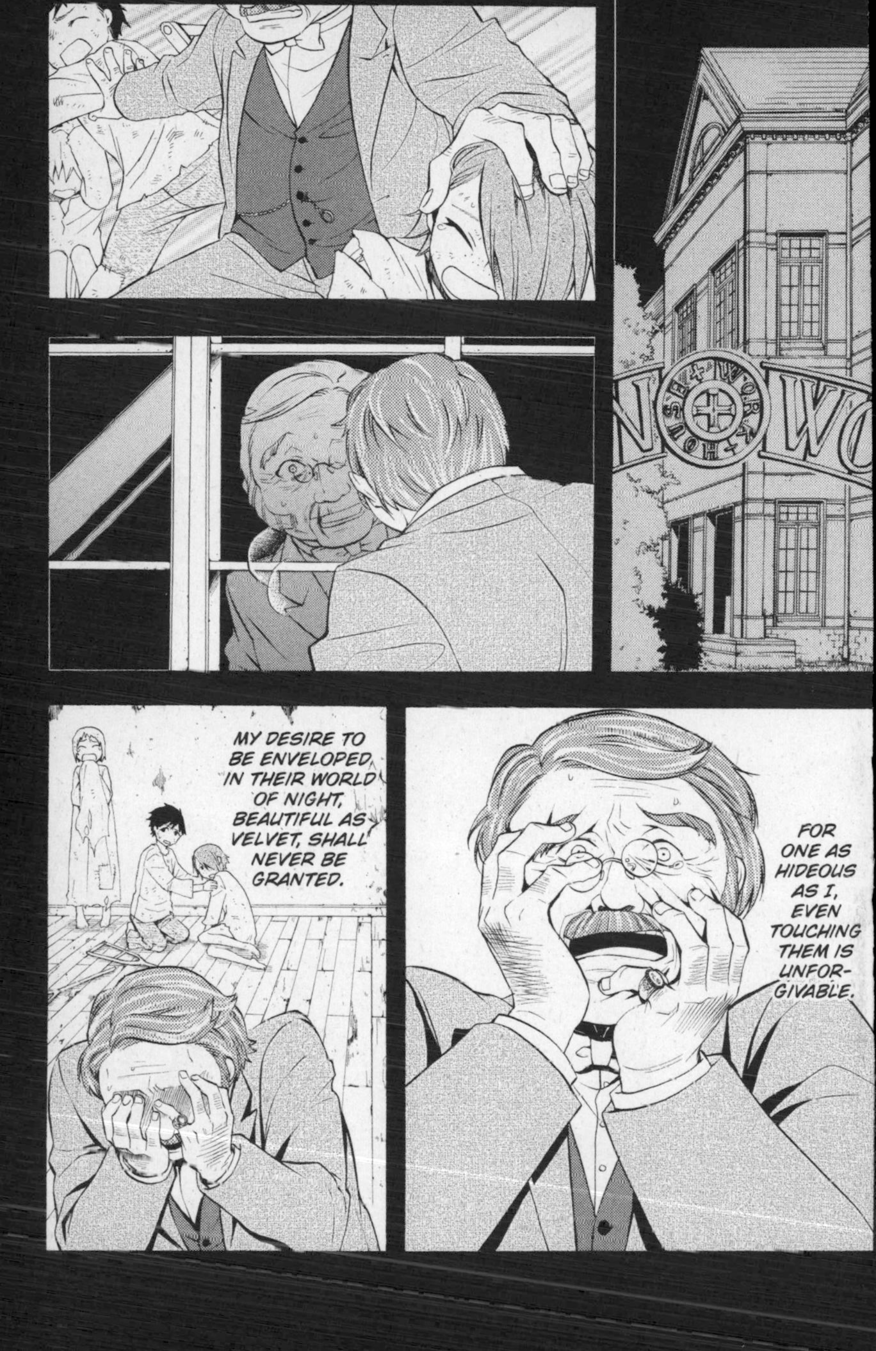
FOR ONE AS HIDEOUS AS I, EVEN TOUCHING THEM IS UNFORGIVABLE.
MY DESIRE TO BE ENVELOPED IN THEIR WORLD OF NIGHT, BEAUTIFUL AS VELVET, SHALL NEVER BE GRANTED.

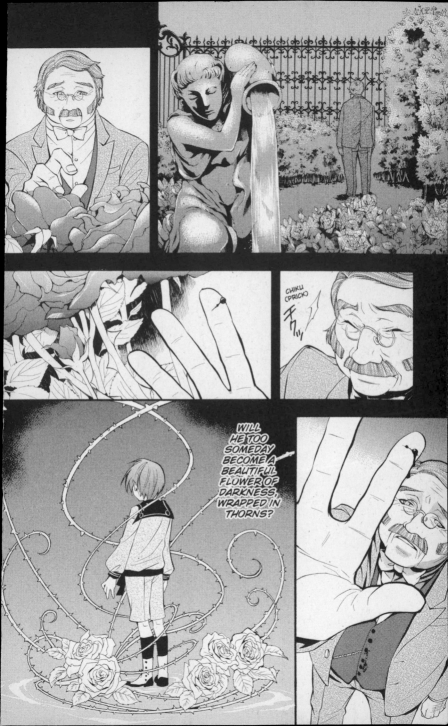

CHIKU
(PRICK)

WILL HE TOO SOMEDAY BECOME A BEAUTIFUL FLOWER OF DARKNESS, WRAPPED IN THORNS?

WILL HE BECOME THE LONE, COLD MOON THAT SHINES IN THAT WORLD OF NIGHT?

SOME-ONE I CAN NEVER REACH...

NOOOO——!!!

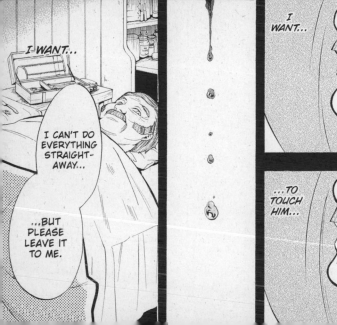

I WANT...

I CAN'T DO EVERYTHING STRAIGHT-AWAY...

...BUT PLEASE LEAVE IT TO ME.

I WANT...

...TO TOUCH HIM...

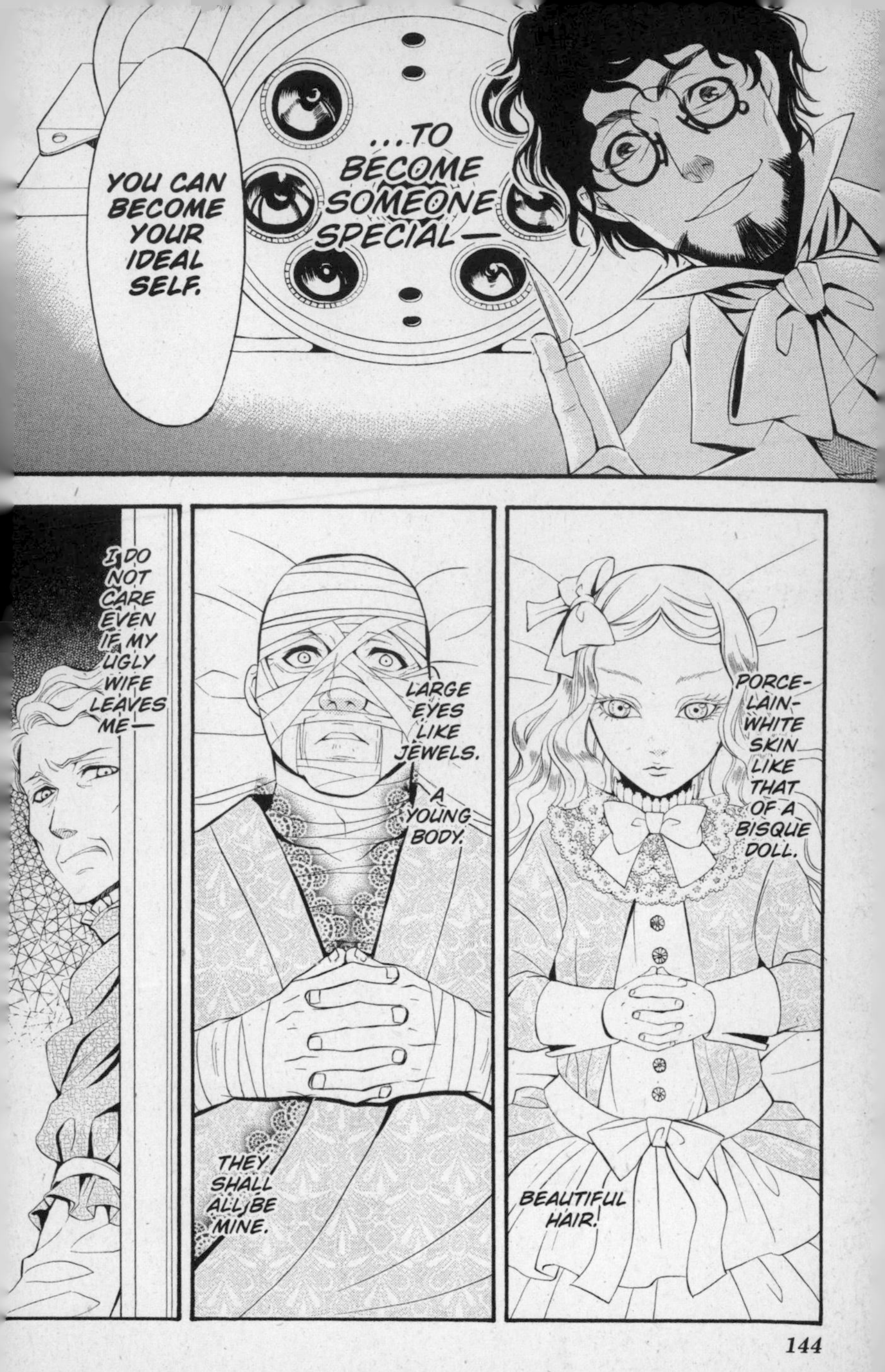
...TO BECOME SOMEONE SPECIAL—
YOU CAN BECOME YOUR IDEAL SELF.
PORCE-LAIN-WHITE SKIN LIKE THAT OF A BISQUE DOLL.
BEAUTIFUL HAIR.
LARGE EYES LIKE JEWELS.
A YOUNG BODY.
THEY SHALL ALL BE MINE.
I DO NOT CARE EVEN IF MY UGLY WIFE LEAVES ME—

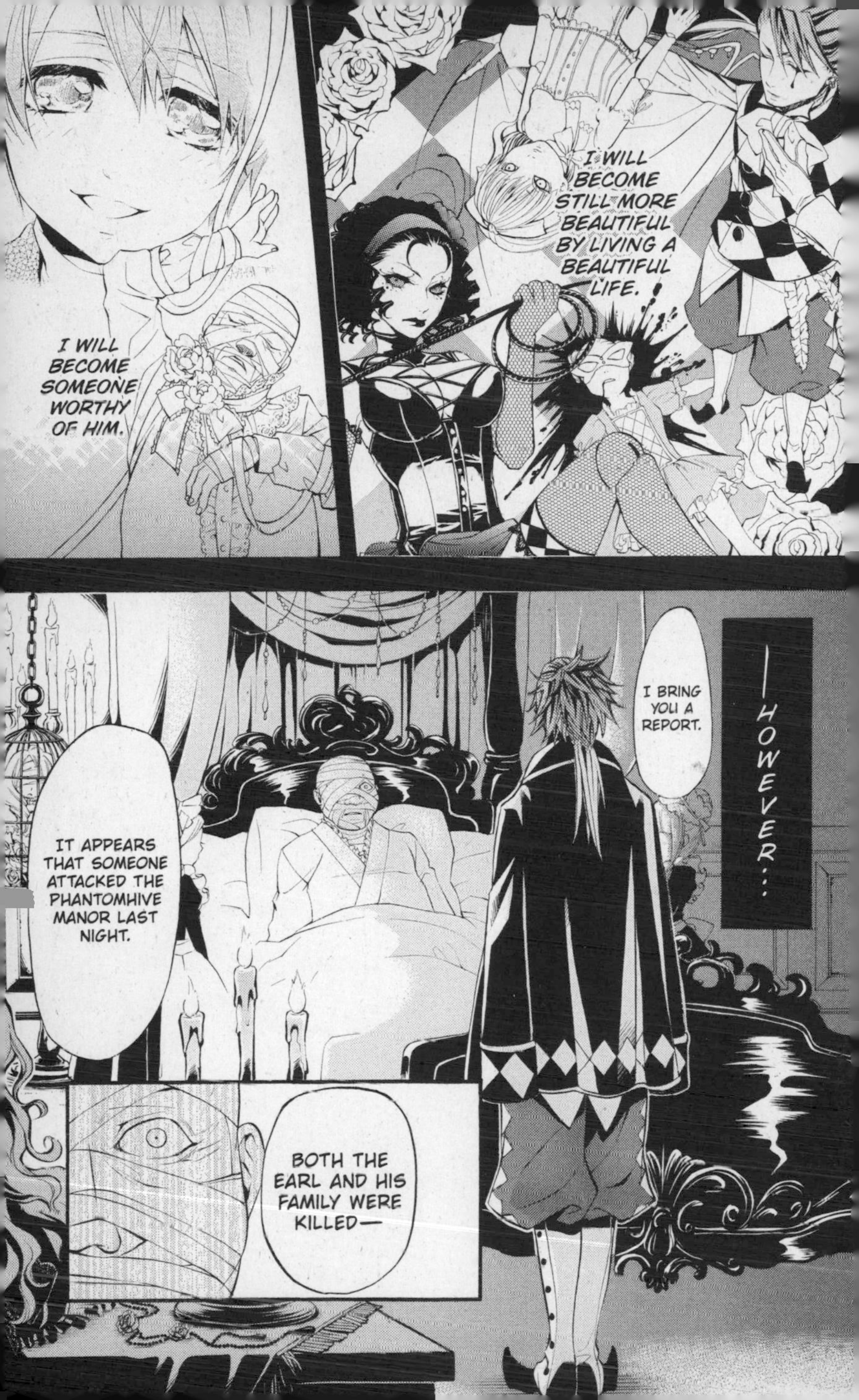
I WILL BECOME STILL MORE BEAUTIFUL BY LIVING A BEAUTIFUL LIFE.
I WILL BECOME SOMEONE WORTHY OF HIM.
—HOWEVER...
I BRING YOU A REPORT.
IT APPEARS THAT SOMEONE ATTACKED THE PHANTOMHIVE MANOR LAST NIGHT.
BOTH THE EARL AND HIS FAMILY WERE KILLED—

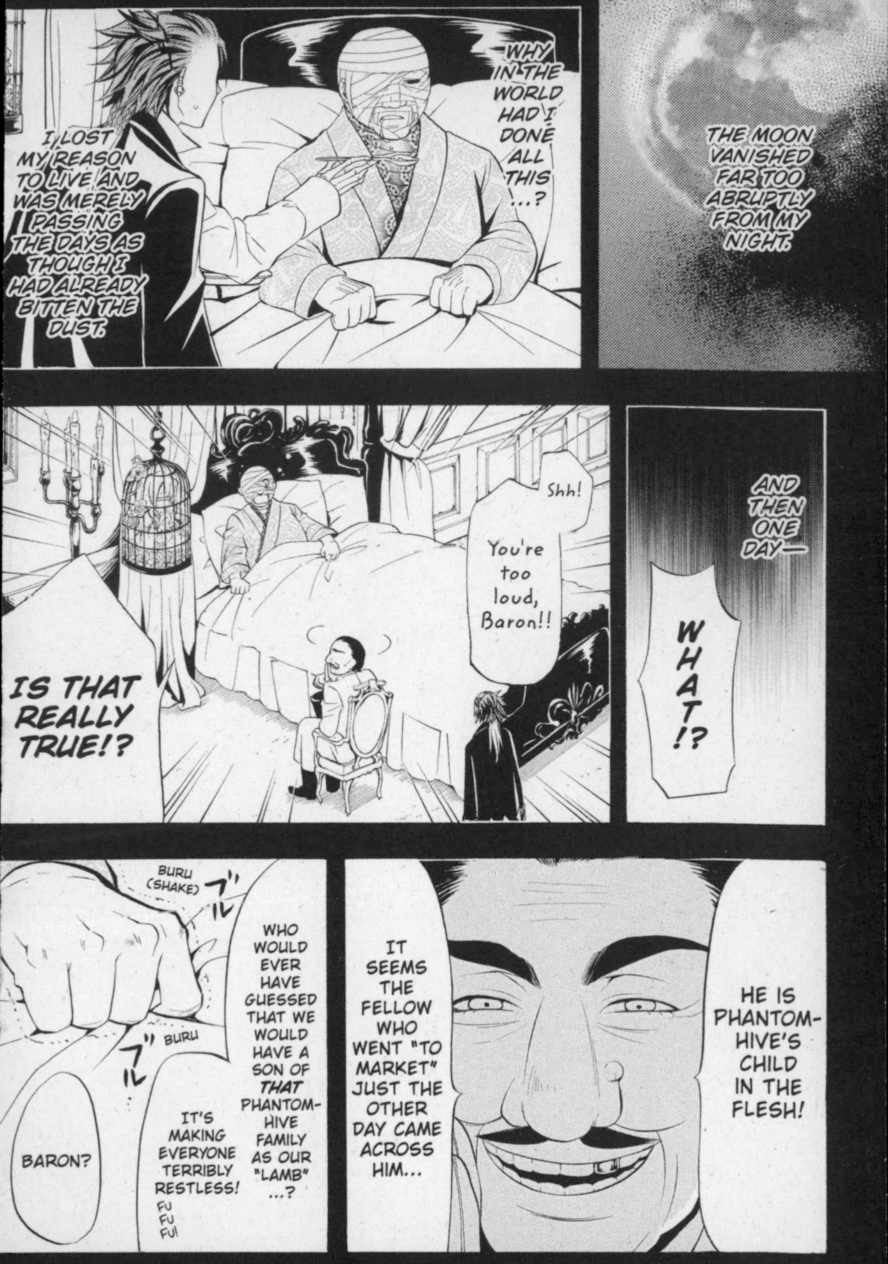
THE MOON VANISHED FAR TOO ABRUPTLY FROM MY NIGHT.
WHY IN THE WORLD HAD I DONE ALL THIS ...?
I LOST MY REASON TO LIVE AND WAS MERELY PASSING THE DAYS AS THOUGH I HAD ALREADY BITTEN THE DUST.
AND THEN ONE DAY—
WHAT!?
Shh!
You're too loud, Baron!!
IS THAT REALLY TRUE!?
HE IS PHANTOM-HIVE'S CHILD IN THE FLESH!
IT SEEMS THE FELLOW WHO WENT "TO MARKET" JUST THE OTHER DAY CAME ACROSS HIM...
BURU (SHAKE)
WHO WOULD EVER HAVE GUESSED THAT WE WOULD HAVE A SON OF *THAT* PHANTOM-HIVE FAMILY AS OUR "LAMB" ...?
BURU
IT'S MAKING EVERYONE TERRIBLY RESTLESS!
FU FU FU!
BARON?

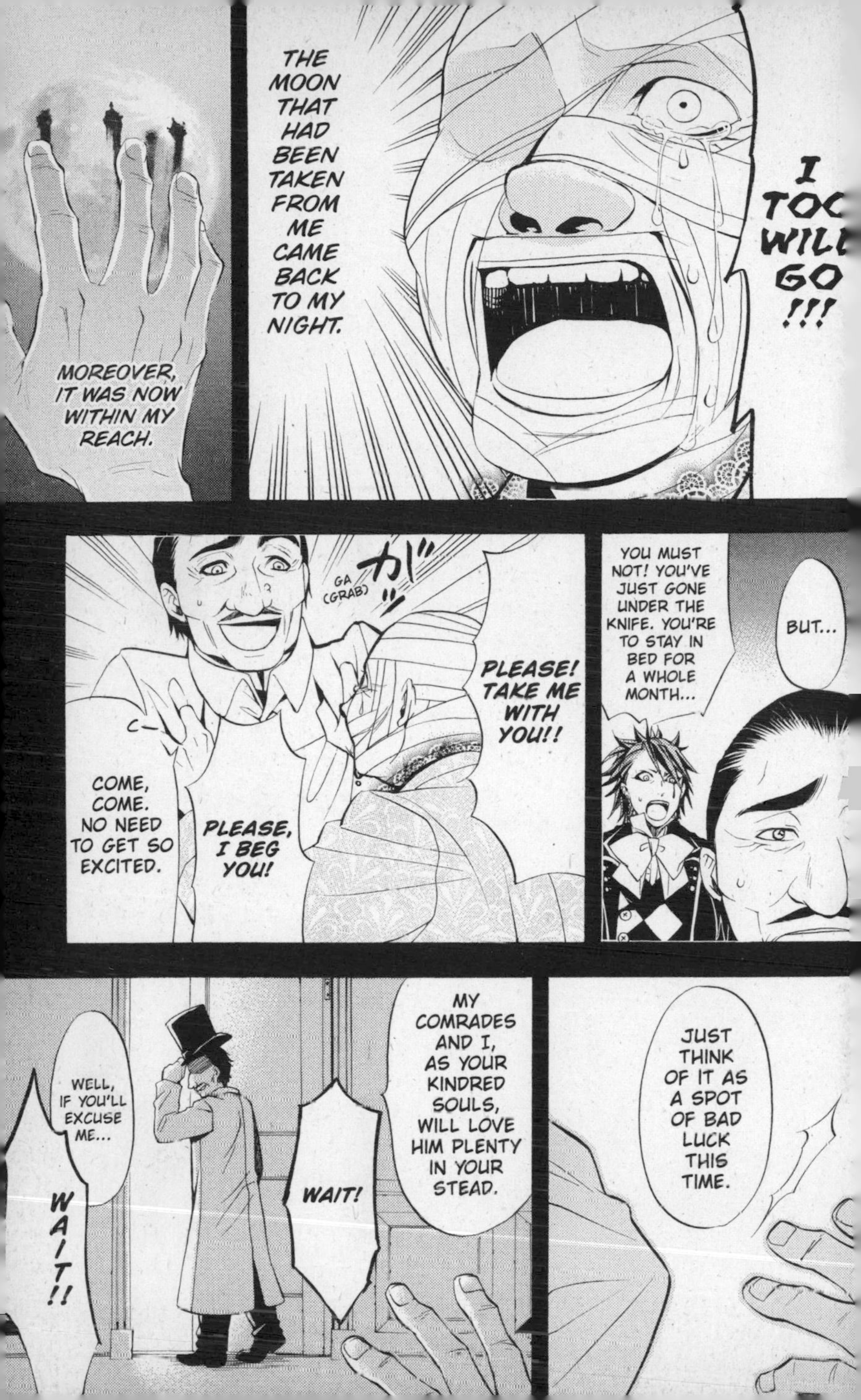
THE MOON THAT HAD BEEN TAKEN FROM ME CAME BACK TO MY NIGHT.
I TOO WILL GO!!!
MOREOVER, IT WAS NOW WITHIN MY REACH.
BUT...
YOU MUST NOT! YOU'VE JUST GONE UNDER THE KNIFE. YOU'RE TO STAY IN BED FOR A WHOLE MONTH...
PLEASE! TAKE ME WITH YOU!!
GA (GRAB)
C—
PLEASE, I BEG YOU!
COME, COME. NO NEED TO GET SO EXCITED.
JUST THINK OF IT AS A SPOT OF BAD LUCK THIS TIME.
MY COMRADES AND I, AS YOUR KINDRED SOULS, WILL LOVE HIM PLENTY IN YOUR STEAD.
WAIT!
WELL, IF YOU'LL EXCUSE ME...
WAIT!!

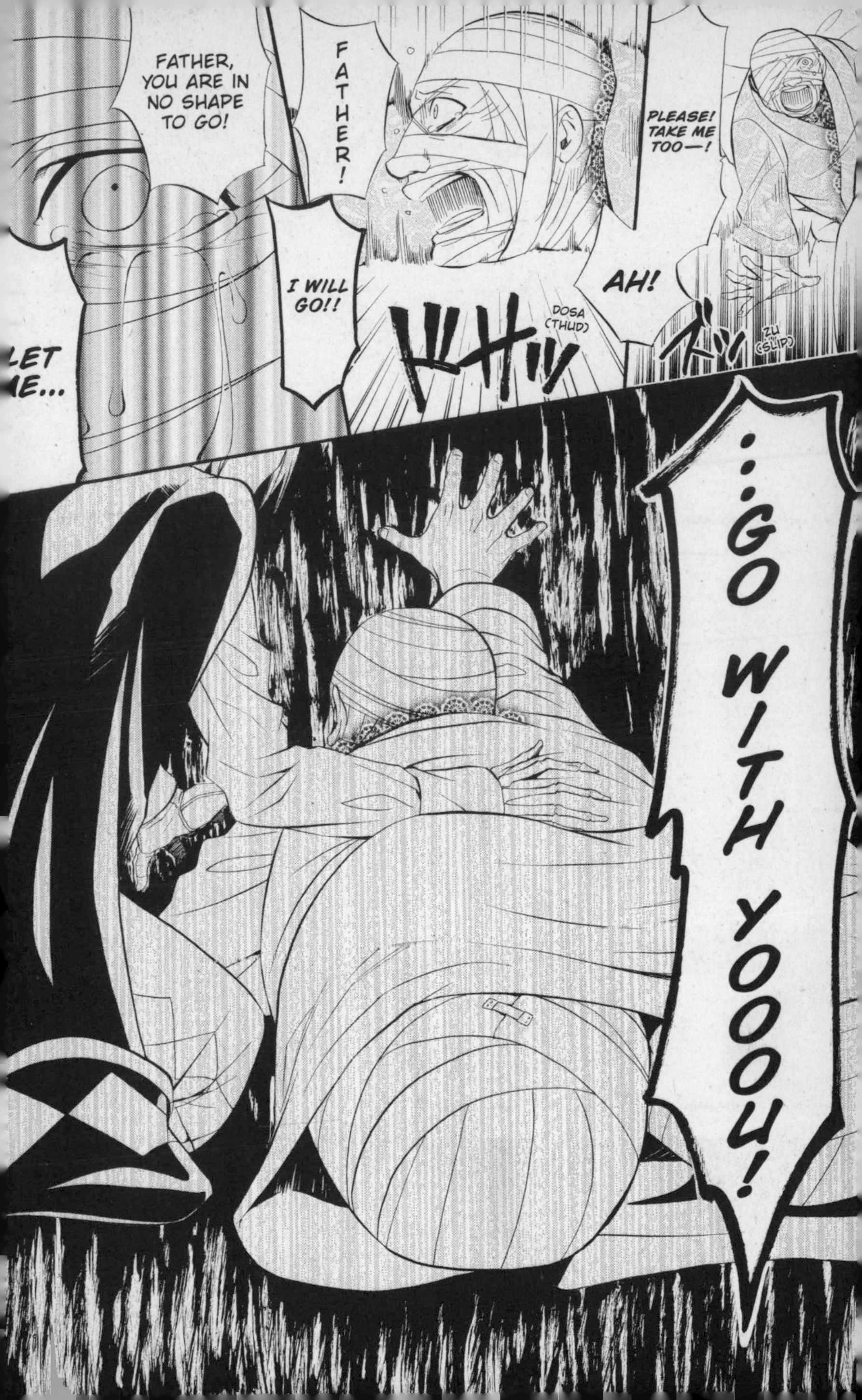
PLEASE! TAKE ME TOO—!
AH!
ズッ
ZU (SLIP)
FATHER!
I WILL GO!!
ドサッ
DOSA (THUD)
FATHER, YOU ARE IN NO SHAPE TO GO!
LET ME...
...GO WITH YOOOOU!

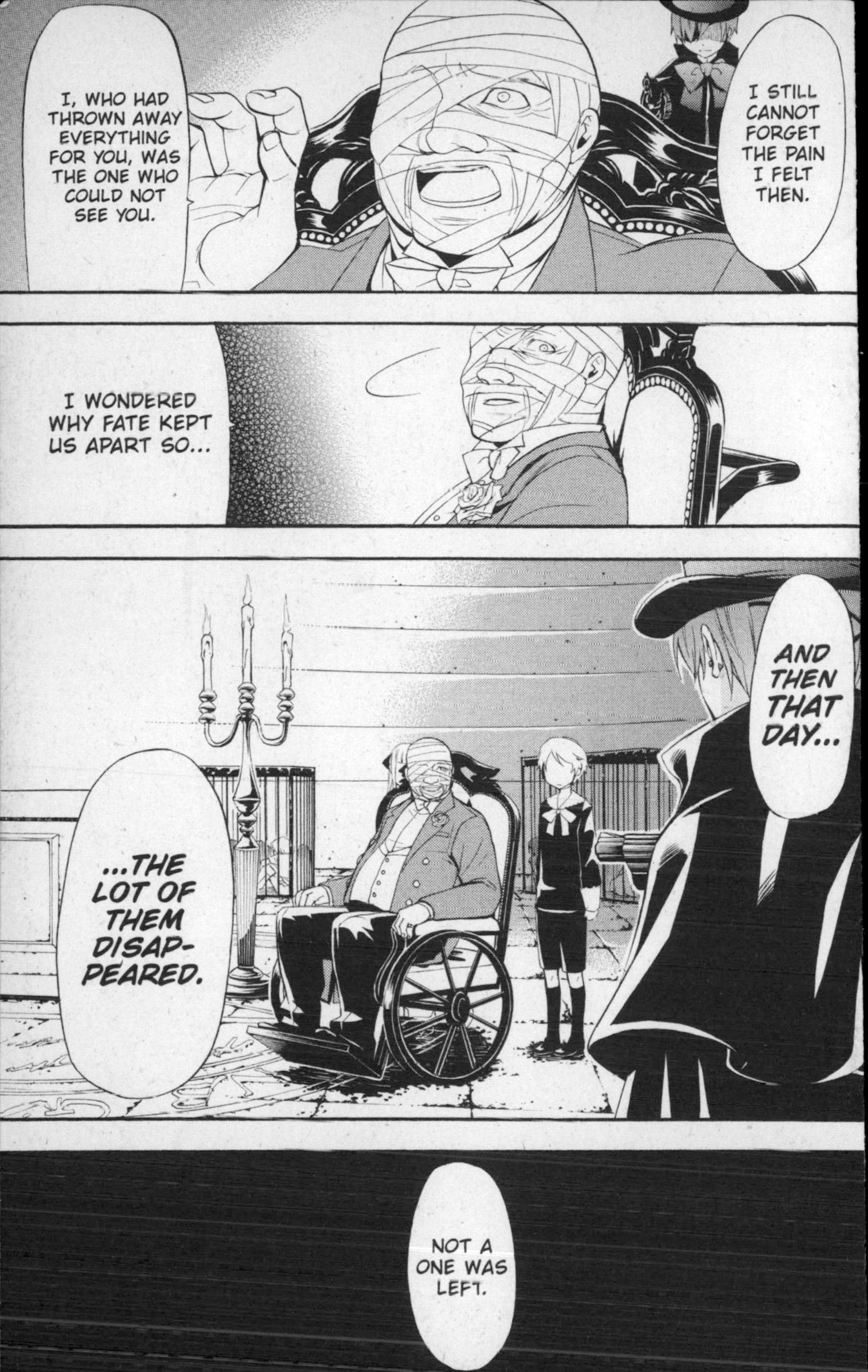
I STILL CANNOT FORGET THE PAIN I FELT THEN.
I, WHO HAD THROWN AWAY EVERYTHING FOR YOU, WAS THE ONE WHO COULD NOT SEE YOU.
I WONDERED WHY FATE KEPT US APART SO...
AND THEN THAT DAY...
...THE LOT OF THEM DISAP-PEARED.
NOT A ONE WAS LEFT.

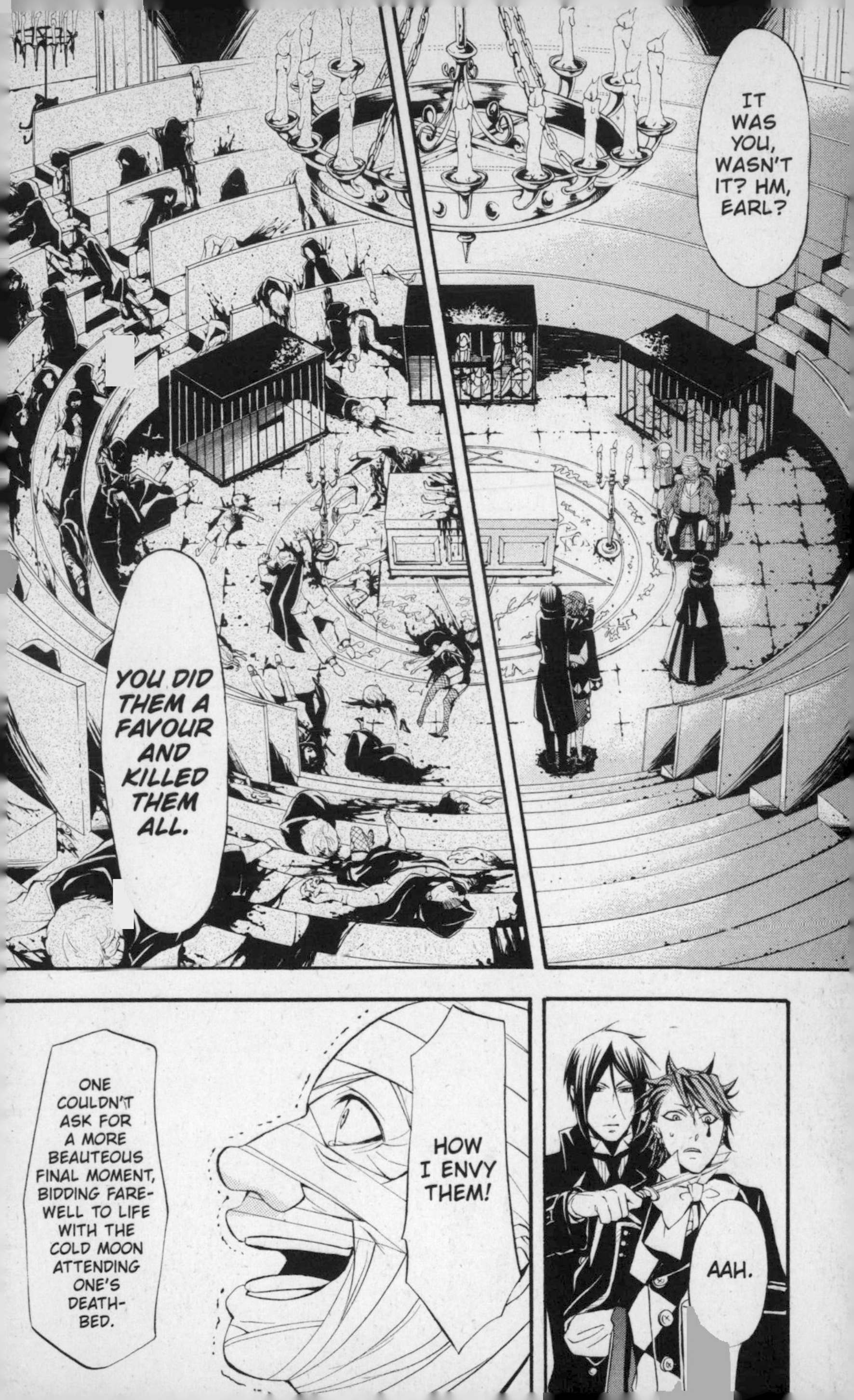
IT WAS YOU, WASN'T IT? HM, EARL?
YOU DID THEM A FAVOUR AND KILLED THEM ALL.
AAH.
HOW I ENVY THEM!
ONE COULDN'T ASK FOR A MORE BEAUTEOUS FINAL MOMENT, BIDDING FARE-WELL TO LIFE WITH THE COLD MOON ATTENDING ONE'S DEATH-BED.

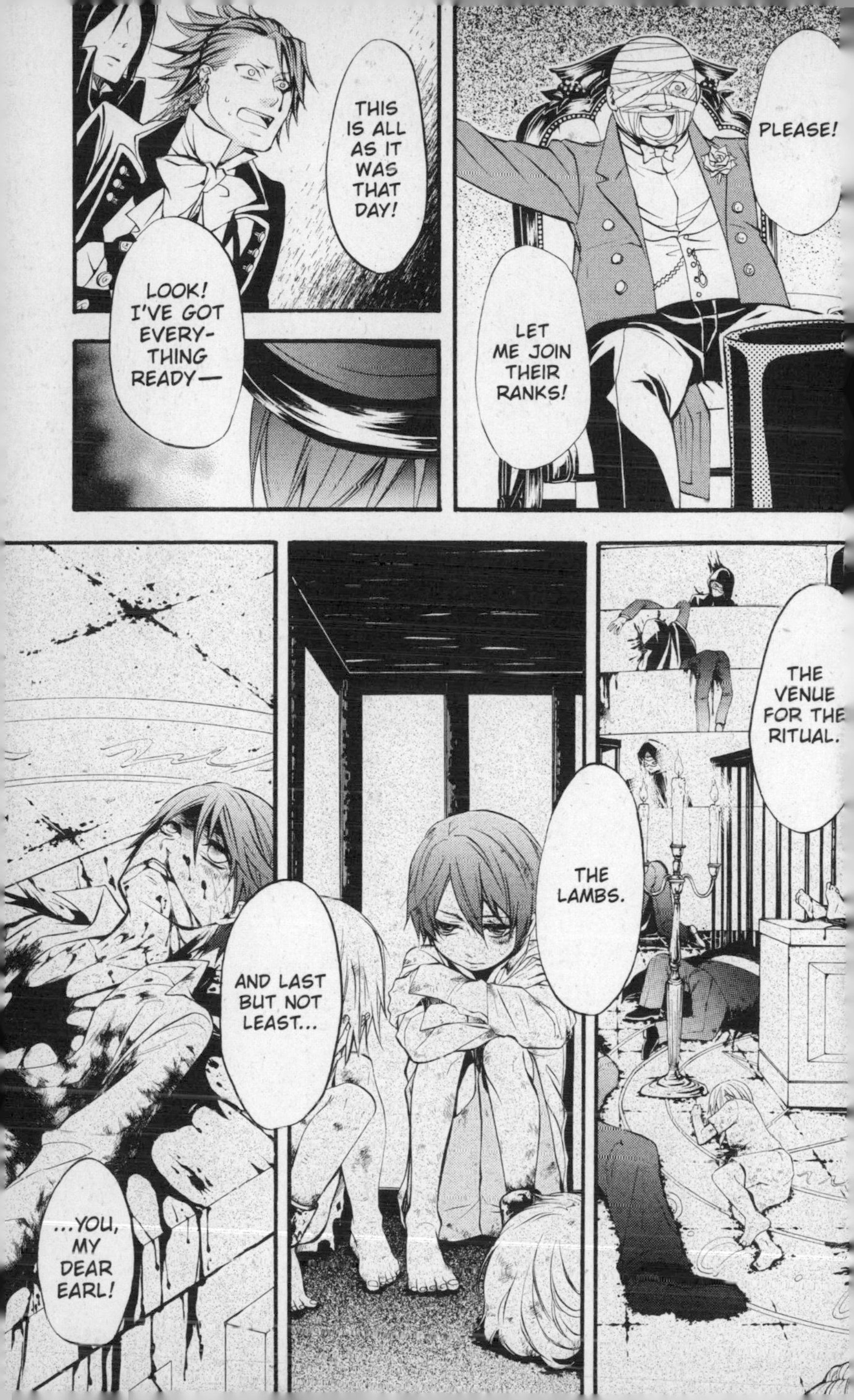
PLEASE!
LET ME JOIN THEIR RANKS!
THIS IS ALL AS IT WAS THAT DAY!
LOOK! I'VE GOT EVERY-THING READY—
THE VENUE FOR THE RITUAL.
THE LAMBS.
AND LAST BUT NOT LEAST...
...YOU, MY DEAR EARL!

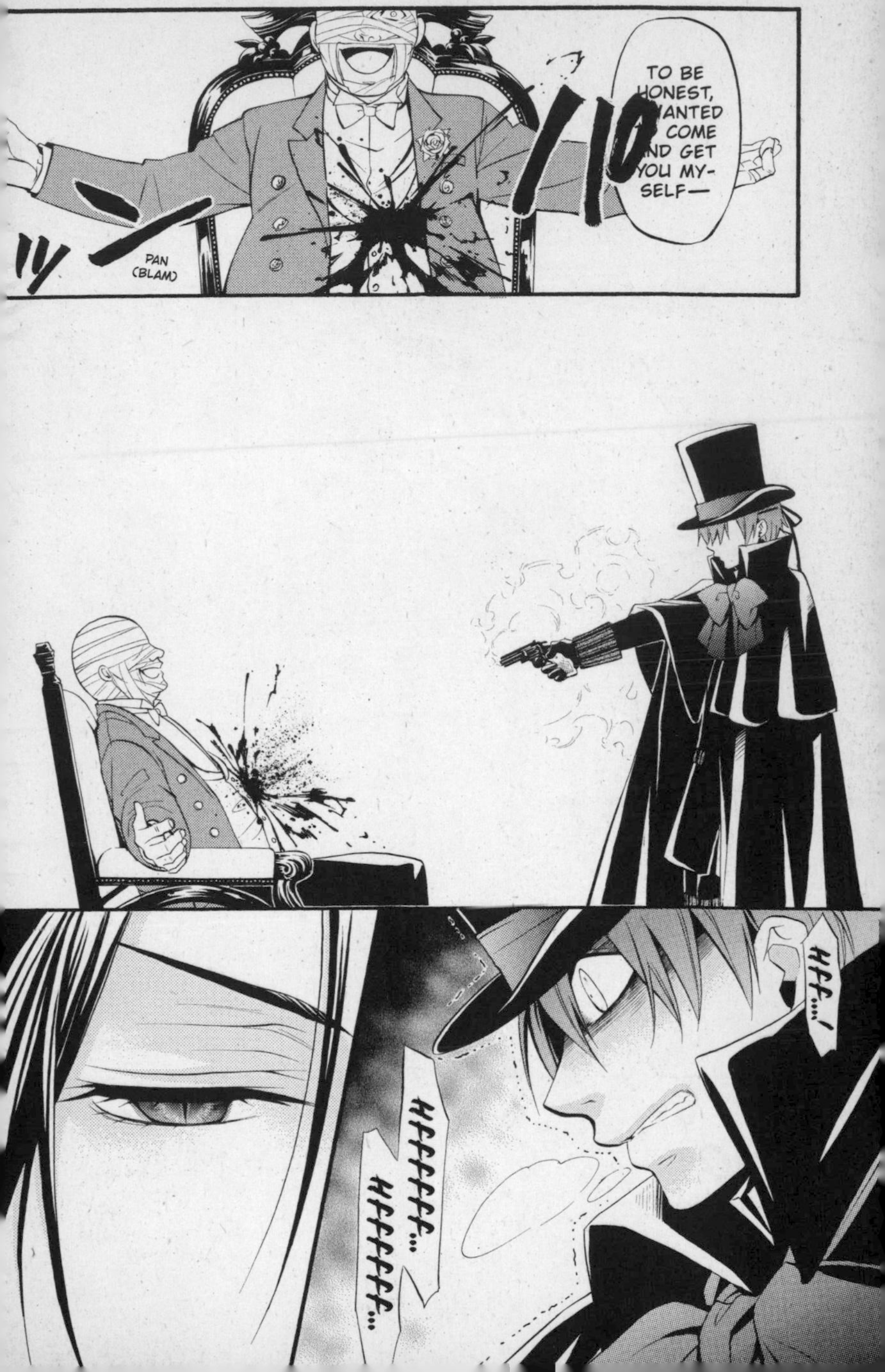
TO BE HONEST, I WANTED TO COME AND GET YOU MY-SELF—
PAN (BLAM)
HFF...!
HFFFFFF...
HFFFFFFF...

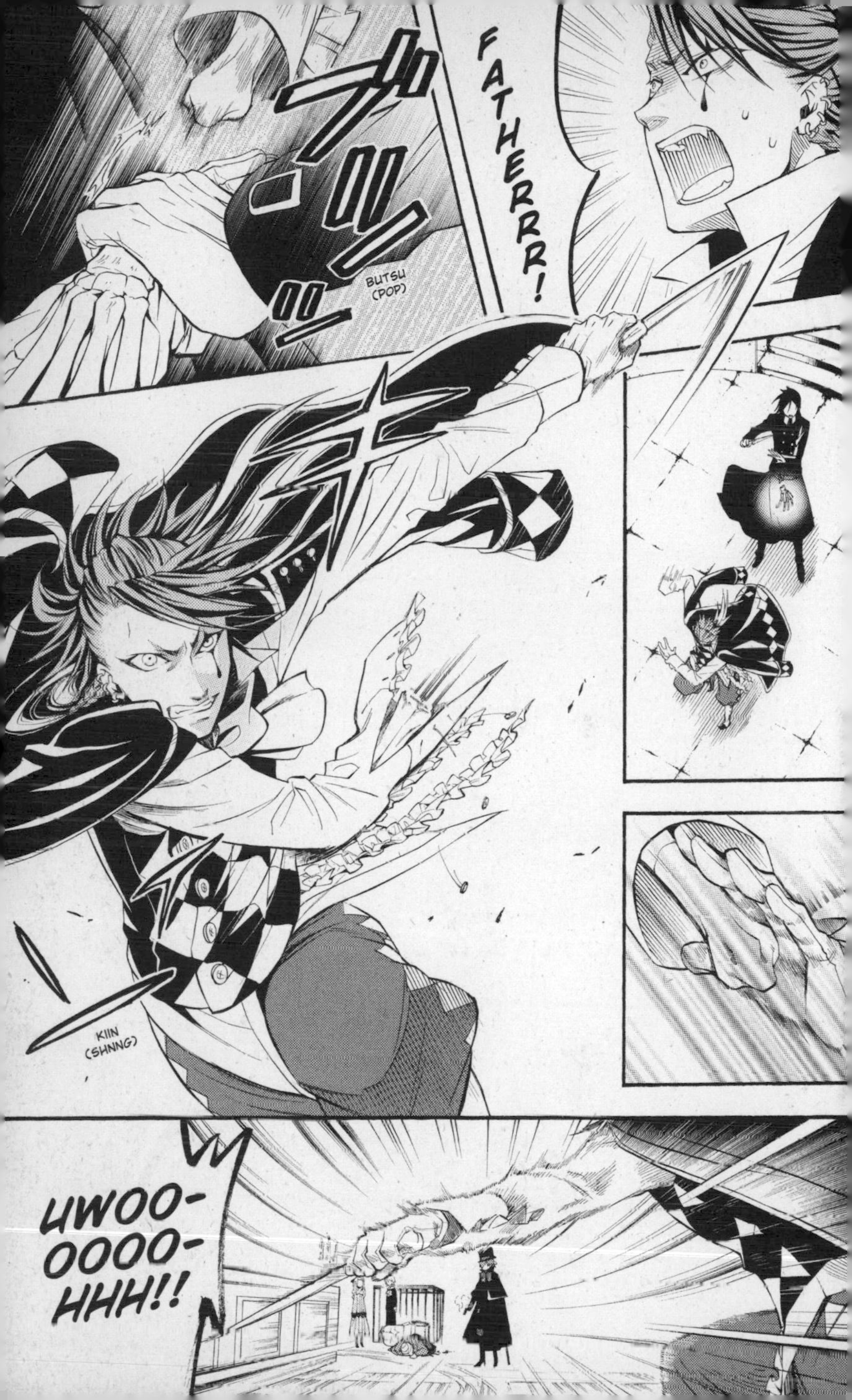
FATHERRR!
BUTSU (POP)
KIIN (SHNNG)
UWOO-OOOO-HHH!!

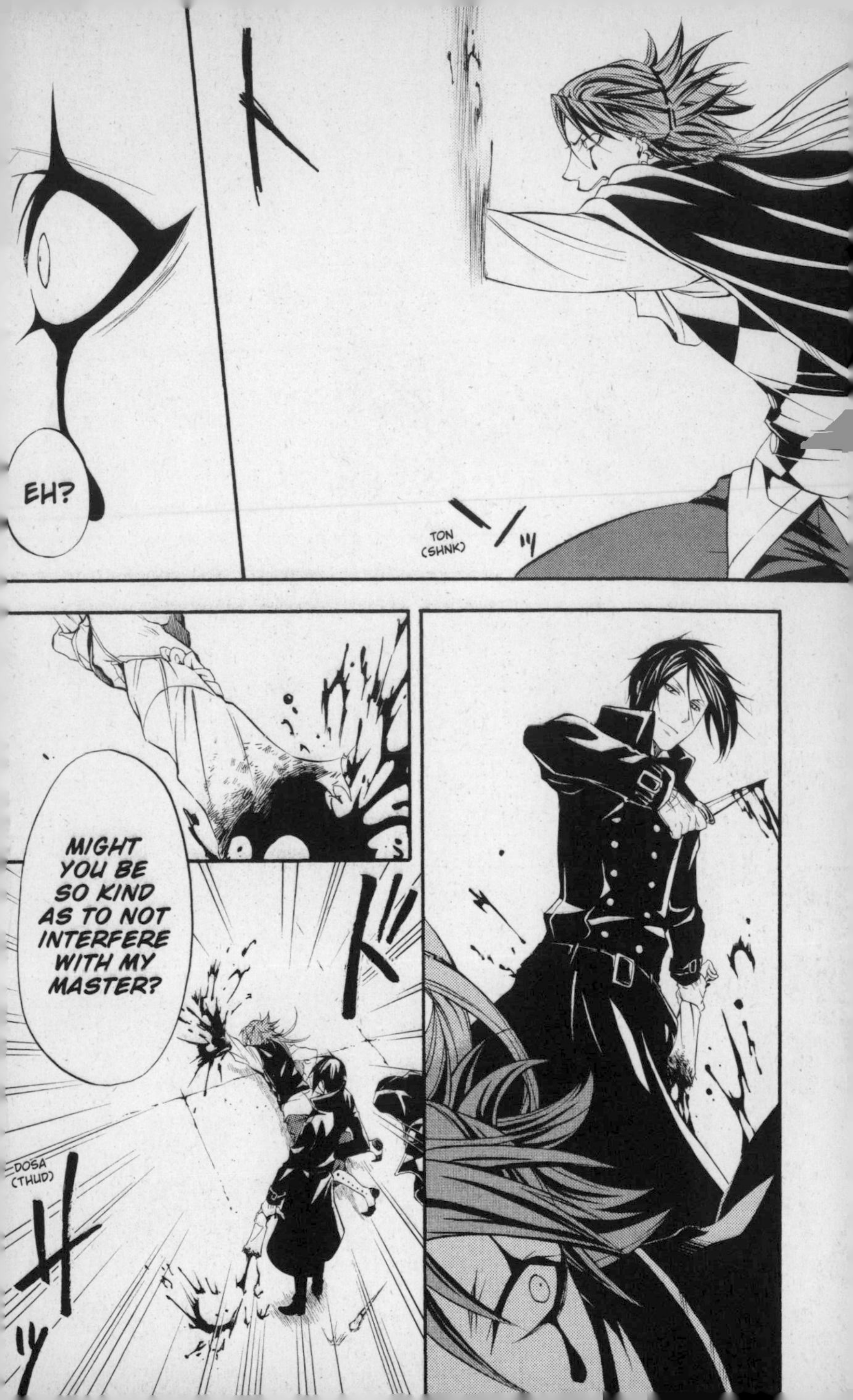
TON
(SHNK)
EH?
MIGHT YOU BE SO KIND AS TO NOT INTERFERE WITH MY MASTER?
DOSA
(THUD)

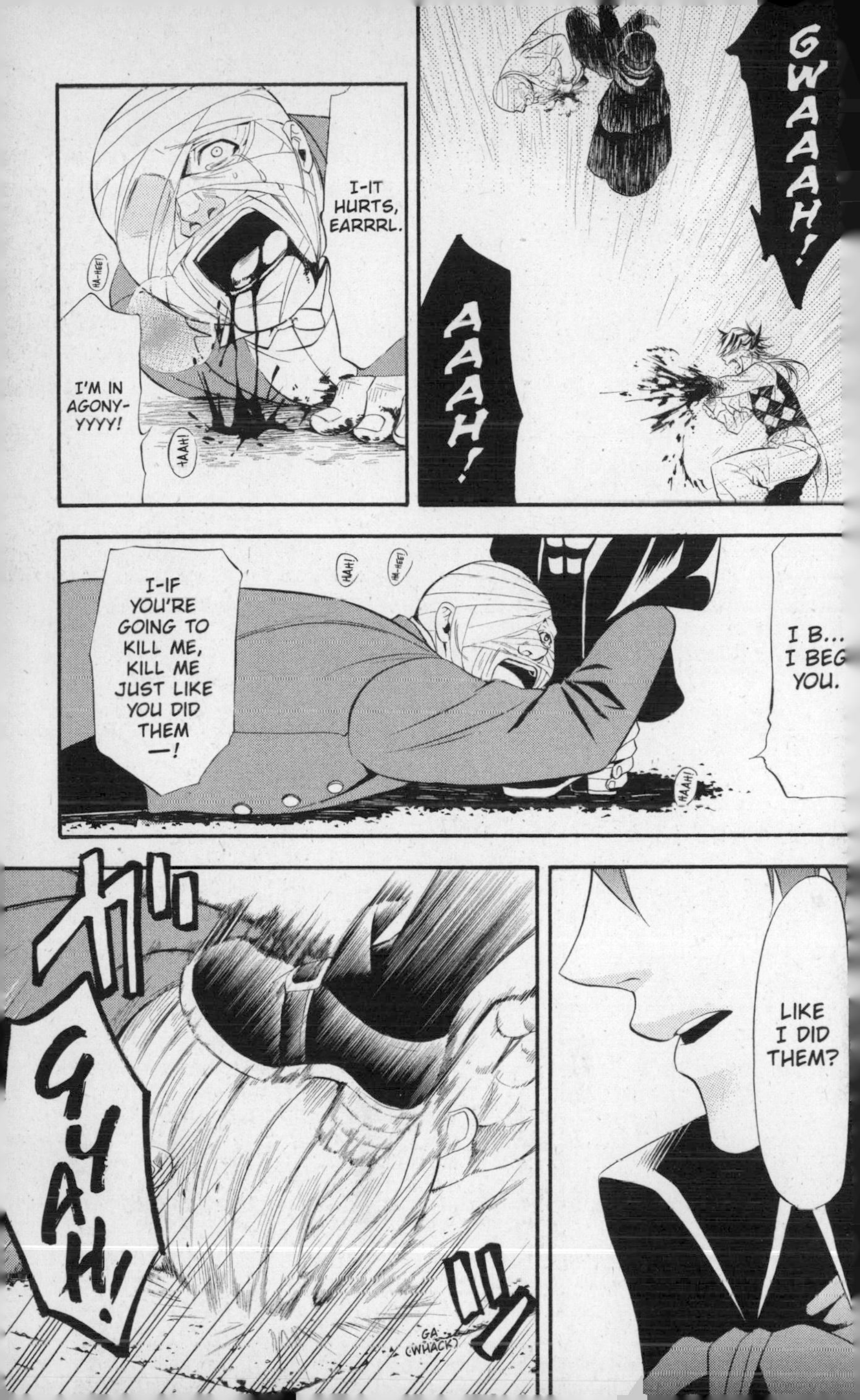
GWAAAAH!
AAAH!
I-IT HURTS, EARRRL.
HA-HEE!
I'M IN AGONY-YYYY!
HAAH!
I B... I BEG YOU.
HA-HEE!
HAH!
I-IF YOU'RE GOING TO KILL ME, KILL ME JUST LIKE YOU DID THEM—!
HAAH!
LIKE I DID THEM?
GYAH!
GA (WHACK)

THEN GET ON YOUR KNEES LIKE A WORM...
...AND PLEAD WITH THE DEVIL.
PLEASE DON'T KILL 'IM!
BE HE AS HE MAY, WE STILL OWE HIM OUR LIVES.
WE, WHO WERE ABANDONED BY OUR PARENTS, BY THIS NATION—
HE SAVED US FROM THE TERROR OF STARVING TO DEATH, WHICH PLAGUED US DAY IN AND DAY OUT.

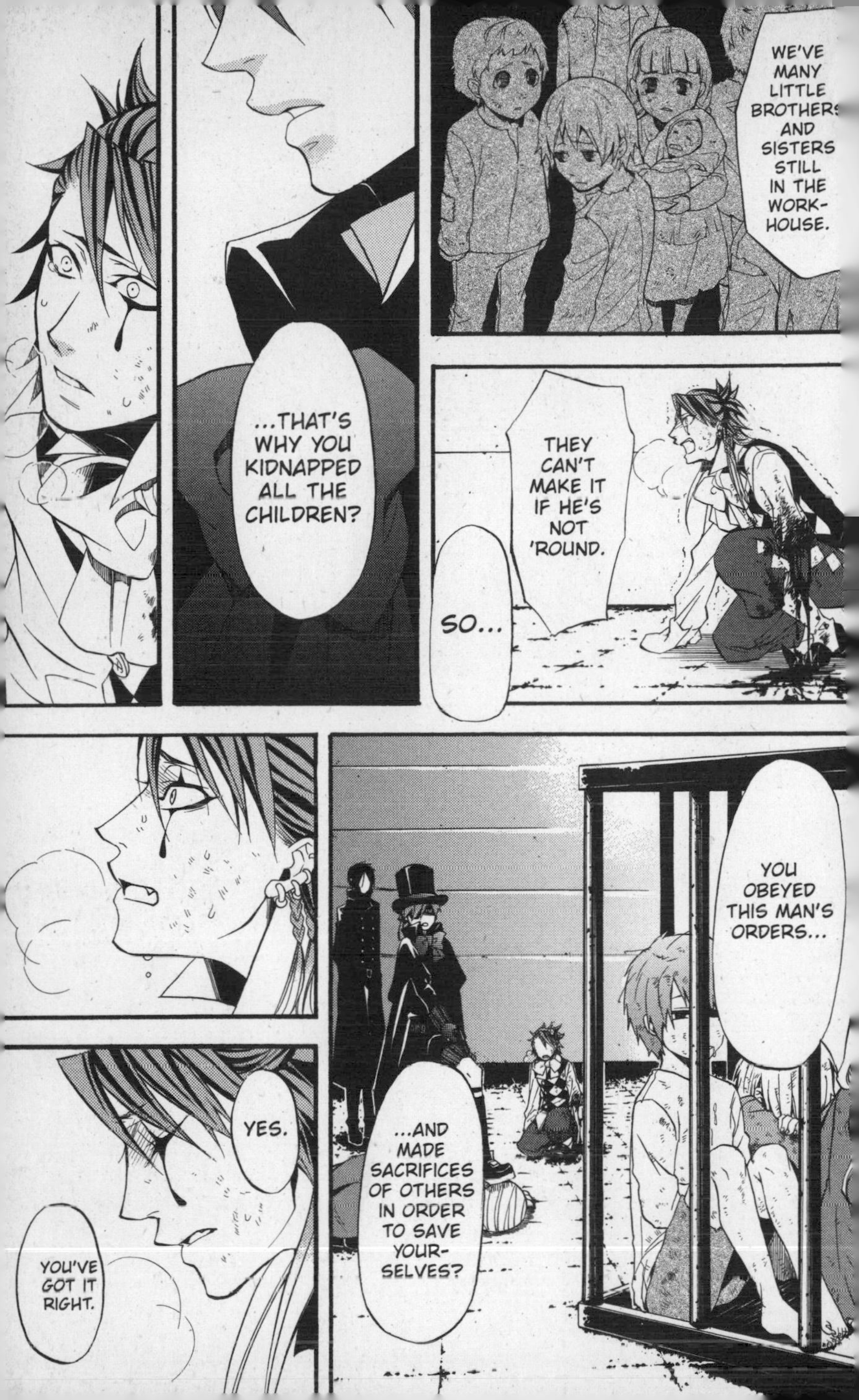
WE'VE MANY LITTLE BROTHERS AND SISTERS STILL IN THE WORK-HOUSE.
THEY CAN'T MAKE IT IF HE'S NOT 'ROUND.
SO...
...THAT'S WHY YOU KIDNAPPED ALL THE CHILDREN?
YOU OBEYED THIS MAN'S ORDERS...
...AND MADE SACRIFICES OF OTHERS IN ORDER TO SAVE YOUR-SELVES?
YES.
YOU'VE GOT IT RIGHT.

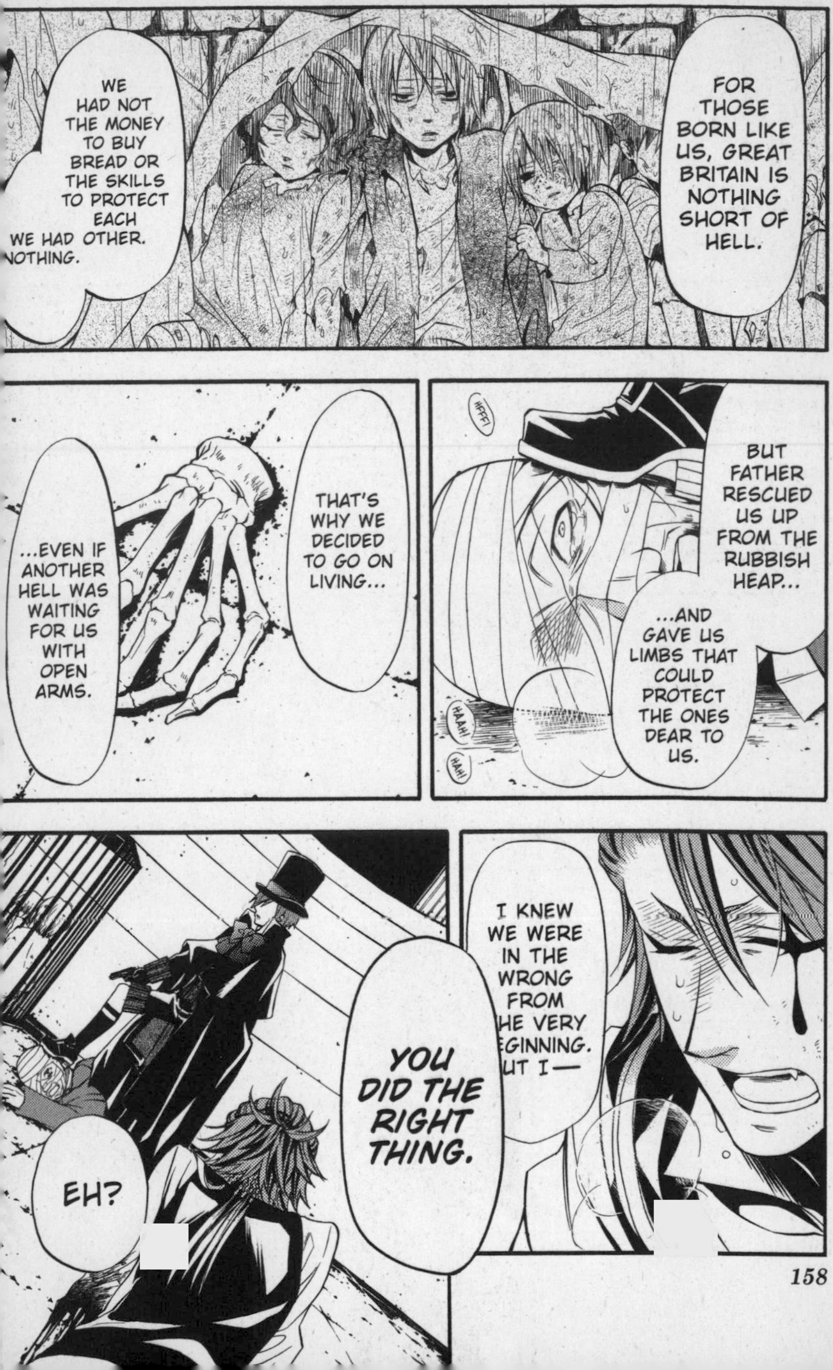
FOR THOSE BORN LIKE US, GREAT BRITAIN IS NOTHING SHORT OF HELL.
WE HAD NOT THE MONEY TO BUY BREAD OR THE SKILLS TO PROTECT EACH OTHER.
WE HAD OTHING.
HFFF!
BUT FATHER RESCUED US UP FROM THE RUBBISH HEAP...
...AND GAVE US LIMBS THAT COULD PROTECT THE ONES DEAR TO US.
HAAH!
HAAH!
THAT'S WHY WE DECIDED TO GO ON LIVING...
...EVEN IF ANOTHER HELL WAS WAITING FOR US WITH OPEN ARMS.
I KNEW WE WERE IN THE WRONG FROM HE VERY EGINNING. UT I—
YOU DID THE RIGHT THING.
EH?

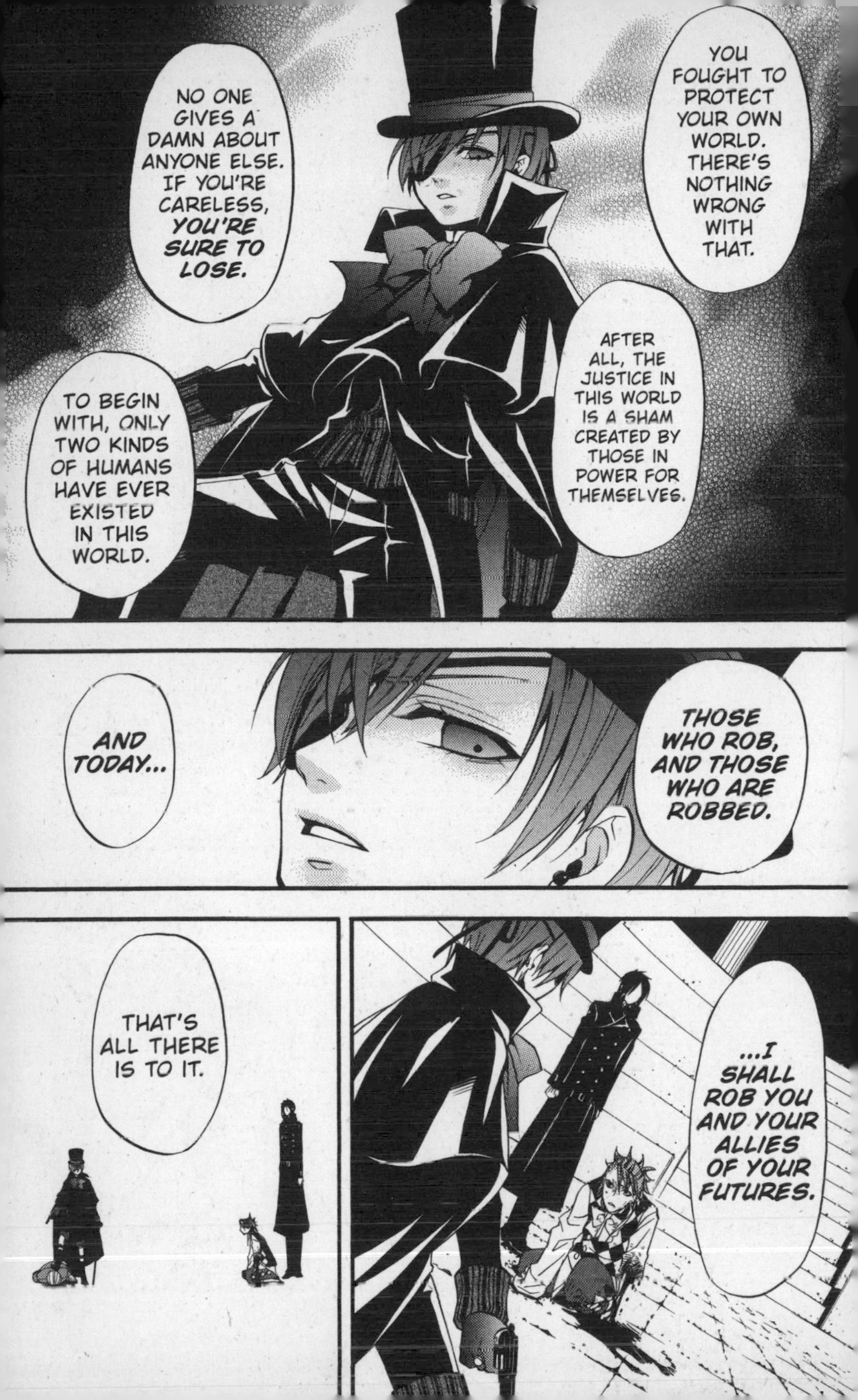
YOU FOUGHT TO PROTECT YOUR OWN WORLD. THERE'S NOTHING WRONG WITH THAT.
AFTER ALL, THE JUSTICE IN THIS WORLD IS A SHAM CREATED BY THOSE IN POWER FOR THEMSELVES.
NO ONE GIVES A DAMN ABOUT ANYONE ELSE. IF YOU'RE CARELESS, *YOU'RE SURE TO LOSE.*
TO BEGIN WITH, ONLY TWO KINDS OF HUMANS HAVE EVER EXISTED IN THIS WORLD.
THOSE WHO ROB, AND THOSE WHO ARE ROBBED.
AND TODAY...
...I SHALL ROB YOU AND YOUR ALLIES OF YOUR FUTURES.
THAT'S ALL THERE IS TO IT.

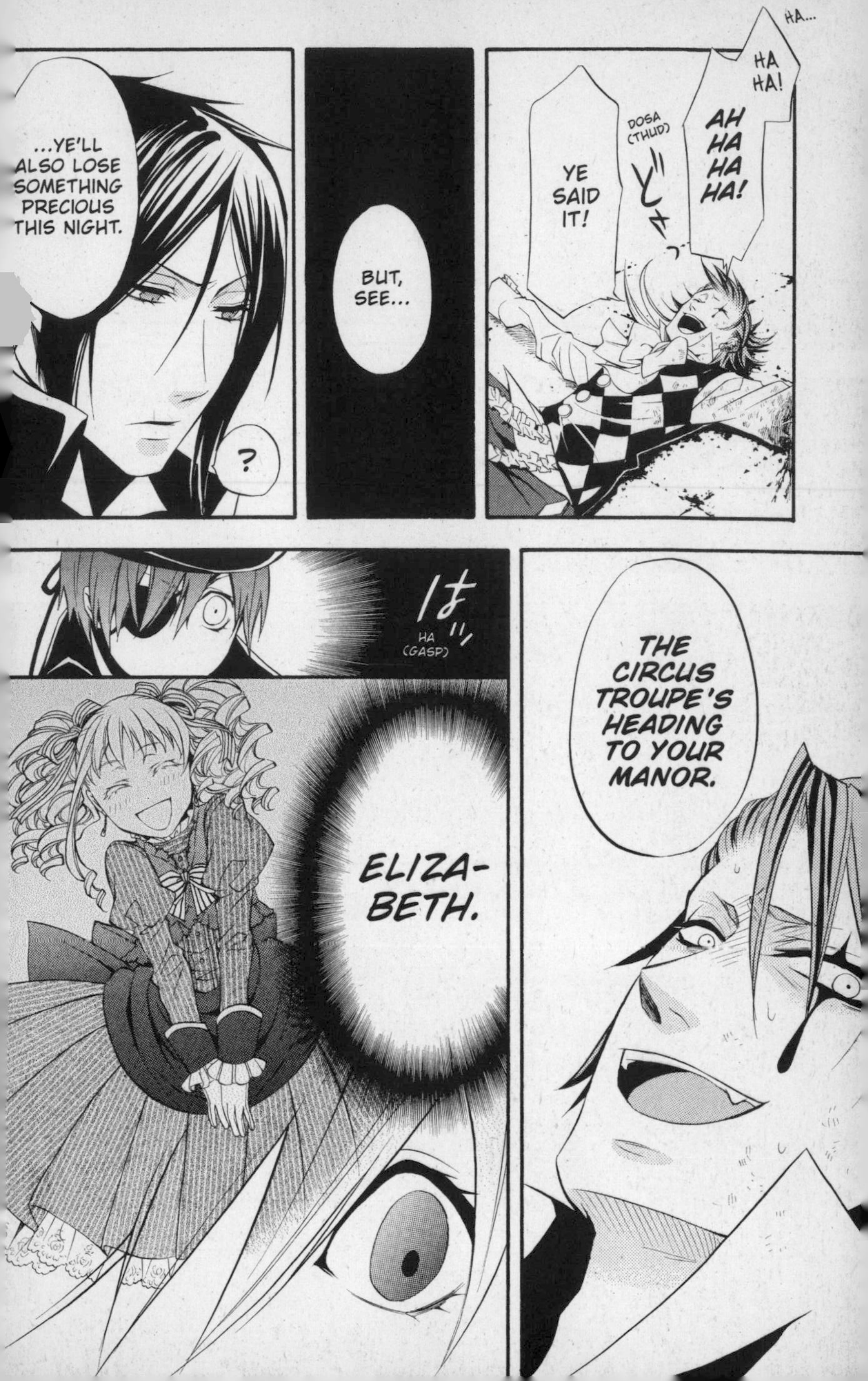
HA...
HA HA!
AH HA HA HA!
DOSA (THUD)
YE SAID IT!
BUT, SEE...
...YE'LL ALSO LOSE SOMETHING PRECIOUS THIS NIGHT.
?
THE CIRCUS TROUPE'S HEADING TO YOUR MANOR.
は
HA (GASP)
ELIZA-BETH.

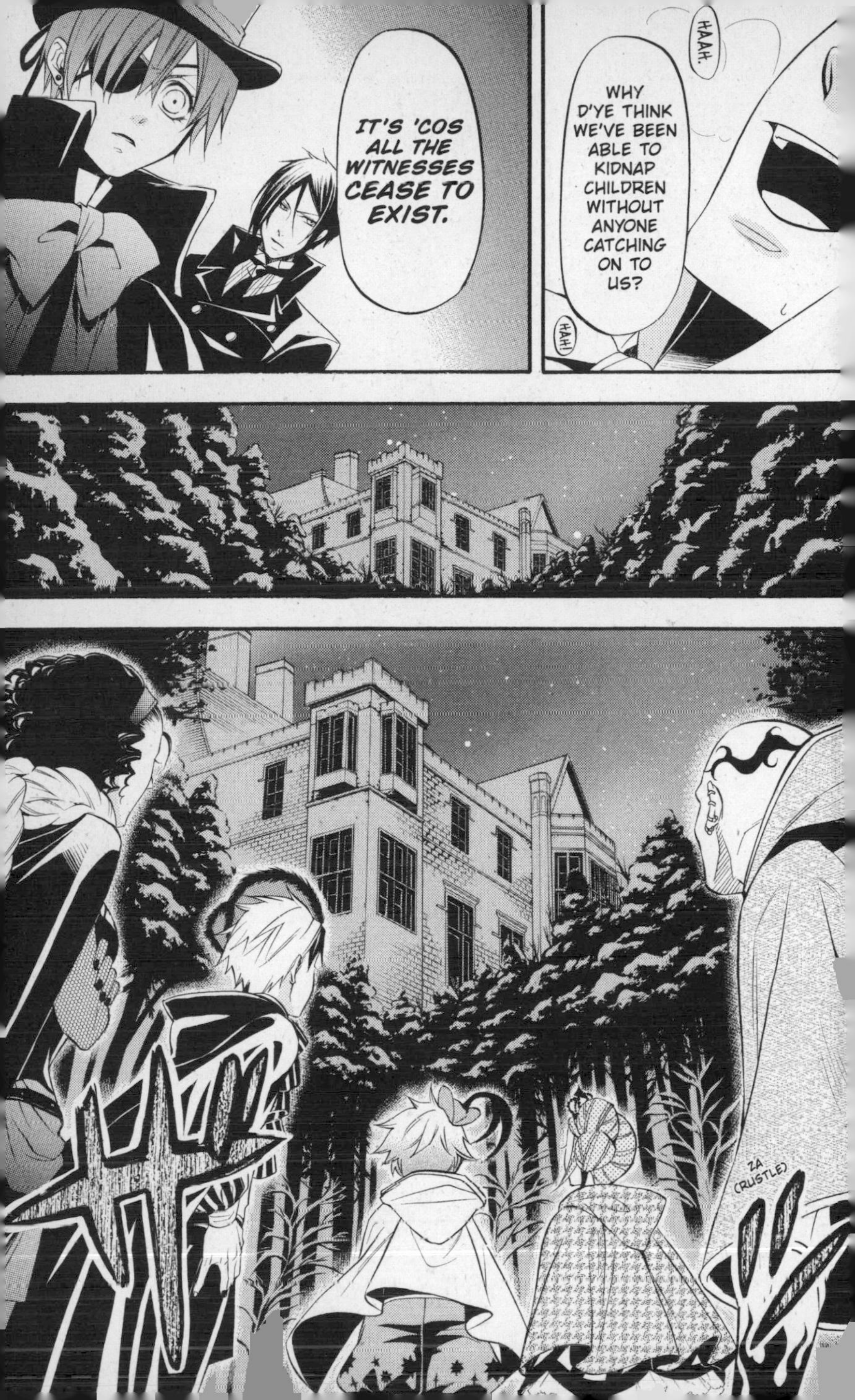
HAAH.
WHY D'YE THINK WE'VE BEEN ABLE TO KIDNAP CHILDREN WITHOUT ANYONE CATCHING ON TO US?
HAH!
IT'S 'COS ALL THE WITNESSES CEASE TO EXIST.
ZA (RUSTLE)

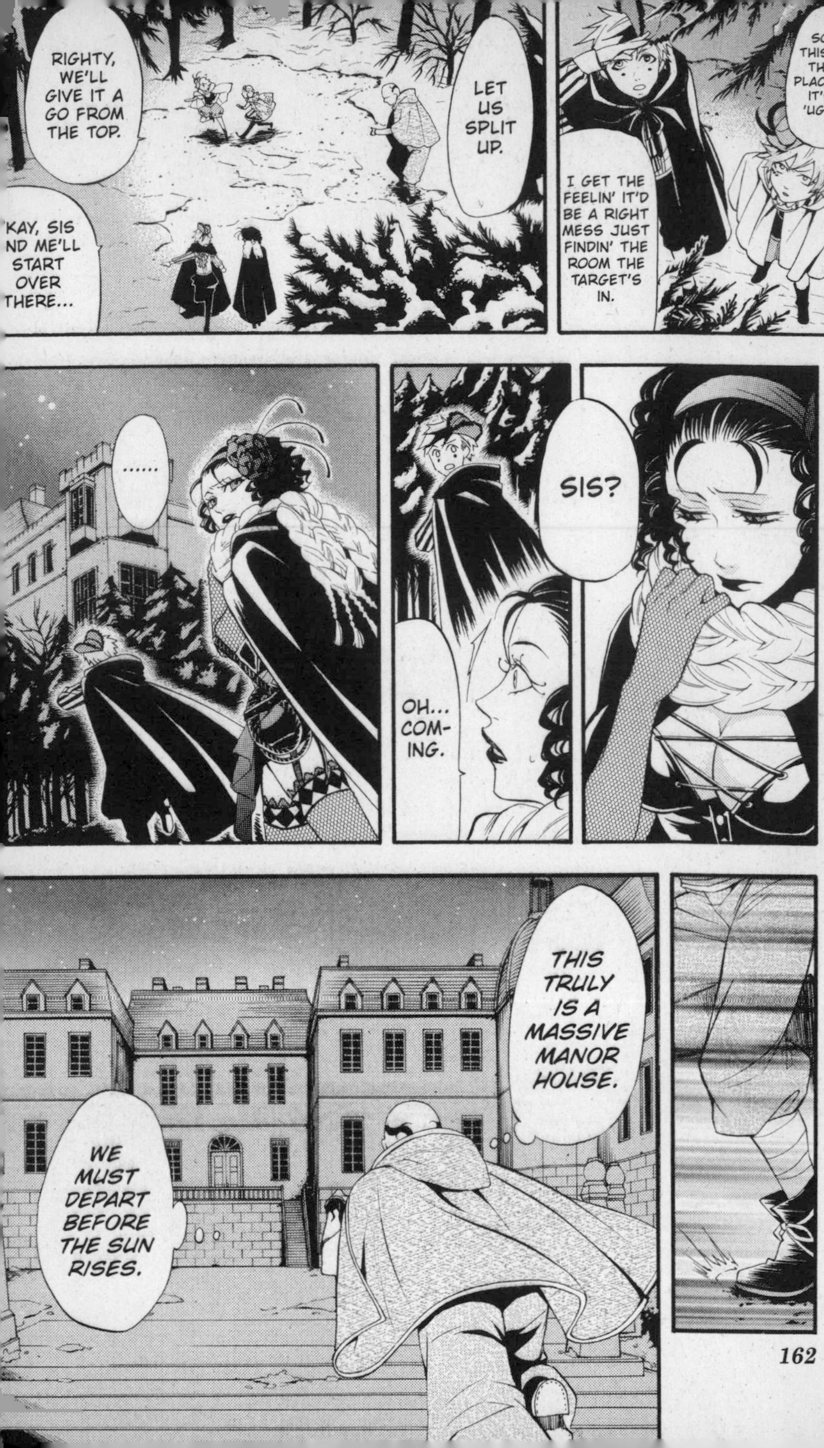

SO THIS'S THE PLACE... IT'S 'UGE.
I GET THE FEELIN' IT'D BE A RIGHT MESS JUST FINDIN' THE ROOM THE TARGET'S IN.
LET US SPLIT UP.
RIGHTY, WE'LL GIVE IT A GO FROM THE TOP.
KAY, SIS ND ME'LL START OVER THERE...
SIS?
OH... COM-ING.
......
THIS TRULY IS A MASSIVE MANOR HOUSE.
WE MUST DEPART BEFORE THE SUN RISES.

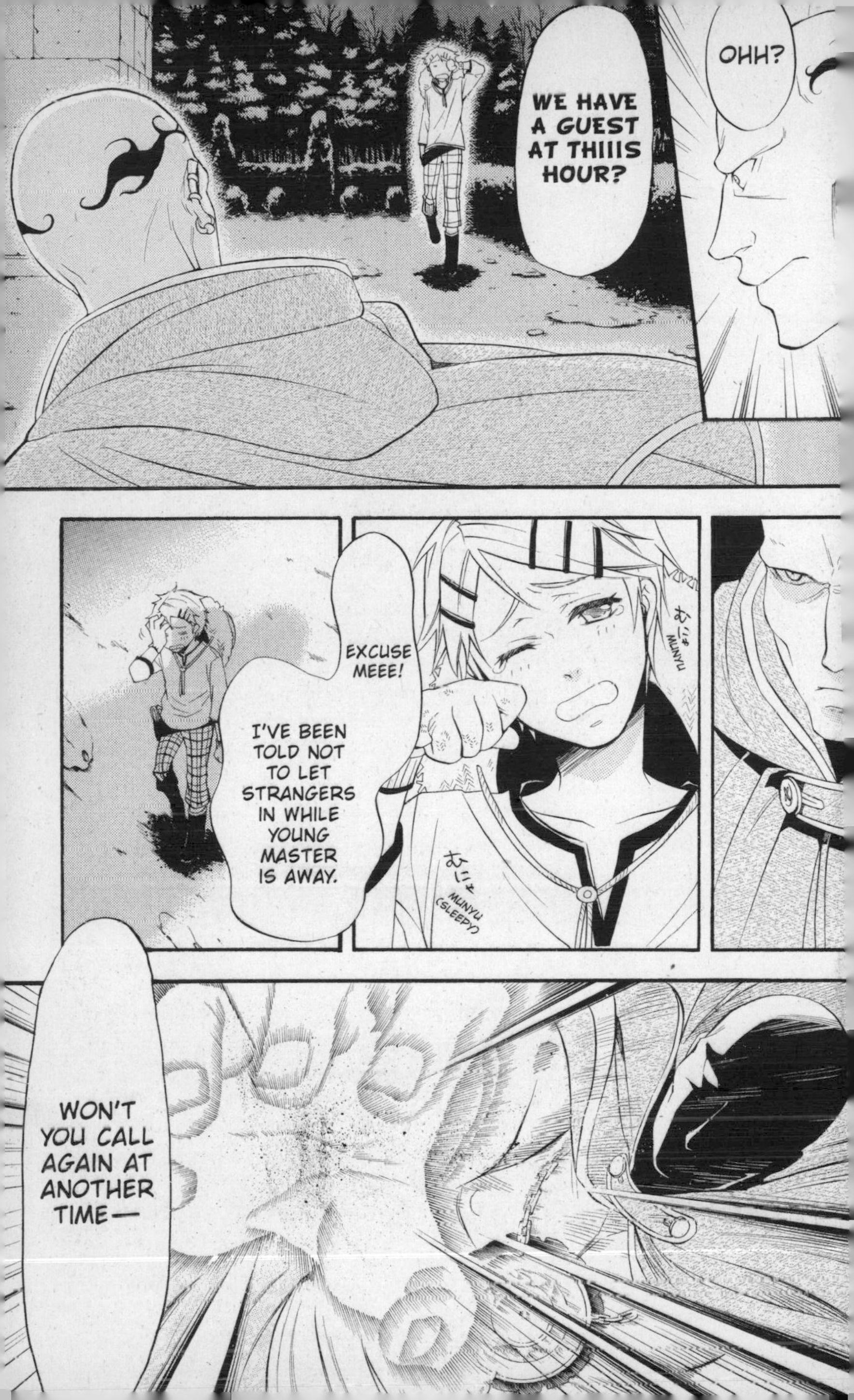
OHH?
WE HAVE A GUEST AT THIIIS HOUR?
むにゅ MUNYU
EXCUSE MEEE!
I'VE BEEN TOLD NOT TO LET STRANGERS IN WHILE YOUNG MASTER IS AWAY.
むにゅ MUNYU (SLEEPY)
WON'T YOU CALL AGAIN AT ANOTHER TIME—

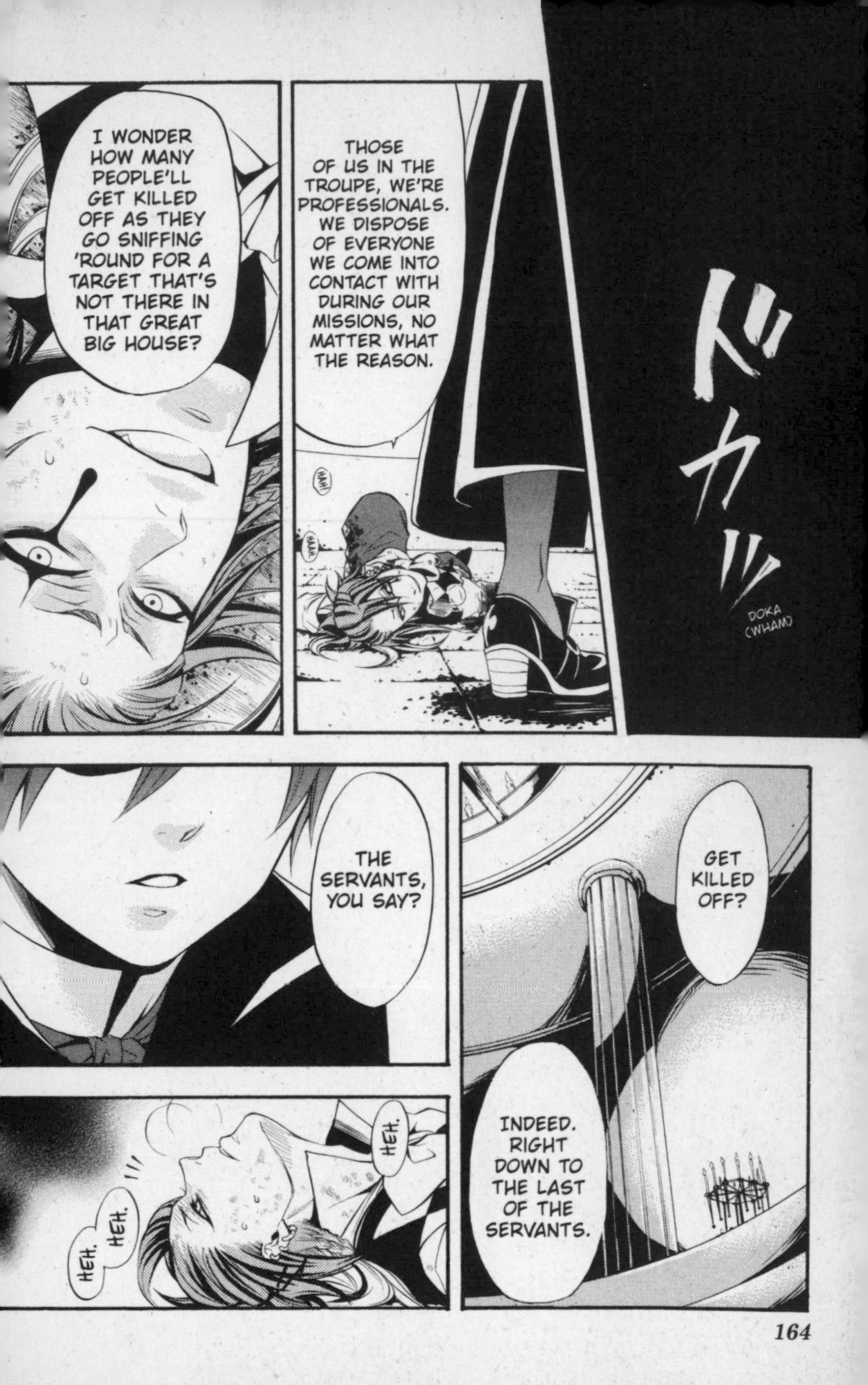
ドカッ
DOKA (WHAM)
THOSE OF US IN THE TROUPE, WE'RE PROFESSIONALS. WE DISPOSE OF EVERYONE WE COME INTO CONTACT WITH DURING OUR MISSIONS, NO MATTER WHAT THE REASON.
HAH!
HAAH.
I WONDER HOW MANY PEOPLE'LL GET KILLED OFF AS THEY GO SNIFFING 'ROUND FOR A TARGET THAT'S NOT THERE IN THAT GREAT BIG HOUSE?
GET KILLED OFF?
INDEED. RIGHT DOWN TO THE LAST OF THE SERVANTS.
THE SERVANTS, YOU SAY?
HEH.
HEH.
HEH.

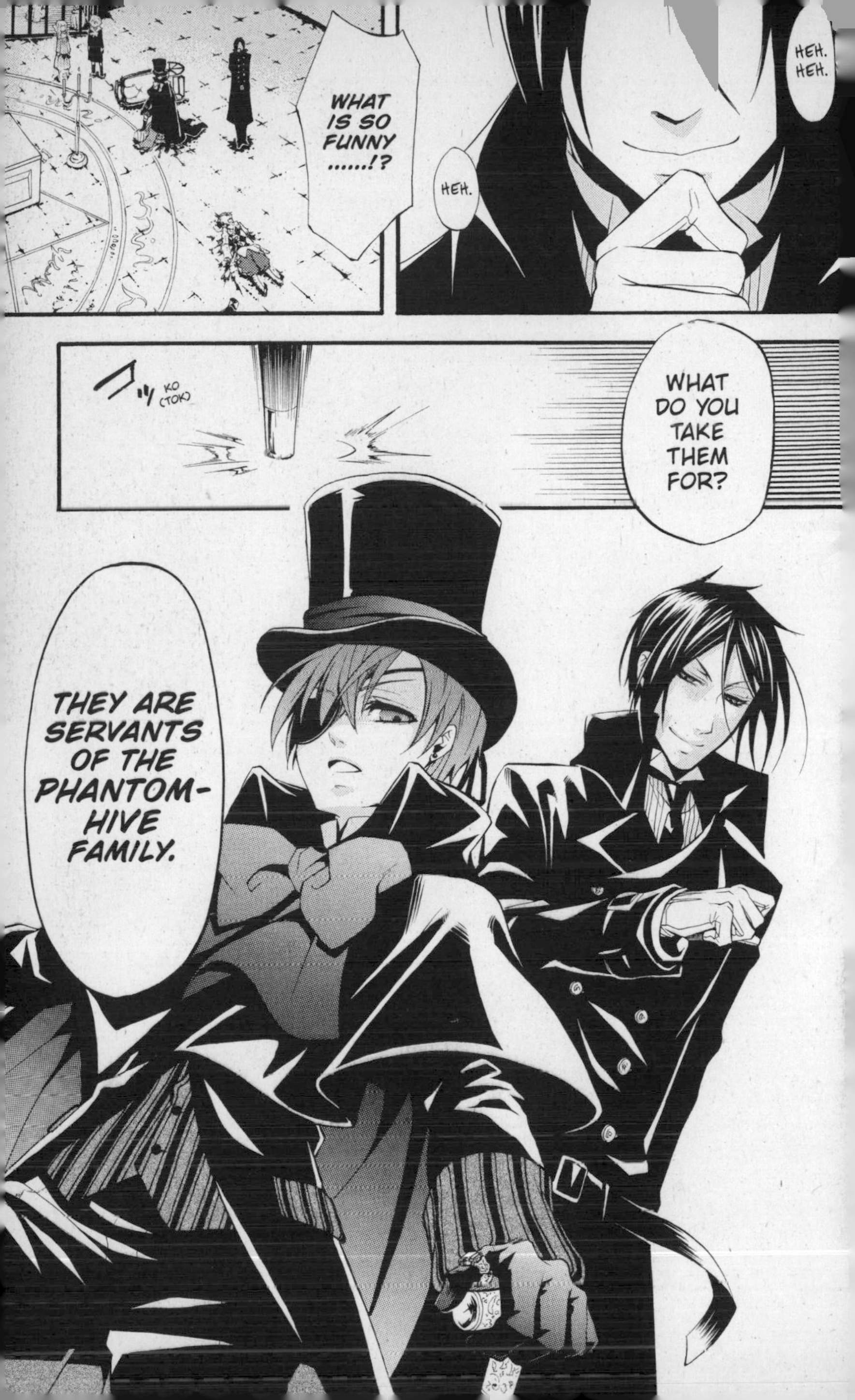
HEH. HEH.
HEH.
WHAT IS SO FUNNY ......!?
WHAT DO YOU TAKE THEM FOR?
KO (TOK)
THEY ARE SERVANTS OF THE PHANTOM-HIVE FAMILY.

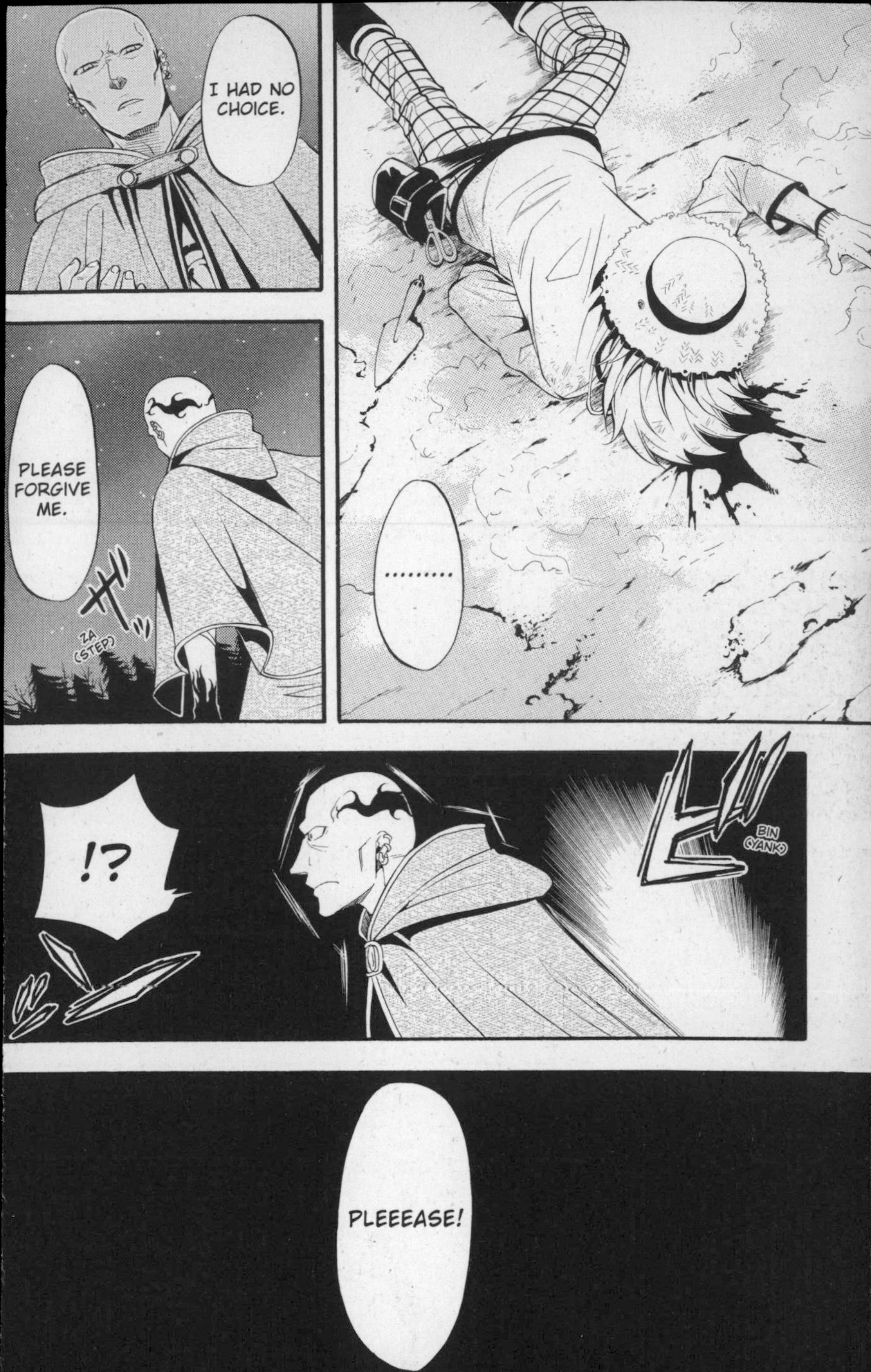
....
I HAD NO CHOICE.
PLEASE FORGIVE ME.
ZA (STEP)
BIN (YANK)
!?
PLEEEASE!

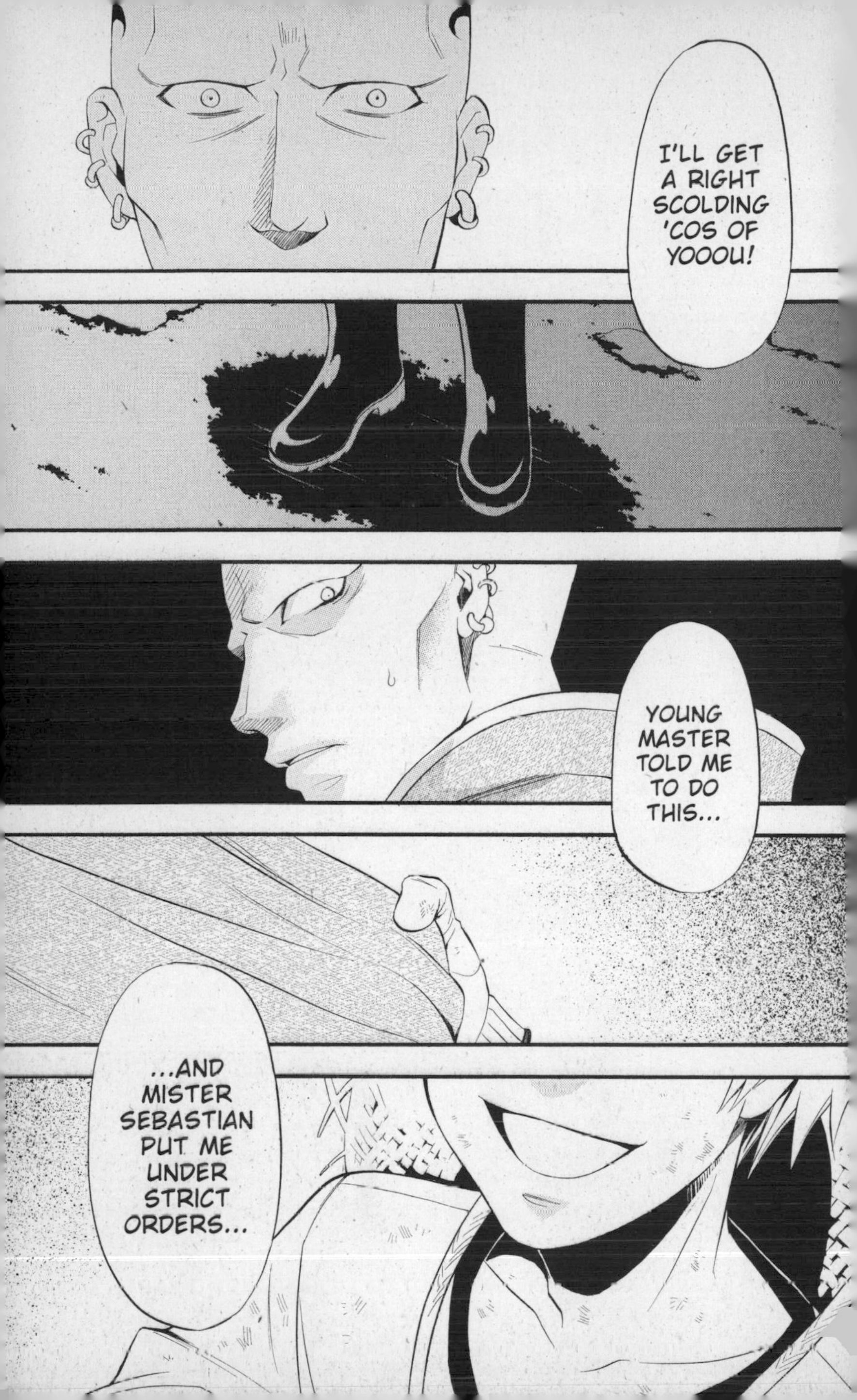
I'LL GET A RIGHT SCOLDING 'COS OF YOOOU!
YOUNG MASTER TOLD ME TO DO THIS...
...AND MISTER SEBASTIAN PUT ME UNDER STRICT ORDERS...

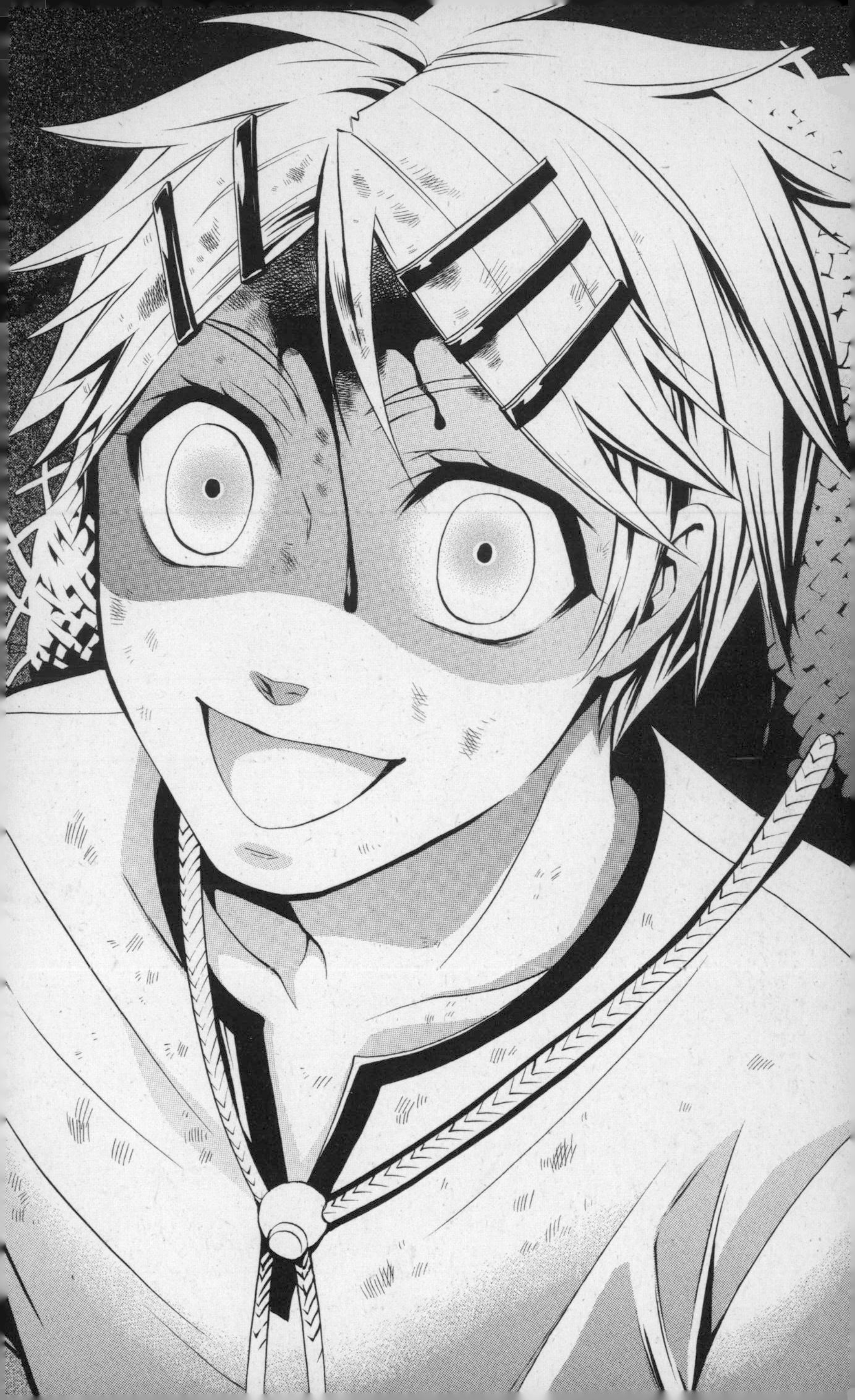

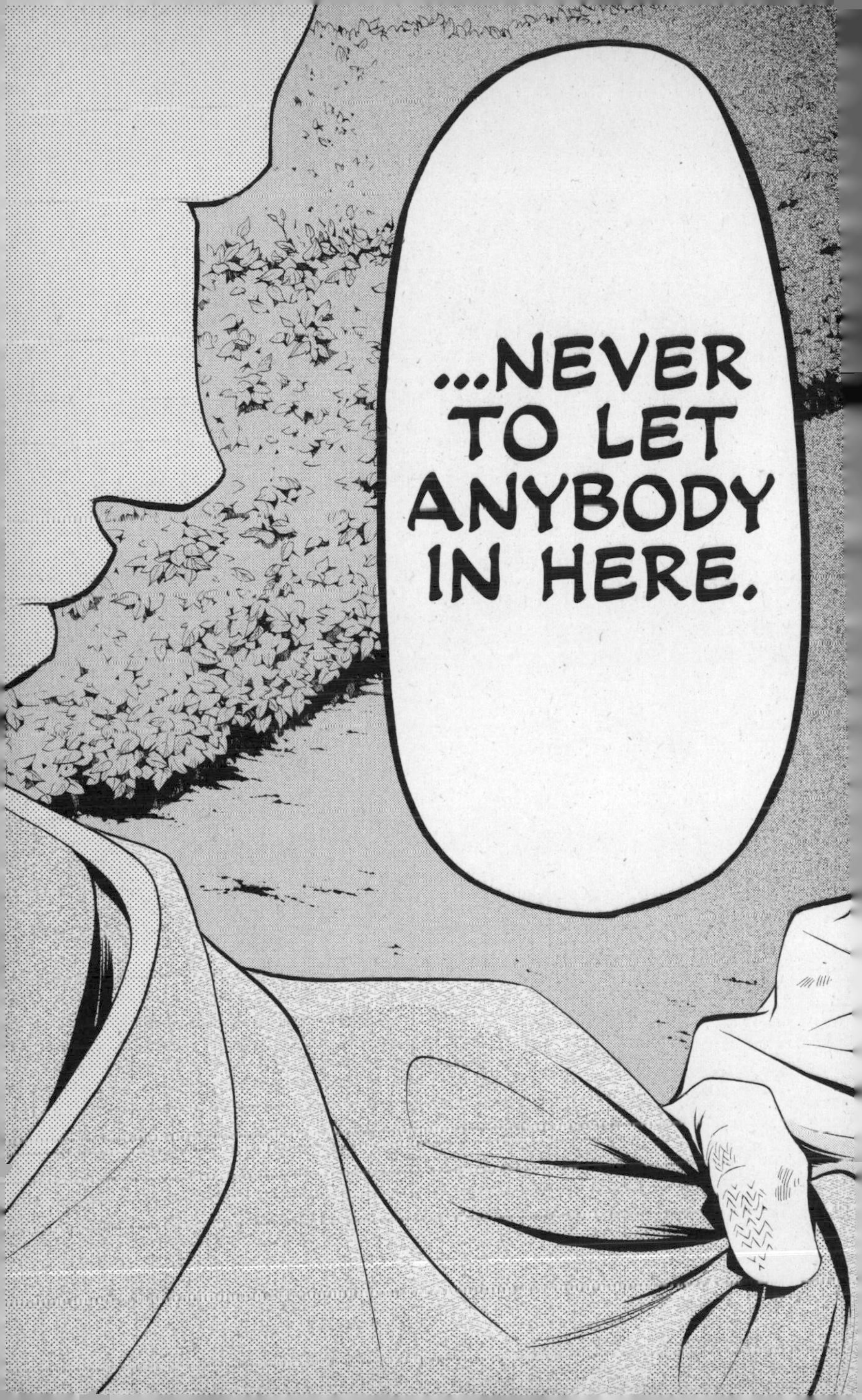
...NEVER TO LET ANYBODY IN HERE.

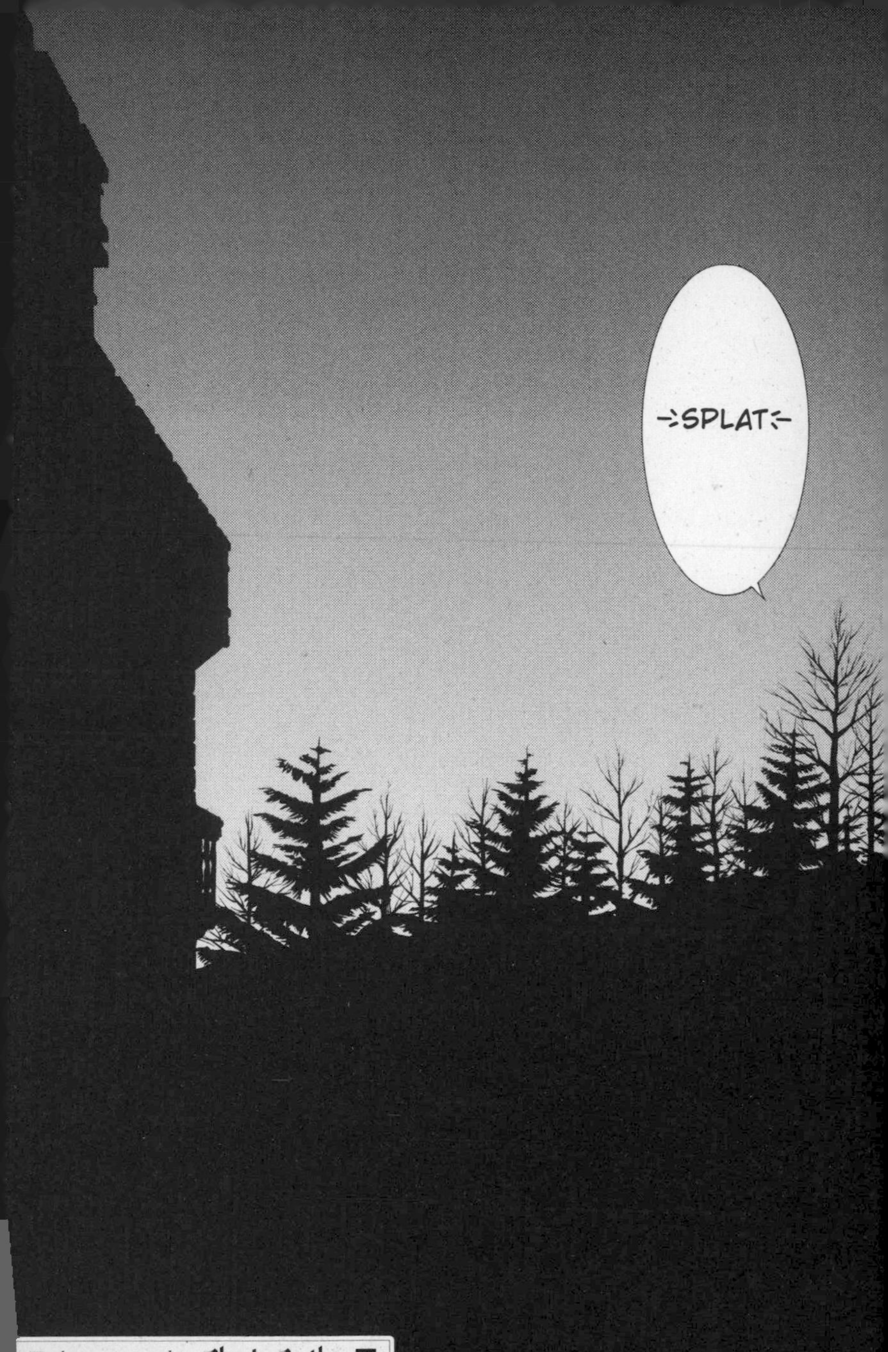
SPLAT

To be continued in **Black Butler 8**

⇒ **Black Butler** ⇐

黒執事

❧

Downstairs

Wakana Haduki

Akiyo Satorigi

SuKe

Kiyo

7

*

Takeshi Kuma

*

Yana Toboso

❧

SpecialThanks

Yana's Mother

for You!

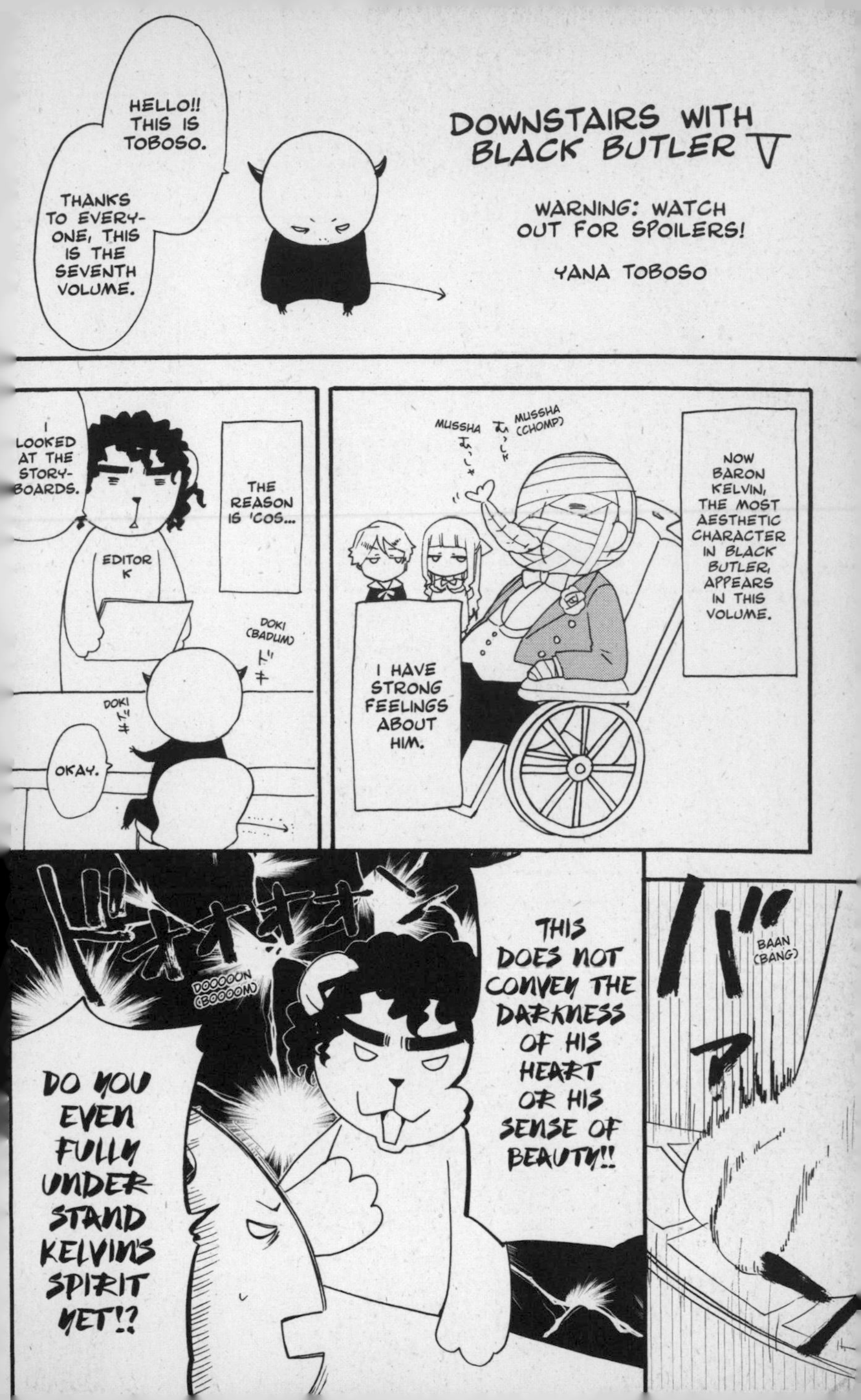
DOWNSTAIRS WITH BLACK BUTLER V
WARNING: WATCH OUT FOR SPOILERS!
YANA TOBOSO
HELLO!! THIS IS TOBOSO.
THANKS TO EVERYONE, THIS IS THE SEVENTH VOLUME.
NOW BARON KELVIN, THE MOST AESTHETIC CHARACTER IN BLACK BUTLER, APPEARS IN THIS VOLUME.
MUSSHA (CHOMP)
MUSSHA
I HAVE STRONG FEELINGS ABOUT HIM.
THE REASON IS 'COS...
I LOOKED AT THE STORYBOARDS.
EDITOR K
DOKI (BADUM)
DOKI
OKAY.
BAAN (BANG)
THIS DOES NOT CONVEY THE DARKNESS OF HIS HEART OR HIS SENSE OF BEAUTY!!
DOOOOON (BOOOOM)
DO YOU EVEN FULLY UNDERSTAND KELVIN'S SPIRIT YET!?

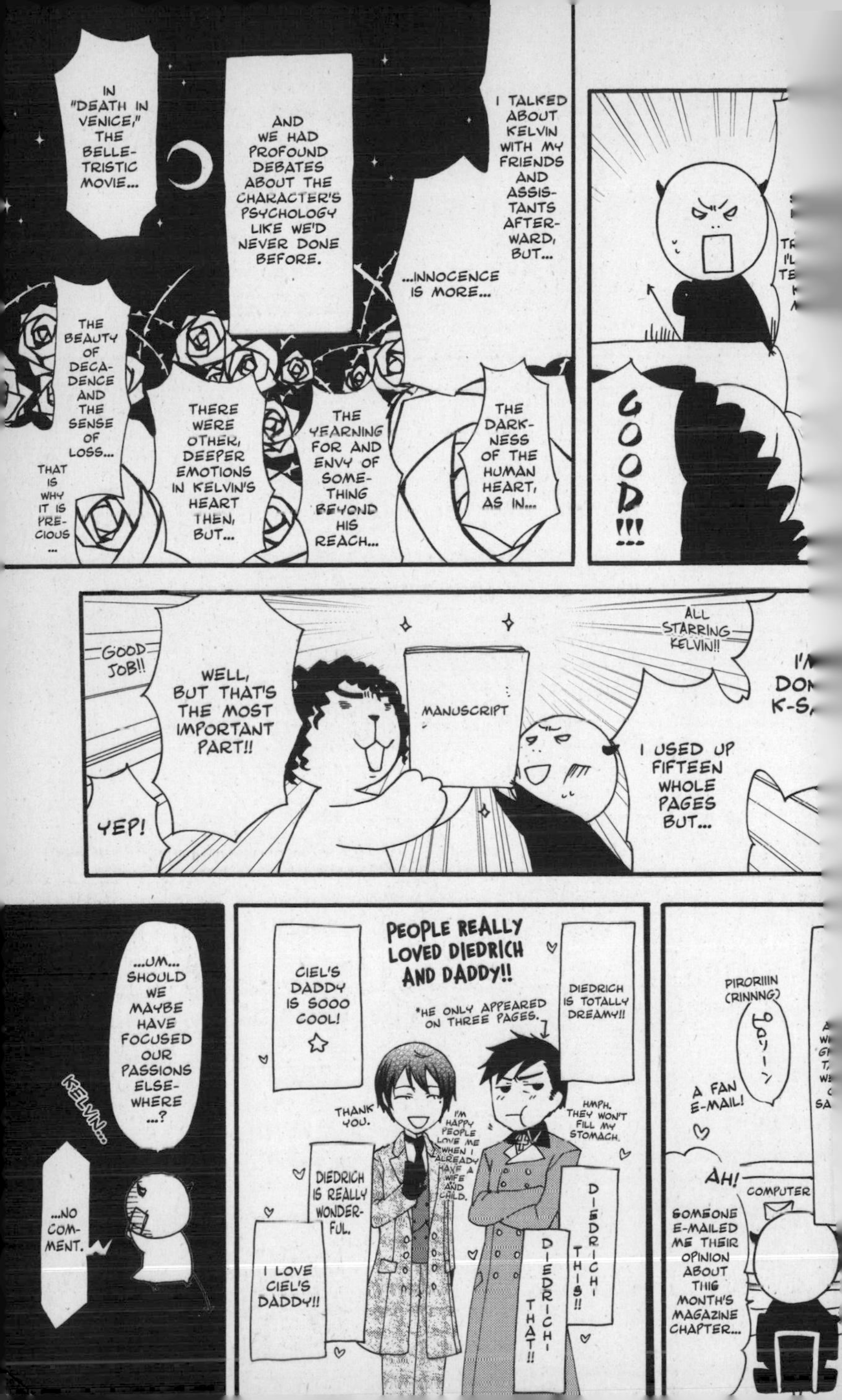
GOOD!!!
I TALKED ABOUT KELVIN WITH MY FRIENDS AND ASSISTANTS AFTERWARD, BUT...
...INNOCENCE IS MORE...
AND WE HAD PROFOUND DEBATES ABOUT THE CHARACTER'S PSYCHOLOGY LIKE WE'D NEVER DONE BEFORE.
IN "DEATH IN VENICE," THE BELLETRISTIC MOVIE...
THE DARKNESS OF THE HUMAN HEART, AS IN...
THE YEARNING FOR AND ENVY OF SOMETHING BEYOND HIS REACH...
THERE WERE OTHER, DEEPER EMOTIONS IN KELVIN'S HEART THEN, BUT...
THE BEAUTY OF DECADENCE AND THE SENSE OF LOSS...
THAT IS WHY IT IS PRECIOUS...
ALL STARRING KELVIN!!
I USED UP FIFTEEN WHOLE PAGES BUT...
MANUSCRIPT
WELL, BUT THAT'S THE MOST IMPORTANT PART!!
GOOD JOB!!
YEP!
PIRORIIIN (RINNNG)
A FAN E-MAIL!
AH!
COMPUTER
SOMEONE E-MAILED ME THEIR OPINION ABOUT THIS MONTH'S MAGAZINE CHAPTER...
PEOPLE REALLY LOVED DIEDRICH AND DADDY!!
DIEDRICH IS TOTALLY DREAMY!!
*HE ONLY APPEARED ON THREE PAGES.
CIEL'S DADDY IS SOOO COOL!
HMPH. THEY WON'T FILL MY STOMACH.
I'M HAPPY PEOPLE LOVE ME WHEN I ALREADY HAVE A WIFE AND CHILD.
THANK YOU.
DIEDRICHI THIS!!
DIEDRICHI THAT!!
DIEDRICH IS REALLY WONDERFUL.
I LOVE CIEL'S DADDY!!
...UM... SHOULD WE MAYBE HAVE FOCUSED OUR PASSIONS ELSEWHERE...?
KELVIN...
...NO COMMENT.

Translation Notes

Page 9
Brother Joker, sister Wendy
In the original Japanese edition, some of the troupe members refer to Joker (and later Peter) as *aniki*, while Beast and Wendy are referred to as *aneki*. This may refer to either the familial bond that the kids from the workhouse have (as brothers and sisters) or seniority among troupe members. For example, Beast refers to Wendy as *aneki*, or "big sis"; however, she clearly appears to be the older of the two. "Ol' timer"/"ol' chap" is also used as an equivalent to the Japanese word *senpai*.

Page 17
College of Arms
The College of Arms, also known as the Heralds' College, is one of the few remaining official institutions which continues to keep records of heraldic devices used in British society in the present day. It was created in the fifteenth century by a group of royal heralds and also has the power to confer coats of arms for England, Wales, and Northern Ireland. As Ciel mentions later on page 24, Scotland has its own heraldic authority in The Court of the Lord Lyon located in Edinburgh.

Page 19
Asthma in Victorian England
The medical world's definition of asthma gradually headed toward a consensus in the nineteenth century, but many physicians would chalk up the symptoms of asthma to other medical problems, and the potential fatality of asthma was often regarded with scepticism. However, this period of industrial development did bring about the invention of inhalation devices to ease the discomfort of asthma sufferers, the ancestors of the modern-day inhaler.

Page 21
Wordsworth
Snake is obviously very well-read. His snakes all seem to be named after famous writers. In this volume, we meet Wordsworth, most likely named for the great English Romantic poet, William Wordsworth, who was instrumental in bringing about the Romantic Age of English literature, alongside his peer, Samuel Taylor Coleridge.

Page 52
Baron Kelvin
There was actually a real Baron Kelvin active at this time. But that is where the similarities end! Sir William Thomson, the first Baron Kelvin, was a world-renowned scientist and engineer active during the Victorian Era; he was in fact knighted by Queen Victoria herself in 1866. The unit of temperature measurement known as the Kelvin was also named for him.

Page 55
Governor-General, viceroy
Prince Soma using this term to refer to himself is humorous because the (British) leader of the British administration in colonial India during the Victorian Era would have been titled the same thing.

Page 72
"Tom, Tom, the Piper's Son"
Joker's song is actually a popular English nursery rhyme. There are two versions of the rhyme; here, Joker is singing the longer version, which is thought to be adapted from another verse which was popular in the seventeenth and eighteenth centuries.

Page 83
Emily
It is likely that Snake's Emily is named for the American poet Emily Dickinson, who was active from 1830 to 1886 and was a contemporary of William Wordsworth. And like her English counterpart, Dickinson, whose work went practically unread in her lifetime, is considered a keystone of the Romantic movement in American literature.

Page 126
Baron Kelvin's speech pattern
Belying his appearance, Baron Kelvin's way of speaking is quite jarring, for he frequently speaks like a child and employs personal pronouns that would only be used by someone much younger. It does match his childish attitude, however.

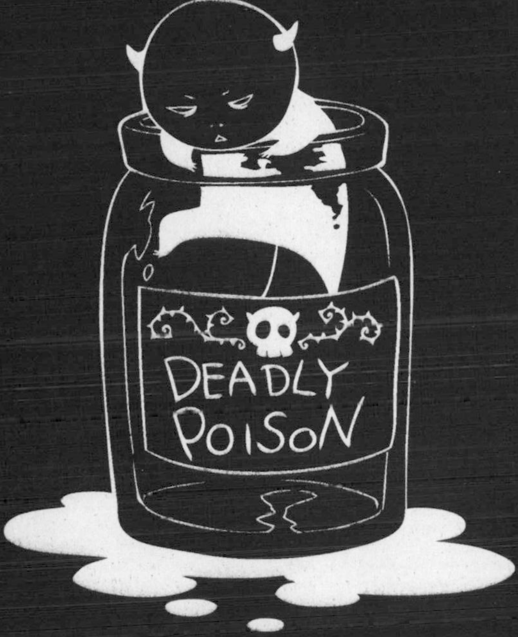
DEADLY
POISON

Yana Toboso

AUTHOR'S NOTE

It's already been two years and several months since Volume 1 was published. In this volume, I drew characters that I hadn't drawn since Volume 1, and I realised that my drawing style has changed quite a bit.

Nothing stays the same. Not myself, or the entire world; we change moment by moment.

And that's what I'm thinking about as Volume 7 hits the shelves.